THE JURISPRUDENCE OF PARTICULARISM

This open access book asks whether there is space for particularism in a constitutional democracy which would limit the implementation of EU law. National identity claims are a key factor in shaping our times and the ongoing evolution of the European Union. To assess their impact this collection focuses on the jurisprudence of Czechia, Hungary, Poland and Slovakia, as they play an essential role in giving life to particularism. By taking particularism as the prism through which they explore the question, the contributors offer a new analytical scheme to evaluate the judicial invocation of identity. This requires an interdisciplinary approach: the study draws on comparative constitutional law, theory, comparative-empirical material and normative-philosophical perspectives. This is a fresh and thought-provoking new study on an increasingly important question in EU law.

The Jurisprudence of Particularism

National Identity Claims in Central Europe

Edited by
Kriszta Kovács

•HART•
OXFORD • LONDON • NEW YORK • NEW DELHI • SYDNEY

HART PUBLISHING

Bloomsbury Publishing Plc

Kemp House, Chawley Park, Cumnor Hill, Oxford, OX2 9PH, UK

1385 Broadway, New York, NY 10018, USA

29 Earlsfort Terrace, Dublin 2, Ireland

HART PUBLISHING, the Hart/Stag logo, BLOOMSBURY and the Diana logo are trademarks of Bloomsbury Publishing Plc

First published in Great Britain 2023

A catalogue record for this book is available from the British Library.

A catalogue record for this book is available from the Library of Congress.

ISBN: HB: 978-1-50996-012-5
ePDF: 978-1-50996-014-9
ePub: 978-1-50996-013-2

Typeset by Compuscript Ltd, Shannon

„Einfach-groß ist der Gedanke, leicht die Ausführung durch Verstand und Kraft. Einheit ist allmächtig, deshalb keine Spaltung, kein Widerstreit unter uns. Insofern wir Grundsätze haben, sind sie uns allen gemein.“

JW Goethe, *Wilhelm Meisters Wanderjahre*
Drittes Buch, Neuntes Kapitel
Stuttgart & Tübingen, Cotta, 1821

"Simple and grand is the thought, easy is its execution by understanding and strength. Unity is all-powerful; no division, therefore, no contention, among us!"

JW Goethe, *Wilhelm Meister's Travels*
trans T Carlyle, Boston, Francis A Niccolls & Co, 1902

Acknowledgements

WHILE WORKING ON this book, I have received support from more people and institutions than I can mention here. The collection arose out of a Marie Skłodowska-Curie research project entitled 'A principle-based EU challenge to East Central European judicial interpretation of constitutional identity'.[1] I thank the European Commission for awarding this research fellowship for the academic years of 2019/2020 and 2020/2021. I also thank the ELTE University Faculty of Social Sciences for granting me research leave from normal teaching and administrative duties during those years. Without the Marie Skłodowska-Curie fellowship and research leave, I would never have had the time to co-write and edit this book.

The fellowship enabled me to test ideas at various conferences at the Georg-August-Universität Göttingen, Lund University, Princeton University and Wissenschaftskolleg zu Berlin, and during COVID times, at online conferences organised by the Council for European Studies, the International Society of Public Law, King's College London, the Law and Society Association, the Manchester Centre for Political Theory and University College London. The fellowship also allowed me to publish an electronic version of the volume under the Gold Open Access model.

I give my heartfelt thanks to the WZB Berlin Social Science Center for being an inspiring academic space and offering continuous research support. Being part of this vibrant and inspiring academic community is an honour and pleasure. I benefited greatly in the early stages of this work from conversations with colleagues at the WZB. I owed a great debt to the Global Constitutionalism Colloquium organised by Mattias Kumm, where I had a chance to discuss topics from this book. The Colloquium is a great place to exchange ideas and learn about the cutting-edge scholarship.

Sincere thanks are due to Stanisław Biernat, Lajos Mészáros, Kateřina Šimáčková, Ján Štiavnický, David Uhlíř, Zuzana Vikarská, and Marek Tadeusz Zubik for taking the time to be interviewed for this book and for generously replying to my questions in writing. I also heartily appreciate the invaluable research assistance of Jasmin Rauch and Maya Vogel.

[1] The project had received funding from the European Union's Horizon 2020 research and innovation programme under the Marie Skłodowska-Curie grant agreement No 794368.

My greatest debt is to my spouse, Gábor Attila Tóth, without whose encouragement and continuous professional support I could have never completed this book. He has helped me at various stages while co-writing and editing this book. It would not have become what it is without his insightful criticism. I am incredibly grateful for his encouragement, suggestions and critical remarks.

Finally, I am grateful to the Hart editorial team for their prompt production of the book and to Roisin Cronin for her skilful editing of my contributions.

Kriszta Kovács
Berlin, November 2022

Contents

PART III
THE EUROPEAN CONSTITUTIONAL CHALLENGE

List of Contributors

Susanne Baer is a public law and gender studies professor at Humboldt University in Berlin. Since 2011, she has served as a judge at the German Federal Constitutional Court. She is also an editorial member of the feminist legal magazine *Streit – feministische Rechtszeitschrift*.

Gary Jeffrey Jacobsohn is the H Malcolm Macdonald Professor in Constitutional and Comparative Law in the Department of Government and professor of law at the University of Texas at Austin. Before coming to the University of Texas, he was in the Department of Political Science at Williams College in Massachusetts for many years. In 2019, he received the Lifetime Achievement Award of the Law and Courts section of the American Political Science Association.

Miluše Kindlová is a senior lecturer at the Department of Constitutional Law, Faculty of Law, Charles University. She worked as a law clerk at the Constitutional Court of the Czech Republic from 2017 to 2019. She earned her degrees from the Faculty of Law, Charles University and the Faculty of Law, University of Oxford.

Kriszta Kovács is a senior researcher of the Cluster of Excellence 'Contestations of the Liberal Script (SCRIPTS)' at WZB Berlin Center for Global Constitutionalism and an associate professor at ELTE University Faculty of Social Sciences, Budapest. She is a former Marie Skłodowska-Curie Fellow and a former adviser to the Hungarian Constitutional Court.

Mattias Kumm is Research Professor 'Global Constitutionalism' at the WZB Berlin Social Science Center and a professor 'Rule of Law in the Age of Globalization' at Humboldt University in Berlin. He is also the Inge Rennert Professor of Law at the New York University School of Law.

Monika Polzin is a professor of public and public international law at the Vienna University of Economics and Business. She was a junior professor at the University of Augsburg, and a visiting professor in Berlin (Humboldt University), Munich (Ludwig-Maximilians-University) and Göttingen (Georg-August-University). From 2018 to 2020, she was a member of the Bavarian Constitutional Court.

Katarína Šipulová is the co-director of the Judicial Studies Institute, Masaryk University Law Faculty in Brno. She earned her PhD at Masaryk University and an MSt degree at the University of Oxford. She previously held a position as the head of the analytical department at the Czech Supreme Court and provided consultation to both the Supreme and Constitutional Court of the Czech Republic.

Max Steuer is an assistant professor at the OP Jindal Global University, Jindal Global Law School, India, and at Comenius University in Bratislava, Department of Political Science, Slovakia. He was visiting researcher at the WZB Berlin Social Science Center, European University Viadrina, Örebro University, the Centre for Socio-Legal Studies at the University of Oxford, and Washington State University as a Fulbright scholarship recipient.

Maya Vogel received her international relations and social sciences BA degree from the University of Erfurt. She was an intern at the Global Constitutionalism Professorship of the WZB Berlin Social Sciences Centre in February and March 2022.

Michał Ziółkowski is an assistant professor of constitutional law at Kozminski University, Poland and the managing editor of the Polish legal journal *The State and the Law*. He received his PhD in constitutional law from the Polish Academy of Sciences. Before being a Max Weber Fellow at European University Institute (2019–2021), he was a judicial clerk (référendaire) in the Bureau of Constitutional Tribunal of the Republic of Poland for many years.

Introduction

Identities, the Jurisprudence of Particularism and Possible Constitutional Challenges

KRISZTA KOVÁCS

In his seminal essay 'Politics and the English language', George Orwell condemns the mechanical use of certain well-worn terms, declaring them meaningless. 'The worst thing one can do with words is to surrender to them'.[1] One wonders, then, what Orwell might think of the omnipresent word 'identity'. For social scientists like Rogers Brubaker and Frederick Cooper, the answer is clear. 'The social sciences and humanities', they argue, 'have already surrendered to the word identity',[2] maintaining that other terms might more effectively do the associated conceptual work. Similar opinions have been expressed in the field of legal studies. Some legal scholars find the concepts of constitutional and national identity inherently flawed, holding that 'the identity discourse is part of the problem that it intends to solve'.[3] Others urge experts on constitutional identity to 'issue a recall on the dangerous product they released in the marketplace of ideas'.[4] What these scholars agree on is that the concepts of constitutional and national identity, as traditional, mythical and monolithic concepts, are not adequate for our current constitutional predicament. They believe that we should abandon these concepts altogether as there are better alternative concepts to constitutional and national identity.

This book addresses these scholarly critiques and takes them seriously – because the language of identity can indeed be used to divide people and thus poses a severe challenge for constitutional democracy based on equal human dignity. The book, however, does not offer a general discussion and critique of

[1] G Orwell, 'Politics and the English Language' 76 *Horizon* 1946.

[2] R Brubaker and F Cooper, 'Beyond "identity"' (2000) 29 *Theory and Society* 1, 1.

[3] F Fabbrini and A Sajó, 'The Dangers of Constitutional Identity' (2019) 25 *European Law Journal* 457, 444.

[4] D Kelemen and L Pech, 'Why Autocrats Love Constitutional Identity and Constitutional Pluralism' (2018) 2 *Reconnect Working Paper* 6–7.

the notion of identity, and it does not take identity as an analytical structure or object of study in and of itself. Identity as a concept has been discussed and contested in many scientific disciplines. Historians, sociologists, social psychologists, and political theorists have taken a critical stand against this concept.[5] These insights from social sciences have greatly informed the legal debates on identity. In contrast, legal scholars came late to the analytical discussion about the concept.

In an ideal world, there would be very little space for the terms 'constitutional identity' or 'national identity' in the legal domain. And even in our non-ideal world, these terms did not play any role in the European legal discourse for a long time. In the past, other concepts resolved the problem of allocations of competencies within the EU. For instance, the concept of sovereignty long framed the discourse: constitutional courts interpreted democracy through the lens of the sovereign state and used the concept of sovereignty to draw boundaries to European integration.[6]

In the 2000s, a conceptual shift happened: the relevance of the concept of sovereignty declined, and the concepts of constitutional and national identity became part of the continent's legal repertoire.[7] The German Federal Constitutional Court (Bundesverfassungsgericht), the French Constitutional Court (Conseil constitutionnel) and the Spanish Constitutional Tribunal (Tribunal Constitucional) started to use the language of 'constitutional identity'[8] to draw certain red lines relating to further European integration. Since then, other European constitutional courts have embedded the language of identity in their own jurisprudence.[9] In parallel, the Lisbon Treaty,[10] which amended the two treaties that form the European Union's constitutional basis, introduced 'national identity' as a justiciable concept to challenge the domestic courts' interpretation. The concept's importance was emphasised by the fact that it was reproduced in the preamble to the EU Fundamental Rights Charter.[11]

Currently, both the concepts of constitutional identity and national identity play a central role as a matter of positive law. Constitutional identity case law

[5] See, eg, KA Appiah and HL Gates, *Identities* (Chicago, The University of Chicago Press, 1995); E Castano and V Yzerbyt, 'The Highs and Lows of Group Homogeneity' (1998) 42 *Behavioural Processes* 219–238; D Bar-Tal, 'Group beliefs as an expression of social identity' in S Worchel et al (eds), *Social identity: International Perspectives* (London, Sage Publications, 1998) 93–113; Brubaker and Cooper (n 2).

[6] R Toniatti, 'Sovereignty Lost, Constitutional Identity Regained' in AS Arnaiz and CA Llivina (eds), *National Constitutional Identity and European Integration* (Cambridge, Intersentia, 2013) 54.

[7] JHH Weiler, 'On the power of the Word: Europe's constitutional iconography' (2005) 3 *International Journal of Constitutional Law* 184.

[8] M Claes, 'National Identity: Trump Card or Up for Negotiation?' in S Arnaiz and CA Llivina (eds), *National Constitutional Identity and European Integration* (Cambridge, Intersentia, 2013) 124.

[9] P Faraguna, 'Taking Constitutional Identities away from the Courts' (2015) 41 *Brooklyn Journal of International Law* 492.

[10] Treaty of Lisbon Amending the Treaty on European Union and the Treaty Establishing the European Community, 2007/C 306/1.

[11] Charter of Fundamental Rights of the European Union, Preamble, 2012/C 326/02.

has prominence in the European constitutional jurisprudence. Its function is to give justifications for the Member States not to obey the primacy of EU law as it is demanded by the Court of Justice (ECJ)[12] by drawing boundaries to the implementation of EU law. The concept of national identity is also present in the European legal space. Article 4(2) of the Treaty on European Union (TEU) obliges the EU to respect the national identities of the Member States. Although EU law explicitly uses the notion of 'national identity', Article 4(2) contextually suggests that national identity has a constitutional relevance.[13]

This book is centrally concerned with the judicial application of these concepts and discusses whether these applications generally correspond with universal constitutional principles. Contrary to what some legal scholars suggest,[14] fundamental rejection of these concepts is likely to be unsuccessful,[15] given the central role that constitutional and national identity clauses play in today's constitutional discourse. Being part of positive law, these clauses are open to interpretation. So, before putting constitutional and national identity into the pantheon of legal keywords, the book will consider whether the concepts of constitutional and national identity as they are used in connection with EU law are inherently flawed or whether they have merely been applied in problematic ways.

What are these problematic applications? In the late twentieth century, a global backlash developed against universal, integrative constitutional principles: human rights, democracy and the rule of law. National identity was rediscovered in common ancestry and shared ethnocultural heritage, which enabled governments to advance exclusivist constitutional agendas. This phenomenon is not limited to the Central European region, so it may not be explained away by references to the unique characteristics of post-socialist states, with their long story of authoritarianism and limited experience of democracy. However, this region, especially the Visegrád 4 countries (V4) – that is, Czechia, Hungary, Poland, and Slovakia – have exhibited, to varying degrees, the most visible signs of exclusionary nationalism in the EU.

Exclusionary nationalism is not new. What is novel is that the V4 countries have cited Article 4(2) TEU as grounds for limiting the authority of EU law. Their claim has been that these countries are different because they reject migration,[16] multiculturalism and 'foreign culture', hence the EU should

[12] The Court of Justice of the European Union comprises two separate courts: The Court of Justice (the higher instance) and the General Court (the lower instance). The higher instance is abbreviated as ECJ.

[13] Toniatti (n 6) 63.

[14] F Fabbrini, D Kelemen, L Pech, and A Sajó (n 3 and n 4).

[15] J Scholtes, 'Abusing Constitutional Identity' (2021) 22 *German Law Journal* 534.

[16] During the Russian War in 2022, the V4 countries' policy and attitude toward migrating people, especially those fleeing Ukraine have changed slightly. However, non-white, non-Christian refugees and Ukrainian Roma refugees are still not welcome in this region. L Tondo, 'Embraced or pushed back: on the Polish border, sadly, not all refugees are welcome' *The Guardian* (London, 4 March 2022).

accommodate their distinctive national identities and allow these countries to refrain from participating in the EU refugee relocation scheme.[17] In a similar vein, V4 countries argue that the 'traditional family' is a value protected as an element of national identity in EU law, so the EU should allow these countries to avoid recognising same-sex marriage.[18]

What is also unique in the case of the V4 is that recently, constitutional judiciaries have played a determining role in invoking the concept of constitutional or national identity. In the 1990s, the V4 constitutional courts were perceived as an integral and crucial part of these societies' transitions toward democracy. They exercised a prominent role in safeguarding constitutionalism and applied various judicial techniques to protect the core of their democratic constitutional structures. For instance, the concept of the 'invisible constitution' became a benchmark of the Hungarian Constitutional Court (Alkotmánybíróság),[19] while the Czech Constitutional Court (Ústavní Soud) and the Slovak Constitutional Court (Ústavný Súd) opted for the 'substantive core' doctrine.[20]

The adoption of the Lisbon Treaty has turned out to be a game-changer. The concept of constitutional or national identity appeared in the constitutional court's jurisprudence in the context of the V4 countries' EU membership. Since the Lisbon Treaty entered into force in 2009, the V4 courts, ostensibly following the German Federal Constitutional Court's (FCC) example, have drawn on the identity discourse and tended to protect the nations' distinctive identities. The Hungarian Constitutional Court (HCC) and the Polish Constitutional Tribunal (Trybunał Konstytucyjny) have even provided an ethnocultural justification for the legal concept of identity. When defining the meaning of identity, they have tended to rely on distinctive historical narratives and selectively chosen historical events from the 'glorious' past of the respective countries to provide a linchpin for future constitutional interpretations. Following their governments, they often treat their countries as victims of 'foreign aggression' with

A Zachová and V Makszimov, 'Visegrad plays hot potato with Ukrainian Roma refugees' *Euractiv* (Brussels, 19 May 2022).

[17] The ECJ rejected this claim by demanding EU law's primacy and held that these countries breached their EU obligations. Joined cases C-715/17, C-718/17 and C-719/17 *European Commission v Republic of Poland, Hungary and the Czech Republic*, Judgment of 2 April 2020. See also joined cases C-643/15 and C-647/15 *Slovak Republic and Hungary v Council of the European Union*, Judgment of 6 September 2017.

[18] The Hungarian, Polish and Slovak governments submitted written observations on the issue in the Case C-490/20 *VMA v Stolichna obshtina, rayon 'Pancharevo'* (Sofia municipality, Pancharevo district, Bulgaria).

[19] The 'invisible constitution' was above and beyond the (frequently amended) text of the 1989 constitution, and the concept was used to develop a coherent constitutional system and fundamental rights. GA Tóth, 'Lost in Transition: Invisible Constitutionalism in Hungary' in R Dixon and A Stone (eds), *The Invisible Constitution in a Comparative Perspective* (Cambridge, Cambridge University Press, 2018) 541–62, 548–49.

[20] See chapters three and four in this volume. The terms 'invisible constitution' and 'substantive core' can be regarded as coextensive, such as the term 'constitutional identity' and the idea of the 'basic structure doctrine', as Mattias Kumm rightly points out in chapter seven.

the greatness to overcome suppression, which becomes an essential component of national identity.[21] Moreover, these constitutional courts invoke identity in areas that are outside the traditional field of constitutionalism, that is, in policy questions such as migration or family law issues.

This book offers an analytical review of these judicial invocations of constitutional or national identity. The use of identity language highlights particularism and historicity, hence the book calls this phenomenon the jurisprudence of particularism.

At this juncture, particularism requires explanation. It is typically contrasted with universalism. However, particularism does not necessarily have to be exclusionist. It can be understood as particularistic manifestations and reflections of universal constitutional principles. When the constitution is concise, uses broad concepts and states the universal constitutional principles somewhat abstractly, the instantiations of these principles as particulars may appear in domestic legislative and judicial arguments. Domestic institutions, especially constitutional courts, may play an essential role in applying universal principles in the given cultural and historical context. Take the example of free speech. The German doctrine of militant democracy introduced after World War II aims to protect the democratic character of the state through a variety of laws and ultimately leads to a specific understanding of free speech limits. By contrast, in the early 1990s, Hungary, newly freed from Soviet-type censorship, embraced the idea of content neutrality and did not restrict hate speech in the vaguely defined interests of social peace or the name of national historical sensibilities. These exemplify two particular approaches to free speech and various levels of protection. Still, both may conform to universal human rights principles because the starting point for these interpretations is the understanding that each person is a human being whose dignity matters. Using the language of constitutional theory, one can say that the German doctrine is not very far from what Jeremy Waldron describes in his book,[22] and the early Hungarian jurisprudence was close to Ronald Dworkin's approach of free speech protection.[23]

Particularism can also mean a non-inclusive attachment to one's own group, in our case, the nation. This arises when the constitution is substantially informed by ethnocultural considerations and historical myths. If such exclusionist

[21] In 2010, the president of the Russian Constitutional Court introduced the concept of identity as a tool to preserve the traditional values of Russian society. Since then, the Court has deployed the concept against the human rights tradition, deeming it alien to the Russian civilization. A Zotéeva and M Kragh, 'From Constitutional Identity to the Identity of the Constitution' 54 *Communist and Post-Communist Studies* 176–195, 180. The Russian Constitutional Court case law on upholding the ban on 'propaganda of non-traditional sexual relations' and the ban on books containing 'historical misrepresentations' could probably guide some Hungarian and Polish judges. ibid, 185–88.

[22] J Waldron, *The Harm in Hate Speech* (Cambridge, Mass, Harvard University Press, 2012).

[23] R Dworkin, *Sovereign Virtue: The Theory and Practice of Equality* (Cambridge, Mass, Harvard University Press, 2000) 351–385, R Dworkin, *Justice for Hedgehogs* (Cambridge, Mass, Harvard University Press, 2011) 371–78.

concerns permeate the whole constitution, it reflects a highly parochial interpretation of universal principles and may even violate them. For instance, the Orbán regime's constitution, officially called the Fundamental Law, projects a mental image of an indivisible and homogeneous ethnic, linguistic, religious and cultural community consisting exclusively of ethnic Hungarians worldwide. It privileges those who identify with the prescribed 'Christian culture' and who accept historical myths that refer to Hungary's past greatness in the same breath as its victimisation. At the same time, the Fundamental Law excludes ethnic, sexual minorities, refugees and 'others' considered not to belong to the nation because they differ in some key respects. The ethnoculturally informed particularism allows only some but certainly not all people to believe that they are part of the same political community. This form of particularism contradicts the egalitarian claim that forms the basis of constitutional democracy: the protection of the human dignity of free and equal individuals.

The ambition of this introduction is to articulate a clear understanding of the frequently contested concepts of national and constitutional identity and trace the recent emergence of the jurisprudence of particularism in Central Europe and the possible basis for a constitutional challenge. Thus, the remainder of this introductory chapter offers some capsule definitions of the key terms – 'personal and communal identity', 'national and constitutional identity' – and provides preliminary notes on these terms and concepts, which we build upon in later chapters. Furthermore, the introduction sets the scene by describing the jurisprudence of particularism, including the most problematic applications of the concepts of identity. After analysing the jurisprudence of particularism in the V4 countries, the book searches for a principle-based tool for a constitutional challenge to the judicial invocation of national identity that has come to be associated with democratic backsliding.

I. PERSONAL VERSUS COMMUNAL IDENTITY

What is meant by personal and communal identity? Let me start from the premise that one may talk about identity in two different senses.[24] First, personal identity is the concept we develop about ourselves. We develop an identity when we search for answers to the question of what separates us from the world around us and what marks the boundaries of our personalities. This may be called the ontological or metaphysical sense of personal identity. Since Aristotle, the notion of 'identity' or 'the idea of sameness' has mainly referred to the identity in this metaphysical sense.[25] Descartes assumes that our personal identity lies in an

[24] For this point, I owe a debt to János Kis.
[25] KT Barnes, 'Aristotle on Identity and Its Problems' (1977) 22 *Phronesis* 48.

immutable essence, the soul; to Aristotle, rationality is the essence of the human being.[26] And as John Locke reminds us, consciousness rather than substance (body or mind) makes a person identical through time.[27]

Yet, we may think of personal identity in another sense, too. Each person has many qualities and characteristics, and they belong to various kinds of social groups. In shaping their lives, individuals decide what they consider to be the circumstances that define their identity. The person's identity is constituted by the qualities and characteristics that they consider essential, that they identify with and that they use to form a community with other individuals who define themselves in the same way. In this sense, personal identity is 'constructed' because it is based on the choice of the individual.

The defining feature of communal identity is that it does not exist in a metaphysical sense; it does not possess ontological status. It is not something naturally given, nor does it enjoy timeless validity. It is an imagined and socially constructed concept.[28] Hence in the case of the communities, the two meanings of identity coincide: their boundaries and their identities in time are defined by the same thing that defines their self-image: that there is a group of people who construct their identity from common cultural elements and traditions and who have enough members who accept this and mutually regard each other as members of the community. The members of the group distinguish themselves from outsiders by creating a communal identity[29] that is designed to maintain inner sameness and continuity and offer a sense of belonging to a collective self.[30] Belonging is the condition of being understood, as Isaiah Berlin points out, and 'to be understood is to share common forms of life'.[31]

In societies, political actors construct and apply this type of communal identity according to the needs of particular historical moments, and they invent traditions, a set of practices of a symbolic nature, which imply continuity with a suitable historical past.[32] They choose which part of the country's history serves as a reference point for identity-making. This is made possible by the fact that history offers several options for political actors to choose when and how to develop a communal identity. It is the presenting of history that establishes and re-establishes identity.[33] History is not a natural science; it cannot be described

[26] For more on this, see F Coulmas, *Identity: A Very Short Introduction* (Oxford, Oxford University Press, 2019) 9.

[27] J Locke, *An Essay Concerning Human Understanding* (Pennsylvania, Pennsylvania State University, 1999) Chapter XXVII. For Erikson, consciousness is also the key to identity. EH Erikson, *Dimensions of a New Identity* (New York, WW Norton and Co, 1979) 113.

[28] B Anderson, Imagined Communities: Reflections on the Origin and Spread of Nationalism (London/New York, Verso, 2017).

[29] B Williams, *Ethics and the Limits of Philosophy* (London, Routledge, 2006) 163.

[30] M Rosenfeld, 'Constitutional Identity' in A Sajó and M Rosenfeld (eds), *The Oxford Handbook of Comparative Constitutional Law* (Oxford, Oxford University Press, 2012) 757.

[31] I Berlin, *Personal Impressions* (London, Pimlico, 1998) 258.

[32] E Hobsbawn, *The Invention of Tradition* (Cambridge, Cambridge University Press, 1992) 1–11.

[33] I Rév, 'Identity by History', in S Greenblatt, I Rév, and R Starn, (1995) 49 *Representation, Special Issue: Identifying Histories: Eastern Europe Before and After 1989*, 8, 9.

and explained in the same way as scientists describe the laws of nature. Hence, one cannot exclude moral categories and judgements from history.[34] But this does not mean that any attempt to present history will be inevitably biased. The reconstruction of history can be a self-reflective process; one that liberates a nation from its past, but presentations of history can also be false and misleading. When might this arise? One such instance might be when the presentation of history in practice means an 'apologetic relationship to one's own national past' and 'historical narratives are replaced by an ideological agenda and a sense of victimisation'.[35]

In any country's past, the theoretical roots of progressive[36] thought and the heroic history of struggling for universal principles like freedom and equality are present and waiting to be discovered. And, of course, any country's history contains reactionary[37] ideas and periods, and they all have dark chapters in which they have denied the universality of human rights. For instance, many identify twentieth century Russia with the atrocious cruelties that were committed under the Stalinist totalitarian regime; however, in 1917, before the Bolshevik seizure of power, Russia was among the first countries to grant suffrage to women.[38] To take another example, German history not only includes the tradition of the Weimar democratic parliamentary system but also that of its predecessor, the Prussian authoritarian regime, not to mention the successor Nazi regime. It is, therefore, crucial to identify which part of a country's history and cultural traditions serve as reference points for the particularistic concretisations of universal constitutional principles and identity-making. The political actors who (re)construct communal identity may relate to the community's history reflexively and critically, but they may also be nonreflexive.[39] For instance, German communal identity is solidly founded on equal human dignity based on an open distancing of the polity from the Nazi past.[40] In Russia, by contrast, an

[34] I Berlin, 'Historical Inevitability' in H Meyerhoff (ed), *The Philosophy of History in our Time* (Hamburg, Anchor, 1959).

[35] A Michnik, 'The Trouble with History: Tradition: Imprisonment or Liberation?' (2009) 22 *International Journal of Politics, Culture, and Society* 445–52.

[36] Progressive, in a sense, Mattias Kumm uses this word in his article. M Kumm, 'The Idea of Thick Constitutional Patriotism and Its Implications for the Role and Structure of European Legal History' (2005) 6 *German Law Journal* 325.

[37] Reactionary, in a sense, Mark Lilla uses this term in his book. M Lilla, *The Shipwrecked Mind on Political Reaction* (New York, The New York Review of Books, 2016).

[38] R Goldberg Ruthchild, 'Women and Gender in 1917' (2017) 76 *Slavic Review* 694.

[39] The Polish thinker Adam Michnik captures it well when he maintains that a sense of shame can be the basis of belonging to a nation: 'He who is ashamed of Polish sins is a Pole.' M Kohn, 'From Lublin to London, Europe's Contested Ideas of National Identity' *The New York Review of Books*, 12 November 2019.

[40] Institutions (eg, the constitutional court) were built on the idea of equal human dignity, and institutional commitment became part of German identity. On the importance of a sense of institution, see R Dahrendorf, 'Germans Lack the Key to Their National Identity', in H James and M Stone (eds) *When the Wall Came Down* (New York-London, Routledge, 1992) 230–33.

aversion to the Stalinist regime is not at the heart of its identity construction.[41] History is not linear but goes in several directions; thus, only a critical and reflexive view can differentiate between better or worse choices when it comes to decisive historical events that can serve as components of communal identity.

II. NATIONAL VERSUS CONSTITUTIONAL IDENTITY

Communal identity in the political sphere can take the form of national or constitutional identity. Conventional wisdom says that there is a dichotomy between the two forms of identity. Our intuitive understanding of the difference between national and constitutional identity is that the former is 'realistic', being closer to local peculiarities and cultural traditions and thus easier to observe. By contrast, constitutional identity embodies universal normative principles that only a handful of people identify with in their day-to-day lives. This book seeks to question this understanding of national and constitutional identity. Both may draw on universal normative principles.[42] Yet political choices determine which of these values gains official recognition as an element of communal identity.

Political actors follow universal patterns even when aiming to construct an idiosyncratic national identity. During the exercise of identity construction, they will likely opt for traditional religious virtues, like loyalty or faith, and they will probably offer special protection to 'traditional marriage'. And the identity components they assemble will most likely include the protection of the majority's language and a narrative about the common past, encompassing the myth of origin and a specific mass culture that has its antecedents in particularities, such as the community's local habits, rituals and symbols.[43] All of these things can be distilled into a single adjective of national identity: ethnocultural. Applying a metaphorical concept – in this case, the idea of the wall identity[44] – we see the emergence of an exclusionist identity that mobilises the 'incomprehensible Alien' to delineate the group from other groups.[45]

Anyone who advocates such an ethnocultural national identity follows Carl Schmitt, who introduced an 'alternative concept of democracy' in the period between the two world wars. He insisted that democracy, properly understood,

[41] On the contrary, the Russian president, Vladimir Putin has embraced the Stalinist cult of fear and control. SS Montefiore, 'Why Putin is beholden to Stalin's legacy' *The New Statesman*, 9 March 2022.

[42] M Kumm, 'Why Europeans Will Not Embrace Constitutional Patriotism' (2008) 6 *International Journal of Constitutional Law* 120.

[43] AD Smith, 'Will and Sacrifice: Images of National Identity' (2001) 30 *Millennium: Journal of International Studies* 571.

[44] F Cerruti, 'Political Identity and Conflict: A Comparison of Definitions' in F Cerutti and R Ragionerie (eds), *Identities and Conflicts* (London, Palgrave Macmillan, 2001).

[45] European Commission, 'The Development of European Identity/Identities: Unfinished Business' (2012).

is an attempt to establish a 'genuine identity' shared by the rulers and the ruled.[46] The ruler may be a directly elected unitary sovereign who acts as an authentic representative of the people's will by symbolically incarnating the identity of the people, and whose primary mission is to guarantee the political entity's self-preservation.[47] The ruled are the people who exist in their ethnic and cultural 'oneness'.[48] This oneness ensures the strict internal homogeneity of the community. The identity of this homogeneous community manifests itself in a self-chosen institutional form.[49] For those who follow Schmitt, the identity of the community is present prior to any constitutional order and has existed since time immemorial. The community consists of members who have 'their roots in the generations that have lived in the nation's territory and share its customs and culture (e.g., language, religion) since childhood'.[50] The underlying foundational idea is that national communities are predicated on genetic affiliation and that the ethnically defined people have a common interest and will. Accordingly, the nation is fully formed prior to the adoption of a constitution or the creation of the state, and national identity is perceived as something given, fixed and unchangeable that exists in nature, outside time.[51]

This vision, however, is a mirage.[52] The scholarship suggests that nationalists merely imagine a common ethnic community. As Anthony Kwame Appiah and Lawrence Friedman insist, there is nothing natural about nations.[53] Different groups are created and accidental entities; thus, national identity is neither self-evident nor the product of ancient tradition. Instead, it is socially constructed to serve the needs of the community, which is likewise invented.[54] 'The line between members and non-members of the nation has nothing to do with consanguinity' because nations are contingent social constructions that never cease to undergo transformations.[55] What nationalists perceive as an 'ancient' tradition has a changing nature, and shared beliefs also mutate from one generation to another. So, in terms of national identity, nothing is fixed or given because all of its components are in a constant state of change.

[46] B Scheuerman, 'Is Parliamentarism in Crisis? A Response to Carl Schmitt' (1995) 24 *Theory and Society* 138.

[47] C Schmitt, *The Concept of the Political* (Chicago, Chicago University Press, 2007) 26.
C Schmitt, *Der Begriff des Politischen* (Berlin, Duncker & Humblot, 1991) 51.

[48] UK Preuss, 'Constitutional Powermaking for the New Polity: Some Deliberations on the Relations Between Constituent Power and the Constitution' in M Rosenfeld (ed), *Constitutionalism, Identity, Difference, and Legitimacy* (Durham, Duke University Press, 1994) 153–54.

[49] C Schmitt, *Constitutional Theory* translated by J Seitzer (Durham, Duke University Press, 2008) 125.

[50] M Haller and R Ressler, 'National and European identity: A study of their meanings and interrelationships' (2006) 47 *Revue Francaise de Sociologie*.

[51] C Geertz, *The Interpretation of Cultures* (New York, Basic Books, 1973).

[52] F O'Toole, 'Celtic Myths' *The New York Review of Books*, 7 March 2019.

[53] LM Friedman, 'Nationalism, Identity, and Law' (1995) 28 *Indiana Law Review* 503; KA Appiah, *The Lies that Bind. Rethinking Identity: Creed, Country, Class, Culture* (New York, Liveright, 2018).

[54] R Brubaker, *Nationalism Reframed: Nationhood and the National Question in the New Europe* (Cambridge, Cambridge University Press, 1996) 276.

[55] S Holmes, 'The Identity Illusion' *The New York Review of Books*, 17 January 2019, 46.

Yet traditionally, the starting point for constructing a national identity was this pre-legal understanding of national identity. In democracies, this understanding of identity has been restricted by universal constitutional principles: the protection of human rights, democracy, and the rule of law. With the advent of this restriction, the understanding of national identity has evolved from a pre-legal to a legal understanding. National identity, in this sense, is connected to the demos-oriented concept of the state-nation[56] or civic nation concept,[57] wherein membership is based upon political criteria: for example, citizenship[58] or residence. This type of identity is either called 'national constitutional identity'[59] or 'constitutional identity'. These terms are interchangeable: they both emphasise that the interpretation of national identity has to move from a pre-legal to a legal approach.[60] This understanding is not sealed off by being based on an assumed ethnic, religious or linguistic homogeneity; on the contrary, it is an integrative 'mirror identity'[61] that focuses on the national contestations of universal constitutional principles and gives concrete form to these principles. While there is always a comparison with other groups, this comparison with 'the others' can be relatively benign, as constitutional identity can remain open to everyone who lives under the same government and shares the same constitutional values. Although some contend that understanding national identity this way results in 'global uniformity' and an elimination of national differences,[62] the commitment to the core constitutional principles is not a commitment to abolishing or flattening national cultures; instead, it calls for interpreting national culture and identity to make it more reflexive and inclusive.

Many scholars have engaged with the relationship between the concepts of national and constitutional identity. Some have suggested that constitutional identity embraces the identity of the community.[63] Others maintain that the

[56] Preuss (n 48).

[57] H Kohn, *The Idea of Nationalism: A Study in Its Origins and Background* (New York, MacMillan, 1944); Y Tamir, *Liberal Nationalism* (Princeton, Princeton University Press, 1995); D Miller, *On Nationality* (Oxford, Oxford University Press, 1995); W Kymlicka, *Multicultural Citizenship* (Oxford, Oxford University Press, 1996); M Ignatieff, *Blood and Belonging: Journey into the New Nationalities* (New York, Farrar, Straus and Giroux, 1995).

[58] Citizenship is a legal institution with equal rights and obligations and is independent of identity-based mutual acceptance. See also M Lilla, *The Once and Future Liberal: After Identity Politics* (New York, HarperCollins, 2018) 86; F Fukuyama, *Identity. The Demand for Dignity and the Politics of Resentment* (New York, Farrar, Straus and Giroux, 2018).

[59] M Claes, 'Negotiating Constitutional Identity or Whose Identity is It Anyway?' in M Claes et al, *Constitutional Conversations in Europe* (Cambridge, Intersentia, 2012) 208.

[60] P Faraguna, 'Taking Constitutional Identities away from the Courts' (2016) 41 *Brooklyn Journal of International Law* 492.

[61] Cerruti (n 44).

[62] R Scruton who accepted honours from Viktor Orbán in 2019 said that Orbán must be congratulated for preserving Hungary's national identity in times when everywhere else there is pressure to accept global uniformity and eliminate national differences. 'Orbán Lauds Sir Roger Scruton, "Loyal Friend of Freedom-loving Hungarians"' *Hungary Today*, 4 December 2019, www.hungarytoday.hu/orban-lauds-sir-roger-scruton-loyal-friend-of-freedom-loving-hungarians/

[63] A Śledzińska-Simon, 'Constitutional Identity in 3D: A Model of Individual, Relational, and Collective Self and its Application in Poland' (2015) 13 *International Journal of Constitutional Law* 124.

relationship between constitutional and national identity is the opposite: the concept of constitutional identity constitutes an element of the state's national identity.[64] It is the state that has an identity; hence, an identity is called a constitutional identity only if it has a constitutional rank.[65] The contributors to this book subscribe to the idea that constitutional identity is distinct from national identity.[66]

Constitutional identity is a contested and difficult to articulate concept, and views differ on the exact meaning of the phrase.[67] Some scholars approach the concept of identity from the perspective of the demos or political people and understand constitutional identity as the people's unique collective self-identity.[68] The main problem with this view is that although constitutions are often bearers of particular conceptions of communal identity, the identity of the community may be different from the identity of the constitution that gives rules to the community.[69] When the constitution is imposed[70] on the community, then the community's self-determination might not be bound up with the constitution. The most blatant manifestations of this phenomenon – ie where the identity of the constitution did not correspond to the identity of the community – were the Stalinist constitutions. These were imposed on Czechoslovakia, Hungary and Poland among others by Soviet forces after World War II. Most of the population considered them sham constitutions that were not their own.

The book therefore prefers another argument that leaves out the community's characteristics from its considerations and understands constitutional identity solely in terms of domestic constitutional law.[71] This approach locates constitutional identity within constitutions themselves and considers constitutional identity as the identity of the constitution.[72] The roots of this idea go

A Khvorostiankina, 'Constitutional Identity in the Context of Post-Soviet Transformation. Europeanization and Regional Integration Processes (the case of Armenia)' (2017) 1 *Armenian Journal of Political Science* 45.

[64] Case C-399/11 *Stefano Melloni v Ministerio Fiscal* [2013] Opinion of Advocate General Bot, para 137.

[65] C Van de Heyning, 'The European Perspective: from lingua franca to common language' in M Claes et al, *Constitutional Conversations in Europe* (Cambridge, Intersentia, 2012) 200.

[66] M Rosenfeld, *The Identity of the Constitutional Subject. Selfhood, Citizenship, Culture, and Community* (London, Routledge, 2009).

[67] Silvia Suteu calls this 'conceptual confusion' in her book. S Suteu, *Eternity Clauses in Democratic Constitutionalism* (Oxford, Oxford University Press, 2021) 94.

[68] Rosenfeld (n 30) 757.

[69] JL Martí, 'Two Different Ideas of Constitutional Identity: Identity of the Constitution v. Identity of the People' in AS Arnaiz and AC Llivina (eds), *National Constitutional Identity and European Integration* (Cambridge, Intersentia, 2013) 19.

[70] A Arato, *Post Sovereign Constitution Making* (Oxford, Oxford University Press, 2018) 75.

[71] A von Bogdandy and SW Schill, 'Overcoming absolute primacy: Respect for national identity under the Lisbon Treaty' (2011) 48 *Common Market Law Review*. G van der Schyff suggests that constitutional identity refers to the individuality or essence of a legal order, a jurisdiction. C Callies and G van der Schyff, *Constitutional Identity in a Europe of Multilevel Constitutionalism* (Cambridge, Cambridge University Press, 2020) 3.

[72] M Troper, 'Behind the Constitution?' in A Sajó and R Uitz (eds) *Constitutional Topography: Values and Constitutions* (The Hague, Eleven 2010); GJ Jacobsohn, 'Constitutional Identity' (2006) 68

back to Aristotle's *Politics*, where he argues that the identity of the polis is not constituted by its walls, but by its constitution.[73] And as Aristotle reminds us, 'whether the community is the same over time depends on whether it has the same constitution'.[74] In this case, Aristotle is not referring to a particular document but to the organising principles of the polis. For him, the constitution is a certain way of organising offices and those who inhabit the polis. Accordingly, the notion of constitutional identity in this book refers to the fact that it is not the physical characteristics or the ethnocultural form of life of the community's members that matters, but the constitution itself.

Today, all countries of the world have either a codified or a non-codified constitution that forms the basis of the organisation of the state: some are democratic constitutions that take the universal constitutional principles (human rights, democracy, and the rule of law) seriously, while others are sham constitutions. Although the sham constitutions often proclaim some or all of these constitutional principles, they actually reinforce the absolute power of a person or a political party, and they tend to recognise human rights in an equivocal and conditional way. Some scholars argue that even such non-democratic constitutions have a constitutional identity,[75] and what is happening in this case is exploitation (or abuse) of constitutional identity.[76] Yet there is a more fruitful way of understanding this phenomenon, and that is to take the qualifier 'constitutional' seriously and recognise constitutional identity as a normative concept.[77] This 'constitutionalist'[78] approach considers moral commitments to the universal constitutional principles as constitutive for the legal order and understands the 'constitutional' in constitutional identity as the set of values defining democratic politics. Viewed in this way, we might understand constitutional identity as referring only to the identity of those constitutions that are perceived as higher regulatory norms and that establish legitimate authority tied to the protection of human rights, democracy, and the rule of law.[79] In this case,

The Review of Politics 361, 387. GJ Jacobsohn, *Constitutional Identity* (Cambridge, Harvard University Press, 2010) 201. See also B Tripkovic, *The Metaethics of Constitutional Adjudication* (Oxford, Oxford University Press, 2017) 13–58.

[73] Aristotle/Barker, E (ed and trans), *The Politics of Aristotle* (Oxford, Oxford University Press, 1946) 98.

[74] F Miller, 'Aristotle's Political Theory', in EN Zalta (ed), (2017) *The Stanford Encyclopaedia of Philosophy* www.plato.stanford.edu/archives/win2017/entries/aristotle-politics/.

[75] See eg, H Zhai, *The Constitutional Identity of Contemporary China – The Unitary System and its Internal Logic* (Leiden, Brill-Nijhoff, 2019).

[76] See chapter one in this volume. See also Scholtes (n 15), R Dixon and D Landau, *Abusive Constitutional Borrowing: Legal Globalization and the Subversion of Liberal Democracy* (Oxford, Oxford University Press, 2021).

[77] M Polzin, 'Constitutional Identity, Unconstitutional Amendments and the Idea of Constituent Power' (2016) 14 *International Journal of Constitutional Law* 424, 433.

[78] Constitutionalist, in a sense, Kumm uses this word in chapter seven. See also M Kumm, 'The Cosmopolitan Turn in Constitutionalism: An Integrated Conception of Public Law' (2013) 20 *Indiana Journal of Global Legal Studies* 605.

[79] W Waluchow, 'Constitutionalism', in EN Zalta (ed) (2018) *The Stanford Encyclopaedia of Philosophy*.

the identity of the constitution may serve as an integrative identity ie, a mirror in which all members of society can equally recognise themselves.

How can such a constitutional identity be determined? When seeking to understand the identity of a constitution, we should consider the whole set of foundational values and rules.[80] The constitutional core can be identified by the sets of norms – including the underlying values, the system of constitutional organs and basic liberties – that provide information on the fundamental structure of a given constitutional order. Scholars should also consider preambles,[81] entrenchment clauses,[82] constitutional amendment procedures,[83] and the designation of the state and of the constituent subject[84] as sources from which we are able to determine a given constitution's identity. Yet constitutional texts themselves have limited potential to offer information on constitutional identity. The words of the constitution need to be interpreted. There may be inconsistencies in the text, and it is the task of the constitutional organs to 'reconcile and accommodate the disharmonic elements'.[85] Socially embedded legislative and juridical institutions have the power to give authoritative interpretations of the constitution. During this interpretative exercise, they focus on the national contestations of universal constitutional principles and give concrete form to these principles. Through the ongoing process of interpreting and applying universal principles, these institutions could actually foster constitutional identity. Constitutions thereby acquire identity through experience.[86] They can grow and adapt to mutable circumstances without losing their identities. Yet, when constitutional change touches the constitutional core, the change results in a modified constitutional identity or an identity that does not deserve the name 'constitutional identity'.[87]

Constitutional identity is thus rooted in the text, reaffirmed by experience and contingent upon the values embedded in the political culture. Jürgen Habermas calls this embeddedness 'constitutional patriotism', that is, a devotion, a 'reflective civic attachment' to these values and the way these values are

[80] Martí (n 69) 24.

[81] L Orgad, 'The Preamble in Constitutional Interpretation' (2011) 8 *International Journal of Constitutional Law* 714.

[82] M Hein, 'Entrenchment Clauses in the History of Modern Constitutionalism' (2018) 86 *Tijdschrift voor Rechtsgeschiedenis* 434–481; Y Roznai, *Unconstitutional Constitutional Amendments – The Limits of Amendment Powers* (Oxford, Oxford University Press, 2017) Roznai calls the constitution's unamendable part its 'genetic code'.

[83] C Grewe, 'Methods of Identification of National Constitutional Identity' in AS Arnaiz and CA llivina (eds) *National Constitutional Identity and European Integration* (Cambridge, Intersentia, 2013) 40.

[84] T Drinóczi, 'Constitutional Identity in Europe: The Identity of the Constitution. A Regional Approach' (2020) 21 *German Law Journal* 105.

[85] Jacobsohn (n 72).

[86] ibid at 364.

[87] K Kovács, 'Changing Constitutional identity via Amendment' in P Blokker (ed), *Constitutional Acceleration within the European Union and Beyond* (London, Routledge, 2018) 199–217.

discussed and established in the democratic context.[88] Only in this democratic context, where the growth of free people is guaranteed, we expect spontaneous enthusiasm and responsible activism for the political community.[89] Without it, constitutional identity will remain fragile and be unable to withstand the test of time.

In short, this book regards the concept of constitutional identity as a socially constructed normative concept that is rooted in the text of the democratic constitution and emerges from the dialogical process of democratic institutions. In this sense, it is not pre-institutional; instead, it is the outcome of the democratic institutional structures and procedures. Although it is centred on the institutions and the democratic principles that govern people's lives, it should be flexible enough to adapt to ever-changing circumstances.

The implication of only recognising constitutional identities that respect universal principles in the international arena is that such constitutional identities would be more compatible with the values at the European and international levels. Constitutional identity, thus defined as entailing the various understandings of the protection of human rights, democracy and the rule of law, can automatically be recognised as national identity, but, as we will see in the following sections, not all national identities can be recognised as constitutional identities even if they are in some form enshrined in the domestic constitution.

III. REGIONAL DYNAMICS: THE EMERGING ETHNOCULTURAL UNDERSTANDING OF NATIONAL IDENTITY

In the second half of the twentieth century, shortly after European states had experienced the terror of Nazi and Soviet totalitarianism, a combination of the concept of constitutional identity and the reflexive account of history served as a tool to facilitate liberal constitutional democracy. In the European constitutions adopted after World War II, the declaration of human dignity as inviolable became a manifesto for a new era of peace and democracy, and political actors tended to understand communal identity in relation to these universal values. Articles 22 and 27 of the first draft of the French Constitution from 1946, Article 3 of the 1947 Constitution of Italy and Article 1(1) of the 1949

[88] Although D Sternberger introduced the German concept *Verfassungspatriotismus*, J Habermas developed the idea further and presented it to the English-speaking world. On his theoretical conception of constitutional patriotism, see, J Habermas, *Eine Art Schadensabwicklung. Kleine Politische Schriften* VI (Berlin, Suhrkamp, 1987) 173–75. See also J Habermas, 'Citizenship and national identity: some reflections on the future of Europe' in R Robertson and KE White (eds), *Globalization: Global Membership and Participation* (London, Routledge, 2003) 155. J-W Müller broadened the framework of the concept in his book *Constitutional Patriotism* (Princeton, Princeton University Press, 2007).

[89] I Bibó, 'Miseries of the East European Small States' in IZ Dénes (ed), *The Art of Peacemaking. Essays by István Bibó* (London, Yale University Press, 2015) 161.

West German Basic Law nicely illustrate how the principle of human dignity occupied a central place in these new constitutional structures.[90] The centrality of equal human dignity meant that these countries committed themselves to a universalistic constitutional project.[91]

After successfully transitioning from authoritarianism to constitutional democracy in 1989, former Soviet satellite states in Central Europe followed this path. These countries' departure from the Soviet past and increasing openness toward European integration played an essential role in their identity formation. Although the constitution-making processes were precipitated by unique events in these countries, they all ended up with more or less similar constitutional narratives at the level of principles. They adopted the core features of constitutionalism: the commitment to human rights, democracy and the rule of law. And in order to reunite with their European constitutional family and provide a forum aiming to achieve the Council of Europe and European Union memberships collectively, Václav Havel, president of Czechoslovakia, Polish president Lech Walesa and Hungarian prime minister József Antall established a loose organisation called the Visegrád group.[92] After Czechoslovakia's disintegration in 1993, the Visegrád group grew to four countries, including the two newly established states of the Czech Republic and Slovakia. The V4's primary mission, fostering European integration, was completed in the 1990s and 2000s when the V4 countries joined the Council of Europe and then the European Union. Yet, now, the convergence toward an identity based on common constitutional values seems to have been only temporary, and a slow process of divergence is underway. What we are witnessing today in these countries is a far-reaching questioning of universal constitutional principles and the rise of exclusivist approaches to nationalism and national identities, which are understood in a pre-legal sense.[93]

The political groups that served as a democratic opposition to the communist regime and played a significant role in Central Europe during the transition have always been divided. They have either belonged to the camp of the modernisers or the traditionalists. The modernisers have embarked upon the project of 'return to Europe' and universal constitutional values. The traditionalists – that is, the national conservatives – have preferred the mission of 'return to our nationhood'.[94] These national conservatives, which later became populist forces,

[90] C Dupré, *The Age of Dignity: Human Rights and Constitutionalism in Europe* (Oxford, Hart, 2015) 53.

[91] For more on this, see chapter eight in this volume.

[92] The name of the Hungarian village Visegrád was chosen because in 1335, the kings of Bohemia, Hungary and Poland met in the castle of Visegrád and agreed to create a commercial system to bypass the Habsburg capital Vienna and obtain access to other European markets. See also Nick Thorpe, 'The castle where a Central European bloc was born' *BBC News*, 21 February 2016.

[93] J Shaw, *The People in Question. Citizens and Constitutions in Uncertain Times* (Bristol, Bristol University Press, 2020) 186.

[94] C Offe, *Varieties of Transition. The East European and East German Experience* (Cambridge, Polity Press, 1996) 62.

and their supporters perceive constitutional revisions adopted after 1989 not as something that is 'homegrown' or organically evolving but something 'imposed' by external forces, such as the international community. Having become a leading force, they are playing a crucial role in creating national identities by characterising their nations as ethnically, culturally, religiously or linguistically homogeneous communities. Can the V4 countries be considered a specific group when it comes to national identity-making? Can the evolution of Czech and Slovak constitutional law and the connected jurisprudence of particularism be compared to that of the Polish and Hungarian? Arguably, it is just a matter of degree.

In Hungary, the ethnocultural national identity has already been entrenched in the Fundamental Law, which refers to the promotion of an ethnic Hungarian and Christian nation. The Fundamental Law insists that 'Hungary's identity' is rooted in its 'historical constitution' and all state institutions should protect it. Accordingly, as chapter six of this volume demonstrates, all three government branches see the world through the lens of this national identity. Ethnocultural identity in Poland is not yet constitutionally entrenched. Although President Andrzej Duda suggested that a referendum should take place on the question of whether the constitution should include a reference to 'the thousand-year Christian heritage as an important source of Polish statehood, culture and national identity', the de facto leader Jaroslaw Kaczyński judged his bid premature.[95] Nevertheless, the fact that 'identity' is not yet among the terms used by the Polish constitution does not mean that identity discourse is not present at the constitutional level. On the contrary, as chapter five reveals, the packed Constitutional Tribunal has rediscovered the potential of national identity to foster its agenda of promoting conservativism.

Unlike the Hungarian and Polish constitutional discourse, the Czech discourse on national identity has not yet reached the constitutional level; nevertheless, leading politicians have instigated nationalism and expressed the desire to protect cultural identity.[96] Former PM Andrej Babiš has vilified the Roma and other 'outsiders' and used fear of refugees to create a sense of external threat to Czech national identity,[97] and former President Miloš Zeman,

[95] Agence France Presse, 'Polish Senate Vote Down President's Referendum Bid' *The National News* 25 July 2018, www.thenationalnews.com/world/europe/polish-senate-vote-down-president-s-referendum-bid-1.754070.

[96] H Hofmannová, '"Small, but Ours": The Czech features of authoritarian methods of governance' (2020) *Charles University in Prague Faculty of Law Research Paper* 9.

[97] S Hanley and MA Vachudova, 'Understanding the illiberal turn: democratic backsliding in the Czech Republic' (2018) 34 *East European Politics* 282. A Babiš: 'In 2030, there will be more Muslims in Brussels than Europeans. I cannot imagine such a situation in the Czech Republic, our people will not accept this. They want the Czechs to be a majority.' Cited by 'Czech Deputy Prime Minister Babiš: I agree with President Zeman and his views about refugees. We cannot kill our continent in the name of humanity' (*britskélisty* 5 December 2005) www.blisty.cz/art/80142-czech-deputy-prime-minister-babis-i-agree-with-president-zeman-and-his-views-about-the-refugees-we-cannot-kill-our-continent-in-the-name-of-humanity.html.

an influential long-term politician, has highly praised Viktor Orbán for his role in defending the Christian values of Europe.[98] The Slovak Republic, since its foundation in 1993, has promoted national identity by laws. The parliament is known for adopting the language act, which instituted a fine for failing to use the Slovak language, and an act that mandates patriotism.[99] Although in the case of national identity, the Slovak political discussion was dominated by the former prime ministers Vladimír Mečiar and Robert Fico,[100] the current ruling party of Slovakia, OĽaNO[101] can also be classified as an identitarian populist party.[102] Whenever these political actors invoke national identity, they refer to a definition centring on the characteristics of the 'real' people and their ancestral greatness, often backed by mythical historical narratives.

One of the most severe consequences of applying an ethnocultural national identity is that the V4 governments have put European integration in peril. For instance, rejecting the notion that Europe is a multicultural continent and invoking fear of a 'foreign culture', the V4 countries refused to comply with the 2015 EU refugee relocation scheme.[103] The V4 group believed the scheme would impose a multicultural societal model that their governments opposed. Thus, Hungary and Slovakia filed two separate actions for annulment against the quota scheme with the ECJ,[104] and the V4 countries released a joint declaration in which they stressed that setting quotas with negative consequences is not a policy that they support.[105] The European Commission launched infringement actions against the Czech Republic, Hungary, and Poland because they did not relocate an appropriate number of asylum-seekers, and the ECJ confirmed that the affected countries had remained in breach of their legal obligations.[106]

Arguing before the ECJ, the V4 governments invoked an ethnocultural understanding of national identity, which they insist gives them exclusive competence for the safeguarding of national security against any abuse of power by the EU.[107] Likewise, V4 governments intervened in an ECJ case concerning

[98] Cited by Hofmannová (n 96) 2.

[99] K Zachalova, 'Patriotism by Decree in Slovakia' *Time* 18 March 2010.

[100] For more on this, see chapter three in this volume.

[101] OĽaNO: Obyčajní ľudia a nezávislé osobnosti (Ordinary People and Independent Personalities).

[102] P Spáč, 'Slovakia' in Vlastimil Havlík et al, *Populist Political Parties in East-Central Europe* (Brno, Munipress, 2012) 227.

[103] Council Decision (EU) 2015/1601 of 22 September 2015 establishing provisional measures in the area of international protection for the benefit of Italy and Greece [2015] OJ L248.

[104] Joined cases C-643/15 and C-647/15 *Slovak Republic and Hungary v Council of the European Union* [2017] OJ C38.

[105] Visegrád Group, 'Joint Statement of V4 Interior Ministers on the Establishment of the Migration Crisis Response Mechanism', Warsaw, 21 November 2016, www.visegradgroup.eu/calendar/2016/joint-statement-of-v4

[106] Joined cases C-715/17, C-718/17 and C-719/17 *European Commission v Republic of Poland, European Commission v Hungary, European Commission v Czech Republic* [2020] OJ C112.

[107] Joined cases C-715/17, C-718/17 and C-719/17 *European Commission v Republic of Poland, European Commission v Hungary, European Commission v Czech Republic* [2020] OJ C112 Opinion of AG Sharpston, para 224.

Bulgaria's refusal to recognise the parentage of a child of a same-sex couple married in Gibraltar. The Bulgarian national parent wanted to have a Bulgarian birth certificate for her child, but the Bulgarian authorities refused her request, arguing that the birth certificate document under Bulgarian law has only one box for the 'mother' and another box for the 'father'. The V4 governments submitted written observations in which they argued that in countries where the conception of the 'traditional family' prevails, this should be protected as an element of national identity within the meaning of Article 4(2) TEU.[108]

This claim is not merely a political claim: in some V4 countries it has already been transformed into a judicial understanding of constitutional identity. The majority of the V4 courts have invoked constitutional identities against what leading V4 politicians have described as attempts by the European Union to impose uniform liberal constitutionalism. The next section briefly outlines these judicial invocations of constitutional – or, in effect, national – identity.

IV. THE JURISPRUDENCE OF PARTICULARISM IN THE V4 COUNTRIES

For two decades after the democratic transition, the V4 constitutional courts played a vital role in revising the legal systems inherited from the Soviet regime to meet new constitutional-democratic standards. Thus, it is not coincidental that these courts have been the first to be attacked by national populists. In Slovakia, a constitutional amendment has been adopted to curtail the Slovak Constitutional Court's (SCC) competences regarding the review of constitutional amendments.[109] In Hungary and Poland, the new systems of government have affected the independence of the (constitutional) courts even more substantially and neutralised the courts as checks on government.[110] Consequently, today, the Hungarian and Polish constitutional courts are more often than not deferential to their respective governments' reasoning on the need to protect the countries' distinctive national identities. Unfortunately, existing case law in the V4 region has also lent them a helping hand.

In the early 2010s, the Polish Constitutional Tribunal (PCT) and the Czech Constitutional Court (CCC) already proclaimed their capacity to conduct

[108] Case C-490/20 *VMA v Stolichna obshtina, rayon 'Pancharevo'* [2021] Opinion of AG Kokott, para 30.

[109] Constitutional Act 422/2020 Coll. Amending the Constitution of the Slovak Republic (9 December 2020) www.nrsr.sk/web/Dynamic/DocumentPreview.aspx?DocID=489083. For more on this, see chapter three in this volume.

[110] Today, both the Polish Constitutional Tribunal and the Hungarian Constitutional Court are composed of justices nominated and elected by the ruling majority. K Kovács and KL Scheppele, 'The Fragility of an Independent Judiciary: Lessons from Hungary and Poland – and the European Union' (2018) 51 *Communist and Post-Communist Studies* 189; GA Tóth (ed), *Constitution for a Disunited Nation: On Hungary's 2011 Fundamental Law* (New York, CEU Press, 2012); W Sadurski, *Poland's Constitutional Breakdown* (Oxford, Oxford University Press, 2019).

identity review, that is, to decide whether the EU respects the constitutional identity of the Member States and the limits of their conferred competences. In 2010, the PCT differentiated between constitutional and national identity, connecting the former to the values of the state's political system[111] and the latter to tradition and culture. By adopting a broad understanding of 'the nation' which covers both the political and the cultural community and relying on the constitution's preamble, the Tribunal provided room for a more historical account of national identity.[112] Likewise, the CCC in the so-called Slovak pension case referred to unique historical conditions by holding that Czech identity draws on a common constitutional tradition with the Slovak Republic that stems from over seventy years of the common state and its peaceful dissolution: It is a 'completely idiosyncratic and historically created situation that has no parallel in Europe'.[113] The HCC's 2016 identity decision[114] fits into this general trend in Central European jurisprudence. Citing the above-mentioned Polish and Czech judgments, the Hungarian judges introduced the notion of 'constitutional self-identity' to the Hungarian legal system.

As things stand, the V4 constitutional courts consider themselves competent to define identity and exercise identity review.[115] Several commonalities in their approach can be noted.[116] First and foremost, their identity case law frequently refers to supposedly common and homogenous (ethno)cultural traditions, often backed by historical myths. Second, when the V4 constitutional courts interpret identity, they lack the exact criteria to select the constitutional essentials. Scholars wishing to understand the haphazard selection may be tempted to seek principled reasons, but there is little point in searching for them. The V4 constitutional courts seemingly decide on the content of identity on a case-by-case basis, and by using the notion of constitutional identity, they often express their understanding of national identity. Consequently, and that is the third similarity, the V4 constitutional courts cast a constitutional, or in effect a national identity as a limit to European integration. And although they emphasise the importance of cooperation with the ECJ, they do not interpret constitutional identity in light of the ECJ's jurisprudence.

[111] Constitutional Tribunal, 24 November 2010, K 32/09, 2.1.

[112] See, eg, Constitutional Tribunal, 21 September 2015, K 28/13.

[113] Decision Pl ÚS 5/12 31 January 2012 of the Czech Constitutional Court: www.usoud.cz/en/decisions/20120131-pl-us-512-slovak-pensions/. For more on the legal background, see Georgios Anagnostaras, 'Activation of the Ultra Vires Review: The Slovak Pensions Judgment of the Czech Constitutional Court' (2013) 14 *German Law Journal* 959.

[114] Constitutional Court of Hungary 22/2016. (XII 5) AB határozat.

[115] In Decision II. ÚS 501/2010, the SCC left a window open for itself to perform a review of EU law, but it has not yet performed identity review.

[116] The narrative of this section is drawn from K Kovács, 'The Rise of an Ethnocultural Constitutional Identity in the Jurisprudence of the East Central European Courts' (2017) 18 *German Law Journal* 1703.

In place of the ECJ, these constitutional courts have often looked to Germany.[117] When deciding on the essence and scope of this review, the V4 constitutional courts frequently refer to the case law of the FCC, although usually ornamentally.[118] Today, the concept of constitutional identity is understood as one of the main attributes of German constitutional case law. The FCC links this concept to the values enshrined by the 1949 Basic Law's non-amendable clause, Article 79(3), which protects the basic principles of Germany's constitutional order, such as the inviolability of human dignity, the principle of democracy and the separation of powers as well as essential elements of the rule of law, federalism and the social state. Thus, the concept of constitutional identity is based on an attachment to the foundational universal values of the democratic constitution. In the FCC's view, it is its task to safeguard these values by performing an identity review.

The V4 constitutional courts claim that the identity review they perform is the same as the identity review performed by their German counterpart. Their reference to the German identity review as a shield against supranational law is not a coincidence. The FCC often bases its identity decisions on an idiosyncratic 'German' understanding of democracy,[119] which risks becoming a kind of self-centred constitutional identity jurisprudence, where the domestic actors are the only ones deemed competent to contribute.[120] This interpretation and the FCC's static conceptual understanding of constitutional identity[121] provide reference points for the V4 constitutional courts.

Ostensibly, German case law serves as a role model for the V4 constitutional courts, but the essence, content and aim of identity review is different than in the V4 jurisprudence. The concept of constitutional identity as developed by the FCC is understood in a politico-constitutional sense; hence, it is an integrative mirror identity, in which all members of the society may recognise themselves. By contrast, the majority of the V4 constitutional courts provide a concept of an exclusionary wall identity, which effectively shuts out 'the other' by referring to historical narratives or sometimes even to ethnocultural considerations that not all residents share. The content of the constitutional identity also differs. In the view of the FCC, the Basic Law's constitutional identity inheres in its non-amendable clauses.[122] By contrast, the V4 constitutional courts do not

[117] J Rideau, 'The Case-law of the Polish, Hungarian and Czech Constitutional Courts on National Identity and the "German Model"' in AS Arnaiz and AC Llivina (eds) *National Constitutional Identity and European Integration* (Cambridge, Intersentia, 2013) 250.

[118] J Komárek, 'Czech Constitutional Court Playing with Matches: The Czech Constitutional Court Declares a Judgment of the Court of Justice of the EU Ultra Vires; Judgment of 31 January 2012, Pl. ÚS 5/12, Slovak Pensions XVII' (2012) 8 *European Constitutional Law Review* 323.

[119] D Halberstam and C Möllers, 'The German Constitutional Court Says Ja Zu Deutschland' (2009) 10 *German Law Journal* 1241, 1258. See also chapter seven in this volume.

[120] B Çali, 'The Two Faces of German Legal Hegemony?' *Verfassungsblog*, 07 October 2020.

[121] See chapter one in this volume.

[122] See chapter two in this volume. M Hong, *Der Menschenwürdegehalt der Grundrechte* (Tübingen, Mohr Siebeck, 2019) 481 ff.

connect the list of values protected by identity review to a non-amendable constitutional provision, and with good reason: most of the V4 constitutions do not render any provisions as non-amendable. There is one notable exception in this regard: the Czech constitution. Yet, the Czech Constitutional Court defines the content of constitutional identity more broadly than the values protected by the non-amendable clause – ie, those affirming the status of the state as democratic and governed by the rule of law. Finally, constitutional courts aim to achieve different outcomes when constructing a constitutional identity. The FCC takes into account Germany's commitments to ensure the success of European integration and gives due regard to EU law supremacy in general, and only claims the need to intervene when the Basic Law would require more baseline protection of fundamental rights[123] and more democratic accountability[124] than EU law. The goal is thus better protection of human rights and democratic principles within the EU and the creation of a culture of constitutional obedience.[125] In contrast, the V4 constitutional courts' jurisprudence applies the concept of constitutional or national identity to allow derogations from some of their governments' obligations under EU law. The HCC even assumes the supremacy of its domestic constitution in its entirety and holds that some parts of EU law do not apply to domestic law because the Fundamental Law promotes very different norms. Sometimes, these country-specific norms of the Fundamental Law directly violate EU law.[126]

In précis, what is characteristic of the V4 jurisprudence of particularism is that constitutional courts tend to apply the concept of constitutional identity to provide cultural and historical explanations for constitutional provisions. So, in effect, they take the pre-legal understanding of national identity as constitutional identity. The underlying assumption is that cultures differ fundamentally from one another, and so do the constitutional rules that structure relations within the society. When judges turn to this type of cultural relativism, they follow, often unconsciously, the national populist authoritarians' self-identification mindset, which assigns particular cultural characteristics, historical narratives and legal categorisations to their own system.[127] Nation, national sovereignty and culture are the terms that provide intellectual cover against challenges made in the name of constitutionalism.

[123] BVerfGE 73, 339 (*Solange II*); 1 BvR 16/13 (*Right to be forgotten I*); 1 BvR 276/17 (*Right to be forgotten II*).

[124] For instance, by demanding enhanced justifications from the European Central Bank in the so called *PSPP* decision (2 BvR 859/15).

[125] KJ Alter, 'National Perspectives on International Constitutional Review: Diverging Optics' in E Delaney and R Dixon (eds), *Comparative Judicial Review* (Cheltenham, Edward Elgar, 2018) 244–271.

[126] C Dupré, 'Human Dignity: Rhetoric, Protection, and Instrumentalization' in GA Tóth (ed) *Constitution for a Disunited Nation: On Hungary's 2011 Fundamental Law* (New York, CEU Press, 2012) 143.

[127] GA Tóth, 'Beyond civilisation and cultural explanations' (Manuscript, 3 December 2020) (On hand with the author).

V. POSSIBLE CONSTITUTIONAL CHALLENGES

National identity became justiciable in the European Union when the Lisbon Treaty came into force in 2009. Since then, domestic courts' interpretations of national identity can be challenged before the ECJ. The relevant first sentence of Article 4(2) TEU reads that 'The Union shall respect the equality of Member States before the Treaties as well as their national identities, inherent in their fundamental structures, political and constitutional, inclusive of regional and local self-government'.[128] Scholars suggest that national identity is a concept in EU law, while constitutional identity is a concept developed by the domestic constitutional courts.[129] However, national identity claims made by Member States and the relevant ECJ case law do not justify making such a sharp distinction between these two concepts. Furthermore, it does not seem to be the case that Article 4(2) is 'merely a confirmation of the realities of the existing relationship between the union and its Member States'; hence, Article 4(2) refers only to the 'national institutional architecture'.[130]

As the *Runević-Vardyn* case clearly illustrates, the ECJ seems to include some cultural elements – like the language of the majority – as part of the national identity concept in Article 4(2). In this case, the ECJ accepted a Member State's argument that the Lithuanian language constitutes a constitutional asset that preserves the nation's identity and held that the specific alphabet constituted a legitimate objective capable of justifying the restrictions on the rights of the Polish minority.[131] It is debatable whether the exclusionist national identity confirmed by the Lithuanian Constitutional Court is compatible with the constitutional core that emanates from EU and domestic constitutional orders.[132] Similarly perplexing is the opinion of Advocate General Kokott in the *VMA* case, which suggests that family law, including the protection of 'traditional' marriage, falls within the scope of national identity.[133] In any event, both cases demonstrate that, even under EU law, there is some space for particularism.

What are the characteristics of this space? National identity claims by the EU Member States can take various forms. They can conform to universal constitutional principles, which occurs when domestic judges interpret and contextualise

[128] For more on this clause, see B Guastaferro, 'Beyond the Exceptionalism of Constitutional Conflicts: The Ordinary Functions of the Identity Clause' (2012) 31 *Yearbook of European Law* 263–318.

[129] E Cloots, *National Identity in EU Law* (Oxford, Oxford University Press, 2015).

[130] Claes (no 59) 228.

[131] C-391/09 *Malgožata Runević-Vardyn and Łukasz Paweł Wardyn v Vilniaus miesto savivaldybės administracija and Others*, para 54.

[132] D Kochenov, 'When Equality Directives Are Not Enough: Taking an Issue with the Missing Minority Rights Policy in the EU' in U Belavusau and K Henrard (eds), *EU Anti-discrimination Law Beyond Gender* (Oxford, Hart, 2018).

[133] Case C-490/20 *VMA v Stolichna obshtina, rayon 'Pancharevo'* [2021] Opinion of AG Kokott, para 76. AG Kokott argues that the ECJ has already implicitly recognised in the Coman case that the rules governing marriage form part of national identity. Case C-673/16 *Relu Adrian Coman and Others v Inspectoratul General pentru Imigrări and Ministerul Afaceriol Interne* [2018] paras 42–43.

these principles in accordance with those very same principles. The aforementioned German understanding of militant democracy or the Czech substantive rule of law doctrine may exemplify this. Nevertheless, there are national identity claims that are not consistent with the European community's underlying values: the protection of human rights, democracy and the rule of law. Thus, not everything that a Member State presents as national identity pertains to its national identity as protected under Article 4(2) TEU. The ECJ pays respectful attention to domestic constitutional courts' interpretations and has proven to be sensitive to the definitions of constitutional identity as expressed by domestic judiciaries. However, domestic constitutions and their interpretations may contain anti-constitutional principles. This arises, for instance, when national identity claims are in large part informed by (ethno)cultural and historical myths. Hence, demonstrating national identity requires more than just inserting a particular provision into domestic constitutional law. But how can legitimate and illegitimate national identity claims be distinguished?

Within the European Union, it is for the ECJ to decide whether a national identity claim is valid as a matter of EU law and can justify derogations from EU law.[134] During this judicial exercise, the ECJ should decide whether it interprets the term 'national identity' in light of the prevailing constitutional structure of the Member State in question or characterises the concept of 'national identity' as autonomous.[135] The first assessment would require the ECJ to be utterly familiar with the twenty-seven different constitutional structures of the EU Member States. Given the ECJ's role, it would be more fitting for it to characterise the concept of 'national identity' as autonomous.[136] If the ECJ did offer an autonomous interpretation of 'national identity', it would be able to control what national identity claims are acceptable. There are some indications in the case law that the ECJ is willing to adopt this approach. ECJ judgments suggest that in the ECJ's understanding, national identity is a legal phenomenon embodied in domestic law from the moment of the foundation of the independent and democratic state.[137]

Although the relevant ECJ judgments do not appear to be manifestations of a coherent, substantive theory of the concept of national identity, they suggest that the ECJ has elaborated some kind of an adjudication scheme and it is adhering to this standard of evaluation. Currently, what the ECJ seems to

[134] Although it flows from the ECJ's established case law, in the *VMA* case, AG Kokott expressly stated that the ECJ is the gatekeeper of national identities. Case C-490/20 *VMA v Stolichna obshtina, rayon 'Pancharevo'* [2021] Opinion of AG Kokott, para 70.

[135] AG Kokott suggests the ECJ to understand it as an autonomous concept of EU law. AG Kokott (n 133) para 70.

[136] See also, A Kaczorova-Ireland, 'What Is the European Union required to Respect under Article 4(2) TEU?: The Uniqueness Approach' (2019) 25 *European Public Law* 57–82, 71.

[137] K Kovács, 'Constitutional or ethnocultural? National identity as a European legal concept' (2022) 8 *Intersections. East European Journal of Society and Politics* 170–90.

respect when interpreting Article 4(2) TEU is the national identity embodied by the domestic legal system from the moment of the foundation of the independent and democratic state. For instance, in the *Sayn-Wittgenstein* case, the ECJ held that the ban on a person using the noble elements of their name constituted a part of the national identity embodied in the legal system of the independent Republic of Austria.[138] Similarly, in the *Bogendorff* case, the ECJ accepted the German constitutional choice to abolish privileges of birth and rank as an element of national identity.[139] And even in the aforementioned *Runević-Vardyn* case, the ECJ took into account that the Lithuanian language is one of the fundamental constitutional values of the independent and democratic Lithuania. All these findings suggest that the ECJ approaches the concept of national identity through the constitutional law framework of the independent and democratic state. This judicial approach is not very far from what this book endorses. The ECJ case law already encompasses the essential elements of it: that the concept of national identity is a legal concept and that it is connected to an independent and democratic state. From here, it would take only a small step forward for the ECJ to recognise that only a constitution of a democratic state has a constitutional identity shaped by the domestic institutions that EU law should respect. The question then remains, how the ECJ can perform a review on domestic measures based on the protection of national identity.

It is already part of ECJ's case law that even in cases concerning national identity claims, the ECJ conducts a proportionality review to determine if the national measure is justified. The scope of proportionality review, however, has been widely discussed by scholars and practitioners. Notable scholars contend that the requirement of proportionality limits the concept of national identity, and they argue for a weak procedural rationality test.[140] However, when they maintain that the ECJ should adopt a formal approach, what they have in mind are the cases in which the constitutional courts refer to fundamental rights or inalienable core principles that they regard as belonging to the EU Member States' mirror identity. The V4 constitutional courts often do not invoke the concept of identity in areas that are inside the traditional field of constitutionalism; instead, they invoke it in policy questions, like migration, national security, social security or family law. Those scholars who acknowledge this difference argue for a strict scrutiny test by saying that invocation of national identity in service of limiting fundamental rights is prima facie suspect, given the danger of national identity being deployed to disadvantage or disparately impact already vulnerable minorities.[141]

[138] See, eg, C-208/09 *Ilonka Sayn-Wittgenstein v Landeshauptmann von Wien*. LFM Besselink, 'Respecting Constitutional Identity in the EU, Case C 208/09, 22 December 2010, Ilonka Sayn-Wittgenstein v Landeshauptmann von Wien' (2012) *Common Market Law Review* 49.

[139] C-438/14 *Nabiel Peter Bogendorff von Wolffersdorff v Standesamt der Stadt Karlsruhe und Zentraler Juristischer Dienst der Stadt Karlsruhe*, para 64.

[140] Van de Heyning (no 65) 203.

[141] J-W Müller, 'Militant Democracy and Constitutional Identity' in G Jacobsohn and M Schor (eds) *Comparative Constitutional Theory* (Cheltenham, Edward Elgar, 2018) 417.

Advocate General Kokott takes a third approach: she suggests that the ECJ should distinguish between national measures linked to what she calls the 'fundamental expression of national identity' and those which concern 'non-fundamental expressions of national identity'.[142] In cases concerning fundamental expressions of national identity, she recommends that the ECJ restrict itself to undertaking limited judicial review based on the requirements arising from Article 2 TEU. According to her, the ECJ should exclude proportionality because, in this instance, the domestic courts carry out proportionality review. For instance, AG Kokott argues that the area of family law falls within the scope of fundamental expressions of national identity; thus, the ECJ should restrict the intensity of its review: it should not carry out a proportionality review; it should only review whether the domestic measure is compatible with Article 2 TEU. Apart from the 'fundamental expression of national identity', the ECJ should perform full scrutiny on domestic measures justified by the protection of national identity, proportionality included. But this distinction raises more questions than answers. The need for such a differentiation is not entirely justified, and it is not apparent why family law constitutes a fundamental aspect of national identity protection.

At this point, it is an open question how the ECJ can best ensure that the universal constitutional principles on which EU law is built continue to be respected when confronted with national identity claims. Therefore, the last part of the book addresses how valid forms of national identity claims can be distinguished from those that violate the EU Member States' constitutional commitments. It also seeks to identify the mechanisms that promise to be most effective in incentivising Member States to fall in line with constitutional commitments.

With these preliminary thoughts, the editor hopes that the readers find interest and insight in the coming chapters and that this collection can become the first of many further studies of judicial invocations of constitutional identity in the V4 region and their possible constitutional challenges.

VI. STRUCTURE OF THE BOOK

The book consists of three parts. Part I presents a defence of the concept of constitutional identity and constructively interprets it as narrowly as possible rather than rejecting the concept altogether. Gary J Jacobsohn examines whether the problematic usages of constitutional identity indicate an inherent defect in the very notion of constitutional identity or rather a failure to engage with its essential attributes. He proposes that the best articulation of the concept of constitutional identity, as exemplified by the FCC's case law,

[142] AG Kokott (n 133) para 92.

does not necessarily correspond to its most problematic applications, as evident in the HCC's jurisprudence. He adds, however, that by solely emphasising the German Basic Law's entrenched guarantees and overlooking the implications of the salient reality, the FCC has inadvertently provided other constitutional courts with a pathway to the past, and with it, a sanctification of the prejudices of the present. Thereafter, the book presents the FCC's pioneering concept of constitutional identity. Monika Polzin describes the content and development of German identity jurisprudence and argues that the concept of constitutional identity as elaborated by the FCC – even though it can be criticised on many levels – is a perfectly legitimate constitutional doctrine.

Based on the German articulation of the concept of constitutional identity outlined in Part I of the book, Part II focuses on how FCC has served as a frame of reference for the V4 constitutional courts as they have sought to empower themselves to exercise identity review. Part II reveals that V4 constitutional courts have applied the concept of constitutional, – or in effect, national – identity quite differently from the FCC. The chapters analyse the relevant constitutional case law and demonstrate that a problematic jurisprudence of particularism is present in every V4 jurisdiction. It exists, albeit in rudimentary form, in the Slovak case, and it is a bit more mature in the Czech jurisprudence. The Polish jurisprudence of particularism has already included (ethno)cultural considerations and exploited the concept of constitutional identity for the benefit of the ruling PiS party. However, it is only in the Hungarian case that particularism centred on ethnocultural national identity is in full bloom.

Part II begins with a chapter describing how the SCC developed its identity discourse. Katarína Šipulová and Max Steuer argue that Slovakia represents a special case among the V4 countries. In the 1990s, it had an episode of nondemocratic rule that led the SCC to avoid identity discourse due to its association with nationalistic, nondemocratic challengers and to instead develop the substantive core doctrine to protect the democratic constitution. However, given recent efforts by the executive and legislative powers to curtail the SCC's competences, the substantive core doctrine may well be dismantled. And without it identity remains a concept that is 'up for grabs' in different interpretations, including those advocating the exclusionary form of the jurisprudence of particularism.

The CCC has not yet provided a comprehensive understanding of constitutional identity. Yet, according to Miluše Kindlová, its case law is one of the primary sources upon which ideas about constitutional identity in the Czech context should be founded and examined. And as we learn from her chapter, the case law demonstrates that the CCC has the substantive and procedural tools to exercise an exclusionary form of the jurisprudence of particularism, even vis-á-vis EU law, if it is convinced that there is no other viable option to protect national sovereignty.

Chapter five is centrally concerned with presenting how the captured PCT has already exploited the concept of constitutional identity to undermine the binding nature and supremacy of Poland's democratic constitution. Michał Ziółkowski explains that when the PCT transplanted the concept of constitutional identity in 2010, it did that carelessly, so that the specific content of the concept remained obscure. This made it extremely vulnerable to exploitation. Recently, the captured PCT has been trying to protect the PiS government's unconstitutional judicial 'reforms' by discovering an identity-centric and particularistic narrative.

The focal point of chapter six is the 2011 Hungarian Fundamental Law, which explicitly defines the community as an ethnic Hungarian and Christian nation, and thereby determines constitutional court decisions and pieces of legislation. This ethnoculturally informed particularism, which aims at protecting ethnic and religious purity, runs counter to universal constitutional principles and hence the foundational values of the EU. Thus, for Hungary to comply with these principles, it would need to adopt a new constitution that would allow it to develop a constitutional identity. The chapter argues that a sufficiently robust constitutional identity can be built upon the emblematic political institutions set up during the two decades of democracy, the constitutionalist principles as interpreted by the independent Constitutional Court, and the crucial EU law achievements as they were implemented in domestic law.

After the detailed analyses of identity jurisprudence in Germany and the V4 countries, Part III discusses the consequences of the tension between the jurisprudence of particularism and universal constitutional principles. In chapter seven, Mattias Kumm provides a general theoretical framework for thinking about questions of constitutional identity that are relevant for employing Article 4(2) TEU. The chapter distinguishes between two conceptions[143] of constitutional identity: the Schmittian (formal) conception and the Constitutionalist (substantive) conception and finds the latter more convincing. The chapter argues that the EU commits Members States to constitutional identities that are not in conflict with constitutionalist principles, which are presumed to be shared in Europe. Hence, un-European national identity claims, that is, identities at odds with these principles, cannot plausibly made under Article 4(2) to justify the nonapplication of EU law.

Finally, the last chapter, written with an eye to the future, explores the supranational mechanisms available to defend constitutionalism. Susanne Baer, Kriszta Kovács and Maya Vogel revisit the meaning of constitutionalism, based on the rule of law and backed up by courts. They first analyse the role of courts within a democratic political system and then revisit what constitutional erosion looks like in some EU Member States. The Hungarian and Polish governments

[143] When we use the concept/conception distinction, we follow Walter B Gallie. However, we agree with Ronald Dworkin that interpretative concepts are indeed contested, but this is not their 'essential' characteristics. WB Gallie, 'Essentially Contested Concepts' (1956) 56 *Proceedings of the Aristotelian Society* 167; R Dworkin, *Law's Empire* (Cambridge, Harvard University Press, 1986).

have been the most prominent actors to seek to undermine the very foundations of the EU community itself. In response to this, the EU launched its rule of law mechanism, which has not been very effective to date. Thus, the chapter poses the question of whether the European constitutional community is capable of dealing with the challenges to transnational democracy and concludes that mechanisms of European constitutionalism should include various measures to ensure that it is upheld – from different forms of litigation before the ECJ to the conditioning of certain subsidies on compliance – with the core constitutional principles of the EU.

Part I

A Defence of Constitutional Identity as a Legal Concept

1

The Exploitation of Constitutional Identity

GARY JEFFREY JACOBSOHN

IN ITS LANDMARK decision in 2009 delineating the nation's terms of engagement with the EU, the German Federal Constitutional Court (FCC) deployed the term *constitutional identity* over thirty times. It did so while affirming, 'The Act Approving the Treaty of Lisbon is compatible with the requirements of the Basic Law, in particular with the principle of democracy'.[1] In addition, the court used the occasion to articulate its collective mindset on the merits of enhanced integration and to establish a jurisprudential framework for determining the constitutionality of any subsequent initiatives in the delegation of sovereign powers to Europe. The court said:

> The Basic Law strives to integrate Germany into the legal community of peaceful and free states, but does not waive the sovereignty contained in the last instance in the German constitution as a right of the people to take constitutive decisions concerning fundamental questions as its own identity.[2]

Guardianship over German constitutional identity carries with it solemn responsibilities. Thus, the German Basic Law (GBL), while not unique among constitutions, is perhaps the most prominent example of a document whose leading principled commitment is to secure the transcendence of the nation's past. By assuming a posture of vigilance in relation to any threats that might compromise the textually entrenched safeguards incorporated within the folds of the document, the court in the *Lisbon* case asserted that among its vital judicial obligations was the exercise of 'identity review'. Inasmuch as the court had years ago famously declared its authority to invalidate an identity-nullifying constitutional amendment,[3] appreciation for the innovative significance of this

[1] *Lisbon Treaty* case [2009] BVerfGE 123, 267, 274.
[2] ibid at 340.
[3] *Southwest* case [1951] BVerfGE 1, 14.

later pronouncement might not have reached a level commensurate with the potential impact of the newly asserted judicial prerogative.

That impact, however, has been considerable, perhaps more so outside the country than within. In Germany the decision was met with measured scepticism, highlighted by a widespread perception that the court had aligned itself with Euro-sceptics eager to impede the progress of further European integration. As one commentator put it, 'The tenor of the Court's judgment … is that "identity trumps integration"'.[4] Still, the court's own language made it difficult to avoid interpreting the underlying thrust of its decision as directed towards more noble ends. 'Through what is known as the eternity guarantee, the Basic Law reacts on the one hand to the historical experience of a creeping or abrupt erosion of the substance of a democratic fundamental order. However, it makes clear on the other hand that the Constitution of Germans … has a universal foundation which cannot be amended by positive law'.[5]

But in recent years the invocation of constitutional identity has come to be associated with less noble ends. As has been pointedly argued, today 'its practical application is liable to create more harm than good'.[6] For the increasing number of commentators holding this view, 'It is time for scholars of constitutional [identity] to issue a recall on the dangerous product they released in the market place of ideas'.[7] Thus, however honourable may have been its earlier deployment by those intent on defending liberal constitutionalism, the idea's appropriation by people eager to facilitate that order's demise has understandably led to a review of its conceptual usefulness. Triggered by constitutional identity's association with the worrisome phenomenon of democratic backsliding, the reassessment finds in this problematic nexus a reason for, in effect, wishing the concept away. As one of the scholars to whom the recall entreaty was directed, I think it is important that the critique of constitutional identity be addressed and taken seriously, and so a rejoinder need not entail a dismissal of the legitimate concerns animating the recently voiced reappraisal of the concept.

I argue that the dangers of constitutional identity are real but in part the result of a misreading of its meaning. After introducing the 'Lisbon problem' in section I, I show in sections II and III how a judicially constructed static conceptual understanding, according to which identity is discovered in text or history and then reified within the setting of an ascendant political movement, has made it possible for compliant courts to advance illiberal and exclusivist constitutional agendas. This is best illustrated in the Hungarian Constitutional

[4] JEK Murkens, '"We Want Our Identity Back": The Revival of National Sovereignty in the German Federal Constitutional Court's Decision on the Lisbon Treaty' (2010) 3 *Public Law* 530, 540.

[5] *Lisbon Treaty* case [2009] (n 1) 218.

[6] F Fabbrini and A Sajó, 'The Dangers of Constitutional Identity' (2019) 25 *European Law Journal* 457.

[7] ibid.

Court's (HCC) decisions concerning European treaty obligations, especially as they relate to the challenging demographics of national migration policies. As we will see, the earlier German efforts to erect constitutional barriers against potential threats to a judicially affirmed self-identity inadvertently paved the way for a later more nefarious deployment of constitutional identity elsewhere, and with it the embrace by well-intended commentators of an understandable general disenchantment with the concept.

Thus, however morally commendable were the exertions of the German Court, some of the reasoning in their *Lisbon* case reflections had the unintended consequence of facilitating outcomes in other jurisdictions very much counter to the spirit of post-war German constitutionalism. In section IV I present a clarifying lens through which the increasingly invoked notion of constitutional identity should be regarded, such that the exclusivist determinations that have engendered the scepticism in the above concerns need not be seen as the unavoidable outcome of this jurisprudential development. What has largely been absent from the judicial exercises in identity review by Member States in the EU is an acceptance of conflict as an enduring aspect of the constitutional predicament. Implicit in this understanding of a nation's constitutional identity is a dynamic of dialogical development, entailing interpretive and political activity reflective of the inevitable disharmonies endemic to the experience of constitutional governance. Such an acceptance is no guarantee that applying the concept of constitutional identity will yield laudable outcomes generally compatible with the precepts of liberal constitutionalism. What it will do, however, is minimise the risks associated with political ambitions incompatible with those precepts.

I. *LISBON*'S FALLOUT

Article 4 (2) of the Treaty on European Union (TEU) in effect invites national courts to address the identity question. It says in part: 'The Union shall respect the equality of Member States before the Treaties as well as their national identities, inherent in their fundamental structures, political and constitutional, inclusive of regional and local self-government'. As has been correctly pointed out, 'Every new step of the integration process will be confronted with the question of whether the direction European integration is taking infringes the fundamental elements or values of a particular Member State's constitutional order as an expression of its individuality – in short, its constitutional identity'.[8] If determining the appropriate multilevel constitutionalist balance

[8] A Schnettger, 'Article 4(2) as a Vehicle for National Constitutional Identity in the Shared European Legal System' in C Calliess and G van der Schyff (eds), *Constitutional Identity in a Europe of Multilevel Constitutionalism* (Cambridge, Cambridge University Press, 2020) 9.

between State and Union is an ongoing challenge for parties to the Treaty, the undertaking is rendered yet more formidable given the diverse ways in which a Member's constitutional identity can be envisaged.[9] For example, not all constitutions include an eternity clause that can, as in Germany, facilitate the formation of a broad consensus over the content of a country's constitutional identity. With its Article 79(3), according to which some provisions of the GBL are deemed unamendable, a clear textual benchmark exists for denoting the substance of German constitutional identity and for imbuing it with an aura of democratic legitimacy.

From the perspective of the principle of democracy, the violation of the constitutional identity codified in Article 79(3) of the Basic Law is at the same time an encroachment upon the constituent power of the people. In this respect, the constituent power has not granted the representatives and bodies of the people a mandate to dispose of the identity of the constitution. No constitutional body has been granted the power to amend the constitutional principles which are essential pursuant to Article 79(3) of the Basic Law. The Federal Constitutional Court monitors this.[10]

Such an unequivocal assertion of constitutional priorities is easily explained, even if its transferability to other locales is limited. Against the backdrop of twentieth-century German history the concern for the constitution's identity extended to the identity of the nation itself. The Basic Law, while not unique among constitutions, is the most conspicuous example of a document that performs a critical redemptive role by essentially repudiating an identity that had over an extended period provided ignoble singularity to the nation. Having experienced the horrors of what it means to be governed unconstitutionally, the inclusion of entrenched limits to paradigm-shifting change signals the codification of the document's guaranteed commitments as The German Constitutional Identity. What is more, viewing the textual affirmations as fixed and immutable underscores an important idea, which is that preventing things from getting marginally better is a price worth paying to ensure that they do not again become radically worse.

The FCC's pronouncement that it would monitor all of this, that henceforth it would be the instrument of 'identity review' in European integration cases, resonated well in other continental courts, including those not featuring entrenchment as part of their constitutional settlement. Despite the diverse understandings of constitutional identity prevailing across these jurisdictions,

[9] 'A characteristic feature of the identity debate in the EU is the ambiguity affecting the identification of the concept'. P Faraguna, 'Constitutional Identity in the EU – A Shield or a Sword' (2017) 18 *German Law Journal* 1617, 1632.

[10] *Lisbon Treaty* case [2009] (n 1) 218.

embrace of the judicial role outlined by the FCC has had wide appeal. As Kriszta Kovács has observed:

> Seemingly, the German Federal Court served as a role model for V4 courts to empower themselves to exercise identity review. In reality the identity reviews exercised by those courts are not identical; the essence, scope and the aim of the identity control are different.[11]

As a general matter, of course, there is a commonality of aims – establishing limits to the primacy of EU law by invoking local constitutional identity-based constraints – but as Kovács and other observers point out, this indigenous summoning of constitutional values varies markedly in the purposes to which defiance of European intrusions attaches.[12] What needs to be explored further, however, are the constitutional logics that lead to different outcomes.

Constitutional identity represents a synthesis of political aspirations and commitments that are expressions of a nation's past, as well as the determination of those within the society who seek to transcend the past. As Hanna Pitkin has said, '[H]ow we are able to constitute ourselves is profoundly tied to how we are already constituted by our own distinctive history'.[13] At least three possible constitutional paths are suggested by this insight, each manifesting a significantly different take on the identity question:

(1) The framers of the text of a new constitution could, as in the German case, make clear their determination to relinquish the document's ties to the past. The nation's distinctive history would serve as a backdrop to the new venture, but in ways explicitly inscribed in the text, the negation of the salient component of that history would henceforth provide a linchpin for subsequent constitutional interpretation.
(2) The framers of the text might make clear their determination to exalt a period in the nation's history as a foundation upon which to build a constitutional identity. As a conveyer of expressive content, the text itself would be of lesser importance than would the associations summoned through intensive excavation of an imagined past.
(3) The framers of the text could invest it with a somewhat subversive significance, such that its future invocations would serve the purpose of altering the course of history by selectively uprooting those patterns of social experience that no longer comport with contemporary aspirations. Unlike #1, in this model the transcendence of the past remains a continuing

[11] K Kovács, 'The Rise of an Ethnocultural Constitutional Identity in the Jurisprudence of the East Central European Courts' (2017) 18 *German Law Journal* 1703, 1705.

[12] See, for example, RD Kelemen and L Pech, 'Why Autocrats Love Constitutional Identity and Constitutional Pluralism,' Reconnect Working Paper No 2, 10. They argue that captured courts serve their autocratic rulers by ostensibly following the lead of the respectable FCC's championing of constitutional identity.

[13] HF Pitkin, 'The Idea of a Constitution' (1987) 37 *Journal of Legal Education* 169.

constitutional project, entailing a transformative societal agenda that is more comprehensive in its ultimate goals than disavowal and negation.

For present purposes I focus on (1) and (2), which are exemplified by Germany and Hungary respectively. Illustrative of the third path is India. Thus, 'The Indian Constitution was perceived by many in the post-colonial world to be a revolutionary document'.[14] That document's endorsement of a socially reconstructive agenda initiated a 'long democratic revolution' or, in Nehru's words, a 'step by step' progression towards validation of the Constitution's identity.[15] Of course, as Armin von Bogdandy has wisely pointed out more generally, 'The [constitutional] text itself has only limited potential for forging identity. A legally binding document is but a first step on the long and winding road from a political design for collective identity to a socially embedded institution that actually fosters such identity'.[16] Indeed, the recent political trajectory in India might very well engender scepticism about the transformative capacity of words on paper.[17]

II. THE CONSTITUTIONAL TEXT

India and Germany are two polities that have provided unusually fertile ground for constitutional theorizing about identity. What is more, through the exertions of these nations' powerful constitutional courts this theorizing has been refined by critical cross-fertilisation, mostly evident in relation to the unconstitutional constitutional amendment issue. Thus it was Germany where the Basic Law's explicitly preservative entrenchment provisions had become the touchstone for the post-War Constitutional Court's recognition of its authority to invalidate an identity-nullifying amendment, that in time figured prominently in the development of Indian jurisprudence.[18] In Germany, however, the constitutional

[14] AK Thiruvengadam, *The Constitution of India: A Contextual Analysis* (London, Bloomsbury Publishing, 2017) 2. Or as another Indian constitutional scholar has said, '[G]iven the appalling living conditions of the majority of the people in the country, the framers understood the burden of the expectations they all carried, and instinctively knew that the new constitution had to be transformative if it had to have any durability or legitimacy.' T Khaitan, 'Directive Principles and the Expressive Accommodation of Ideological Dissenters' (2018) 16 *International Journal of Constitutional Law* 389, 403.

[15] Parliamentary Debates V xii–xiii, Pt. 11, 8820–22, 5/16/1951. In SC Kashyup, *Jawaharlal Nehru and the Constitution* (New Delhi, Metropolitan Book Co, 1982) 147.

[16] A von Bogdandy, 'The European Constitution and European Identity: Text and Subtext of the Treaty Establishing a Constitution for Europe' (2005) 3 *International Journal of Constitutional Law* 295, 314.

[17] Consider in this regard the view of James Madison in *Federalist #48*: 'Will it be sufficient to mark, with precision, the boundaries of these departments, in the constitution of the government, and to trust to these parchment barriers against the encroaching spirit of power?' If Madison's challenge to the efficacy of written guarantees in protecting a people's rights calls attention to the restricted potential of a constitutional text, then it surely must stimulate a similar concern for parchment promises of societal transformation.

[18] The German constitutional theorist, Dietrich Conrad, was the key figure in transferring the German understanding to the Indian subcontinent. His work was cited by Indian justices in several of the Indian cases concerning amendment provisions found unconstitutional by the Supreme Court.

text has been foundational in a way that has not been the case in India, where amendment invalidation rests upon the less certain constraints of 'basic structure' jurisprudence.[19]

The more certain limitations in the textually explicit provisions of the GBL have meant that what has become foundational for constitutional identity in that country has at times functioned as a 'hard shield', establishing judicially enforceable limits on the progression of European integration.[20] For those believing the brandishing of the shield to be an act of dubious merit, the danger resides chiefly in the perceived loss that can be anticipated from a failure to align national policies with rules and norms adopted at the Union level. But there is a jurisprudential aspect to this exercise of identity review that requires serious consideration as well. Thus, jurists committed to a 'textualist' understanding of their institutional role subscribe to the view that constitutional interpretation commences with the language of the constitution, and where the meaning of the document's words are clear, their inquiry must conclude. While practitioners of this legal orientation are more likely to be found on American courts, the centrality of the text matters deeply, regardless of whether it figures prominently in an elaborately articulated judicial philosophy.

Consider in this regard the important declaration in the German *Lisbon Treaty* case that serves as a critical predicate for the court's embrace of identity review:

> Within the order of the Basic Law, the structural principles of the state laid down in Article 20 of the Basic Law, i.e., democracy, the rule of law, the principle of the social state, the republic, the federal state, as well as the substance of elementary fundamental rights indispensable for the respect of human dignity are … not amenable to any amendment because of their fundamental quality.[21]

The generality of these 'structural principles' should not detract from the salient fact that the only reason they are assigned the lofty status of non-negotiable requirements is that they are deemed essential to the achievement of constitutionalism. They make a claim of universality, such that the moral truths they are said to embody are precisely the ones whose recognition is required for a constitution to exist in more than name only. The operative assumption of post-war constitutional jurisprudence in Germany has been that there exists an 'objective ordering of values' according to which the Constitutional Court's adjudication of cases will culminate in rulings supportive of the country's constitutive obligations.[22]

[19] The 'basic structure' doctrine first entered Indian jurisprudence in the landmark case of *Kesavananda Bharati v State of Kerala* [1973] 4 SCC 225.

[20] Faraguna (n 9) 1629. See also M Claes, 'National Identity: Trump Card or Up for Negotiation?' in AS Arnaiz and CA Llivina (eds), *National Constitutional Identity and European Integration* (Cambridge, Intersentia, 2013).

[21] *Lisbon Treaty* case [2009] (n 1) 217.

[22] The German 'objective order of values' (*eine objektive Werteordnung*) fact refers to fundamental constitutional principles in the sense that, as the FCC once affirmed, it functions in that nation's jurisprudence 'as a yardstick for measuring and assessing all actions in the area of legislation, public administration, and adjudication'. *Lüth Case* [1958] BVerfGE 7, 198.

Again, the textual entrenchment of these commitments in the Basic Law must be seen against the backdrop of the earlier totalitarian experience, but the document itself does not invoke that history; in fact, its preamble, a place where frequently the past finds explicit reference in national constitutions, does not mention either the discredited Nazi period or, indeed, any celebrated bygone point of reference. In making the case for identity review, the FCC alludes to the lessons of history, while emphasising the a-historical nature of the constitution's entrenched principles:

> Through what is known as the eternity guarantee, the Basic Law reacts on the one hand to the historical experience of a creeping or abrupt erosion of the free substance of a democratic fundamental order. However, it makes clear on the other hand that the Constitution of the Germans, in accordance with the international development which has taken place in particular since the existence of the United Nations, has a universal foundation which cannot be amended by positive law.[23]

Notice that in the court's view the eternity clauses draw their special status as unamendable provisions from principles external to the local context. German constitutional identity in effect assumes a seemingly generic form corresponding with principles commonly linked to liberal constitutionalism. As a reading of other courts' *Lisbon* rulings reveals, the FCC is hardly unique in referencing such principles, but what we might portray as German exceptionalism, its constitution is perhaps the paradigmatic case of a nation constituted by its constitution.[24] While textual acknowledgments of these principles in other documents should not reflexively be greeted with dismissive scepticism, their constitutive significance must be viewed in the context of additional touchstones of identity that are given pride of place within their fundamental law. Elsewhere I have distinguished between principles and values, the second term distinguishable from the first by its connection to the local environment and the traditions and histories that leave a decisive imprint on the constitutional identity of a given polity.[25] To be sure, the categorical boundaries separating these different types are anything but precise; still, however contestable, for present purposes it will be useful to conceive of the latter as comprising a culturally determined

[23] *Lisbon Treaty* case [2009] (n 1) 218.

[24] The American Constitution is typically cited in this way. But as important as constitutional principles are to American identity, in addition to not standing as a bar to radical amendments, they do not apply uniformly across different levels of government, and they do not, as they do in Germany, possess a jurisprudentially delineated objective quality that extends their application from the public domain to the private. On this latter point see, M Kumm, 'Who is Afraid of the Total Constitution? Constitutional Rights as Principles and the Constitutionalization of Private Law' (2006) 7 *German Law Journal* 341, 350. For a comparison of the relative importance of American and German constitutional principles to national identity see, GJ Jacobsohn, 'A Lighter Touch: American Constitutional Principles in Comparative Perspective' in K Orren and JW Compton (eds), *Cambridge Companion on the United States Constitution* (Cambridge, Cambridge University Press, 2018).

[25] GJ Jacobsohn, 'Constitutional Values and Principles' in M Rosenfeld and A Sajó (eds), *Oxford Handbook in Comparative Constitutional Law* (Oxford, Oxford University Press, 2012) 777.

meaning that provides it with a particularistic significance that effectively severs the idea from any universalistic claims.

Before seeing how this plays out in the Hungarian case, one aspect of the strongly textual character of the court's handling of constitutional identity – its static quality – warrants special consideration. As we will see, it is this property that is similarly present in the type 2 model of Member State/EU treaty interactions. Thus, despite the very different purposes for which the followers of a more historical account of constitutional identity exercised their judicial authority, the German precedent of the *Lisbon* case laid bare how national resistance to European integration could benefit from an inadequately articulated framing of the identity question. What ostensibly served the interests of liberal constitutionalism could be adapted to the advancement of its opposite.

The post-*Lisbon* controversy in Germany had very little to do with the goal of protecting the principles embedded in the constitution's eternity provisions. Most of the pointed criticism the court received for its protective efforts focused instead on the alleged Euro-scepticism of the decision. In the European Court of Justice (ECJ), the critics did not find an institution any less committed to the constitutionalist goals of the Karlsruhe tribunal; and so they saw in the court's cautious approach to European integration a regrettable foreclosing of a desirable dialogical process of judicial and political interaction that, in essence, presumes the inherent mutability of constitutional identity. In this account, it is illusory to isolate a specific identity – Germany's – from the larger historical narrative of which it is a part – Europe's – and believe that the former will or should remain unaffected by the connection. Thus, the identity challenge 'calls for judicial dialogue to settle a balance between centripetal and centrifugal dynamics'.[26] It should not be presumed that once discovered an identity – in this case the German constitutional identity – simply is what it is and must be preserved as such. It develops over time, which is to say it is not an entity inhabiting a constitutional text, there to be found and maintained as is by those to whom it applies.[27]

[26] R Toniatti, 'Sovereignty Lost, Constitutional Identity Gained' in AS Arnaiz and CA Llivana (eds), *National Constitutional Identity and European Integration* (Cambridge, Intersentia, 2013) 67.

[27] As J Kokott's astutely observes, '[T]he special openness for integration is also a part of the constitutional identity of the Basic Law.' J Kokott, 'Report on Germany' in A-M Slaughter, A Stone and J Weiler (eds), *The European Court and National Courts – Doctrine and Jurisprudence: Legal Change in its Social Context* (Oxford, Hart, 1998) 103. Highlighted is an intriguing dilemma: since the fixed and unalterable substance of German constitutional identity is directly linked to universal principles embedded in international law, and since the court arrogated to itself the responsibility of defending the core meaning of that identity, then its assigned preservative task should require for its fulfilment an active engagement with sources outside the indigenous scope of sovereign authority. And so, constitutional identity 'is a dynamic notion, that evolves and changes through and along constant and continuous social spontaneous processes'. Toniatti (n 26) 67. Consequently, 'It has to develop over time, which means that it *can* in fact develop over time'. FC Mayer, 'Rashomon in Karlsruhe: A Reflection on Democracy and Identity in the European Union: The German Constitutional Court's Lisbon decision and the changing landscape of European constitutionalism' (2011) 9 *International Journal of Constitutional Law* 757, 785.

These critics recognised that a theory of constitutional identity that cannot account for its prospective mutability is an incomplete theory.[28] They rightly construed identity as an interactive process whereby a constitution, much like a person, develops its distinctive character or individuality through engagement with its environment, within the broader context of its being. Their concerns comport with the philosopher Charles Taylor's insight, 'My own identity crucially depends on my dialogical relation with others'.[29] The same relationship arguably pertains at the state level, which implies an openness to the evolutionary possibilities in a nation's constitutional identity. Thus, whether or not one agrees with how the substance of identity has come to be understood, that such an understanding may have assumed an unalterable, unyielding status in the course of judicial scrutiny, betrays a fundamental misconception about the nature of the concept in question.

This presumption, present in more recent decisions of the FCC, is largely missing in the *Lisbon* opinion, the result of which was that the defence of constitutional identity was readily translatable into a conventional discussion of sovereignty. The numerous judicial expressions of concern about constitutional identity incorporate comparable apprehensions that speak both to the substantive competences affected by the terms of the Treaty and the methods by which governing authority has been exerted in their derivation. For example, the *Lisbon* court concludes: 'From the perspective of the principle of democracy, the violation of the constitutional identity codified in Article 79(3) of the Basic Law is at the same time an encroachment upon the power of the people. In this respect the constituent power has not granted the representatives and bodies of the people a mandate to depose of the identity of the constitution'.[30]

To depose is to remove or overthrow. The constituent power has *fixed* its construction of identity into the constitutional text, thereby affirming the sanctity of its sovereign will and implying that any refinement in the meaning of that rendering without the authoritative intervention of the people would be tantamount to an overthrow.[31] Thus, the judges stipulate that the Basic Law's

[28] The mutability of constitutional identity is a concept well entrenched in the constitutional patriotism literature. As Jan-Werner Müller writes, 'Identity was not to be understood in static … terms – it was constituted precisely by a continuous civic self-interrogation and open argument about the past, and not least, the purging of problematic continuities with that past. In short, it was understood as a *process*'. J-W Müller, *Constitutional Patriotism* (Princeton, Princeton University Press, 2007) 34. See also M Kumm, 'The Idea of Thick Constitutional Patriotism and its implications for the role and structure of European legal history' (2005) 6 *German Law Journal* 319, 353: 'The idea of constitutional patriotism … provides a basic focal point for a plurality of identities that can challenge, complement and enrich one another'.

[29] C Taylor, *The Ethics of Authenticity* (Cambridge, Harvard University Press, 1991) 48.

[30] *Lisbon Treaty* case [2009] (n 1) 218.

[31] Monika Polzin has called to my attention several more recent decisions in which the FCC has adopted a less Euro-skeptical orientation, which has resulted in a more dynamic understanding of German constitutional identity. In its identity control order of 15 December 2015, the court outlined for the first time the procedural requirements for such control. The powers of review, it maintained, are to be exercised with restraint and in a manner open to European law. BVerfGE 140, 317, para 46. In this regard, see as well the right to be forgotten decisions. Here the FCC held

goal of European integration must be achieved without any surrender of the nation's sovereignty, which is here defined as the 'right of the people' to undertake constitutive decisions concerning the substance of identity. That collective right – elsewhere described as 'the right to free and equal participation in public authority' – is inviolable and immune from balancing because it is 'enshrined in human dignity'.[32]

Indeed, specifically with regard to dignity it is accordingly sufficient in the court's calculations to invoke the text of Article 1 as if the inviolability of the principle therein codified established a clear and immutable essence whose safeguarding is the principal responsibility of the FCC.[33] But does the inviolability of a principle and its subsequent constitutional entrenchment signify that a defence of the principle requires acceptance of its unchanging meaning? As the court once said:

> [We] cannot separate our recognition of the duty to respect human dignity from its historical development .... [A]ny decision defining human dignity in concrete terms must be based on our present understanding of it and not on any claim to a conception of timeless validity.[34]

While dignity's centrality in the objective order of German values makes it an object of obvious interest, its similar standing in the European scheme of codified values – Article 1 of the Charter of Fundamental Rights of the European Union replicates the Basic Law's language – can hardly escape notice. The fact, however, that it is a common and prominent presence in many of the neighbourhood's other constitutional arrangements, both national and supranational, does not diminish its distinctive symbolic weight in a political order whose pivotal break with the past was the basis for the nation's political transformation. Clearly, then, comparing and assessing different documents in terms of the constitutive meaning of their inscribed commitments requires more than simply

that fundamental rights of the GBL can in certain instances be interpreted in light of the European Charter of Fundamental Rights. 'Given that both the Basic Law and the Charter are rooted in a common European rights tradition, the fundamental rights of the Basic Law, too, must be interpreted in light of the Charter'. Order of the First Senate of 6 November 2019 – 1 BvR 16/13 – (*Right to be forgotten I*) para 60. Very important too, the FCC in the second right to be forgotten case decided that it will, where appropriate, also directly apply the European Charter in its decisions. Order of the First Senate of 6 November 2019 – 1 BvR 276/17 – (*Right to be forgotten II*). See in this regard, D Thym, 'Friendly Takeover, or: the Power of the "First Word". The German Constitutional Court Embraces the Charter of Fundamental Rights as a Standard of Domestic Judicial Review' (2020) 16 *European Constitutional Law Review* 187. 'Two decisions of November 2019 on the "right to be forgotten" mark a tectonic shift that will profoundly transform German constitutional law and scholarship and will reinforce the shift towards a composite framework of axiomatic "unity in diversity" in the pan-European human rights jurisprudence on the basis of the Charter of Fundamental Rights, the European Convention and national constitutions.' ibid at 2.

[32] *Lisbon Treaty* case [2009] (n 1) 211.

[33] Such an exercise has occurred, as the FCC in 2015 applied its identity review to justify its refusal to implement a European Arrest Warrant, which, according to the court, would have violated an individual's human dignity as guaranteed under Articles 79(3) and 1(1). 2 BvR 2735/14 (2015).

[34] *Life Imprisonment* case [1977] BVerfGE 45, 187, 229.

observing the parchment use of identical language. Scholars and jurists should be sceptical, therefore, of extrapolating identity directly from the words emblazoned in a constitutional text.[35]

What is more, the very fact of incorporation in eternity clauses underscores the identitarian significance of textual language even as awareness of less exceptional uses in other documents argues for a degree of humility in affirming any fixed or static meaning to the substance of that identity.[36] But in designating itself the instrument of *identity review*, and by embracing a fundamentally static textual interpretation of constitutional identity, the continent's most powerful national court has become the institutional epicentre for assessing the precise character of supranational 'respect' for indigenous constitutional essentials. As such it has also become a source of emulation for other national courts, some of whom care less than the German judges about the primacy of their constitutional texts, and at least as much about the rewards of a non-dynamic invocation of constitutional identity.

III. HISTORY

The rhetorical outer limit of displeasure with the court's decision in the *Lisbon Treaty* case is surely to be found in this gloomy appraisal: '30 June 2009 will be remembered as a black day in the history of Europe'.[37] Other more temperate assessments echoed the gist of this dark evaluation, to the effect that the judgment's decidedly sovereigntist bent represented a serious threat to the European integration project. The burden of the critical accounts of the court's massive opinion was that lamentably the justices aligned themselves with the legion of Euro-sceptics in Germany and elsewhere. Further, the methodology for doing so involved a protective invocation of German constitutional identity that will purportedly lead to the creation of a false dichotomy between the values

[35] Again, Monika Polzin has pointed out to me a decision that manifests a Euro-friendly approach with respect to identity review and human dignity. The FCC in this instance clarified that the application of identity control will be limited to exceptional cases where the protection of human dignity at the European level fails. In most cases the Charter and the Basic Law are presumed to be reinforcing. BVerfG, 2 BvR1845/18 ao, 1 December 2020, para 40.

[36] In evaluating the importance of the constitutional text for establishing a polity's constitutional identity it surely is worth reflecting on the relative ease with which the provisions of the document can be formally changed. Where modification is burdensome – or in the case of Germany's eternity clauses, forbidden – the text may be presumed to carry more identity-laden significance than in systems that incorporate a more amenable amendment mode of textual adaptation. The fact that Hungary is among the ten or so other EU Member States that do not establish high barriers to constitutional change is therefore notable as we consider the less text-based derivation of constitutional identity.

[37] A Grosser, 'The Federal Constitutional Court's *Lisbon* Case: Germany's "Sonderweg" – An Outsider's Perspective' (2009) 10 *German Law Review* 1263, 1263.

and principles of the nation and the larger political community. 'The Union is presented as a foreign entity, not as part of Germany's identity'.[38]

Others found such accounts wildly excessive in the face of a judgment that in actual fact approved the substance of the Treaty with only a modest disclaimer about an easily remedied flaw in the legislative process by which it was ratified.[39] For the European courts that followed suit in accepting the *Lisbon* terms, the methodology of constitutional identity provided ample flexibility should the ultimate course of their Treaty jurisprudence take them to a place that the court in Karlsruhe might well find morally or politically unacceptable.[40]

To take one example, the Polish Constitutional Tribunal, citing 'the judgment of the Federal Constitutional Court of Germany of 30 June 2009 [on] the issue of "constitutional identity"', made clear that this issue would also have a determinative role in guiding the conduct of Polish jurists.

> What is worth noting … is the fact that the Federal Constitutional Court redefined its own role as a guard of 'constitutional identity', in the light of the Treaty of Lisbon; courts with a constitutional function may not be deprived of the responsibility 'for the boundaries of their constitutional empowerment for integration and for the safeguarding of the inviolable constitutional identity'. In the opinion of the Federal Constitutional Court, its competences arise from the sovereignty of Germany as a Member State of the Union.[41]

Unlike the FCC, however, which had the Basic Law's unamendable provisions upon which to rest its claims about constitutional identity, the Polish Court was much less definitive on how its derivation of that concept's meaning would proceed. And tellingly, its characterisation of the German methodology was correspondingly vague. Thus, 'The understanding of the elements of identity arises from the context of historical and cultural experiences'.[42]

While the opinion on the Lisbon Treaty largely equates Polish constitutional identity with that of the EU, its heavy reliance on the constitution's

[38] R Bieber, 'An Association of Sovereign States' (2009) 5 *European Constitutional Law Review* 391, 397.

[39] As was pointed out in a moderately critical account of the *Lisbon* decision, 'There is probably no other judgment in the history of the Karlsruhe Court in which the argument is so much at odds with the actual result'. C Schönberger, 'Lisbon in Karlsruhe: Maastricht's Epigones at Sea' (2009) 10 *German Law Review* 1201.

[40] While the German *Bundesverfassungsgericht* established the most important precedent for identity review, F-X Millet reminds us that it was the French *Conseil constitutionnelle* that first relied on constitutional identity as a barrier against an EU Directive. See his, 'Constitutional Identity in France: Vices and – Above All – Virtues' in C Calliess and G van der Schiff (eds), *Constitutional Identity in a Europe of Multilevel Constitutionalism* (Cambridge, Cambridge University Press, 2020) 134.

[41] Judgment of 24 November 2010 Ref No K 32/09, para III.3.

[42] ibid.

preamble provides room for a more historical account should future circumstances render such a development politically desirable:

> [T]he purposes of the European Union are fully identical with the purposes of the Republic indicated in the basic law. The basis for full axiological identity is the equivalence of the axiological inspiration of the Union and the Republic confirmed in the Preamble to the Treaty on European Union and the Preamble to the Constitution.[43]

While that latter source is correctly cited for its appeal to principles broadly shared on the European continent, it also includes value-steeped language that could be readily adapted to the fulfilment of the illiberal objectives of some future potential autocrat. 'Beholden to our ancestors for their labours, their struggle for independence achieved at great sacrifice, for our culture rooted in the Christian heritage of the Nation and in universal human values …'. Indeed, as a cogent study of later developments concluded:

> Since the Treaty of Lisbon decision, constitutional identity has turned out to be a device of resistance rather than cooperation between the Polish and EU orders. Moreover, the national sovereignty rhetoric used during the electoral campaign in 2015 by the political leaders of the current government not only awoke the sentiment of a strong nation state but also laid the ground for political introversion, revisionism, xenophobia, lack of solidarity, and non-cooperation.[44]

Why is this so important? As Wojciech Sadurski notes, '[2015] witnessed the beginning of a fundamental authoritarian transformation: the abandonment of dogmas of liberal democracy, constitutionalism, and the rule of law that had been so far taken for granted'.[45]

In Hungary the transformation proceeded differently, as the 2011 Fundamental Law had, much like the GBL, specified a more accessible conduit to the material core of constitutional identity than was available to the Polish Tribunal in its 2010 *Lisbon* decision. That core of course was decidedly different than in Germany, history no longer serving as an implicit object of rejection but as a source of meaning. József Szájer, the prominent leader of the Fidesz party charged with drafting the new Constitution, said it well. Asked why the Fundamental Law referred to the historic constitution, he insisted it

> had to define its position with respect to the thousand-year tradition that had always secured for Hungary a position at the forefront of Europe … A constitution defines a country's identity – it condenses what we think of our history, achievements and

[43] ibid at para III.2.2.

[44] A Śledzińska-Simon and M Ziółkowski, 'Constitutional Identity in Poland: Is the Emperor Putting on the Old Clothes of Sovereignty?' in C Calliess and G van der Schiff (eds), *Constitutional Identity in a Europe of Multilevel Constitutionalism* (Cambridge, Cambridge University Press, 2020) 266.

[45] W Sadurski, *Poland's Constitutional Breakdown* (Oxford, Oxford University Press, 2019) 3.

> attainments. … Hungary's previous constitution did not fulfil this function of defining the nation's identity.[46]

Szájer might well have had that previous constitution in mind when a year earlier the Constitutional Court rejected a petition aimed at establishing the unconstitutionality of the act of promulgation of the Lisbon Treaty:

> [T]he Constitutional Court came to the conclusion that even if the reforms of the Lisbon Treaty were of paramount importance, they did not change the situation that Hungary maintains and enjoys her independence, her rule of law character and her sovereignty. Consequently, the application was rejected in all its elements.[47]

However compatible this ruling was with the thinking of the Fidesz leader regarding competing competences of Hungary and the EU, given what he was later to say of the constitution's deficiencies, the absence in that opinion of a specific reference to constitutional identity should not have been surprising. Nor should it be surprising that in contrast with the German treaty decision's frequent allusion to constitutional identity, its Hungarian counterpart, although similarly deferential to national sovereignty, did not frame its response in the language of identity.

What is more, while the HCC's emphatic commitment to the rule of law was appropriately attentive to a core principle of constitutionalism, that very commitment also had an abstract quality to it that, standing alone, comports with the emerging critique of the 1989 transition that saw in the earlier hinge moment a neglect of what was specific to Hungarian constitutional identity. Thus, in the understandable effort to uphold the rule of law through the establishment of legal continuity, an opportunity was arguably lost to advance a positive articulation of constitutional identity.[48] 'There was no regime change' was the appropriate motto for the proponents of the identitarian critique.[49]

[46] B Ablonczy et al, *Conversations on the Fundamental Law of Hungary* (Budapest, Elektromedia, 2012) 27.

[47] HCC Decision 143/2010. (VII 14).

[48] The famous and controversial *Lustration* case of 1992, in which the HCC explicitly held the rule of law to be a constitutional priority over the competing claim of substantive justice, may be seen in retrospect as a precursor for the proponents of the later constitutional transformation and their firmly held views concerning the inadequacy of the post-1989 understanding of Hungarian constitutional identity. See, eg, A Jakab, 'What is Wrong with the Hungarian Legal System and How to Fix it' *Max Planck Institute for Comparative Public Law & International Law (MPIL) Research Paper No. 2018–13* (arguing that 'The crucial problem of institution-building in the 1989/90 constitutional system … was that issues of justice, of dealing with the past (ie the narrative) were swept under the carpet following a peculiar interpretation of the formal rules'). Also, D Robertson, 'A Problem of their Own, Solutions of their Own: CEE Jurisdictions and the Problems of Lustration and Retroactivity' in W Sadurski, A Czarnota, and M Krygier (eds), *Spreading Democracy and the Rule of Law? The Impact of EU Enlargement for the Rule of Law, Democracy and Constitutionalism in Post-Communist Legal Orders* (Dordrecht, Springer, 2006). Yaniv Roznai and I discuss this case at some length by way of the very differently decided Czech lustration case in GJ Jacobsohn and Y Roznai, *Constitutional Revolution* (New Haven, Yale University Press, 2020) chapter 3.

[49] U Korkut, *Liberalisation Challenges in Hungary: Elitism, Progressivism, and Populism* (London, Palgrave MacMillan, 2015) 60.

Viktor Orbán and József Szájer could in essence deny the import of the constitutional transition in 1989 for its alleged failure to establish a clear identity for the Hungarian nation; his 'revolution of the voting booth' could then be defended as satisfying the people's hunger for the constitutional overhaul that had, in his supporters' view, yet to be achieved.[50]

How that identity was instantiated is by now an oft-told tale by European legal scholars, who place the development within the broader regional context of resistance to EU prescribed migrant relocation quotas. Thus, the constitutional courts of the Visegrád countries (V4) have advanced a self-protective jurisprudence, availing themselves of Article 4(2) TEU for the purpose of renouncing identity-threatening EU legal obligations. The Hungarian court has been in the forefront of this effort; my reflections will not seek to build on the ample and burgeoning literature that has been spawned by its rulings, except to highlight the historical dimension and its relevance to the exploitation of constitutional identity.[51]

Had things worked out differently, which is to say as planned, the court would not have had to carry as much of the identity burden as ultimately came to pass. In the course of events in Hungary the failure to adopt the Seventh Amendment left the judiciary with the mission of attaining the amendment's goals through its own devices.[52] That amendment – later adopted in 2018 – would have added the following language to the Fundamental Law: 'We hold that the defence of our constitutional self-identity, which is rooted in our historical constitution, is the fundamental responsibility of the state'. But as the HCC's 2016 decision on the State's obligations concerning EU refugee acceptance measures made clear, existing language in the Fundamental Law was adequate to the task of implementing the spirit of the failed amendment.[53] How, then, is this any different from what we saw in Germany, where the text of the extant document was the direct source of understanding for that nation's constitutional identity?

[50] KL Scheppele, 'Guardians of the Constitution: Constitutional Court Presidents and the Struggle for the Rule of Law in Post-Soviet Europe' (2005) 154 *University of Pennsylvania Law Review* 1758.

[51] See, for example, K Kelemen, 'The Hungarian Constitutional Court and the Concept of National Constitutional Identity' (2017) 15–16 *Ianus-Diritto e finanza*; T Drinóczi, 'Hungarian Constitutional Court: The Limits of EU Law in the Hungarian Legal System' (2017) 11 *Vienna Journal on International Constitutional Law* 139. G Halmai, 'The Misuse of Human Dignity and Constitutional Identity: The Case of Hungary' https://me.eui.eu/wp-content/uploads/sites/385/2018/11/Dignity_identity_Hungary_Halmai.pdf; K Kovács (n 11).

[52] As G Halmai points out, by this time the court had been 'captured' by the Orbán government, leading it to do the bidding of those in power. 'After the failed constitutional amendment, the Constitutional Court, loyal to the government, came to the rescue of Orbán's constitutional identity defence of its policies on migration.' G Halmai (n 51) 7.

[53] It is not a perfect analogy, but something similar occurred in the United States with respect to gender equality. Thus, with the failure to adopt the Equal Rights Amendment it was left to the Supreme Court to secure much of the equality that the amendment would have guaranteed by expansively interpreting the Fourteenth Amendment's equal protection clause. Indeed, the court would have gone further in equating its outcome with the proposed amendment had not one judge – Justice Lewis Powell – withheld his vote to do so by arguing that the ERA, if passed (it was under consideration at the time), would have obviated any need for the court to reach the result through its interpretation. *Frontiero v Richardson*, 411 US 677 (1973).

The question's importance is only underscored by the Hungarian court's embrace of the same role assumed by its German counterpart. 'Respecting and safeguarding the sovereignty of Hungary and its constitutional identity is a must for everybody … and, according to Article 24(1) of the Fundamental Law, the principal organ for the protection is the Constitutional Court'.[54] And another textual site – Article R(3) – is cited as the source for the applicable judicial interpretive standards: 'The provisions of the Fundamental Law shall be interpreted in accordance with their purposes, the National Avowal and the achievements of our historical constitution.' But tellingly, several paragraphs later, the court assigns the constitutional text a pointedly attenuated role in discovering constitutional identity. 'The Constitutional Court established that the constitutional self-identity of Hungary is a fundamental value not created by the Fundamental Law – it is merely acknowledged by the Fundamental Law'.[55] The significance of this assertion is perhaps best appreciated in the discordant sentiments of a concurring judge:

> This approach would actually tear apart Hungary's constitutional identity from the text of the Fundamental Law, creating a kind of invisible Fundamental law to be protected by the Constitutional Court – with a content interpreted according to an uncertain methodology.[56]

As in Germany, the text is where the inquiry into constitutional identity begins. And as in Germany the inquiry cannot end within the confines of the text. Thus, to the extent that certain provisions in the Basic Law are deemed unamendable, it is by virtue of their alignment with principles external to the local setting. Their status within the objective ordering that is the hallmark of German constitutional jurisprudence means that their content – ie, German constitutional identity – cannot be accessed without going beyond the document. Once this connection is made, however, the constitution's text assumes its status of interpretive eminence, such that the identity of the broader constitutional order is for all practical purposes henceforth contained within the folds of the document. 'The constituent power of the Germans which gave itself the Basic Law wanted to set an insurmountable boundary to any future development'.[57] Entrenchment epitomizes the constitutional reality.

The Hungarian National Avowal's exaltation of the 'historical constitution' may, as the concurring judge complained, generate 'an uncertain methodology' for those charged with the protection of Hungary's constitutional identity, but if, in accordance with the Avowal, future generations are 'to make Hungary great again', it will happen as a result of the recognition of 'our country [as] a part of Christian Europe one thousand years ago'. If this does not create

[54] HCC Decision 22/2016 (XII 5), para 55.
[55] ibid at para 67.
[56] ibid at para 107.
[57] *Lisbon Treaty* case [2009] (n 1) para 216.

an 'insurmountable boundary' to future development, it surely establishes a restricted pathway in which the past serves as a more or less fixed marker of constitutional legitimacy. And as I argue in the next section, the judicial misuse of the concept of constitutional identity clears the way for 'illiberal democratic' rule.

IV. THE FAILURE OF DISHARMONIC RECOGNITION

After citing the threat posed by the millions of migrants targeting Europe, another concurring judge in the landmark 2016 case discussed above wrote:

> [T]he need to protect Hungary from the proliferations of tensions from the Western part of the Union [shows] the future primary importance of the Hungarian Constitutional Court's procedure of sovereignty and constitutional identity control, the foundations of which have been laid down in this decision.[58]

The use of euphemistic language cannot quite conceal the larger point of the opinion, which is consistent with the basic thrust of the Court's decision: Hungarian constitutional identity supports policies antagonistic to the predominant EU position respecting the treatment of refugees.

Not that Hungary stands alone in this regard. As Gábor Halmai notes, 'The behaviour of the Hungarian government, supported by the other three Visegrád countries, during the refugee crisis, has taught us that the strengthening of populist and extreme nationalist movements across Europe is incompatible with the values of the liberal democracy, and that membership in the European Union is not a guarantee for having liberal democratic regimes in all Member States'.[59] That behaviour was vividly on display in the case brought before the HCC by Amnesty International in 2019, in which a section of the Criminal Code aimed at those working in the field of asylum was held not to be in violation of the Fundamental Law.[60]

The Orbán government had insisted that the EU plan to relocate asylum seekers would undermine Hungary's Christian identity. While population movements involving the influx of many ethnic groups into the country have been very common throughout Hungarian history, the predominantly Muslim aspect of the recent refugee crisis has focused attention on the ethnocultural evolution

[58] HCC Decision 22/2016 (n 54) para 93.

[59] G Halmai, 'Illiberal Constitutionalism? The Hungarian Constitution in a European Perspective' in S Kadelbach (ed), *Verfassungskrisen in der Europäischen Union* (Baden-Baden, Nomos, 2018) 101. See also, Z Körtvélyesi and B Majtényi, 'Game of Values: The Threat of Exclusive Constitutional Identity, the EU and Hungary' (2017) 18 *German Law Journal* 1721.; N Chronowski, 'The New Hungarian Fundamental Law in the Light of the European Union's Normative Values' (2012) *Revue Est Europa* 111.

[60] The controversial so-called 'Stop Soros' law criminalised various forms of aid to illegal immigrants. The Parliament had approved the measure overwhelmingly by a 160–18 vote.

of constitutional identity since the nation's 'revolution under law'. The court's rejection of Amnesty International's petition avoided the confrontational rhetoric that often accompanied the government's migration policy pronouncements, but its validation of that policy was explicitly predicated on the exclusivist reasoning of the 2016 case. Thus, 'in the presently nineteenth point of the National Avowal, Hungary has made the protection of Hungarian sovereignty and of the constitutional identity a clear requirement to rely upon'. And, in that 'our identity rooted in our historic constitution is a fundamental obligation of the State', there is ample justification for regulating 'the uncontrollable masses that have illegally crossed the external borders of the European Union during a short period of time'.[61]

That the HCC has embraced the concept of constitutional identity for exclusivist purposes is at this point a widely shared view, one that is held also as applying to the other V4 courts. This assessment provides a sharp contrast with the approach of the FCC, whose identity review jurisprudence did not evoke a similar illiberal motivational agenda. As Kovács notes, 'The concept of constitutional identity as developed by the FCC is understood in a political – constitutional sense. By contrast V4 courts tend to provide an ethnocultural background for the concept of identity'.[62] While surely correct, the contrast may obscure an underlying commonality, namely a failure in both judicial settings adequately to wrestle with the nuance and complexity of constitutional identity.

We saw in the previous section that a strong reliance on text and history can lead to a static representation of constitutional identity, thus empowering those charged with its formal articulation to establish fixed constitutional meanings that advance their political projects, whether noble or ignoble. Constitutional identity, however, exists neither as a discrete object of invention, nor as a heavily encrusted essence embedded in a society's culture, requiring only to be discovered. As I have argued elsewhere, it is the disharmony internal to a constitutional text or between the text and the social context in which it is situated that is the driving force behind a nation's evolving constitutional identity.[63] A perfectly harmonious constitution is an illusion. In India, to cite one non-European example, there are two powerful claims on constitutional identity, both firmly rooted in centuries of conflict and contestation. Since independence one of these claims – for a secular composite culture nation – has mostly been in ascendance, but the other – for a Hindu nation – has at times posed a distinct threat to the

[61] HCC Decision 3/2019. (III 7) para 46.

[62] Kovács (n 11) 1720. Katalin Dobias writes in a similar vein: 'The Fundamental Law's aim was to re-imagine and ethno-religious (rather than political) community by constitutionalising an exclusionary rather than inclusive political identity'; K Dobias, 'The Role of Constitutional Identity in the Responses to the Terror Attacks in France and Refugee Management Crisis in Hungary' (2015) *Annual Review of Constitution Building Processes* 101, 113.

[63] GJ Jacobsohn, *Constitutional Identity* (Cambridge, Harvard University Press, 2010) 4–5, 351–53.

hegemony of the predominant view. Over time the identity that has emerged reflects the entrenched realities of both visions. The constitutional text embodies them, as does the history of constitutional construction and interpretation. And along the way there have been efforts to reinvent the past, most notably by those determined to create a history expunged of the truths that complicate their ethno/religious story.

This is when the invocation of constitutional identity should arouse heightened concern; specifically, when its derivation and application is managed in wilful or careless neglect of the disharmonic reality that is endemic to the constitutional condition. Or put differently, constitutional identity becomes concerning, and in some cases dangerous, when it is inspired by a felt need to eliminate contradiction or incongruity. Expunging dissonance from its core meaning enables guardians of constitutional identity to achieve a desired outcome without confronting the obstacles that would otherwise make the attainment more problematic. As Anne Applebaum writes in her study of authoritarianism, 'The noise of argument, the constant hum of disagreement – these can irritate people who prefer to live in a society tied together by a single narrative'.[64] A notable contemporary example is playing out in Israel in the debate over the Knesset-passed Basic Law on the Nation-State of the Jewish People. The Law's omissions have meant that the balance between Jewish and democratic values was arguably no longer the operative reality. What has occurred, critics said, was nothing short of a re-founding of the state, an assault upon its secular identity. As the petition to the Supreme Court contesting the legitimacy of the law stated, 'The act of grounding the constitutional identity of the state in exclusionary principles negates the legitimacy of the entire constitutional and political regime'.[65] It is perhaps worth observing that hours before the passage of the Basic Law, Prime Minister Benjamin Netanyahu met with Viktor Orbán in Jerusalem, calling him a 'true friend of Israel'. As one Israeli commentator put it, they 'have a keen understanding of their respective nations' histories and have been very adept at using it to their political advantage in domestic politics and, increasingly, on the global stage'.[66]

[64] A Applebaum, *The Twilight of Democracy: The Seductive Lure of Authoritarianism* (New York, Doubleday, 2020), 109. Applebaum shows how history can be very useful to authoritarians by the invocation of 'restorative nostalgia'. 'The nation is no longer great because someone has attacked us, undermined us, sapped our strength. Someone – the immigrants, the foreigners, the elites, or indeed the EU – has perverted the course of history and reduced the nation to a shadow of its former self. The essential identity that we once had has been taken away and replaced with something cheap and artificial'. ibid at 75.

[65] Adalah Petition to the Supreme Court on the constitutionality of the Basic Law on the Nation-State of the Jewish People.

[66] IB Zion, 'Netanyahu greets Hungary's Orbán as "true friend of Israel"' *AP news*, 19 July 2018; A Pfeffer, 'Netanhyahu and Orbán: An Illiberal Bromance Spanning from D.C. to Jerusalem', *Haaretz*, 18 July 2018. In Israel, where a persistent and fragile political equilibrium is traceable to the dual commitments of the nation's founding, the course of constitutional identity is impelled by the discord of ordinary politics within limits established by commitments from the past. The disharmony internal to a constitutional text will ordinarily not be as prominent as it is in Israel. Indeed,

To be sure, the disharmonies in the Hungarian Fundamental Law and the other V4 constitutions are less stark than the Israeli Declaration of Independence's avowal that the state be both Jewish and democratic, but they are in their own way constitutionally challenging in comparable ways. While Israel is a paradigmatic instance of competition between seemingly irreconcilable visions of national identity that has shaped the course of that nation's unconventional constitutional development, one need only glance at the Hungarian Avowal to observe that its commitment to both Christian nationhood and democracy presents the possibility for a creative synergy that, when deployed in a dialectical relationship with energised forces in the larger social order, can lead to a dynamic constitutional identity not beholden to exclusivist goals.[67] But the deeper commitment to the 'historical constitution' has seemingly foreclosed this possibility, the result of which is encapsulated in Orbán's designated constitutional identity: 'illiberal democracy'.

Still, before too tightly embracing such a conclusion we need to reflect on the fact that while the National Avowal includes ample historical allusions to a past that comports with contemporary illiberal ambitions, it also incorporates several mentions of ideals that are normally associated with the liberal constitution. Perhaps most discernibly, it affirms, 'We hold that human existence is based on human dignity'. In so doing, it aligns the Hungarian text with the similar sentiments inscribed in the governing documents of both Germany and the EU, thus presenting us with an obvious question: why should we not, as of course we do in these other jurisdictions, expect the dignity declaration to push Hungarian legal outcomes to a constitutionally liberal destination? And does not the textually disharmonic language of the dual commitments promise a dynamic interpretive framework for the delineation of constitutional identity?

Here, again, the German precedent is important. As explained in the previous section, the unamendable provision that elevated dignity to its inviolable position within the document's objective ordering of values led the FCC essentially to conflate the affirmation of constitutional identity with a defence of

in many polities it will be deftly obscured in the mists of compromise language authored by determined constitution-makers. But Israel's evolving formal constitution only renders more transparent than elsewhere a process that is unusual in that nation mainly for the quality of its translucence.

[67] Ireland represents an instructive contrast with Hungary. At the time of the drafting of the 1937 Irish Constitution Eamon de Valera asserted, 'Since the coming of St. Patrick fifteen hundred years ago, Ireland has been a Christian and Catholic nation. … She remains a Catholic nation'. Quoted in B Chubb, *The Politics of the Irish Constitution* (Dublin, Institute of Public Administration, 1991) 27. The document's Preamble begins famously 'In the Name of the Most Holy Trinity …'. Juxtaposed with this religious prioritising is a commitment to democratic principles that, however, are not subordinated, as they are today in Hungary, to the dictates of the 'historic constitution'. Even as applied to the abortion issue, the dual Christian and democratic commitments intersect creatively to achieve a dynamic constitutional identity. As noted by Mary Robinson, the former President of Ireland, 'Our identity must be constantly rediscovered, or re-created, if we are to come to terms with … changing circumstances'. Quoted in C James, 'Céad míle fáilte? Ireland Welcomes Divorce: The 1995 Irish Divorce Referendum and the Family (Divorce) Act of 1996' (1997) 8 *Duke Journal of Comparative and International Law* 175, 179.

national sovereignty. The eternity implication codified in the contents of Article 1 established a clear and immutable core whose safeguarding was to be the principal responsibility of the Constitutional Court. If there is a concern in any of this it lies not in the commendable exercise of identity review over a commitment that is constitutive of German post-War nationhood; rather, it has to do with the potential lost opportunities to refine the meaning of dignity by not engaging dialogically with extra-sovereign authorities whose own commitments to the same principle are almost surely sincere.

Indeed, dignity's perceived scope and significance are not the same in all legal systems. A formal acceptance of dignity is no guarantee that its substantive meaning will resonate in comparable ways across borders, or even within them at different times. As Michael Rosen has noted, 'History shows the existence of different strands in the meaning of dignity, strands that come together and move apart at different times'.[68] Such is prominently the case in Germany where the dual histories of Kantian and Catholic thought have come to shape and define the concept, sometimes as competitive traditions with contrasting policy and constitutional implications (for example on the abortion question), and sometimes in ways that converge to a similar place. With regard to the project of supra-national legal development and the Basic Law's declared openness to the advancement of European integration, the evolution of identity-laden provisions – in particular those notable for their entrenchment in the document – ought not to be isolated from parallel efforts in the broader community. Yet ironically, the text's enhanced protected status for particular guarantees may also impede their subsequent substantive enhancement.

To see, then, in the unentrenched aspiration for human dignity in the Hungarian Fundamental Law reassurance that it will yield a salutary outcome as it interacts with the ethno-centric sections of the National Avowal is to underestimate the potential of Article R(3)'s 'historical constitution' directive for illuminating dignity in a manner consistent with an illiberal constitutional identity. It is not that the textual provision respecting human dignity is to be rendered null and void; instead, it will receive its meaning from an extra-textual source rooted in a past that is both real and constructed. If what happened in Germany can be understood as the replacement of a brutally anti-egalitarian idea of dignity, in which social honour is owed to an ascriptively defined class of people,[69] with one emphasising equality and human rights, then the reliance in Hungary on an exclusivist historical narrative to delineate a constitutional identity threatens to install a version of that older account into the heart of Europe.[70]

[68] M Rosen, *Dignity* (Cambridge, Harvard University Press, 2012) 8.

[69] See in this regard, JQ Whitman, 'On Nazi "Honour" and the New European Dignity' in C Jourges and NS Gholeigh (eds), *Darker Legacies of Law in Europe: The Shadow of National Socialism and Fascism Over Europe and Its Legal Traditions* (Oxford, Hart, 2003) 245.

[70] The disparate array of responses in Europe to the 2015 refugee crisis is a revealing case in point. At the height of the emergency, a Serbian official said, 'What we expect from the EU is to tell us what the form of good behaviour is. Is it what Germany is doing, where refugees are welcomed with medicine and food? Or is it where they are welcomed with fences, police and tear gas?' *New York Times*, 18 September 2015, A9. And consider this rejoinder from the German foreign minister to

V. CONCLUSION

All constitutions are crafted over time in the sense that their meaning and identity evolve gradually in ways determined by a dynamic impelled by their internal tensions and contradictions and their confrontations with a social order over which they have limited influence. In time a constitutional order is constructed and shaped, and the ambitions inscribed in, or attributed to, the constitution will have been realised or not or, more likely, approximated to a greater or lesser degree. In reflecting on Article 4 (2) TEU as a vehicle for the expression of national constitutional identities within a communal European legal order, Anita Schnettger writes, 'Collective identity is, in the first place, not a static identity but rather an imagined and constructed one. As such, it is also accepted that a homogeneous group is not a necessary pre-condition of national identity …'.[71] And writing more generally, Francis Fukuyama argues that the remedy for identity abuses is not to abandon identity; rather, '[it] is to define larger and more integrative national identities that take into account the de facto diversity of existing liberal democratic societies'.[72] Unfortunately, these valuable insights have in recent years often not prevailed in the workings of the V4 courts, as the derivation of constitutional identity has increasingly come to neglect sources of meaning that rely on complexity, diversity, and fluidity.

Prior to becoming one of these identity-abusing courts, the Constitutional Court of the Czech Republic perceptively grasped the essential character of constitutional identity. In its *Lisbon 1* decision, it said of the Member State courts' relationship to the EU, that it 'should continue to be a dialogue of equal partners, who will respect and supplement each other's activities, not compete with each other'.[73] Further, 'In a modern, democratic law-based state, state sovereignty is not an aim in and of itself, in isolation, but is a means to fulfilling … fundamental values on which the construction of a constitutional law-based state stands'.[74] Specifically as applied to the concept that has been the focus of this chapter, the court's view of fulfilment amounts to 'a procedural understanding of constitutional identity [that] allows for its continuous rediscovery through dialogue that maintains its legitimacy'.[75] Such an understanding is incommensurate with the more constrained and inflexible account that may follow from the lofty heights of a formally unbending text or the exploitative historic validation of contemporary parochialism.

his Czech counterpart's assertion of the primacy of national sovereignty in connection with policy towards migrants. 'We can, as Europe, say that we will shut all borders, and not let anyone else in'. But in doing so, 'we would betray our values'. *New York Times*, 12 September 2015, A9. The idea, then, that there has been convergence within the European community on the practical implications of a continent-wide commitment to human dignity can only be described as illusory.

[71] Schnettger (n 8) 14.

[72] F Fukuyama, *Identity: The Demand for Dignity and the Politics of Resentment* (New York, Farrar, Straus and Giroux, 2018) 123.

[73] 2008/11/26 – Pl ÚS 19/08: *Treaty of Lisbon I*, para 197.

[74] ibid at para 209.

[75] Dobias (n 62) 105.

2

Identity and Eternity: The German Concept of Constitutional Identity

MONIKA POLZIN

'An idea that is not dangerous is unworthy of being called an idea at all'.

Oscar Wilde

THE GERMAN FEDERAL Constitutional Court (FCC) established the current German doctrine of constitutional identity[1] in its famous *Lisbon* judgment.[2] The doctrine is based on the eternity clause, ie Article 79(3) of the German Basic Law (GBL). According to the FCC, Article 79(3) of the Basic Law constitutes an absolute limit for the protection of the constitutional identity.[3] Article 79(3) states that constitutional amendments affecting the division of the Federation into Länder, their general participation in the legislative process, or the principles laid down in Articles 1 and 20 shall be inadmissible. The German constitutional discourse therefore inextricably links identity and eternity. However, the notion of constitutional identity predates the eternity clause and the current German Constitution. During the Weimar Constitution of 1919, similar concepts were used in order to justify implicit limits for constitutional amendments (see under section I). During the drafting of the GBL, neither the idea nor the notion of constitutional identity had any relevance. The drafters incorporated the eternity clause in order to protect the newly gained democracy as such (see under section II). The present doctrine of constitutional identity was then established by the FCC by case law on constitutional limits for European integration and, in particular, the *Lisbon* judgment. The court

[1] Further English publications are, for example, D Thym, 'Attack or Retreat? Evolving Themes and Strategies of the Judicial Dialogue between the German Constitutional Court and the European Court of Justice' in M Claes, M de Visser, P Popelier and C Van de Heyning (eds), *Constitutional Conversations in Europe* (Cambridge, Intersentia, 2012), 235; C Callies, 'Constitutional Identity in Germany: One for Three or Three in One' in C Callies and G von der Schyff (eds), *Constitutional Identity in Europa of Multilevel Constitutionalism* (Cambridge, Cambridge University Press, 2020).

[2] BVerfGE 123, 267.

[3] BVerfGE 129, 124 (169), cf BVerfG, 2 BvR 1685/14, 30 July 2019, para 119.

has developed a fully-fledged legal doctrine of constitutional identity concerning the EU and implied a potential but still drafted doctrine of constitutional identity in relation to general international law (see under section III).

As the notion of constitutional identity is both vague and glamorous at the same time, it has found many followers, copyists and some dubious developers.[4] Therefore, it is essential to distinguish between generally legitimate uses of the German concept of constitutional identity and illegitimate misuses of the idea and notion (see under sections IV–VII).

I. A BRIEF LOOK AT THE HISTORICAL BACKGROUND: IDENTITY BEFORE ETERNITY

The idea of constitutional identity was first developed during the Weimar Constitution of 1919,[5] which did not contain material limits for constitutional amendments. Article 76 of the Weimar Constitution stated that the constitution could be amended through the legislative process.[6] Constitutional amendments needed a two-thirds majority in the Reichstag (the then parliamentary assembly) and in the Reichsrat (the then assembly of the representatives of the Länder, which, however, only had the right to an objection) or the majority of the votes in a referendum. Based upon Article 76, the majority of the contemporary constitutional lawyers (eg Anschütz[7] and Thoma[8])[9] argued that there were no material

[4] See, eg, Hungarian Constitutional Court Decision 22/2016. (XII 5), at para 67, available at: www.hunconcourt.hu/uploads/sites/3/2017/11/en_22_2016-1.pdf. See regarding the misuse discussion, eg, G Halmai, 'Abuse of Constitutional Identity: the Hungarian Constitutional Court on Interpretation of Article E) (2) of the Fundamental Law' (2018) 43 *Review of Central and East European Law* 23; J Scholtes, 'Abusing Constitutional Identity' (2021) 22 *German Law Journal* 534. See also chapter six in this book.

[5] See extensively M Polzin, 'Constitutional Identity, Unconstitutional Amendments and the Idea of Constituent Power' (2016) 14 *International Journal of Constitutional Law* 411, 415–21.

[6] Article 76 of the Weimar Constitution reads as follows: 'The Constitution can be amended via legislation. However, a decision of the Reichstag regarding the amendment of the Constitution only takes effect when two-thirds of those present consent. Decisions of the Reichsrat regarding amendment of the Constitution also require a two-thirds majority of the votes cast. If a constitutional amendment is concluded by initiative in response to a referendum, then the consent of the majority of enfranchised voters is required. If the Reichstag passes a constitutional change against the objection of the Reichsrat, the President is not permitted to promulgate this statute if the Reichsrat demands a referendum within two weeks'. English translation of the Weimar Constitution in: C Schmitt, *Constitutional Theory* trans J Seitzer (Durham, Duke University Press, 2008).

[7] G Anschütz, *Die Verfassung des Deutschen Reiches, Kommentar für Wissenschaft und Praxis* 14th edn (Berlin, Verlag von Georg Stilke, 1933) 401–06 on Article 76.

[8] R Thoma, 'Das Reich als Demokratie' in R Thoma and G Anschütz (eds), *Handbuch des Deutschen Staatsrecht* 1 (Tübingen, Mohr, 1930) §16, 186, 199; R Thoma, 'Die juristische Bedeutung der grundrechtlichen Sätze der deutschen Reichsverfassung im Allgemeinen' in HC Nipperdey (ed), *Die Grundrechte und Grundpflichten der Reichsverfassung, Kommentar zum zweiten Teil der Reichsverfassung* (Berlin, Hobbing, 1929) 43.

[9] Other proponents of this view were, inter alia, S Jeselsohn, *Begriff, Arten und Grenzen der Verfassungsänderung* (Carl Winters Universitätsbuchhandlung, 1929) 62–64 (especially at 62);

limits on constitutional amendments. They based their arguments on the wording of Article 76 itself and on the theoretical assumption that the Reichstag was both the legislature and constitution-making body.[10] The constitution was not perceived as standing above the legislature. Rather, the constitution was at the disposition of legislature.[11] The reason for this assumption was that the Weimar Constitution did not provide for a special body (such as a constitutional assembly) for constitutional amendments, and, therefore, there was no *constituent power*.[12]

Against this background, the anti-democratic constitutional thinkers Bilfinger and Schmitt developed different theoretical arguments to reason implicit material limits governing constitutional amendments in 1928. Both thinkers used notions of 'identity and continuity of the constitution as an entirety'[13] (Schmitt) and 'the identity of the constitutional system'[14] (Bilfinger) to justify implicit limits on constitutional amendments.[15] Bilfinger's theory – relatively unknown today – is based on the assumption that a constitution is a closed ('harmonious')[16] systematic order and an implied rejection of the idea of constitutional disharmony.[17] Bilfinger argued that the legislative branch of the state did not have the right to 'disrupt the constitutional system or turn it upside down'.[18] Thus, an intrusion into the identity of a constitutional system could not be regarded as a constitutional amendment but as a destruction of the Constitution.[19] The legislature had the duty to preserve the fundamental core of a constitution.[20] He expanded on his theory in 1929, arguing that the character of a constitution itself justified the legal rule that its fundamental provisions are unamendable.[21] A constitution that allowed its own abrogation could not, in his view, be described as a constitution.[22]

M Kraft-Fuchs, 'Prinzipielle Bemerkungen zu Carl Schmitts Verfassungslehre' (1930) 12 *Zeitschrift für Öffentliches Recht* 511, 532.

[10] Anschütz, (n 7) 401; W Jellinek 'Das verfassungsändernde Reichsgesetz' in R Thoma and G Anschütz (eds), *Handbuch des Deutschen Staatsrechts* 2 (Tübingen, Mohr, 1931) 182.

[11] Anschütz, (n 7) 401; J Schlesinger, 'Der pouvoir constituant' (1933) 15 *Zeitschrift für Öffentliches Recht* 104, 110.

[12] See eg, R Thoma, 'Grundbegriffe und Grundsätze' in R Thoma and G Anschütz (eds), *Handbuch des Deutschen Staatsrechts* 2 (Tübingen, Mohr, 1931) §71, 108, 153; W Jellinek (n 10, 182; cf more generally H Kelsen, *Allgemeine Staatslehre* (New York, J Springer, 1925) 253.

[13] C Schmitt, *Verfassungslehre* (Berlin, Duncker & Humblot, 1928) 105.

[14] C Bilfinger, *Der Reichssparkommissar* (Berlin, W de Gruyter & Company, 1928) 17.

[15] In the present context, constitutional amendments mean express amendments to the wording of the constitution.

[16] Bilfinger (n 14), 16–17.

[17] Regarding the importance of constitutional disharmony see chapter one of this book.

[18] Bilfinger (n 14), 17. Translation provided by the author.

[19] ibid.

[20] C Bilfinger, 'Verfassungsfrage und Staatsgerichtshof' (1931) 20 *Zeitschrift für Politik* 81, 86.

[21] C Bilfinger, *Nationale Demokratie als Grundlage der Weimarer Verfassung, Rede bei der Feier der zehnjährigen Wiederkehr des Verfassungstages gehalten am 24. Juli 1929* (Tübingen, M. Niemeyer Verlag, 1929) 17.

[22] ibid, especially clear at 18.

Schmitt's well-known theory justifies material limits on constitutional amendments according to his particular idea of the constituent power. He drew upon the notion that the constituent power is 'the comprehensive foundation of all other "powers"'[23] and, from this theoretical assumption, derived material limits on constitutional amendments. According to Schmitt, the will of the constituent power (in principle: the people or the monarch)[24] provided the basis for the validity of a constitution.[25] Only the constituent power had the capacity to decide fundamental questions concerning the 'type and form of its own political existence'.[26] These fundamental decisions (with regard to matters such as the form of government, human rights or the separation of powers) constituted the 'constitution in the positive [ie real] sense' that had to be distinguished from the written constitution.[27] Schmitt here applied an understanding of the notion of constitution that was widespread at this time. He distinguished between the essential norms of a constitution, which formed part of the material constitution, and other provisions, which did not have the value of a constitutional norm.[28] Consequently, the Weimar Constitution was regarded as consisting of two different kinds of provisions: those representing the fundamental decisions and, thus, constituting the ('true') constitution and other, less-important provisions that were simply 'constitutional laws'.[29] According to Schmitt, Article 76 of the Constitution covered only the latter provisions – in other words, the constitutional laws – that could be amended by the constituted powers.[30] Provisions that were the ('true') constitution could not be amended under Article 76. They could only be amended by the people, the constituent power.[31] Schmitt wrote:

> The limits for constitutional amendment follow from the rightly understood notion of constitutional change. A competence given only by a constitutional law to amend the constitution means that one or several constitutional laws can be changed, but only on the condition that the identity and continuity of the constitution as a whole are preserved.[32]

Schmitt expressly argued that the unamendable parts of the Weimar Constitution could not be listed or specified.[33] He only mentioned some examples,

[23] Schmitt (n 13) 77.

[24] Schmitt (n 13) 23, 75 et seq, see also 81 on the 'organisation of a "minority"' as the constituent power.

[25] ibid at 9, 75–76.

[26] ibid at 75.

[27] ibid at 21.

[28] C Schmitt, *Die Diktatur* 3rd edn (Berlin, Duncker & Humblot, 1964) IX.

[29] Schmitt (n 13) 20, 76, 104.

[30] ibid at 101–02.

[31] ibid at 27, 105 and 177.

[32] ibid at 103.

[33] C Schmitt 'Zehn Jahre Reichsverfassung' (1929) 58 *Juristische Woche* 2313 reprinted in: C Schmitt, *Verfassungsrechtliche Aufsätze aus den Jahren 1924–1954* 2nd edn (Berlin, Duncker & Humblot, 1957) 34, 40.

eg, replacing the system of democratic elections with a system consisting of ('workers') councils ('Rätesystem').[34]

Besides, Schmitt did not specify how the people could act as the constituent power. He argued that a 'regulated procedure, through which the activity of the [constituent power] would be bound' did not exist.[35] Neither constitutional laws nor the constitution could regulate the use of the constituent power by the people.[36] Instead, the people would use 'their [constituent power] through some recognisable expression of their direct comprehensive will, which is targeted at a decision on the type and form of the existence of political unity'.[37]

II. THE APPEARANCE OF ETERNITY: THE DRAFTING OF THE BASIC LAW

The drafting of the GBL after the Second World War led to the creation of Article 79(3) that introduced material limits on constitutional amendments.[38] However, the authors of the Basic Law did not refer to the concepts and ideas of Schmitt and Bilfinger. The (published) discussions do not address the distinction between constituent power and constituted powers,[39] the distinction between constitution and constitutional law,[40] or the notion of constitutional identity. Instead, because of the historical events that occurred during the Weimar Republic and the rise to power of the Nazi party,[41] two aspects were important to the drafters. Firstly, during the preparatory work of the Constitutional Convention on the Isle of Herrenchiemsee, material limits on constitutional amendments were proposed. This had the objective to protect the free and democratic order as given by natural law and to safeguard the constitution from destruction.[42]

[34] Schmitt (n 13) 152.

[35] ibid at 130. See also at 132.

[36] ibid at 128.

[37] ibid at 130–31.

[38] See in detail Polzin (n 5) 421–24.

[39] cf U Steiner, *Verfassunggebung und verfassunggebende Gewalt des Volkes* (Berlin, Duncker & Humblot, 1966) 211. For a different view see E-W Böckenförde, 'Die verfassunggebende Gewalt des Volkes – Ein Grenzbegriff des Verfassungsrechts' in UK Preuß (ed), *Zum Begriff der Verfassung* (Frankfurt am Main, Fischer, 1994) 58, 70.

[40] However, in a debate in the Bundestag in 1954, the constitutional lawyer C Schmid (former Chairman of the main committee of the Parliamentary Council) in substantive terms relied on Schmitt's distinction between constitution and constitutional law with a view to determining the limits on constitutional amendments (see 17. Sitzung des Deutschen Bundestages, 26. Februar 1954 in: 18. Verhandlungen des Bundestages, 2. Wahlperiode 1953, Stenographische Berichte (1954) 573.

[41] Dispelling the myth that Article 76 of the Weimar Constitution or an overbroad reading of this provision enabled the accession to power of the Nazi regime in March 1933, see, inter alia, H Dreier, *Gilt das Grundgesetz ewig?* (München, Carl Friedrich von Siemens Stiftung, 2008) 54–55; C Gusy, '*Demokratische Verfassungsänderung Selbstschutz oder Selbstpreisgabe der Verfassung*' (2012) 20 *Der Staat* 159, 179–80, both with further references.

[42] 'Bericht über den Verfassungskonvent auf Herrenchiemsee vom 10. bis 23. August 1948' in Deutscher Bundestag and Bundesarchiv (eds), *Parlamentarischer Rat 1948–1949, Akten und*

Secondly, the main argument favouring the eternity clause adopted by the subsequent Bonn Parliamentary Council, whose function was to draft the final text of the German Constitution, was the desire to deny potential future revolutions their legitimacy (in accordance with the yardsticks of the GBL).[43] The father of the eternity clause, the free-democrat Thomas Dehler, wanted to prevent a situation where a new revolutionary movement could – as the Nazis had done – rely on a constitution to gain legitimacy for their idea. Consequently, he came to utter the often-quoted words that an eternity clause is necessary to 'destroy a revolution's mask of legitimacy'.[44]

III. THE GERMAN CONSTITUTIONAL COURT AND THE RE-INVENTION OF CONSTITUTIONAL IDENTITY

After adopting the GBL, the notion of constitutional identity initially stayed without attracting particular attention in German constitutional thought. Some writers used it to analyse and interpret the eternity clause in the light of Schmitt's writings and concepts.[45] It only became famous when the FCC prominently re-introduced the notion in the *Lisbon* judgment. However, the court has used the similar phrase 'identity of the constitution' already in its *Solange I* decision of 29 May 1974[46] in order to justify limits of the supremacy of European Law.

A. The *Solange* Cases

In the *Solange* cases, constitutional identity was not used within the framework of the eternity clause but the framework of Article 24(1) of the GBL.[47] Article 24(1) allows Germany to transfer sovereign powers to international organisations and was, at the time, the legal basis for participating in European integration.

In the *Solange I* decision, the court had to decide whether the fundamental rights protected by the GBL limited the supremacy of European law (in the case at hand: regulations). It decided that, in principle, regulations had to conform

Protokolle, Der Verfassungskonvent auf Herrenchiemsee 2 (Boppard, Harald Boldt Verlag, 1981) 504, 558.

[43] See also Dreier (n 41) 59; P Kirchhof 'Die Identität der Verfassung' in J Isensee and P Kirchhof (eds), *Handbuch des Staatsrechts* 3rd edn (Heidelberg, C.F. Müller, 2004) §21 marginal n 42.

[44] Deutscher Bundestag and Bundesarchiv (eds), *Parlamentarische Rat 1948–1949, Hauptausschuß*, Vol 14/2 (Berlin, W De Gruyter & Co, 2009) n 36, 1094, 1118.

[45] See in detail Polzin (n 5) 424–26.

[46] BVerfGE 37, 271, 279; see also A von Bogdandy and S Schill, 'Overcoming Absolute Primacy: Respect for National Identity under the Lisbon Treaty' (2011) 49 *Common Market Law Review* 1417, 1434.

[47] Polzin (n 5) 426–27.

to the fundamental rights of the GBL, since at the time (1974) there was no adequate protection of fundamental rights at the European level.[48] The court also justified its decision using the notion of constitutional identity.[49] The court stated that Article 24(1) of the GBL had to be construed and interpreted in the overall context of the GBL. This concludes that Article 24(1) does not allow a change of the fundamental structure of the constitution, which is the basis of its identity, through the legislation of an international organisation in the absence of a constitutional amendment.[50] These basic structures were regarded as unamendable. According to the court, Article 24(1) does not provide any authority – for the legislation of an international body or for the German legislature itself – to alter the constitution's basic structure by means of an amendment to the European treaties.[51] The FCC reiterated its finding in its *Solange II* decision in 1986.[52]

B. Maastricht and a Short Disappearance of the Notion of Constitutional Identity

Following the *Solange II* decision, the notion of 'constitutional identity' first disappeared from the language of the FCC.[53] One reason might be that, in 1992, Article 23(1) of the GBL was introduced as the legal basis for the transfer of sovereign powers to the European level.[54] Article 23(1) expressly points to the eternity clause in Article 79(3) of the GBL as a limitation for European integration. Thus, the court did not refer to the notion of 'constitutional identity' in its decisions on the Common Organisation of the Market in *Bananas*,[55] *Maastricht Treaty*,[56] *Constitutional complaints challenging the euro*[57] and the *European Arrest Warrant*.[58] In those decisions, it also examined whether the measures concerned were in conformity with Article 79(3) of the GBL. Of particular

[48] BVerfGE 37, 271, 280–81.

[49] ibid at 280. See also C Tomuschat, 'The Defence of National Identity by the German Constitutional Court' in AS Arnaiz and CA Llivina (eds), *National Constitutional Identity and European Integration* (Cambridge, Intersentia, 2013) 205, 208.

[50] BVerfGE 37, 271, 279. See, regarding contemporary criticism, HP Ipsen, 'BVerfG versus EuGH re "Grundrechte"' (1975) 10 *Europarecht* 1, 12–13.

[51] BVerfGE 37, 271, 279–80.

[52] BVerfGE 73, 339, 375–76.

[53] Polzin (n 5) 427–29.

[54] Gesetz zur Änderung des Grundgesetzes [Law Amending the Basic Law] Dec. 21, 1992, *Bundesgesetzblatt* I 2086.

[55] BVerfGE 102, 147.

[56] BVerfGE 89, 155 (translation available in 98 ILR 196). However, the court did use the phrases 'core of the Basic Law system' and 'amendment-proof core of the Basic Law' (translation in 98 ILR 196, 220).

[57] BVerfGE 97, 350, 368–70.

[58] BVerfGE 113, 273, 295–98.

importance in this context is the court's *Maastricht* judgment. In this judgment, the court for the first time examined whether European integration itself (ie, the Act of approving the Treaty of Maastricht) was in accordance with the GBL. At the basis of the eternity clause, it started to develop general limits on the transfer of sovereignty rights to the European level. These limits based on Article 79(3) of the GBL were the democracy principle and – discussed in an obiter dictum[59] – the loss of German statehood (which is not expressly protected by Article 79(3) and is read into the eternity clause).[60]

C. *Lisbon*: Rebirth

In 2009 the court revisited the notion of 'constitutional identity' in its well-known *Lisbon* judgment, which examined the constitutionality of the act of approval of the Treaty of Lisbon. The court made the connection between constitutional identity as defined in Article 79(3) and the distinction between the constituted powers, including the amendment power and the constituent power derived from the democratic principle.[61]

From the perspective of the principle of democracy, the violation of the constitutional identity codified in Article 79(3) of the GBL is at the same time an encroachment upon the constituent power of the people. In this respect, the constituent power has not granted the representatives and bodies of the people a mandate to dispose of the identity of the constitution. No constitutional body has been granted the power to amend the constitutional principles, which are essential pursuant to Article 79(3) of the Basic Law. The FCC monitors this.[62]

Only the constituent power of the people can – to the extent, which it is not limited by natural law principles[63] – determine the constitutional identity and

[59] See also C Tomuschat, 'Die Europäische Union unter der Aufsicht des Bundesverfassungsgerichts' (1993) 20 *Europäische Grundrechte Zeitschrift* 489, 496.

[60] Statehood as a value protected by Article 79(3) GBL was first proposed by P Kirchhof (*Brauchen wir ein erneuertes Grundgesetz* (Heidelberg, C.F. Müller, 1992) 37). This line of argument was quickly accepted by a majority of the German doctrine (see also O Bryde, 'Verfassunggebende Gewalt des Volkes und Verfassungsänderung im deutschen Staatsrecht: Zwischen Überforderung und Unterforderung der Volkssouveränität' in RBP Widmer (eds), *L'Espace Constitutionnel Européen/Der Europäische Verfassungsraum/The European Constitutional Area* (Schulthess 1995) 329, 342 n 342.) There are, however, also important authors rightly arguing against the protection of statehood by the eternity clause. See eg extensively C Möllers, *Der Staat als Argument* 2nd edn (Tübingen, Mohr Siebeck, 2011) ch 1; critically also M Nettesheim, 'Wo "endet" das Grundgesetz?' (2012) 51 *Der Staat* 313, 319.

[61] BVerfGE 123, 267, 343–44. See also Polzin (n 5) 429–31.

[62] ibid at 344 at para 218. In addition, the court held that it is competent to decide whether the constitutional identity is violated by acts of organs of the European Union (ibid at 353–55). See also in detail, the later decision *Mangold* (BVerfGE 126, 286, 302 and 307).

[63] BVerfGE 123, 276, 343 para 217. See also Polzin (n 5): 'It may remain open whether, due to the universal nature of dignity, freedom and equality alone, this commitment even applies to the constituent power, i.e. to the case that the German people, in free self-determination, but in a continuity of legality to the rule of the Basic Law, gives itself a new constitution [citation omitted] (…).'

provide the people with a new constitution. Therefore, 'the sovereign statehood of a constitutional state'[64] could only be abandoned in favour of establishing a European federal state according to the 'declared will of the German people'. The manner in which the German people can exercise this will is not apparent from the judgment. However, one can infer that the court intended to refer to Article 146 of the GBL.[65]

The current version of Article 146 was introduced in the context of German reunification. It provides, '[t]his Basic Law, which since the achievement of the unity and freedom of Germany applies to the entire German people, shall cease to apply on the day on which a constitution freely adopted by the German people takes effect.' It replaces an earlier version of the provision, which stated that the Basic Law 'shall cease to apply on the day on which a constitution freely adopted by the German people takes effect' and related to a new constitution to be adopted by a reunified Germany.

This rewording of Article 146 has led to intense discussions among legal writers with regard to the purpose and function of the new Article 146 of the GBL and its relationship to Article 79(3).[66] The approach, taken by the court in its *Lisbon* judgment, accords with the argument that Article 79(3) does not apply within the context of Article 146, and, in particular, with arguments by the Constitutional Court Justice, Peter M Huber. According to these arguments, Article 146 addresses the constituent power of the people, which is regarded as a power in the legal sense outside the constitution, while Article 79(3) addresses only the constituted powers. The constituent power has only conferred limited competence on the constituted powers and has reserved its right to decide on the provisions protected by Article 79(3). Consequently, the material limits contained in Article 79(3) do not apply within the scope of Article 146.[67]

D. The Aftermath

Since its *Lisbon* judgment, the court has further detailed the doctrine of constitutional identity. In the *Outright Monetary Transactions* decision of 14 January 2014,[68] the court underlined (partly deviating from the *Lisbon*

[64] BVerfGE 123, 267, 347 paras 226, 228.

[65] The court refers to article 146 GBL in relation to the issue of legal standing (ibid at 331–33) and relies on it (at least indirectly) in two further sections of its judgment (ibid at 343 and 349).

[66] See in detail M Polzin, *Verfassungsidentität* (Tübingen, Mohr, 2018) 117–32.

[67] Particularly clear: PM Huber, in M Sachs (ed), *Grundgesetz Kommentar* 6th edn (Munich, CH Beck, 2011) preamble, marginal no 26–27 and Article 146 marginal no 7–14; see an earlier work: PM Huber, 'Die Anforderungen der Europäischen Union an die Reform des Grundgesetzes' (1994) *Thüringer Verwaltungsblätter* 1, 7; similarly also HD Jarass, in HD Jarass and B Pieroth (eds), *Grundgesetz Kommentar* 11th edn (Munich, CH Beck, 2011), preamble marginal no 2. For detail on Article 146 GBL: B Stückrath, *Art. 146 GG: Verfassungsablösung zwischen Legalität und Legitimität* (Berlin, Duncker & Humblot, 1997).

[68] BVerfGE 134, 366.

judgment)[69] that the idea of constitutional identity is an inherent and absolute legal doctrine required by the GBL that is different from the notion of national identity stipulated by Article 4(2) of the Treaty on the European Union (TEU).[70] It emphasised that the eternity clause sets an 'ultimate limit' on the application of EU law within Germany, as the principles enshrined in Article 79(3) of the GBL 'may not be balanced against other legal interests'.[71] As a consequence, the protection of the core content of the Basic Law lies in the hands of the German Constitutional Court alone and does not fall within the competence of the ECJ, which, based on Article 4(2) TEU, treats national identity as an interest that can be balanced against others.[72]

Moreover, in the identity control order of 15 December 2015, the court outlined the procedural requirements for German identity control. It stated that an infringement of the provisions protected by Article 79(3) of the GBL, in particular, human dignity (Article 1)[73] and the essential core of the principles protected by Article 20,[74] such as the rule of law or the principle of democracy, as adopted by the European Union can be asserted by constitutional complaint.[75] Accordingly, the court controls whether the European Union acts[76] in accordance with the constitutional provision protected by Article 79(3). In this context, the guarantee of human dignity as protected by Article 1 of the GBL is of particular importance,[77] as it is the only human right that individuals can invoke in this context. The final decision of such an act of identity control can be that the respective act of the European Union is inapplicable in Germany as it contravenes the constitutional identity of the GBL, which is, in turn, a limitation of the primacy of EU law.

However, the court also underlined that the powers of review are to be exercised with restraint and in a manner open to European law.[78] In particular, the court will ask the ECJ for a preliminary ruling pursuant to Article 267(3) TFEU before its final decision and will use the interpretation provided by the ECJ when deciding on the merits of constitutional identity control.[79] In addition, strict

[69] In the *Lisbon* judgment (BVerfGE 123, 267) the court underlined the general consonance between the concept of German constitutional identity and Article 4(2) TEU (see, in particular, paras 234 and 332).

[70] BVerfGE 134, 366, para 29. However, in the later judgement on identity control (BVerfGE 140, 317, para 44) the court argues that his concept is rather inherent in the concept of Article 4(2) TEU.

[71] ibid.

[72] ibid.

[73] See also BVerfG 2 BvR 1685/14, 30 July 2019, para 156.

[74] Art 20 para 1–3 GBL states: '(1) The Federal Republic of Germany is a democratic and social federal state. (2) All state authority is derived from the people. It shall be exercised by the people through elections and other votes and through specific legislative, executive and judicial bodies. (3) The legislature shall be bound by the constitutional order, the executive and the judiciary by law and justice.'.

[75] BVerfGE 140, 317, para 42–50.

[76] The same applies to Acts adopted by German authorities that are determined by European Union law. See BVerfG, 2 BvR 890/16, Order of 6. September 2016, para 32 et seq.

[77] BVerfGE 140, 317, para 49.

[78] BVerfGE 140, 317, para 46.

[79] BVerfGE 140, 317, para 46.

admissibility requirements apply: 'The complainant must substantiate in detail to what extent the guarantee of human dignity that is protected by Article 1 GG is violated in the individual case'.[80]

In its order on identity control dated 1 December 2020,[81] the court further developed the European law friendly application of the identity control. It clarified that the guarantee of fundamental rights as provided by the Charter of Fundamental Rights of the European Union generally excludes an infringement of the principles of human dignity[82] as protected by Articles 1(1), 23(1)3 and 79(3) of the GBL.[83] Therefore, the application of the identity control will be limited to exceptional cases, where the protection of human dignity at the European level (evidently) fails. Thus, identity control has become the last safety device against a failure to protect human dignity at the European level.

IV. THE UNCLEAR SIDELINE: CONSTITUTIONAL IDENTITY AND PUBLIC INTERNATIONAL LAW

The role of the doctrine of constitutional identity regarding the relationship between constitutional law and public international law is, in the absence of a coherent and concluding case law, still unclear. However, three observations can be made. Firstly, the FCC still uses the *Solange I* formula in the framework of Article 24 of the GBL and not the constitutional identity doctrine as developed in the *Lisbon* judgment (see under IV.A.). Secondly, constitutional identity may constitute an absolute limit for a public international law friendly interpretation of the constitution if the application of the European Convention of Human Rights (ECHR) is concerned (see under IV.B.). And thirdly, if international treaties are concluded in close connection with European integration, constitutional identity becomes relevant (see under IV.C.).

A. Article 24(1) of the Basic Law and *Solange I*

After the adoption of Article 23 of the GBL,[84] the FCC continued to use the formula developed in the *Solange I* decision[85] when examining treaties transferring

[80] BVerfGE 140, 317, para 50.

[81] BVerfG, 2 BvR 1845/18 ao, 1 December 2020.

[82] This approach is in line with the right to be forgotten landmark cases (see Order of the First Senate of 6 November 2019 – 1 BvR 16/13 – (*Right to be forgotten I*) and Order of the First Senate of 6 November 2019 – 1 BvR 276/17 – (*Right to be forgotten II*), which also underline that the human rights protection on the European and national level are rooted in a common tradition (*Right to be forgotten I*, para 60) and that there is generally the same level of protection.

[83] ibid at para 40.

[84] See above under section II.

[85] BVerfGE 37, 271, 279. See in more detail under section I.

competencies to an intergovernmental institution under Article 24(1) of the GBL.[86] According to the *Solange* case law, Article 24(1) contains implicit limits and does not contain the possibility to change the basic structure of the German constitution.[87] However, the Court has not – except for one non-acceptance order dated 12 May 2015[88] – used the notion of identity of the constitution as referred to in the *Solange I* decision and has not yet (December 2020) referred to the constitutional identity concept based on Article 79(3) as developed in the *Lisbon* judgment.[89]

This equates with the case law regarding the constitutional limits for the application of acts of International Organisations in Germany and the possibility of legal protection. Here, the court also follows the *Solange* case law and regards constitutional complaints against these international acts only as admissible if the claimant can substantiate that the respective organisation does not generally safeguard and manifestly protect unconditionally guaranteed fundamental rights as required by the GBL.[90]

B. Constitutional Identity and the European Convention on Human Rights

The ECHR is a human rights treaty setting up an international court that has the competence to decide about individual complaints against member states for the violation of the ECHR.[91] Therefore, the ECHR has an exceptional position within the framework of the GBL and is not treated as a 'normal' international treaty that has the status of a federal law in accordance with Article 59(2)1 of the GBL. Rather the ECHR in the interpretation of the European Court of Human Rights is regarded as an interpretation aid for the fundamental rights and rule-of-law based principles in the Basic Law by the FCC.[92] The main reason is Article 1(2) of the GBL which stipulates that 'The German people therefore acknowledge inviolable and inalienable human rights as the basis of every community, of peace and of justice in the world'. Article 1(2) is understood as 'a maxim for the interpretation of the Basic Law' and as a confirmation that the

[86] Examples are: BVerfGE 68, 1, 93; BVerfGE 59, 63, 83; BVerfG, Non-Acceptance Order 4 April 2001 – 2 BvR 2368/99, paras 14 et seq.

[87] See above under Section I.

[88] BVerfG, 2 BvR 2954/10, Order of Non-Acceptance of 12 May 2015, para 24.

[89] The court did not refer to the notion of constitutional identity in the following non-acceptance orders after the *Lisbon* judgment: BVerfG, 2 BvR 1848/07, 27 April 2010, para 13; BVerfG, 2 BvR 2954/10, 12 May 2015, para 24.

[90] See the following non-acceptance orders: BVerfG, 2 BvR 1848/07, 27 April 2010, para 13; BVerfG, 2 BvR 2253/06, 27 January 2010, para 19; BVerfG, 2 BvR 1458/03, 3 July 2006, paras 21–22; BVerfG, 2 BvR 2368/99, 4 April 2001, para 18.

[91] See Article 34 of the ECHR.

[92] The Constitutional Court applies the ECHR in the interpretation of the European Court of Human Rights irrespective of whether it is contained in a judgment against Germany or in any other decision of the Strasbourg Court (BVerfGE 128, 326, 368–69).

fundamental rights are a manifestation of international human rights, which have incorporated the latter as a minimum standard.[93] However, this international law friendly constitutional interpretation also has limits.[94] In its judgment on the constitutionality of the security prevention the FCC wrote without further explanation,[95] that 'the core content of the constitutional identity of the Basic Law under Article 79(3) of the Basic Law' is an absolute limit for the interpretation of the GBL in conformity of the ECHR.[96]

C. Constitutional Identity and International Treaties Connected with the European Integration

The latest extension of the doctrine of constitutional identity is that the FCC found it applicable in relation to public international law treaties based on Article 59(2)1 of the GBL that were concluded in close relationship with the European Integration. Relevant are the *EFS* judgment,[97] the *ESM* decisions,[98] and the judgment on the act of approval to the Agreement on a Unified Patent Court of 19 February 2013 in conjunction with the Agreement on a Unified Patent Court.[99]

The treaty-related use of constitutional identity is not a fully developed legal concept and can be clearly distinguished from the European integration-related doctrine of constitutional identity. This is mainly because according to the case law of the FCC and the general view in German literature, international treaties do have the status of federal law in accordance with Article 59(2)1 of the GBL.[100] The consequence is that the act of approval of an international treaty (and therefore also the content of an international treaty) has to conform to all provisions of the Basic Law and not only the core protected by the eternity clause.[101] Otherwise, the act of approval is void,[102] or a previous constitutional amendment is necessary.[103]

The relevance of the treaty law related concept of constitutional identity is, for the time being, purely procedural and has its origins in the *Maastricht*

[93] BVerfGE 128, 326, 369; BVerGE 111, 307, 329.

[94] BVerfGE 111, 307, 317; BVerfGE 128, 326, 367.

[95] See also M Payandeh and H Sauer, 'Menschenrechtskonforme Auslegung als Verfassungsmehrwert: Konvergenzen von Grundgesetz und EMRK im Urteil des Bundesverfassungsgerichts zur Sicherungsverwahrung' (2012) *JURA* 289, 295.

[96] BVerfGE 128, 326, 371.

[97] BVerfGE 129, 124.

[98] BVerfGE 132, 195 and BVerfGE 135, 317.

[99] BVerfG 2 BvR 739/17, 13 February 2020.

[100] BVerfG, 2 BvL 1/12, Order of 15 December 2015, para 74 with further references.

[101] See, eg, BVerfGE 30, 272–91, para 29.

[102] An example is BVerfGE 72, 200.

[103] See, eg, BVerfGE 36, 1, 14.

judgment. In the *Maastricht* judgment, the FCC started to interpret Article 38 of the GBL and held:

> Art. 38 of the GBL forbids the weakening, within the scope of Article 23 of the GBL, of the legitimation of State power gained through an election, and of the influence on the exercise of such power, by means of a transfer of duties and responsibilities of the Federal Parliament, to the extent that the principle of democracy, declared as inviolable in Article 79(3) in conjunction with Article 20(1) and (2) of the GBL, is violated.[104]

The consequence was that the complainants could argue that the TEU possibly led to an unconstitutional loss of power of the German Parliament.[105] In the *EFS* judgment,[106] this approach was further transferred to international treaties connected to European integration. The Constitutional Court decided that the interpretation of Article 38 of the GBL as developed in the *Maastricht* judgment also applies 'to comparable commitments entered into by treaty, which are connected institutionally to the supranational European Union, if the result of this is that the people's democratic self-government is permanently restricted in such a way that central political decisions can no longer be made independently'.[107]

In the later decisions on the constitutionality of the European Stability Mechanism and the Fiscal Compact, the Constitutional Court examined whether the Act approving the Treaty of 2 February 2012 establishing the European Stability Mechanism and the Act approving the Treaty of 2 March 2012 on Stability, Coordination and Governance in the Economic and Monetary Union conformed to Article 79(3) of the GBL.[108] The court examined whether the act of assent satisfied the requirements of Articles 38(1), 20(1) and (2) in conjunction with Article 79(3) of the GBL.[109] Furthermore, the court introduced the duty of the constitutional organs during the ratification process to ensure that the Treaty establishing the European Stability Mechanism was not interpreted in such a way that it would violate the principles protected by Article 79(3) of the GBL and that Germany would not be bound to the treaty with such an interpretation were adopted.[110]

[104] BVerfGE 89, 155, 172. English translation: Wegen et al, 33 ILM 388 (March 1994).

[105] ibid at 173; see also BVerfGE 123, 267, 330 f.

[106] See in this context the dissenting opinion of Justice Lübbe-Wolff on the Order of the Second Senate of 14 January 2013, para 15: 'Without admitting to any innovation, it was recently held that the same applies to legislation on international treaties submitting the exercise of sovereign rights to other bonds and influences (cf BVerfGE 129, 124 <168>)'.

[107] BVerfGE 129, 124, 168.

[108] BVerfGE 132, 195, 251 et seq; BVerfGE 135, 317 (paras 183 et seq).

[109] ibid.

[110] BVerfGE 131, 195, 256–57, 260.

V. CONSTITUTIONAL IDENTITY AND ULTRA VIRES CONTROL

In the aftermath of the *Lisbon* judgment, the FCC also re-defined the relationship between identity and ultra vires control. The purpose of the ultra-vires control is to determine whether the European Union acted within its competencies. It was developed by the Constitutional Court in the *Kloppenburg* decision[111] and the famous *Maastricht* judgment[112] and further specified in the *Mangold* decision in July 2011.[113] The *Maastricht* judgment justified the ultra vires control with the idea that fundamental changes of the European Treaties are not covered by the original act of approval and therefore inapplicable in Germany.[114] The famous passage reads as follows:

> The important factor is that the Federal Republic of Germany's membership and the rights and obligations which arise from it, in particular the legally binding direct activity of the European Communities in the domestic legal territory, have been defined foreseeably for the legislator in the Treaty, and that the legislator has standardized them to a sufficiently definable level in the Act of Consent to the Treaty (…). This also means that any subsequent substantial amendments to that programme of integration provided for by the Maastricht Treaty or to its authorizations to act are no longer covered by the Act of Consent to ratify this Treaty (…). If, for example, European institutions or governmental entities were to implement or to develop the Maastricht Treaty in a manner no longer covered by the Treaty in the form of it upon which the German Act of Consent is based, any legal instrument arising from such activity would not be binding within German territory. German State institutions would be prevented by reasons of constitutional law from applying such legal instruments in Germany. Accordingly, the German Federal Constitutional Court must examine the question of whether or not legal instruments of European institutions and governmental entities may be considered to remain within the limits of the sovereign rights accorded to them, or whether they may be considered to exceed those limits (…).[115]

The *OMT* judgment modified this approach. Here the court argued for the first time that both the identity and ultra-vires control are based upon Article 79(3) of the GBL.[116] The court wrote:

> The fundamental elements of the principle of democracy enshrined in Article 20(1) and (2) GG are part of the constitutional identity of the Basic Law, (…). In conjunction with Article 38(1) sentence 1 GBL, the principle of democracy protects citizens (…) also from institutions, bodies, offices, and agencies of the European Union that

[111] BVerfGE 75, 223, 227.
[112] BVerfGE 89, 155, 187 f.
[113] BVerfG, NJW 2010, 3422, 3423 ff.
[114] See also P Kirchhof, § 183 Der deutsche Staat im Prozeß der europäischen Integration' in Isensee/Kirchhof (eds), *Handbuch des Staatsrechts VII* (1992) paras 63 et seq; Critically: FC Mayer, 'Verfassung im Nationalstaat: Von der Gesamtordnung zur europäischen Teilordnung?' (2015) *Veröffentlichung der Vereinigung der Deutschen Staatsrechtslehrer* 75, 7 (40 f).
[115] BVerfGE 89, 155 (188).
[116] BVerfGE 142, 123 para 153.

> exceed their competences in a manifest and structurally significant way (…). (…) the issue of whether the boundaries of the democratically legitimated European integration under Article 23(1) sentence 2 GBL are exceeded by such acts in a manifest and structurally significant manner and thereby violate the principle of the sovereignty of the people is determined by the Court in its ultra vires review (Ultra-vires-Kontrolle) (…) Both the identity review and the ultra vires review are derived from Article 79(3) GBL but constitute independent types of review using different standards.[117]

The reason for this approach is again procedural. The Constitutional Court allows the individual to claim evident excess of competence of the European Union based on Article 38(1)1 of the GBL.[118] The reason is that Article 38(1)2 in connection with Articles 20(1), (2) and 79(3) contains the 'right to democracy',[119] which protects the citizens against acts of the European Union that are outside the powers transferred to them by the relevant Acts of Approval.

If institutions, bodies, offices, and agencies usurp functions and powers that have not been transferred to them by the European integration agenda laid down in the Act of Approval, they violate the core of the principle of the sovereignty of the people protected by Article 1(1) GBL, because they subject the citizens to a public authority that they have not legitimated and that – given the institutional structure of the organs of the European Union (…) – they cannot freely, equally and effectively influence'.[120]

The court confirmed and further detailed this approach in later decisions regarding *CETA*,[121] the *European Banking Union*[122] and the famous *PSPP* judgment.[123] Even though the court now (in my view wrongly)[124] bases the ultra vires control on Article 79(3) of the GBL; the ultra vires control can be clearly distinguished from the identity control and the idea of constitutional identity. Here, the court examines not whether the European Union violated core values of the German Constitution as such, but whether an act 'manifestly exceeds EU competences, resulting in a structurally significant shift in the division of competences to the detriment of the Member States'.[125] The latter is generally the case, 'if the exercise of the competence in question by an institution, body, office, or agency of the European Union were to require a treaty amendment in accordance with Article 48 TEU or an evolutionary clause'.[126] The court, therefore, guards the universal principle of law that no institution can act outside its competencies rather than defend national particularities.[127]

[117] ibid at 121. English translation provided by the FCC.
[118] ibid at paras 127 et seq.
[119] ibid at paras 133, 147 and 85.
[120] ibid at para 135.
[121] BVerfGE 143, 65 para 50–51 and 59.
[122] BVerfGE 151, 202 paras 114, 141–50.
[123] BVerfG, Judgment of the Second Senate of 5 May 2020 – 2 BvR 859/15 –, paras 98, 105–13, see already: BVerfGE 146, 216, paras 44 et seq, 63 and 123.
[124] See in detail Polzin (n 66) 189.
[125] See BVerfG, Judgment of the Second Senate of 5 May 2020 – 2 BvR 859/15 –, para 109 with further references.
[126] ibid.
[127] More critical Thym (n 1) 247.

VI. IDENTITY AND ETERNITY: THE CORE PROBLEMS

To conclude, the FCC firstly established a fully developed European integration-related legal doctrine of constitutional identity and a possible concept in progress in relation to general international law. The European integration-related constitutional identity is an absolute limit for the transfer of competencies to the European Union and the application of European Union law. It can even be asserted through constitutional complaints. However, the newest case law indicates that identity control relating to human dignity is to secure this guarantee only in very exceptional cases. Its ultimate purpose is to protect the core of the German Basic Law that guarantees the universal core of a democratic and constitutional state as well as the vertical power delimitation between the European Union and the Member State. Finally, we can also note that the Constitutional Court has not (yet) used the notion of constitutional identity when examining constitutional amendments unconnected to European integration.[128]

However, the doctrine of constitutional identity was established by a sheer magnitude of judicial creativity and is far from uncontroversial in German constitutional doctrine.[129] In addition to the discussion about whether constitutional identity is a constitutionally required limit for the application of European law,[130] there are two core constitutional points of criticism.

Firstly, the doctrine of constitutional identity is connected to the idea of a constituent power outside the constitution and the distinction between amending and constituent power. The latter is regarded as the sole power that can decide upon the constitutional identity. This becomes particularly clear in the famous formulation of the FCC in the *Lisbon* judgment.

> In this respect, the constituent power has not granted the representatives and bodies of the people a mandate to dispose of the identity of the constitution. No constitutional body has been granted the power to amend the constitutional principles which are essential pursuant to Article 79(3) of the GBL.[131]

Even though the FCC, in contrast to the theory of Schmitt, seems to regard the constituent power as an entrenched power that might be articulated through Article 146 of the GBL, this approach is problematic as it offers the possibility to overcome the eternity clause and the protected core of the Basic Law.

The second problem is directly related to the notion of constitutional identity itself. On the one hand, there is still some subtle ambiguity in the case law of the German court when it comes to the definition of 'constitutional

[128] See, eg, BVerfGE 94, 49; BVerfGE 109, 279.

[129] See, eg, A Ingold 'Die verfassungsrechtliche Identität der Bundesrepublik' (2015) 140 *Anstalt des öffentlichen Rechts* 1; M Nettesheim, 'Ein Individualrecht auf Staatlichkeit? Die Lissabon-Entscheidung des BVerfG' (2009) *Neue Juristische Woche* 2867; C Schönberger, 'Identitäterä: Verfassungsidentität zwischen Widerstandsformel und Musealisierung des Grundgesetzes' (2015) 63 *Jahrbuch des öffentlichen Rechts der Gegenwart* 41; extensively see Polzin (n 66).

[130] Polzin (n 66) 177–97.

[131] See section III.

identity'. It seems unclear whether it is a limited concept and simply an alternative expression for the provisions protected by Article 79(3) of the GBL, or if it is a possibly independent legal concept that goes beyond Article 79(3).[132] For the time being, the court has generally relied[133] on the values protected by Article 79(3), particularly the democracy principle, when further specifying the content of constitutional identity.[134] On the other hand – and that is the key issue – the notion of constitutional identity is a device that can be used to broaden the scope of Article 79(3) due to its indeterminacy and softness – in particular concerning the European integration.[135] Such an approach contradicts the democratic principle that requires a restrictive interpretation of Article 79(3) as the eternity clause constitutes an absolute limit for the democratic process. In addition, the right to examine whether a constitutional amendment conforms to the eternity clause gives the Constitutional Court a powerful position in the constitutional system. It allows the court to have the very last word on the content of the constitution as the legislative branch (which has the competence to change the German constitution with a 2/3 majority in accordance with Article 79(2)) is unable to overturn a decision declaring an amendment unconstitutional. Therefore, Article 79 – as an exceptional provision[136] – is interpreted restrictively in accordance with the case law of the FCC when it examines constitutional amendments unrelated to the European integration.[137] In its landmark decision on these 'classical constitutional amendments', the court held that the eternity clause does not prevent the German legislature from modifying inherent parts within the constitutional system and fundamental constitutional principles through a constitutional amendment.[138]

Thus, the notion of constitutional identity is a direct contradiction of the principle of restrictive interpretation of the eternity clause. It is also a device which can lead to a power shift from the Constitutional Court to the detriment of the German legislative branch.

However, despite this criticism, the German doctrine of constitutional identity is based on a legitimate idea as it aims at protecting the core values of the GBL, which in turn are the core elements of a democratic and constitutional state.

[132] See on the different school of thoughts on Article 79(3) GBL as a limit for the transfer of power, Callies (n 1) 168–69.

[133] One exception is an obiter dictum of the 1st Senate of the German Court (BVerfGE 125, 260 (324) – *Data Retention*. The Court wrote 'the prohibition to gather and record the exercise of freedom by citizens in its entirety belongs to the constitutional identity of the Federal Republic of Germany (…).' [translation provided by the author].

[134] See, eg, BVerfGE 132, 195, para 213; BVerfGE 135, 317 paras 159, 164, 177, 179; BVerfG, 2 BvR 1685/14 and others, 30 July 2019, para 156; BVerfG 2 BvR 859/15 and others, 5 May 2020, para 115.

[135] See Polzin (n 66) 136–141.

[136] BVerfGE 30, 1, 25.

[137] BVerfGE 109, 279, 310.

[138] BVerfGE 30, 1, 25; BVerfGE 84, 90, 121; BVerfGE 94, 12, 34; BVerfGE 94, 49, 103; BVerfGE 109, 297, 310.

The main concern against the German doctrine is the missing rule of law approach. Such a situation would exist if the German concept of constitutional identity was not based on the distinction between the amending power and an imagined constituent power outside the constitution, whose empowerment remains somehow unclear. Instead, it should be based on an idea that was also immanent in the making and drafting of the German eternity clause: namely, that certain provisions are so important for a democratic state that they have to be protected as such and are therefore contained in the eternity clause of the GBL. A pertinent example of such an approach is Hans Nawiasky's statement:

> The newest development in constitutional law has led to the general insight, that there are unchangeable constitutional provisions, which cannot be amended by legal means. Those provision can only be eliminated through extralegal force – i.e. a revolution or coup d'état – that cannot be regarded as legal. Such unamendable provisions theoretically have a higher rank than the constitution itself, as they are binding on the constitution. They can be described as the fundamental norms of a state.[139]

VII. CONSTITUTIONAL IDENTITY: DIFFERENT USES AND POSSIBLE MISUSES

Constitutional identity is a relatively new and enigmatic notion in German constitutional discourse as well as constitutional law and theory in general. Constitutional identity relates either to a constructed identity of the 'self' in relation to the constitution, or the identity of a constitution itself.[140] However, in the absence of a universal or uniform definition or scope of application of constitutional identity,[141] constitutional identity can have different meanings and the distinction between legitimate and illegitimate uses can become tricky. Therefore, the normative concept of constitutional identity developed by the FCC is firstly distinguished from other normative and theoretical constitutional identity discourses (A) before possible misuses of the German concept are described (B).

A. The Different Constitutional Identity Discourses

The present chapter only focuses on the normative concept of constitutional identity developed by the FCC. It concerns constitutional identity as a legal

[139] H Nawiasky, *Die Grundgedanken des Grundgesetzes für die Bundesrepublik Deutschland* (Stuttgart, W. Kohlhammer, 1950) 123. Translation by the author.

[140] JL Martí, 'Two Different Ideas of Constitutional Identity: Identity of the Constitution v. Identity of the People' in AS Arnaiz and CA Llivina (eds), *National Constitutional Identity and European Integration* (Cambridge, Intersentia, 2013) 17.

[141] cf M Rosenfeld, 'Constitutional Identity' in M Rosenfeld and A Sajó (eds), *The Oxford Handbook of Comparative Constitutional Law* (Oxford, Oxford University Press, 2012) 756.

concept. Its purpose is to describe limitations for constitutional amendments in general, including limits for the further development of the European Union and applying European and possibly international law in Germany. Here, constitutional identity is used as the 'identity of the constitution'. On an abstract level, the major question in this context is whether a constitution remains the same despite any amendments made to it, or whether it is fundamentally altered by those amendments so that it becomes an entirely different one.

The German constitutional identity concept is partially overlapping with two other normative constitutional identity discourses,[142] namely the constitutional respective national identity discourse centred on Article 4(2) TEU[143] and the less developed discourse on the relationship between important constitutional values and public international law.[144]

However, the FCC's normative approach is – even though there are some similarities – different from the theoretical constitutional identity discourse.[145] In the latter, constitutional identity is understood as a particular collective identity of a people or a nation that is also expressed, determined and shaped by the constitution.[146] This discourse focuses on the relationship between national culture and the constitution.[147] The most important author in this respect is Gary Jeffrey Jacobsohn.[148] He asks the difficult theoretical question: 'How does one come to know the identity of a constitution?'[149] His answer is 'that this identity exists neither as a discrete object of invention nor as a heavily encrusted essence embedded in a society's culture, requiring only to be discovered. Rather, identity emerges dialogically and represents a mix of political aspirations and commitments that are expressive of a nation's past, as well as a determination of those within the society who seek in some ways to transcend this past'.[150] It is fundamental that the process of shaping a constitutional identity is driven

[142] On the different identity discourses see M Polzin, 'Constitutional Identity as a Constructed Reality and a Restless Soul' (2017) *German Law Journal* 1595, 1597–599.

[143] See on this discourse inter alia F-X Millet, 'L'union européene et l'identité constitutionnelle des États membres' (LGDJ ed, 2013); AS Arnaiz and CA Llivina (eds), *National Constitutional Identity and European Integration* (Cambridge, Intersentia, 2013); L Burgorgue-Larsen (ed), *L'identite constitutionnelle saisie par les juges en Europe* (Paris, Pedone, 2011); P Faraguna, 'Constitutional Identity in the EU–A Shield or a Sword?' (2017) 18 *German Law Journal* 1617.

[144] See, eg, A Peters, 'Rechtsordnungen und Konstitutionalisierung: Zur Neubestimmung der Verhältnisse' (2010) 65 *Zeitschrift für Öffentliches Recht* 3, 54.

[145] See also in this regard chapter eight in this volume.

[146] See G Jacobsohn, *Constitutional Identity* (Cambridge, Harvard University Press, 2010) 8; M Rosenfeld, *The Identity of the Constitutional Subject* (London, Routledge, 2009), Rosenfeld (n 141) 760.

[147] For this perspective see RC Post, 'The Supreme Court, 2002 Term-Forward: Establishing the Legal Constitution: Culture, Courts and Law' (2003) 117 *Harvard Law Review* 8 ('[C]onstitutional law and culture are locked in a dialectical relationship, so that constitutional law both arises from and in turn regulates culture.').

[148] See also chapter one in this book.

[149] Jacobsohn (n 146) 7.

[150] ibid.

by disharmony, either in the text of the constitution or in the society itself – in particular historical and political contestations.[151]

B. Misuses and Legitimate Uses

Lastly, the critical question is how to distinguish between generally legitimate use and the further development of the German normative concept of constitutional identity as well as possible misuses. This question has become particularly important, as the notion of constitutional identity is (relatively) new and vague. Therefore, it can easily be relied on to prevent the application of European and international law on the national level for a multitude of reasons, such as to protect a particular imagined idea of a historical nation.[152]

Any delamination has to begin with the two ultimate purposes of the German concept of constitutional identity: to protect the core elements of a given constitution, which constitute the essence of a democratic and rule of law-based constitutional order. Thus, if the concept of constitutional identity is not used in order to protect the core of a constitution itself or protect the core of a constitution that is neither democratic nor a rule of law-based constitution, the concept of constitutional identity is misused.

The normative concept of constitutional identity is therefore not a suitable legal doctrine for limiting the application of European or possibly international law in order to protect an autocratic or dictatorial regime. The main problem in all these misuse cases would be to determine whether the relevant constitution is still a democratic and rule of law-based constitution as well as the core content of the relevant constitution. This is a question that deserves more thorough analysis and beyond the scope of the present chapter.

[151] ibid at 13, 351–55.

[152] See regarding the use by the Hungarian Constitutional Court in chapter six of this book.

Part II

National Identity Claims in the Visegrád 4 Countries

3

From Minimalism to the Substantive Core and Back: The Slovak Constitutional Court and (the Lack of) Constitutional Identity

KATARÍNA ŠIPULOVÁ AND MAX STEUER[1]

HAS THE SLOVAK Constitutional Court (SCC) engaged with the concept of constitutional identity? If so, what are its key tenets and how has it evolved? Recent scholarship has explored the constitutional identity discourse in Czechia,[2] Hungary[3] and Poland[4] regarding the relationship between national constitutional orders and EU law (Hungary, Czechia), as well as authoritarian populist attacks in Hungary and Poland.[5] Yet, these phenomena have so far remained largely unexplored in Slovakia, despite its moving history. Unlike in the rest of the Visegrád group, the fall of communism did not continue as a democratic success story in early 1990s Slovakia. Instead, the country faced four years of the semi-authoritarian rule of Vladimír Mečiar,[6] which halted the progress of integration into EU and seriously impeded the establishment of early democratic institutions.

[1] We would like to thank the editor of the volume as well as the participants at an online book workshop and the research seminar of the Judicial Studies Institute for valuable feedback. The chapter is updated with developments until June 2022.

[2] D Kosař and L Vyhnánek, 'The Constitutional Court of Czechia' in A von Bogdandy, P Huber and C Grabenwarter (eds), *The Max Planck Handbooks in European Public Law: Volume III: Constitutional Adjudication: Institutions* (Oxford, Oxford University Press, 2020).

[3] G Halmai, 'Abuse of Constitutional Identity. The Hungarian Constitutional Court on Interpretation of Article E) (2) of the Fundamental Law' (2018) 43 *Review of Central and East European Law* 23.

[4] A Śledzińska-Simon and M Ziółkowski, 'Constitutional Identity in Poland: Is the Emperor Putting On the Old Clothes of Sovereignty?' in C Calliess and G van der Schiff (eds), *Constitutional Identity in a Europe of Multilevel Constitutionalism* (Cambridge, Cambridge University Press, 2020).

[5] See the introductory chapter in this volume.

[6] Classifications of Mečiar's regime differ, using terms such as 'troubled democracy': H Kitschelt, *Post-Communist Party Systems: Competition, Representation, and Inter-Party Cooperation* (Cambridge, Cambridge University Press, 1999) 42, mixed case: Commission on Security and Cooperation in Europe, 'Human Rights and Democratization in Slovakia', or even one-party

While it acceded to the EU in 2004, Slovakia continues to be a puzzling case three decades later. At the very end of 2020, the Slovak parliament, riddled with Covid-19-related restrictions and disputes, rapidly passed a startling amendment to the Constitution, aiming to strip the SCC of the power to review any constitutional act or constitutional amendment.[7] The controversial decision came only a year after a breakthrough judgment of the SCC which annulled a constitutional act allowing security screening of judges.[8] Interestingly, this was also the very first time the SCC identified judicial independence as part of the substantive core of the Constitution and hence one of the core criteria of the constitutional review of an act of any public authority. Even more importantly, we argue this was the closest the SCC came to the articulation of Slovakia's constitutional identity.

The strike against the SCC came in a reaction to the court's emancipation in the last couple of years, which culminated in the unconstitutional constitutional amendment judgment. The social and political upheaval after the murder of Slovak journalist Ján Kuciak due to his investigative work, and his fianceé, Martina Kušnírová, exposed a vast corruption network in the public sphere – including the judiciary. It culminated with 2020 parliamentary elections which brought to power a new government led by a populist, Igor Matovič, who promised his voters that he would clean the system of old cadres and break the corruption networks, strengthening both judicial independence and the rule of law.[9] The SCC itself suffered significant partisan pressure when the outgoing government, suspecting its looming loss in the coming election, (unsuccessfully) attempted to pack the SCC with close allies. In what follows we explain how the SCC's reactionist approach to constitutional identity backed the court into a corner and turned it into a target of the populist government in 2020. In doing so, we pay homage to existing scholarly works suggesting that constitutional identity needs to be understood in a broader context, as it develops dialogically from past experience, as well as future aspirations.[10]

Our chapter provides the very first analysis of the SCC's interaction with the concept of constitutional identity.[11] While many constitutional courts

authoritarian system: JJ Linz and A Stepan, *Problems of Democratic Transition and Consolidation: Southern Europe, South America, and Post-Communist Europe* (Baltimore, Johns Hopkins University Press, 1996) 38–55; PC Schmitter and TL Karl, 'What Democracy Is … and Is Not' (1991) 2 *Journal of Democracy* 75.

[7] The SCC refused the petition against the change of the SCC's constitutional competences in April 2022 (PL ÚS 8/2022).

[8] PL ÚS 21/2014.

[9] See manifesto of Ordinary People and Independent Personalities, political party led by former PM Matovič. Obyčajní ľudia a nezávislé osobnosti, 'Úprimne, odvážne pre ľudí' www.obycajniludia.sk/wp-content/uploads/2020/02/OLANO_program_2020_FINAL_online.pdf.

[10] See chapter one in this volume.

[11] Hereinafter, when we talk of constitutional identity, we simply mean how the SCC understands and conceptualises the term constitutional identity, and do not aspire to offer our own definition.

interpreted constitutional identity in response to historical legacies (experience with non-democratic regimes) or external challenges (supranational commitments and EU law in particular),[12] Slovakia is a different story. Unlike in the case of the Hungarian or Polish constitutional courts, constitutional identity has not played a central role for the SCC and its articulations in its case law has remained limited.

We analyse the references to constitutional identity in the case law of the court between 1990–2020 and discuss existing reflections in Slovak domestic scholarship with an emphasis on the relationship between constitutional law and EU law. We argue that the SCC's reluctant engagement with the concept of constitutional identity can be explained by three interrelated factors. First, Mečiar's use of nationalism for easy electoral gains in the 1990s[13] placed the SCC in opposition to ethnonationalist claims. The SCC embraced a minimalistic approach,[14] that is, avoiding references to theories and abstract concepts such as constitutional identity, and limiting itself to narrow and shallow decisions on the circumstances of a case. The SCC benefited from this judicial minimalism, as it sufficed to offset Vladimír Mečiar's most blatant autocratisation efforts, while it also shielded the SCC from at least some decision costs. Second, the accession to the EU in 2004 offered Slovakia an opportunity to lock in desired democratic policies.[15] This sentiment was also reflected in the SCC's case law. The court did not grasp accession to the EU as an opportunity to recognise challenges of EU law's supremacy and juxtapose it against the concept of constitutional identity. Unlike in the rest of the Visegrád group, the court made a striking acknowledgment of EU law's supremacy, which resulted from the legacy of Mečiar's regime. Third, lacking clear wording of constitutional identity in the text of the Constitution or the past democratic legacy, the SCC, challenged by decades of competence and power disputes between executive and legislative actors, eventually developed a doctrine of the substantive core of the Constitution. Since core challenges of the Slovak constitutional system that reached the SCC addressed mostly separation of powers disputes, principles of the rule of law and judicial independence became the cornerstone of this doctrine. The whole existence of the SCC is also characterised by contestation of judicial independence: part of the political elite attempted to capture the judiciary from the inside, pack the courts with loyal justices and eliminate checks and balances.

[12] See the introductory chapter in this volume.

[13] Cf E Harris, 'Nation before Democracy? Placing the Rise of the Slovak Extreme Right into Context' (2019) 35 *East European Politics* 538.

[14] CR Sunstein, *One Case at a Time: Judicial Minimalism on the Supreme Court* (Cambridge, Mass, Harvard University Press, 2001).

[15] A Moravcsik, 'The Origins of Human Rights Regimes: Democratic Delegation in Postwar Europe' (2000) 54 *International Organization* 217.

The chapter on the SCC hence demonstrates that constitutional courts may develop their reading of constitutional identity in a reactive way. The lack of textual hooks in the text of the Slovak Constitution, combined with experience of political unrest, tradition of judicial minimalism, and dominance of separation of powers disputes in the SCC's case law, eventually led the court to ground its approach to constitutional identity in the substantive core doctrine. This doctrine represents a reading of constitutional identity which aims at integrating democracy, human rights and the rule of law.

We argue that locking in the principle of judicial independence became important both for the SCC's self-preservation and for its understanding of the threats to the Slovak judiciary in general. Therefore, the government's attempt to interfere in judicial independence via the security screening of judges spurred the court to quash several provisions of the constitutional act. However, in doing so the SCC also created a space for a pushback from the populist government,[16] which demanded more accountability for the 'non-democratic' judiciary[17] by curtailing the court's formal powers in an accelerated procedure. This is important for the broader literature examining legislative reactions to judicialisation of politics.[18]

The chapter proceeds as follows. In section I we briefly sketch the institutional background that frames the SCC's decision-making capabilities. In section II we examine the building blocks laid down in jurisprudence under Vladimír Mečiar's semi-authoritarian regime, showing how the court managed to push back against the core challenges with a minimalist strategy. Then, we proceed to explain why Slovakia's accession to the EU and subsequent developments prompted the SCC not to turn to constitutional identity, but instead to articulate grounds of what came later to be known as the substantive core doctrine (section III). In section IV we elaborate on the emphasis on judicial independence in the substantive core doctrine against the backdrop of corruption scandals and some political parties' court-curbing attempts. Finally, we discuss the advantages and risks of the combination of a limited debate on the relationship between the Slovak Constitution and the EU and the substantive core doctrine, with judicial independence among its central principles (section V). We conclude by assessing the fundamental challenge launched against the SCC by the post-2020 governing majority that set out explicitly to curtail its competence to review constitutional acts and amendments.

[16] See, eg, L Buštíková and P Baboš, 'Best in Covid: Populists in the Time of Pandemic' (2020) 8 *Politics and Governance* 496.

[17] Explanatory statement for Constitutional Act No 422/2020 Coll, 6–7. www.nrsr.sk/web/Dynamic/DocumentPreview.aspx?DocID=484567.

[18] Eg, MA Graber, 'The Nonmajoritarian Difficulty: Legislative Deference to the Judiciary' (1993) 7 *Studies in American Political Development* 35; K Pócza (ed), *Constitutional Politics and the Judiciary: Decision-Making in Central and Eastern Europe* (London, Routledge, 2018).

I. SETTING THE STAGE: FORMAL AND INSTITUTIONAL LOCUS OF THE SCC

The SCC was established under two conflicting narratives: first, the democratisation efforts after the Velvet revolution (in Slovak called 'the Tender revolution') of November 1989, and second, nationalist sentiments that contributed to the dissolution of the short-lived democratic Czecho-Slovak Federal Republic and the establishment of independent Slovakia in 1993. The former manifested themselves in the effort to gain inspiration from Western democratic traditions and to signal Slovakia's commitment to a 'return to Europe', ultimately via accession to the Council of Europe and the EU. The latter resulted in a hasty constitution-drafting process[19] orchestrated mainly by the future first Slovak Prime Minister, Vladimír Mečiar. Mečiar's race towards an independent Slovakia, motivated by both a personal vendetta against federal politicians who sought to remove him from power and a will to concentrate more power in his hands,[20] left little time to consider the intended role of the newly established SCC.

As a result, the design of the SCC copied many of the competences of its federal predecessor. The SCC was established as an institution with a wide range of formal powers,[21] which were not sufficiently discussed.[22] It was tasked with safeguarding constitutionality and its competences included extensive constitutional review of legislation, as well as the abstract interpretation of constitutional and legal statutes and provisions.[23] The first ten justices were appointed without much controversy, with Mečiar's ruling party (Hnutie za demokratické Slovensko) playing a prominent role.[24]

The Slovak political regime between 1994 and 1998 is typically characterised as semi-authoritarian.[25] The ruling party took absolute control of the state's

[19] D Malová, 'Slovakia: From the Ambiguous Constitution to the Dominance of Informal Rules' in J Zielonka (ed), *Democratic Consolidation in Eastern Europe: Volume 1: Institutional Engineering* (Oxford, Oxford University Press, 2001) 347.

[20] J Suk, *Labyrintem revoluce* (Prague, Prostor, 2009).

[21] J Drgonec, *Ústavné právo procesné* (Munich, CH Beck, 2017); M Steuer, 'Constitutional Court of the Slovak Republic' in R Grote, F Lachenmann and R Wolfrum (eds), *Max Planck Encyclopedia of Comparative Constitutional Law* (Oxford, Oxford University Press, 2019) <https://oxcon.ouplaw.com/view/10.1093/law-mpeccol/law-mpeccol-e803>.

[22] Like the Federal Constitution, the Slovak Constitution was criticised for its rushed creation in narrow political elites' circles, hidden away from broader civic and public discussion (see, eg, I Grudzińska-Gross, *Constitutionalism in East Central Europe* (Czecho-Slovak Committee of the European Cultural Foundation 1994); J Malenovský, 'O legitimitě a výkladu české Ústavy na konci století existence moderního českého státu' (2013) 152 *Právník* 745).

[23] A Bröstl, J Klučka and J Mazák, *Ústavný súd Slovenskej republiky. Organizácia, proces, doktrína* (PHARE Foundation, 2001).

[24] M Leško, *Mečiar a mečiarizmus: Politik bez škrupúľ, politia bez zábran* (Prešov, VMV, 1996).

[25] Kitschelt (n 6); Schmitter and Karl (n 6); Linz and Stepan (n 6).

economy and used privatisation processes to vest the control of key businesses in people with close ties to the party. Mečiar's regime limited the freedoms of its political opponents and allowed the creation of vast corruption and patronage networks between politicians and oligarchs.[26] The judiciary suffered under Mečiar's regime, never executing a real personal and substantive functional transition from the communist legacy.[27]

The Constitutional Court soon became the arbiter of many competence disputes between Mečiar and his political opponents (especially the President of the Republic), demarking the core principles of separation of powers and the limits of competences of the executive power. The SCC, however, benefited from the fact that Mečiar initially underestimated its importance, and later did not manage to pack it with more ideologically aligned justices.[28]

Nevertheless, the deficiencies of the hastily formed constitutional design, which mechanically adopted many of the federal provisions, soon became obvious. After Mečiar lost the 1998 parliamentary election, the new political elite vested considerable effort into the integration into the EU. Slovakia perhaps best illustrates Moravcsik's hypothesis of young democratic regimes committing to international law to lock in preferred democratic policies. EU accession and membership became a symbol of Slovakia's return to the family of democratic regimes. Given the lack of historical experience with democracy and negative legacy of the first independent government, it was the integration project and democratic conditions laid upon the candidate countries by the European Commission that had a formative impact on Slovak political institutions and an understanding of its constitutional identity.

A substantive part of the reforms enacted between 1998 and 2004 was the reconstruction of judicial governance and the strengthening of judicial independence.[29] The SCC gained several new competences, including review of individual petitions. The appointment system for SCC justices was modified as well, increasing the number of judicial seats to 13, and changing their seven-year renewable terms to twelve-year non-renewable ones. The parliament (National Council of the Slovak Republic, NRSR) lost the competence to appoint and dismiss judges of general courts. Instead, drawing heavily on the recommendations of the Venice Committee and European Commission, the new government transferred those competences to the newly established National Judicial Council (90/2001 Coll). Nevertheless, the Judicial Council governed by the

[26] Eg, E Harris and K Henderson, 'Slovakia since 1989' in SP Ramet and CM Hassenstab (eds), *Central and Southeast European Politics Since 1989* (Cambridge, Cambridge University Press, 2019) 195–99.

[27] D Kosař, *Perils of Judicial Self-Government in Transitional Societies* (Cambridge, Cambridge University Press, 2016) 238–43.

[28] The mandates of the first constitutional court justices ended in 2000.

[29] Kosař (n 27) 243–46.

majority of judges proved to be an ill fit for the post-communist country with an unreformed judiciary. It became occupied by people close to Mečiar's Minister of Justice Harabin, later president of the Supreme Court, who soon captured the judiciary from the inside and closed it against any reform attempts.[30] In the coming years, judicial independence sank again, and Slovak courts lost considerable public confidence.[31]

Still, 1998–2006 was a period marked by a euro-optimistic atmosphere and the rebuilding of state institutions. In 2004, Slovakia successfully joined the EU.[32] It was also a tranquil period for the SCC, obstructed only by the failure to appoint new justices to replace three sitting members of the SCC, who left to serve in the EU judiciary. In 2006, a fairly young party, SMER-SD, led by Robert Fico, won the parliamentary election[33] and formed a close alliance with the President, Ivan Gašparovič. It was this association that in 2007 determined the composition of the SCC.[34] Although several justices were reappointed,[35] the bench contained few experts on constitutional scholarship.

With the exception of a two-year period, Fico remained in power until the 2020 parliamentary election.[36] While at this time he demonstrated pro-EU commitment, his government also allowed the formation of wide corruption networks between politicians and oligarchs, destroying the independence of the state prosecution and ordinary judiciary.[37] His influence on the composition of the SCC was, however, brought to a halt in 2014, when pro-EU liberal President Andrej Kiska replaced Gašparovič and adopted an assertive approach to the SCC, defending the idea of the most highly qualified jurists being appointed to the bench.[38] The post-2014 era was marked by disputes between Fico and the

[30] S Spáč, K Šipulová and M Urbániková, 'Capturing the Judiciary from Inside: The Story of Judicial Self-Governance in Slovakia' (2018) 19 *German Law Journal* 1741; Kosař (n 27).

[31] M Urbániková and K Šipulová, 'Failed Expectations: Does the Establishment of Judicial Councils Enhance Confidence in Courts?' (2018) 19 *German Law Journal* 2105.

[32] We detail the constitutional framework for the accession and the SCC's interpretation of this framework in section III.

[33] D Malová, 'Slovakia' in J-M de Waele, F Escalona and M Vieira (eds), *The Palgrave Handbook of Social Democracy in the European Union* (London, Palgrave Macmillan, 2016) 554–56.

[34] With the mandates of six other justices ending on 21 January 2007, the court was left with only four sitting justices, insufficient for delivering any decision in the plenum, which required at least seven votes.

[35] These justices were appointed in 2000; thus, the constitutional amendment in 2001 that prohibited reappointment did not apply to them. As a result, a few justices served 19 consecutive years at the court.

[36] Societal uproar after the murder of Kuciak and Kušnírová forced Fico to resign. However, he remained in power informally as the chairman of SMER-SD.

[37] M Vagovič, *Vlastnou hlavou* (Bratislava, Premedia 2016); Bertelsmann Stiftung, 'BTI 2020 Country Report: Slovakia' (2020) <https://bti-project.org/content/en/downloads/reports/country_report_2020_SVK.pdf>.

[38] Between 1993 and December 2020, Slovak constitutional justices were selected and appointed by the President of the Republic, who selected them from a double number of nominees submitted by the single chamber parliament.

Presidents (both Kiska and his successor Čaputová) over the composition of the SCC. Due to the parliament's inability to select enough candidates, Kiska left two chairs at the SCC empty for three years (2014–2017). The dispute ended with a ruling of the SCC (I ÚS 575/2016) which found that the President had violated the right of several candidates to access public office by refusing to appoint them to a vacant position.

The Parliament run by SMER-SD attempted to use the very same court-packing strategy[39] again in 2019, after nine of 13 constitutional justices finished their mandates. The Parliament, seeking to secure the appointment of people close to the outgoing government, presented President Kiska with a very limited list of names to choose from. PM Fico himself voiced an interest in joining the SCC as its new president. Both attempts turned out unsuccessful for Fico. President Kiska once again did not make appointments, and the dispute was resolved only after the Parliament had backed down and nominated a sufficient number of candidates, at which time Čaputová replaced Kiska in office.

It is important to note that this latest 2019 selection of SCC justices attracted unprecedented public interest. The investigation of the murder mentioned above revealed, among other things, deeply rooted corruption in judicial ranks and led to a heightened period of political mobilisation, demanding accountability and justice. As we discuss in section IV below, this public sentiment has paradoxically not squared well with the SCC's attempt to set limits to the executive investigation of judges' backgrounds. The emphasis on judicial independence and the nascent articulation of Slovakia's constitutional identity did not attract its zealous supporters, even among Slovak constitutional scholars.[40]

The 2020 parliamentary elections have been followed by massive changes in the official support for prosecutions of public officials suspected of corruption, judges among them. The call for prosecutions and accountability also targeted the SCC. In May 2020 one of its justices resigned after the media published a secret service report on his communication with oligarch Kočner, accused of ordering Kuciak and Kušnírová's murder and several economic frauds. This all culminated in an unprecedented step being taken by the new coalition government which, amid the Covid-19 pandemic and state emergency at the very end of 2020, restricted the SCC's competence to review constitutional laws. These challenges, particularly the petition to invalidate the constitutional amendment restricting the court's own competences, provided ample opportunity for the court's robust (self-)articulation of its role, and of the principles contained in Slovak constitutionalism as well.

[39] For more on the use of similar strategies see D Kosař and K Šipulová, 'How to Fight Court-Packing?' (2020) 6 *Constitutional Studies* 133.

[40] J Štiavnický and M Steuer, 'The Many Faces of Law-Making by Constitutional Courts with Extensive Review Powers: The Slovak Case' in M Florczak-Wątor (ed), *Judicial Law-Making in European Constitutional Courts* (London, Routledge, 2020) 198–99.

In what follows we discuss the emergence of the SCC's reactionist approach to the concept of constitutional identity, arguing that the court avoided the concept of constitutional identity partly due to its association with a nationalist, anti-democratic challenger in the 1990s and opted for a minimalist approach. Given the negative national historical legacy and readiness to embrace the supremacy of EU law, the SCC stayed clear of nationalistic particularism[41] and instead reacted to domestic challenges to constitutionalism. This reactionist approach led the SCC gradually to develop the doctrine of the substantive core of the Constitution, which placed core emphasis on the separation of powers doctrine and judicial independence.

II. NEW COUNTRY WITH NO CONSTITUTIONAL IDENTITY? JUDICIAL MINIMALISM IN THE PRE-ACCESSION ERA

Unlike the Hungarian Fundamental Law,[42] the Slovak Constitution on its own does not explicitly include any notion of identity, and in contrast to those of Germany and the Czech Republic,[43] the constitutional text does not even encompass any eternity clause or identification of core principles,[44] nor does it recognise tiered constitutional design,[45] which could be used for constructing such a clause. In this section we demonstrate how the lack of explicit articulation, when coupled with the political context of 1994–1998, facilitated the absence of constitutional identity from the SCC's terminology. According to the Preamble to the Constitution

> *We, the Slovak nation*, bearing in mind the political and cultural heritage of our ancestors and the centuries of experience from the struggles for national existence and our own statehood, mindful of the spiritual heritage of Cyril and Methodius and the historical legacy of Great Moravia, [...] *together with members of national minorities and ethnic groups* [...] that is, we, the citizens of the Slovak Republic adopt through our representatives this Constitution [emphasis added].[46]

The Preamble (although mentioning the commitment to 'a democratic form of government') exhibits tenets of nationalism due to separating 'the Slovak nation' as the primary constitution-maker from the 'national minorities and ethnic groups' as playing a secondary role, and bringing up the citizenship

[41] For a definition and discussion of the concept, see the introductory chapter in this volume.

[42] See chapter six in this volume.

[43] See chapters two and four in this volume.

[44] In contrast, see Article 9.2 and 1 of the Czech constitution. For more on this, see chapter four in this volume.

[45] J Drgonec, *Ústava Slovenskej republiky s úvodným komentárom* (Vantaa, Heuréka, 2004).

[46] Constitution of the Slovak Republic. See the English translation at www.constituteproject.org/constitution/Slovakia_2017?lang=en.

principle as secondary to the nationhood principle.[47] The importance of the Preamble, particularly in the context of national identity, cannot be underestimated, as it provides a tone for the text that follows, captures the historical conditions affecting the text, and formulates the key values of the constitution-maker.[48] Interestingly, the Preamble also reflects the overall atmosphere of the hasty constitution-drafting process created by Mečiar, who relied on national identity as the driving force of his political campaign, severing the ties with the Federation.

The SCC, however, repeatedly refused to recognise the interpretative power of the Preamble. In a decision on the Act on State Language,[49] the SCC stated that preambles are not a source of law; they only represent introductory ('non-normative') statements for a given act and cannot be reviewed. The generality of this statement was confirmed in its 1999 decision interpreting the President's competence to grant amnesties and pardons,[50] where the SCC rejected any normative content which could follow from the Preamble. The SCC's case law on the Preamble remains underdeveloped. Nevertheless, the important takeaway is that the SCC avoided further engagement with the controversial wording of the Preamble and also sent a signal of itself as a court loyal to 'written law' in its interpretive practice.[51] In other words, the SCC eliminated a potential threat to democracy represented by the nationalist impulses of the Preamble that might be tapped into by authoritarian actors.[52] We can only hypothesise to what extent the spirit of the Preamble, which, unlike in the Czech case,[53] was hostile to the legacy of the democratic First Czechoslovak Republic and was tied to Mečiar's nationalistic rhetoric, played a role in the SCC's stance. Nevertheless, we argue that the refusal to acknowledge the Preamble's interpretative force paved the way for the court later to develop the substantive core doctrine instead of embracing the concept of constitutional identity.

The SCC's approach in relation to the Preamble, which avoided substantive, conceptual engagement with abstract ideas, also fits into its overall positioning in the 1990s, sometimes known as the 'first term' of the court under the presidency of Milan Čič. The political conflicts between the President and the

[47] This distinguishes the Slovak preamble from its Czech counterpart which constructs a political nation from its very beginning. For more see J Marušiak, 'Ústavy SR a ČR a ich úloha v procese konštituovania národných identít' in Vladimír Goněc and Roman Holec (eds), *Česko-slovenská historická ročenka 2012. Češi a Slováci 1993–2012: Vzdalování a přibližování* (VEDA 2013) 109.

[48] I Halász, *Minulosť a symbolika v ústavách štátov strednej Európy* (Bratislava, Ústav státu a práva AV ČR, 2019) 11; see also JO Frosini, 'Constitutional Preambles: More than Just a Narration of History' (2017) *University of Illinois Law Review* 603.

[49] PL ÚS 8/96.

[50] Art 102 s 1j); I ÚS 30/99.

[51] Štiavnický and Steuer (n 40) 185–86.

[52] Zs Körtvélyesi, 'From "We the People" to "We the Nation"' in GA Tóth (ed), *Constitution for a Disunited Nation: On Hungary's 2011 Fundamental Law* (New York, Central European University Press, 2012) 113–17.

[53] See chapter four in this volume.

Prime Minister intensified considerably after 1994. Although Mečiar lost a vote of confidence in March 1994, he still managed to turn the public preferences around, won the next election, and prevented the opposition from gaining any position in the NRSR committees. The level of governmental control pervaded all spheres of political and social life, but targeted most harshly Mečiar's political opponents, President Kováč but also the SCC. Having noticed the affinity between the two actors' views on key political issues, Mečiar called the SCC the 'unhealthy element on the political scene'.[54]

Characterised by the 'constructive use of silence' and a commitment to 'passive virtues',[55] the court has nevertheless been able to resist Mečiar's key autocratisation efforts using the minimalist approach. It has received a helping hand from the President, who was the petitioner in several key cases concerning the limits of governmental power. It is in this struggle that the role of the president *in interaction with the SCC* became particularly important in comparative terms.

Even in refusing the Preamble, the SCC had, in theory, two other sources on which to base a definition of constitutional identity: the first was the wording of Article 1 of the Constitution, which identifies Slovakia as a sovereign, democratic state governed by the rule of law, not bound by any ideology or religion and committed to general rules of international law. The second one was the brief but very formative case law of the Federal Czechoslovak Constitutional Court which, in the review of the Big Lustration Act,[56] introduced a value-oriented definition of the new democratic regime which later became a foundation stone for all future transitional justice jurisprudence of both successors' constitutional courts.[57]

Despite these resources, however, the SCC in this period remained confined to a minimalist approach, avoiding any grand theoretical considerations even when under pressure from Mečiar. References to constitutional identity were altogether missing from its case law. With competence disputes between core state institutions being the source of some of the most salient decisions of the court, the principle of the separation of powers appeared in its case law. However, even in its most illuminative articulation,[58] the SCC did not provide any conceptual footing for it beyond the context of the particular case. Hence, the court underwent its first major change in composition (in 2000) 'untainted' by more in-depth conceptual discussions in the spirit of the decisions of the

[54] D Malová, 'The Role and Experience of the Slovakian Constitutional Court' in W Sadurski (ed), *Constitutional Justice, East and West: Democratic Legitimacy and Constitutional Courts in Post-Communist Europe in a Comparative Perspective* (The Hague, Kluwer Law International, 2010) 355.

[55] Sunstein (n 14) 5.

[56] PL ÚS 1/92, on a review of Act No. 451/1991 Coll. Big Lustration Act (Velký lustrační zákon), and PL ÚS 5/92.

[57] PL ÚS 1/92.

[58] PL ÚS 16/95.

CFCC. It took the developments of the early 2000s to achieve a gradual change in this attitude.

III. SUBSTANTIVE CORE: PASSIVE ARTICULATION IN A EURO-OPTIMISTIC ATMOSPHERE

The SCC's commitment to minimalism began to change in the 2000s, when the court furthered the idea of the substantive rule of law to encompass human rights and freedoms. The very first articulation of the principle dates back to 1998, when the court subtly derived 'legal certainty' and 'justice (substantive rule of law)' from Article 1 of the Constitution.[59] However, it elaborated on the latter only in 2002, arguing that in the substantive rule-of-law state, 'particular emphasis is placed on the protection of those rights which are subject to constitutional regulation'.[60] With this decision the court no longer seemed to insist on the minimalist position that had excluded substantive review of human rights.[61]

The explanation for this change, we argue, is twofold. Firstly, the formal powers of the court were extended in 2001 to encompass individual complaints of human rights violations. Unsurprisingly, the court's human rights jurisprudence grew in quantity and more engagement with the human rights provisions of the Constitution was required. Secondly, the looming accession of Slovakia to the EU directed the court's attention to human rights which are embraced by EU law as well.[62] Therefore, we proceed by examining the extent to which the court explored the relationship between the Constitution and EU law, including possible disjunctions between the two.

Before we return to the case law, a few words on the relationship between EU law and the Slovak Constitution are needed.[63] EU law gained a prominent constitutional position thanks to the constitutional amendment having been drafted in a Euro-friendly atmosphere, where both the political and judicial elites strove to prove their place in Western Europe and democratic society even more vehemently than after 1989.[64] Formally, the relationship of Slovakia with the EU was defined in Article 7(2), which, inter alia, states that 'The Slovak Republic may [...] transfer the exercise of a part of its rights to the [EU]. Legally binding acts of the [EU] shall have primacy over the laws of the Slovak Republic'. The

[59] I ÚS 10/98, 9.

[60] I ÚS 54/02, 12–13.

[61] Cf R Procházka, *Mission Accomplished: On Founding Constitutional Adjudication in Central Europe* (New York, Central European University Press, 2002) 176.

[62] Article 2 TEU.

[63] In the 1990s the Constitutional Court had identified the Constitution as the basic and highest law of the state, supreme over all other sources of law (PL ÚS 32/95).

[64] The EU's institution and monitoring process by the European Commission had its part in Mečiar's loss of preferences and eventual electoral defeat.

transfer clause[65] in the first sentence of this paragraph reflects the optimistic atmosphere and Slovakia's enthusiasm for fostering integration with the EU. The peculiar way in which the SCC reflected the transfer of the exercise of rights might seem surprising when compared with the Czech and German constitutions which limited delegation by the constitutional identity[66] or substantive core of the constitution.[67] Furthermore, due to a very pro-EU atmosphere, the legislator introducing provisions on EU law forgot to include transitional provisions in the constitutional amendment, formally thus making EU law effective even before the real accession. In this context, Kühn and Bobek point out that it is quite puzzling that Slovak courts did not feel the need to articulate a big overreaching doctrine of voluntary consistent interpretation of Slovak law with EU law before the accession. None of the Slovak courts attempted to use European Communities' or EU law as an interpretative argument before accession.[68] The Slovak approach is, however, understandable in light of the almost uncontested pro-EU atmosphere of the late 1990s.

In 2005 a group consisting of the members of the Slovak Conservative Institute and several think-tanks contested Article 7 after the government issued its approval of the Treaty establishing a Constitution for Europe 2002 (TCE) on 11 May 2005. The petitioners claimed that their right to participate in the administration of public affairs had been violated by the NRSR, which approved the Treaty without a preliminary referendum. The petitioners claimed that the approval should have been validated by a new referendum under Article 7(1), as the EU now represented a union of states, closely resembling a state formation.

The SCC's judgment[69] is surprising in many respects. The SCC stated that although the TCE had shifted the integration project in the direction of a state formation, the EU would still preserve several specifics and characteristics distinguishing it from a state or a state formation with other countries. On the other hand, the SCC stressed that the Union respects the national identity of individual members encompassed in their core political and constitutional systems.[70] Although the EU gained plenty of signs and functions characteristic of a state, the SCC claimed that it was not for the member state or its authorities to decide on the legal nature of the EU independently of other members. Moreover, the SCC found that holding a referendum on accession to the EU was prohibited by Article 93(3) of the Slovak Constitution, as the Charter of Fundamental Rights is a part of the treaties and the Constitution forbids the holding of a

[65] D Krošlák, *Ústavné právo* (Warsawa, Wolters Kluwer, 2016) 135; see also J Filip, 'K formulaci evropských klauzulí v ústavním právu' (2010) 18 *Časopis pro právní vědu a praxi* 217.

[66] See chapter two in this volume.

[67] See chapter four in this volume.

[68] Z Kühn and M Bobek, 'Europe Yet to Come: The Application of EU Law in Slovakia' in A Lazowski (ed), *The Application of EU Law in the New Member States: Brave New World* 1st ed (The Hague, TMC Asser Press, 2010) 357.

[69] II ÚS 171/05.

[70] Article 4(2) TEU.

referendum on human rights. Even more importantly, the SCC precluded any future potential referendum on any act of Slovakia within the EU, stating that such an act, even if it significantly alters the conditions of cooperation between member states of the Union, is to be considered under Article 7(2), which does not require a mandatory referendum.

The SCC's approach differs from several of its Visegrád counterparts, which fought hard to protect their competence to decide whether the EU acts within its competences and respects the national identity of the Member States.[71] According to the SCC, Slovakia delegated rather than transferred its competences to the EU indefinitely (ie, in theory, the legislator could 'take them back' in the future). Yet, the decision did little to explore the ramifications of this distinction or to guide the SCC's future thinking on EU integration.

In another important decision aiming to clarify the relationship between EU law and national constitutional law, shifting the constitutional provisions even closer to EU law, the SCC found that every national court applying EU law has the obligation to secure the effect of that law and therefore has to set aside any national provision that conflicts with it. This obligation includes constitutional laws and does not come with a requirement to refer the issue to the SCC first.[72] This took the principle of euro-conform interpretation much further than in most EU countries whose courts opted for the protection of constitutional norms above the effectiveness of EU law. For Slovakia, EU law gained supremacy over constitutional order, even if it meant changing the interpretation of the constitutional provisions away from their original meaning. The court did not depart from this approach in a later small chamber decision in which the petitioner contested the European Commission's overriding of a Slovak general court's decision on granting state aid.[73] Although it nominally referred to the *Solange* doctrine of the German Federal Constitutional Court and the *Lisbon I* decision of the Czech Constitutional Court, de facto it adopted a much more deferential standard that had not set a barrier to the review of EU law-related matters being reserved exclusively to EU institutions.

To sum up, the early post-accession years were characterised by a very open and very friendly position of the SCC towards EU law.[74] The SCC proved to

[71] See, eg, Constitutional Court of the Czech Republic, PL ÚS 5/12.

[72] PL ÚS 3/09.

[73] II ÚS 501/2010, para 20. See also Z Vikarská and M Bobek, 'Slovakia: Between Euro-Optimism and Euro-Concerns' in A Albi and S Bardutzky (eds), *National Constitutions in European and Global Governance: Democracy, Rights, the Rule of Law: National Reports* (The Hague, TMC Asser Press, 2019) 872–73.

[74] The SCC on several occasions also openly accepted an opportunity to submit a preliminary question to the CJEU: see eg PL ÚS 8/04 and A Blisa, P Molek and K Šipulová, 'Czech Republic and Slovakia: Another International Human Rights Treaty?' in M Bobek and J Adams-Prassl (eds), *EU Charter of Fundamental Rights in the Member States* (Oxford, Hart, 2020); J Mazák, 'Príspevok Ústavného súdu Slovenskej republiky při uplatňovaní práva plnění povinností na komunitárnej úrovni' (2005) 14 *Jurisprudence* 11; I Macejková, 'Právo Európskej únie v rozhodovacej činnosti Ústavného súdu Slovenskej republiky' in A Krunková (ed), *Európska únia a jej vplyv na organizáciu a fungovanie verejnej správy v Slovenskej republike* (Košice, Univerzita P J Šafárika, 2016).

be very willing to accept the doctrine of the supremacy of EU law before the Slovak Constitution,[75] without engaging with the substantive puzzles that might emerge as a result (eg in the event that the Slovak Constitution provided for higher standards of human rights protection than EU law).[76] EU integration helped strip Mečiar of his power and EU integration was expected to work as a strong and important safeguard. Yet, the court continues to avoid the more difficult questions, eg, having declined to consider the Charter of Fundamental Rights in judicial review.[77]

IV. SOBERING UP: TOWARDS CONSTITUTIONAL IDENTITY

While the SCC post-accession never faced a similarly hostile political context to that in the 1990s, it became the arbiter of central constitutional disputes, some of them again centred on the relationship between core state institutions, including the judiciary and the SCC itself. At this time, two central characteristics of the court's (very limited) references to identity emerged: the resurgence of the central focus on the head of state, and the attribution of a central role to judicial independence in the separation of powers and the growing self-awareness of the SCC via its development of the substantive core doctrine in (a somewhat delayed) reaction to the autocratisation efforts of the Mečiar government. We will address each of these trends in turn, with reference to key judgments.

The scope of presidential powers became a contested issue in the 2012–2014 electoral term and resulted in the first judgment in which the SCC ever explicitly used the term *constitutional identity*.[78] The case revolved around the refusal of President Gašparovič to appoint Jozef Čentéš, a candidate for the position of General Prosecutor. Čentéš claimed that President Gašparovič violated his right to access public office by not appointing him to the post. The petitioner claimed that the time between the approval of his election by the NRSR and the President's inactivity, which stretched for over 18 months, was unconstitutionally long.

The SCC found the President to be overstepping his competences, which had also[79] led to a violation of the petitioner's right of access to a public office.[80] The

[75] Krošlák (n 65) 148; J Čorba et al, *Uplatňovanie európskeho práva na Slovensku* (Bratislava, Kalligram, 2003).

[76] M Steuer, 'Constitutional Pluralism and the Slovak Constitutional Court: The Challenge of European Union Law' (2018) 8 *The Lawyer Quarterly* 108.

[77] PL ÚS 10/2014. See also J Mazák and M Jánošíková, 'Prienik Charty základných práv Európskej únie do vnútroštátneho práva na príklade Slovenskej republiky' [2016] *Acta Universitatis Carolinae Iuridica* 9.

[78] The exact same reference was reproduced in a more recent judgment concerning the validity of the 2019 presidential election results (PL ÚS 16/2019, para 270).

[79] I ÚS 397/2014.

[80] III ÚS 427/2012.

SCC recognised 'the Game of Thrones' in appointments shortly before the end of the electoral term to be a natural element of the democratic constitutional system in general, and an integral part of Slovak constitutional history and difficult political development in the 1990s.[81] Referring to this complicated historical development of the independent Slovakia, the SCC declared that

> the President is a significant element of the constitutional identity of the country. [S/he] represents statehood and sovereignty. It is not a regular public office [...] The President does not decide on individual rights. Similarly, however, the President does not stand above the constitution, although he [she] may interpret the constitution and this interpretation is not always subjected to constitutional review.[82]

The recognition of the centrality of the figure of the President has not led the SCC to any further elaboration on the concept of constitutional identity. The judgment is nevertheless important for the contextual understanding of the importance which the SCC attributed to the division of competences and the role of the principle of checks and balances in Slovak democracy. This is well demonstrated by the emphasis laid in the SCC on the responsibility of the head of state regarding constitutional values.[83]

The emphasis on the role of the president has not been connected to the rise of the *substantive core* doctrine in the SCC's case law. This idea was floated in (Czecho)Slovak legal doctrine for some time in the 2010s,[84] particularly after the adoption of the *Melčák* judgment where the Czech Constitutional Court invalidated a constitutional law on early parliamentary election. Experts on the Slovak Constitution were not united, however, on the question whether, despite the absence of an eternity clause, there is an *unamendable core* of the Constitution encompassing central values that define the Slovak political community.[85] The SCC did not offer an answer until the landmark judgment of 2019 (delivered only a few days before the end of the term of the justices (re)appointed in 2007, including SCC President Ivetta Macejková).

Crucially for the pathway towards the substantive core doctrine, the SCC has become a staunch defender of judicial independence. The court went further in a series of decisions in which it invalidated legislation creating a Special Court to adjudicate on serious criminal offences,[86] or freezing judicial salaries due to the economic downturn.[87] As the freezing of salaries affected the SCC justices'

[81] See above, eg, II ÚS 65/97, I ÚS 61/96, or I ÚS 7/96.

[82] ibid at para 59.

[83] Moreover, the presidential competences were further narrowed down in the judgments concerning the appointment of constitutional justices: III ÚS 571/2014, I ÚS 575/2016.

[84] Eg, B Balog, *Materiálne jadro ústavy Slovenskej republiky* (Žilina, Eurokódex, 2014); R Procházka, *Ľud a sudcovia v konštitučnej demokracii* (Prague, Aleš Čeněk, 2011).

[85] See also J Drgonec, *Ústavné právo hmotné* (Munich, CH Beck, 2018) 65–83.

[86] PL ÚS 17/08.

[87] Eg, PL ÚS 99/2011, PL ÚS 27/2015, PL ÚS 8/2017.

income as well, these decisions came across as particularly inward-looking, protecting independence for the justices' rather than broader society's sake.

The 2016 general elections resulted in the third administration led by PM Robert Fico, with his coalition including the nationalist Slovak National Party. The coalition soon found itself under pressure from the civil society, as indications of corruption of high public officials proliferated. The already fragile atmosphere became even more brittle in 2017 due to a fictional movie entitled 'Abduction', loosely based on the abduction of President Kováč's son in 1995, allegedly orchestrated by Mečiar's regime as retaliation for the President's resistance. After President Kováč's term ended, the Slovak parliament put off a new selection while being unable to agree on his successor. In the meantime, Mečiar executed the presidential competences and used the opportunity to issue two controversial decisions on amnesties.[88] The first one concerned the blocked 1997 referendum relating to Slovakia's accession to NATO and the proposal to establish the direct election of the President.[89] The second set of amnesties related to the kidnapping of President Kováč's son to Austria.[90] Both decisions on amnesty stipulated the close of criminal investigation in these cases, closely tied to the political conflicts at the time. The former case concerned the Ministry of the Interior's actions while, in the latter, several independent media outlets connected the case to power disputes between the President and Mečiar and suggested the involvement of the Slovak Information Agency (controlled by Mečiar's nominee).

The screening of the movie reopened unhealed and unaddressed past crimes of Mečiar's regime. The government quickly used the momentum and passed an amendment to the Constitution vesting the NRSR with official power to abolish amnesties and the SCC with a new responsibility to review the annulment acts within 60 days. In this way, Fico distracted the public from his own scandals, seemingly listening to calls for justice 20 years after the end of Mečiar's rule.

Shortly after the constitutional amendment, the NRSR adopted two acts annulling Mečiar's amnesties. Lawyers addressed the amendment as a new constitutional transition or moment in Slovak history. The NRSR justified its decision by claiming that amnesties kept worrying Slovak society, pointing to the indivisibility of human rights from the rule of law concept and Slovakia's international obligation to investigate forced disappearances.

Like the NRSR, the SCC identified the topic as extremely sensitive and important for society. It also explained the position of the institution of the amnesty in different regimes and its relation to the system of checks and balances. The

[88] Decision of 3 March 1998, No 55/1998 Coll, Decision of 7 July 1998, 214/1998 Coll.

[89] E Láštic, *V rukách politických strán: Referendum na Slovensku 1993–2010* (Bratislava, Univerzita Komenského, 2011).

[90] J Mazák and L Orosz, 'Quashing the Decisions on Amnesty in the Constitutional System of the Slovak Republic: Opening or Closing Pandora's Box?' (2018) 8 *The Lawyer Quarterly* 1.

SCC also concluded that the original wording of the Constitution, assigning the President (and PM who acted as his substitute) unlimited competence, was too generous, bringing with it a huge risk of arbitrariness.[91] The substantive democratic rule of law state is incompatible with unlimited exercise of state power.

The judgment represented the first occasion on which the SCC finally defined the content of the term 'principles of democratic state and law' (Article 1(1) of the Constitution), emphasising that no constitution is neutral, as constitutions are embedded in values and principles mirroring the societal understanding of the good. These principles are respected by the state,[92] cannot be derogated from[93] and – important in face of the 2020 curtailment of the SCC's competences – represent the 'core of the constitutional review'.[94] Although not all principles are explicitly mentioned in the Constitution, they may still underlie its provisions.

The SCC in the main tackled two issues: (1) whether the amnesties were against the principles of the democratic state and the rule of law, and (2) whether it was acceptable for a democratic Parliament to abolish an amnesty granted by the PM.

The SCC found that Mečiar had acted in clear breach of the constitutional prohibition of arbitrariness. The amnesties interfered with several core principles, such as the separation of powers, transparency, public control and legal certainty. But the most important element of the judgment was the SCC's rationalisation of the search for the substantive protection of the rule of law. The SCC stated that both its previous case law and the ECtHR's decision in *Lexa v Slovakia* (App No 54334/00) were formalistic, while the substantive protection of constitutional principles including the rule of law permitted its reconsideration. While the annulment of the amnesties clearly has retroactive effect and goes against legitimate expectations of victims, the discrepancy between the acts of PM Mečiar and the constitutional principles of Slovakia was too great. Adhering to the principle of legal certainty in such a situation would, according to the SCC, be too formalistic.

A reference to constitutional identity occurs in dissenting opinions by two justices, Milan Ľalík and Peter Brňák, who analysed the effect of the judgment on Slovakia's constitutional identity.[95] The justices opposed the act in which the NRSR attributed itself more competences (competence to annul the amnesties via a constitutional act) than originally envisaged by the Constitution. According to the justices, this moved the NRSR into a position which was not envisaged by the Constitution and the SCC's judgment had de facto erased any limits to the

[91] PL ÚS 7/2017, 88.
[92] PL ÚS 12/01.
[93] Here, the Court referred to the case PL ÚS 16/95. As discussed above, back in 1995 the content of the principles was not defined by the SCC.
[94] PL ÚS 7/2017, 121–22.
[95] PL ÚS 7/2017, dissenting opinion of P Brňák and M Ľalík, 21.

NRSR's powers of constitutional change. Both justices pointed out that, while today the NRSR is relatively liberal-democratic, this might not always be the case, and some constitutional fundamental principles are more protected by the force of the law than by a societal consensus. According to the dissenting justices, the majority decision, by rejecting the 'antidemocratic nature' of the SCC, opted for 'cheap populism' and even 'denied' the existence of constitutional identity articulated in the principles of democracy and the rule of law as declared in Article 1 of the Constitution.[96] Brňák's and Ľalík's narrative gained traction in Slovak constitutional jurisprudence neither on the invocation of constitutional identity nor on the critique of the judgment. The amnesties decision, however, marked the entry of the substantive core doctrine from a few works of constitutional scholarship into mainstream political discourse.

The tug of war between the president and the legislature over the appointment of constitutional justices prompted the debate on changing the appointment model. While the constitutional amendment proposal introducing the change failed, a new Constitutional Court act (314/2018 Coll) was adopted in 2018, introducing public hearings for the candidates.[97] These hearings frequently featured a question on the substantive core being put to the candidates, with the actors involved recognising how the doctrine might facilitate the invalidation of constitutional laws.[98] The question was not merely a logical follow-up to the SCC's amnesty decision. At that time, the court had another petition to adjudicate on, which alleged the incompatibility with the Constitution of the introduction of background checks on sitting general court judges[99] by the National Security Authority.[100] This measure was part of the partisan actors' effort to roll back judicial independence at a time of public distrust of the Slovak judiciary.

The court decided the judicial security clearance case in 2019, after more than four years of deliberation, by invalidating several provisions of the constitutional amendment in addition to implementing legislation. In doing so, the majority of the SCC justices offered a fully-fledged subscription to the substantive core doctrine on this occasion, though without a single reference to constitutional identity. With the substantive core doctrine in mind, the SCC not only derived the competence to protect the substantive core against direct amendments to the Constitution, but also, in a rare move globally,[101] altogether

[96] PL ÚS 7/2017, dissent, at para 34.

[97] M Steuer, 'The First Live-Broadcast Hearings of Candidates for Constitutional Judges in Slovakia: Five Lessons' (*Verfassungsblog*, 5 February 2019) https://verfassungsblog.de/the-first-live-broadcast-hearings-of-candidates-for-constitutional-judges-in-slovakia-five-lessons/.

[98] Š Drugda, 'Changes to Selection and Appointment of Constitutional Court Judges in Slovakia' (2019) 102 *Právny obzor* 14.

[99] Appointed before 1 September 2014.

[100] Constitutional Act No 161/2014 Coll where it added Article 154d (1) to (3) to the text of the constitution as well as amendments to several pieces of ordinary legislation.

[101] Y Roznai, 'Who Will Save the Redheads? Towards an Anti-Bully Theory of Judicial Review and Protection of Democracy' (2020) 29 *William & Mary Bill of Rights Journal* 1, 16–17.

invalidated the constitutional amendment. The judgment completes the transformation of the emphasis on the substantive rule of law into a fully-fledged substantive core doctrine[102] with a central role for judicial independence.[103] At the same time, it has also generated several critical commentaries,[104] not only denouncing the court's invalidation of the *particular* constitutional amendment (which would have become 'toothless' with the invalidation of the ordinary legislation that executed the provisions, as the dissenting justices highlighted), but leaning towards questioning the *SCC's very competence* to exercise constitutional amendment review with reference to its mission set out in Article 124 of the Constitution. To appreciate the significance of this critique we must turn to the political context of 2019–2020.

V. CONSTITUTIONAL IDENTITY FOUND – AND LOST AGAIN?

The 2019 decision on judicial security clearances came almost a year after the murder of the journalist Ján Kuciak and his fiancée that led to massive societal upheavals. Although the initial charges did not include the judiciary, as investigations progressed allegations of corruption in high judicial office spread. One of the Slovak constitutional justices, Mojmír Mamojka, resigned also due to leaks of his text messages with Marián Kočner, the man chiefly suspected of having ordered the murder and being involved in other corruption scandals.[105] Given the composition of the new governing coalition (which possessed a constitutional majority in the NRSR) after the 2020 general elections, investigations progressed and several judges were charged, some with having admitted violations of the law shortly after they had been presented with the charges.

This atmosphere has not been conducive to a robust defence of judicial independence in the substantive core of the Constitution, as it tended to endorse

[102] It should be noted though that the principle of democracy (which is inseparable from the rule of law in the wording of Article 1 of the Constitution) is still largely neglected in the judgment and can be discerned only in a majoritarian fashion. Notably, the SCC accepted that a valid referendum on the constitutional amendment would prevent the referendum results from being reviewable by the SCC, thereby subscribing to a decisionist notion of the constituent power as residing in the hands of the people understood through a majoritarian lens (PL ÚS 21/2014, para 177).

[103] Cf JE Moliterno et al, 'Independence without Accountability: The Harmful Consequences of EU Policy Toward Central and Eastern European Entrants' (2018) 42 *Fordham International Law Journal* 481, 516.

[104] M Káčer and J Neumann, *Materiálne jadro v slovenskom ústavnom práve. Doktrinálny disent proti zrušeniu sudcovských previerok* (Prague, Leges, 2019); O Preuss, 'Slovenský „Melčák", nukleární zbraň jako dar novému ústavnímu soudu' (2019) 6 *Jurisprudence* 1.

[105] M Terenzani, 'Judge from Threema Resigns from Constitutional Court' (*spectator.sme.sk*, 13 May 2020) https://spectator.sme.sk/c/22403918/mamojka-ends-at-constitutional-court-over-kocner-allegations.html.

unrestrained majoritarianism constrained only by partisan contestation.[106] The backlash against the court's articulation of the principle manifested itself when the new coalition gained a constitutional majority making it capable of enacting constitutional amendments.[107] At this time, in late 2020, distrust in the judiciary was buttressed by the arrest of several prominent judges on corruption charges. The constitutional majority went further than that, surpassing even PM Mečiar's formal efforts to curtail the court's powers. In an extensive amendment to the Constitution,[108] from which public attention was further diverted by the Covid-19 pandemic, the constitutional majority launched a frontal attack on the substantive core doctrine. Article 125(4) of the Constitution was amended to include a sentence stating that 'the Constitutional Court does not decide on the compatibility of a constitutional law with the Constitution'.[109] This particular modification was not part of the initial draft that was subject to public consultation and was presented less than three weeks before its approval.

In a historically rare setting, the SCC President appeared before the deputies to argue against this particular amendment;[110] yet the amendment passed with 91 out of the 141 participating MPs voting in favour. Some opposition representatives announced, shortly after the approval of the amendment, that they would petition the SCC to review it. The petition triggered a Catch-22 situation of the SCC reviewing the legislator's curtailment of its own competences via a competence that the latter aims to curtail. The SCC, nevertheless, rejected the petition. It repeated that the substantive core doctrine includes the protection of human rights, democracy and the rule of law and that the NRSR is not the unconstrained sovereign. However, it also retained only a very narrow leeway for amendment review in those cases that create extreme interference in the substantive core of the Constitution.[111]

In sum, the SCC's journey towards a substantive core doctrine has just begun, as it needs to withstand the current challenge from the governing majority,

[106] Cf R Dworkin, 'What Is Democracy?' in GA Tóth (ed), *Constitution for a Disunited Nation: On Hungary's 2011 Fundamental Law* (New York, Central European University Press, 2012).

[107] The model previously in place would have led to 12 out of 13 seats on the SCC becoming vacant in the same electoral term, and the difficulties with it were illustrated by the SCC appointment saga of 2014–2020: see, eg, M Steuer, 'The Guardians and the Watchdogs: The Framing of Politics, Partisanship and Qualification by Selected Newspapers during the 2018–2019 Slovak Constitutional Court Appointment Process' (2019) 102 *Právny obzor* 34.

[108] The amendment also included the establishment of the Supreme Administrative Court for Slovakia, transforming the Administrative Collegium of the Supreme Court.

[109] Constitutional Act that amends the Constitution of the Slovak Republic 2020 [422/2020 Coll]. Constitutional acts include direct constitutional amendment as well as acts adopted as constitutional acts by a three-fifths majority (eg, Constitutional Act on State Security at the Time of War, State of War, State of Emergency, and State of Necessity [227/2002 Coll]).

[110] SITA, 'Fiačan nesúhlasí, aby Ústavný súd nemohol skúmať súlad ústavných zákonov s Ústavou' (*Sme*, 12 March 2020) https://domov.sme.sk/c/22547894/fiacan-nesuhlasi-aby-ustavny-sud-nemohol-skumat-sulad-ustavnych-zakonov-s-ustavou.html.

[111] PL ÚS 8/2022, para 27.

which might signal its capacity to resist similar pressures with more malevolent aims from the perspective of democratisation. Yet particularly if the 2020 coalition's effort to curtail the court's competences succeeds, the substantive core doctrine will be shattered, with few doctrinal reservoirs standing in the way of new, authoritarian populist interpretations of the Constitution. Furthermore, the fact that longstanding democratic actors have supported the amendment can easily legitimise future similar legislative actions by political elites interested in the neutralisation of the threat that the SCC poses to unrestrained exercise of power by any means at their disposal.

VI. CONCLUSION

As demonstrated by the example of the SCC, extensive formal powers of a constitutional court do not necessarily prompt it to engage in particularism vis-à-vis EU law. This chapter told the story of the SCC, which enriches the debate on how constitutional courts develop their interpretation of constitutional identity and helps us to understand why they invoke ideas of particularism.

Three factors explain the SCC's reluctant engagement with the concept of constitutional identity: (1) the ethnonationalist rhetoric of the first PM, Mečiar, which tainted the ideas of nationalistic particularism, as the democratic actors wished to be perceived as an integral and committed member of the Western democratic community, (2) the uncontested nature of EU law, and (3) challenges faced by the SCC which mostly lay in the separation of powers disputes between key political actors (the SCC included).

As we have shown, the SCC has a peculiar place within the Visegrád group. It transformed itself from a minimalist constitutional court to a protector of the substantive core of the Constitution, built on its understanding of the separation of powers and the rule of law. We pointed out the reactionist character of this substantive core doctrine, as the SCC identified its tenets in reaction to the major challenges it faced since the 1990s. Out of these, competence disputes between individual key political actors played the core role, and resulted in the case law, which stressed, for example, the constitutional competences of the President, or later the judicial independence, as the 'significant element of the constitutional identity'.

When reading the SCC's case law in its best light,[112] this understanding of the substantive core contains a potential to safeguard political interferences and unconstitutional steps of executives. The conflict between the SCC and the populist Slovak government since 2020, however, also demonstrates its shortcomings. We might hypothesise to what degree the SCC invited the pushback from the government by raising the stakes too high. First, the SCC's cemented

[112] R Dworkin, *Law's Empire* (Cambridge, Mass, Harvard University Press, 1986) 252, 338.

division of competences clashes with the government's and especially former PM Igor Matovič's calls for 'more direct democracy'.[113] Second, the complicated history of the Slovak judiciary and its engagement in the informal corruption networks, opened the window for negative interpretation of the SCC judgment on judicial independence, and part of the public understood it as a sign of SCC protecting the old cadres. The view that the SCC's judgment defied the attempts to clean the judiciary and restart processes leading to more judicial accountability and strengthening the rule of law dominated in media coverage and pre-election debates.[114] This broader context helped the government to execute a strike against the SCC in the period of the pandemic, without an outcry from society, in the same year as the rest of the EU Member States pointed fingers at interferences in judicial independence in Poland and Hungary. The Slovak story therefore demonstrates the contextual sensitivity of how constitutional courts interpret and develop the concept of constitutional identity.

In the context of the EU and Slovakia's membership of the V4, the SCC subscribes to the supremacy of EU law as articulated by the Court of Justice, rather than trying to define how EU values are intertwined with those of the Slovak Constitution. This, on the one hand, distinguishes Slovakia from its V4 counterparts but, on the other, might not provide a robust basis for defence against particularistic constitutional identity claims distinguishing between Slovakia's values and those of the EU.[115] The absence of a connection between the EU values and the substantive core doctrine in the court's case law appears to create an ideational barrier between the interpretation of Slovakia's core constitutional values and its EU membership.

While it remains unlikely that the court would succumb to ethnonationalist inclinations any time soon, it faces the risk of marginalisation. With the recent effort of the executive and the legislature to curtail the SCC's competences,[116] the substantive core doctrine may well be deconstructed before it gains a firm position in the constitutional canon – if the SCC itself does not defend it. The SCC retains a basis for resisting the government's step, as it previously identified the review of any legislative or political step impacting on the substantive core of the Constitution as the backbone of constitutional review as such.

[113] Obyčajní ľudia a nezávislé osobnosti (n 9) 42.

[114] See, eg, M Kováčik, 'Najväčšia predvolebná debata: Lídri povedali, ako chcú zmeniť Slovensko' (*HNOnline*, 24 February 2020) https://hnonline.sk/parlamentne-volby-2020/2099737-najvacsia-predvolebna-debata-hn-hntelevizia-expres; M Paulík, 'Previerky sudcov znova na stole. V hre je zmena Ústavy' (*HNOnline*, 24 February 2020) https://hnonline.sk/parlamentne-volby-2020/2100018-previerky-sudcov-znova-na-stole-v-hre-je-zmena-ustavy.

[115] In 2020 such a position was articulated by former PM Robert Fico who spoke against Slovakia distancing itself from the efforts of the Hungarian and Polish governments to defend their own interpretation of the rule of law in a way at odds with the substantive content of EU values.

[116] See, eg, the statement of the minister of justice. B Dobšinský, 'Mária Kolíková: Nie je namieste, aby nám Ústavný súd hovoril, čo je ústava' (*Aktuality.sk*, 12 August 2020) https://www.aktuality.sk/clanok/846317/kolikova-nie-je-namieste-aby-nam-ustavny-sud-hovoril-co-je-ustava-podcast/.

4

Instruments and Elements of Particularism in the Context of Constitutional Identity: The Czech Constitutional Court

MILUŠE KINDLOVÁ[1]

THERE SEEMS TO be no clear-cut understanding of what constitutional and national identities are, nor what they precisely encompass in the Czech Republic. Both terms have appeared in the Czech academic debate particularly under the influence of their usage in an EU-wide integration context; until then debates on other notions such as sovereignty, the raison d'être of the state or Czech statehood resembled the current 'identity' discourse. In the Czech language, constitutional identity (*ústavní identita*) is usually understood as pertaining either to the constitution of the Czech state or to the Czech state pursuant to its constitution,[2] while national identity (*národní identita*) is usually perceived as a concept bound with the Czech nation (*národ*, which can carry either a more or less political or ethnocultural understanding),[3]

[1] The chapter was written in the framework of the Cooperatio project of Charles University in Prague (Social Sciences, LAWS). The author thanks Kriszta Kovács for her valuable editorial input and Katarína Šipulová, Max Steuer and Jan Malíř for their reading of the draft chapter and providing very helpful comments.

[2] Eg, D Kosař and L Vyhnánek, 'Ústavní identita České republiky' (2018) 10 *Právník* 854 (the revised English version of this paper appeared as D Kosař and L Vyhnánek, 'Constitutional Identity in the Czech Republic: A New Twist on the Old Fashioned Idea?' in C Calliess and G van der Schyff (eds), *Constitutional Identity in a Europe of Multilevel Constitutionalism* (Cambridge, Cambridge University Press, 2019), J Baroš and I Pospíšil, 'Čl. 112 (Pojem ústavního pořádku)' in P Rychetský et al, *Ústava České republiky. Ústavní zákon o bezpečnosti ČR: komentář* (Prague, Wolters Kluwer, 2015) 1115.

[3] Eg, P Maršálek, 'Evropská integrace, unijní občanství a česká národní identita' (2014) 2 *Acta Universitatis Carolinae – Iuridica* 73. National identity can be understood as either identity of the Czech political (civic) nation or the Czech cultural nation.

or also sometimes with the Czech state.[4] However, the terms are frequently used interchangeably, which on the one hand confirms and on the other hand deepens their indeterminacy. This indeterminacy is a disappointing factor when we consider how important the legal and political implications these concepts entail at the state, EU and international levels.[5]

The Czech Constitutional Court (CCC) very seldom used the vocabulary of constitutional identity and national identity and has not comprehensively explained its broader understanding of the concepts, their contents or structure. This leaves more space for various doctrinal conceptions of Czech constitutional or national identity and for diverse analytical approaches in this endeavour, sometimes inferring how the CCC in fact understands these concepts.[6]

For instance, an influential analysis by D Kosař and L Vyhnánek finds the Czech constitutional identity either in the sphere of the entrenched principles of the Czech Constitution (the 'eternity clause' of Article 9(2)) as construed by the CCC (the 'thin' version of constitutional identity), or in the 'substantive core of the constitution' sometimes understood as a complex of essential features forming the integrity of the constitution, which is broader than the entrenched principles pursuant to Article 9(2) of the Constitution (the 'thick' version of constitutional identity).[7] These authors also present the notion of 'popular constitutional identity' as a concept describing possible perceptions of constitutional identity in the eyes of Czech society, which might differ from the understanding of the Czech constitutional identity as distilled by the authors from the cases of the CCC and which may, on the other hand, influence the

[4] R Zbíral, 'Koncept národní identity jako nový prvek ve vztahu vnitrostátního a unijního práva: poznatky z teorie a praxe' (2014) 2 *Právník* 112.

[5] F Fabbrini and A Sajó, 'The Dangers of Constitutional Identity' (2019) 25 *European Law Journal* 457. In the Czech context, O Preuss, 'Demokratický právní stát tesaný do pískovce' (2016) 24:3 *Časopis pro právní vědu a praxi* 365.

[6] The recent Czech academic literature on the concepts of constitutional identity and national identity in the context of the Czech Republic include Kosař and Vyhnánek (n 2); Zbíral (n 4); Preuss (n 4); Maršálek (n 3); K Hvížďala and J Přibáň, *Hledání dějin, O české státnosti a identitě* (Prague, Karolinum, 2018); J Kysela and P Ondřejek (eds), *Stát jako kolos na hliněných nohou* (Prague, Leges, 2016), P Molek, *Materiální ohnisko jako věčný limit evropské integrace?* (Brno, Muni Press, 2014), M Tomoszek, 'Ústavní identita jako vyjádření ústavní filosofie' in T Sobek, M Hapla et al, *Filosofie práva* (Brno, Nugis Finem Publishing, 2020).

[7] Kosař and Vyhnánek (n 2) 94. However, legal academia is not uniform in the issue of what this 'substantive core of the constitution' entails beyond the principles protected by Article 9(2), which provides that 'Any changes in the essential requirements of a democratic state governed by the rule of law are impermissible.' Molek (n 6) discusses, for instance, the principle of republicanism (149–150). Preuss (n 5) adds unitarity of the state and the parliamentary system of government. Moreover, the CCC's cases seem to use the term 'substantive core' as equivalent to the entrenched principles pursuant to Article 9(2) of the Constitution (eg, ruling of 10 September 2009 File No Pl ÚS 27/09). The resulting uncertainty as to how to understand and use this notion of 'substantive core' is, in addition, complicated by the fact that the term 'core' (*jádro*) is sometimes replaced by a 'centre' or 'focus' (*ohnisko*), probably understood synonymously. It is also possible to find another expression: the 'hard' core of the constitution (with the potential implication that there is also a part of the core which is not 'hard'?).

identity perceptions held or supported by other participants in the governmental process.[8]

In the light of one of the main aims of this monograph – studying the jurisprudence of particularism[9] in Visegrád countries in the identity and the membership of the EU contexts – this chapter also focuses on the concept of constitutional identity in the Czech Republic. However, given the fact that the CCC has not clearly articulated the concept in its case law thus far (there are just a few remarks in this respect)[10] and that it is not entirely obvious what the understandings of constitutional judges (whose 'internal point[s] of view'[11] are crucial) are, the chapter takes a rather cautious approach and does not aim to present the CCC's understanding of constitutional identity. In order to do so, a much more explicit articulation of the concept in the case law would be needed. Also, even though this may be a subjectively perceived feeling of the author of this chapter based on her informal debates with colleagues (including

[8] Kosař and Vyhnánek (n 2), 94.

[9] Kriszta Kovács explains particularism as 'particularistic judicial interpretations of universal constitutional principles' and finds the question of whether constitutional democracies can coexist with 'legitimate space for particularism' a central issue of the volume. See the introductory chapter in this volume.

[10] In ruling of 26 November 2008 File No Pl ÚS 19/08 (*Lisbon I*) the CCC mentions 'abandoning of value identity' as a reason for the exercise of its power of review whether any act of an EU body exceeded the powers transferred to the EU, para 120. In this case, the Government as a participant in the proceedings treated 'the essentials of the democratic state governed by the rule of law' protected by the eternity clause of Article 9(2) as synonymous with the identity of the Constitution and related it to the maintenance of 'the value system on which the Constitution as a whole rests' (para 35 – summary of participants' claims). Ruling of 10 September 2009 File No 27/09 (*Melčák*) calls principles protected by Article 9(2) as 'fundamentally identifying the constitutional system of the Czech Republic'. These formulations in the two cases may be considered as the nearest confirmation that the CCC places constitutional identity in Article 9(2) of the Constitution. On the other hand, ruling of 14 February 2012 File No Pl ÚS 5/12 (*Slovak Pensions*) mentions constitutional identity with potentially different connotations when it refers to 'the constitutional identity of the Czech Republic … drawing from the common constitutional tradition with the Slovak Republic, that is from the over seventy years of the common state and its peaceful dissolution, i.e., from a completely idiosyncratic and historically created situation that has no parallel in Europe'. One resolution of the CCC's senate (section) talks about Lebanon as a democratic state governed by the rule of law whose constitutional identity covers the protection of religious minorities (resolution of 15 December 2020 File No II ÚS 3318/20, para 9). Finally, ruling of 18 February 2020 File No Pl ÚS 4/17 (*Conflict of Interests*) does not use the term constitutional identity but talks about the obligation of the EU to respect 'national identity' of Member States pursuant to Article 4(2) TEU and the 'entitlement of the Member State to maintain room for the development of its political and constitutional system', while mentioning the 'constitutional principles of democracy, free and democratic elections and free competition among political parties and political forces' and 'principles of the democratic state governed by the rule of law' in this connection (paras 159–60). It is noteworthy that, in her dissenting opinions to two of the recent decisions of the CCC (resolutions of 5 May 2020 File No Pl ÚS 10/20 and File No Pl ÚS 13/20), Judge Kateřina Šimáčková referred to two provisions in the Czech Charter of Fundamental Rights and Freedoms (the right of Czech citizens not to be deprived of their citizenship against their will and the right of all individuals rightfully present in the Czech territory to freely leave the country) as to the components of the Czech constitutional identity, specifically stressing their historic dimension of disrespect during the Communist regime.

[11] HL Hart, *The Concept of Law* 2nd edn (Oxford, Oxford University Press, 1994) 89.

constitutional judges-academics and their legal clerks), so far, the meaning of the concept has not been 'internalised' in any more solid form by Czech constitutional academia.

This chapter's analysis is inspired by a theoretical study of constitutional identity in the sense of the 'identity of the constitution' proposed by Drinóczi, dealing with a three-part template: the designation of the state and the constituent subject, the procedural sameness element of the constitution and the principles protected by the eternity clause.[12] After a brief introduction into the Czech Constitution and the concept of the 'constitutional order', the chapter will first analyse constitutional provisions regulating the amendment process in order to examine the 'procedural sameness' aspect of the identity of the constitution. Then substantive principles entrenched in the Constitution will be examined. The next part of the chapter will look at how the Constitution textually designates the state and how the constituent subject is presented there. In all three sections, the relevant case law of the CCC will be dealt with. This analytical structure can be used as a useful framework in which the elements of universalism can be explored as well as elements and instruments of particularism in the CCC's case law.

As regards national identity in the sense of the identity of the Czech nation, it will be dealt with only very partially and only to the extent necessary to put the 'identity of the constitution' in its broader context. This should not suggest that the issue of (formation, search for) national identity is of lesser importance, because the history of Czechoslovakia and the Czech Republic, as well as of older territorial entities in this region, proves the opposite.[13]

[12] T Drinóczi, 'Constitutional Identity in Europe: The Identity of the Constitution. A Regional Approach' (2020) 21 *German Law Journal* 105. In her text, the author discusses three possible holders of constitutional identity – the people or nation; the state; and the constitution. She concludes that linking the term of constitutional identity with the people, nation or the state makes no sense from a legal perspective because it does not bring anything new above what is not already expressed under such notions as national identity, legitimacy or state sovereignty. Therefore, she recommends legally conceptualising the term constitutional identity as 'the identity of the constitution'. Because – as she writes – 'from the European case law it seems that the term "constitutional identity" is used in many ways – confrontationally and cooperatively – to preserve the uniqueness of the constitution and, consequently, the sameness of the state and its people', she approaches constitutional identity as the expression of what of its collective identity the 'constitutional subject as constituent deemed to be as important' as to incorporate in the constitution. She then focuses on three types of provisions in constitutions in which constitutional identity in this sense is traditionally expressed – (1) designation of the state and of the constitutional subject – constituent people, (2) 'procedural sameness' and (3) the entrenched principles (117–22). The modification of the analysis in this chapter is the addition of the concept of formal legal continuity as another aspect of the 'procedural sameness' element of the identity of the constitution because it is a traditional analytical tool used in the Czechoslovak and Czech constitutional theory and is relevant in the CCC's case law, as well.

[13] The conflicts between different perceptions of national identities during the existence of Czechoslovakia and their implications for the eventual dissolution of the federation are studied by E Stein, *Czecho/Slovakia: Ethnic Conflict, Constitutional Fissure, Negotiated Breakup* (Ann Arbor, University of Michigan Press, 2000) or J Rychlík, 'The "Velvet Split" of Czechoslovakia (1989–1992)' (2018) 57 *Politeja* 169.

The chapter will suggest two main conclusions regarding the Czech Republic. First, the CCC, as it can be inferred from its case law, does not strongly subscribe to the idea of particularism. Second, the CCC has, however, developed several 'defensive' instruments which may be used to promote and assert particularism, even vis-à-vis the EU law, if it considers some crucial constitutional values are at stake. The chapter will also suggest that especially the issue of the identification of the constituent subject might reveal a sensitive area.

I. PRELIMINARY INTRODUCTION TO THE CZECH CONSTITUTION: THE PRINCIPLE OF LEGAL CONTINUITY

The Constitution of the Czech Republic was adopted by the Czech National Council, the legislative body of the Czech Republic – then a Member State of federal Czechoslovakia – on 16 December 1992.[14] From a legal perspective, following the dissolution of the federation on 31 December 1992, the already existing Czech Republic gained independence on 1 January 1993.[15] The Constitution, containing the main structure of the governmental system, forms only one component of the broader so-called 'constitutional order' (*ústavní pořádek*, the Czech equivalent of *bloc de constitutionnalité*). Apart from the Constitution, it comprises, inter alia, the Charter of Fundamental Rights and Freedoms (the Czech Charter) adopted originally by the Czechoslovak Federal Assembly in 1991, and constitutional statutes adopted pursuant to the Constitution.[16] In principle, the Czech Republic took over all legal regulations of the former federation applicable in its territory, making inapplicable only those which relied on the existence of the federal system and the membership of the Czech Republic in it, and with the exception of some repealed former constitutional statutes.[17] In this sense, the principle of legal continuity was adopted but the CCC's case law on several occasions stressed that this continuity was accompanied by 'value discontinuity' with the pre-1989 political regime.[18] Importantly, the CCC has

[14] Constitutional Act No 1/1993 Coll, the Constitution of the Czech Republic.

[15] The Czech Republic was established on 1 January 1969 as a Member State of the Czechoslovak federation (eg V Sládeček et al, *Ústava České republiky. Komentář* 2nd ed (Praha, CH Beck, 2016) 1261 and J Filip, *Ústavní právo České republiky. Základní pojmy a instituty. Ústavní základy ČR. Díl 1* 4th edn (Brno, Masarykova universita and Doplněk, 2003) 167. However, the opinion that the Czech Republic came to being as a new state on 1 January 1993 also appears in academic texts: J Kysela, *Ústava mezi právem a politikou: úvod do ústavní teorie* (Praha, Leges, 2014) 127. The difference between these opinions is largely of only academic interest but it is, nevertheless, noteworthy considering that it relates to the very beginning of the state's existence.

[16] Article 112(1) of the Constitution.

[17] Constitutional Act No 4/1993 Coll, on Measures Related to the End of the Czech and Slovak Federative Republic, and Article 112 of the Constitution.

[18] Eg, ruling of 21 December 1993 File No Pl ÚS 19/93 or ruling of 26 March 2003 File No Pl ÚS 42/02. The principle of 'value discontinuity' with the past legal regime was firstly asserted in the ruling of the Federal Constitutional Court of 26 November 1992 File No Pl ÚS 9/01 (Lustration I).

included international human rights treaties binding on the Czech Republic into the constitutional order and also proclaimed that unwritten constitutional principles form part of constitutional law.[19]

II. THE IDENTITY OF THE CONSTITUTION: PROCEDURAL SAMENESS AND THE ENTRENCHED PRINCIPLES

A. Two Views of 'Procedural Sameness'

The 'procedural sameness' aspect of the identity of the Constitution is sometimes understood in the sense of a requirement that the constitutional subject (the people or the nation) should be kept as the 'final determinant of the constitutional text,' with an emphasis on the importance of the 'pluralistic and inclusive constitution-making process' and referenda in the adoption of constitutional amendments.[20] The main rationale behind this requirement can be found in the perceived need to maintain the genuine legitimacy link between the people (nation) and the constitution (and its development).[21]

From another, strictly formal legal perspective, the element of 'procedural sameness' in the identity of the constitution may imply that, to maintain the constitution's identity, each constitutional amendment must be adopted pursuant to the relevant competence and procedural norms laid down in the existing constitution ('formal legal continuity'). If an amendment is adopted outside of these rules, it cannot belong to the same constitution but belongs to a new one (a new constitutional system has been established).[22]

Studying the Czech Constitution and the formal amending process in the light of these two procedural approaches, the following picture unfolds. First, the constitutional system of the Czech Republic is clearly based on the preference of indirect, representative democracy, including the process of constitutional amendments.[23] Article 9(1) of the Constitution stipulates that the Constitution can be 'amended or changed by constitutional statutes', which require the consent of qualified majorities in both chambers of the Parliament. Organising a constitutional referendum (in fact any direct exercise of state authority by

The ruling was one of the most formative decisions of the short-lived Federal Constitutional Court and was very influential for the future case law of the CCC.

[19] Ruling of 25 June 2002 File No Pl ÚS 36/01 and ruling of 17 December 1997 File No Pl ÚS 33/97.

[20] Drinóczi (n 12) 120.

[21] ibid.

[22] Different types of legal/state continuity belong to traditional topics of Czechoslovak and Czech constitutional studies. This view of formal legal continuity is described in Z Neubauer, *Státověda a theorie politiky* (Praha, Jan Laichter, 1947) 34.

[23] M Kindlová, 'Formal and Informal Constitutional Amendment in the Czech Republic' (2018) 4 *The Lawyer Quarterly* 512.

the people) requires prior adoption of a constitutional statute.[24] Equally, in the context of international and EU law, pursuant to Article 10a of the Constitution, any delegation of 'certain powers' of the authorities of the Czech Republic to an international organisation or institution requires the adoption of a treaty approved by the same 'constitutional' majorities in chambers of Parliament unless, again, a constitutional statute establishes that the approval must be given in a referendum.[25] The entry to the EU was the only extraordinary occasion on which such a referendum occurred.[26]

In this situation, the standard process of amending the constitutional order is only via constitutional statutes adopted by the Parliament. Their procedural democratic legitimacy is mediated through the elected members of the Parliament, ie deputies and senators. In fact, the legacy of the way in which the Czech Constitution was adopted in December 1992 and in which Czechoslovakia ended its existence in the same year (by means of a constitutional statute adopted by the federal parliament) persists until today and one of the important consequences of this state of affairs is obvious – the impact of the people on the creation, interpretation and understanding of constitutional identity can, in a certain sense, be only indirect.[27]

B. The Entrenched Principles and their Effect in the Constitutional System

The Czech Constitution is one of those constitutional texts which contain a version of an eternity clause. It appears in Article 9(2) and is complemented by an interpretative provision in Article 9(3). Unlike in, for instance, the German Basic Law or Portuguese or Greek constitutions, the clause contains no specific

[24] Article 2(2) of the Constitution.

[25] Article 10a in conjunction with Article 36(4) of the Constitution.

[26] Constitutional Act No 515/2002 Coll, on the Referendum on the Entry to the European Union.

[27] The reserved approach of the authors of the Constitution to direct democracy was, in the view of several commentators, a continuation of the practice in which citizens were not given the opportunity to directly decide on the dissolution of Czechoslovakia and which let this political decision to an agreement primarily between the leaders of two political parties winning the 1992 elections in the Czech Republic and the Slovak Republic respectively. This happened despite the existence of a federal constitutional act which regulated a process through which people in either republic could, inter alia, decide to leave the federation, and despite the fact that no relevant political party on the Czech side had the division of Czechoslovakia in their election manifestos. More information in Z Jičínský, 'Ústavněprávní a politické problémy vzniku České republiky a charakteristika sociálně-demokratického návrhu Ústavy ČR' in A Gerloch and J Kysela (eds), *20 let Ústavy České republiky (Ohlédnutí zpět a pohled vpřed)* (Plzeň, Aleš Čeněk, 2013) 43 or V Šimíček, 'Art. 2' in L Bahýlová et al, *Ústava České republiky: Komentář* (Prague, Linde Praha, 2010) 52. The lack of mandate of the elected representatives to decide the end of Czechoslovakia is still considered a smear on the entire process by some authors (eg, J Reschová, 'Paradoxy česko-slovenských vztahů' (2018) 3 *Acta Universitatis Carolinae Iuridica* 11 who points out how this fact is often subdued by the general understanding of the entire process as a successful project – 'a quick, transactionally least expensive and politically least demanding' 12).

principles but, instead, protects as unamendable the 'essentials of the democratic state governed by the rule of law'. The latter provision extends the protection to the 'foundations of the democratic state' and proclaims that it is impermissible to remove or threaten them by means of interpretation of legal norms. Both provisions are the Constitution's reaction to the experience under the Nazi and Communist totalitarian regimes and aim to prevent a similar threat in the future.

Because of the very general text of Article 9(2), it has been mainly upon the CCC to construe the provision and conceptualise its effect in the constitutional system and upon the constitutional doctrine to further systematise the concept and critically assess its working. The CCC refuses to provide any detailed catalogue of principles protected by Article 9(2) but has indicated some of them in its case law. In the *Lisbon I* ruling, the CCC cited inviolability of natural rights, human dignity, sovereignty of the state, democratic state governed by the rule of law, the protection of minorities, the prohibition of discrimination, plural democracy, solidarity in particular as regards socio-economic rights and free competition of political parties as entrenched principles.[28]

Importantly, the CCC has already applied Article 9(2) as a strong interpretative weapon against the Parliament even acting in its derivative constitutional power by maintaining that no constitutional amendment can contravene Article 9(2) principles and may not be construed in a way that would diminish the attained procedural level of protection of human rights in the Czech Republic.[29]

The protection of the essentials of the democratic state governed by the rule of law pursuant to Article 9(2) combined its force with the requirement of 'procedural sameness' of constitutional amendments in the sense of Article 9(1) in the *Melčák* case, which apparently until today was the most important case decided by the CCC. In this ruling, the CCC annulled a constitutional statute, adopted by the required qualified majorities in both chambers of Parliament, which shortened the fifth electoral period of the Chamber of Deputies (ie, one of the two parliamentary chambers). Pursuant to the majority opinion of judges, the amendment in issue did not comply with the constitution-amendment rules because it did not 'change or amend' the Constitution (in a general way) as required by Article 9(1) but rather ad hoc bypassed it (for the individual electoral period just running), while the conditions for a possible exception in this

[28] *Lisbon I* ruling (n 10) para 93. All domestic commentaries of the Czech Constitution devote to the topic, eg, Bahýľová et al (n 27) 153–63 or Sládeček et al (n 15) 109–114.

[29] Ruling of 25 June 2002 File No Pl ÚS 36/01. In this ruling, the CCC included human rights treaties binding on the Czech Republic in the constitutional order. The broader context of the case is discussed in J Malíř and J Ondřejková, 'Law-Making Activity of the Czech Constitutional Court' in M Florczak-Wątor (ed), *Judicial Law-making in European Constitutional Courts* (London, Routledge, 2020) 120–21.

regard stipulated by the CCC were not met. In other words, according to the CCC, Parliament acted ultra vires, outside of the competence stipulated by Article 9(1) of the Constitution. At the same time, the court found a violation of the principle of the general character of legal regulations and of the principle of retroactivity which it subsumed under the entrenched principles guaranteed by Article 9(2).[30]

Some of the main cases in which the protection of the essentials of the democratic state governed by the rule of law was peculiarly significant directly concerned the relationship of the Czech legal system to the EU law and European integration as such. In that respect, the CCC also dealt, inter alia, with the above-mentioned provision of Article 10a of the Constitution on the delegation of 'certain powers of the authorities of the Czech Republic to an international organisation or institution', as well as with the basic characteristics of the state in Articles 1(1) and (2) of the Constitution (republican and unitary character, sovereignty, respect for fundamental rights, observing international obligations). It should be noted that the text of the Constitution as amended by the so-called 'Euro-Amendment' provided a relatively broad scope for the CCC's interpretation of the legal consequences of the accession to the EU.[31] In the cases mentioned below, the CCC formulated the basic tenets of the relationship of the Czech and EU legal systems as viewed by the CCC. On the one hand, the CCC postulated the openness of the Czech legal space to the application and primacy of EU law and its preparedness to construe even the constitutional order in an EU-friendly way. On the other hand, the CCC put emphasis on the existence of certain constitutional limits or barriers in this regard. The cases may also be read as rulings which paved the way towards the possibility of the CCC's 'ultra vires review' and 'identity review' in the context of EU membership.[32]

In 2006, in the *Sugar Quotas III* case, the CCC noted the defensive aspects of the above-mentioned provisions and proclaimed that the 'delegation of certain powers' to a supranational organisation (and thus also the effects of law resulting from such a delegation)[33] is not and must not be without limits:

> In the Constitutional Court's view, this conferral of a part of its powers is naturally a conditional conferral, as the original bearer of sovereignty, as well as the

[30] *Melčák* ruling (n 10). The critique of the ruling appears in Y Roznai, 'Legisprudence Limitations on Constitutional Amendments? Reflections on the Czech Constitutional Court's Declaration of Unconstitutional Constitutional Act' (2014) 8(1) *Vienna Journal on International Constitutional Law* 29.

[31] The 'Euro-Amendment' of the Constitution is a colloquial name of the Constitutional Act No 395/2001 Coll which strengthened the position of international law in the domestic legal system and created the option for the Czech Republic to join the EU. More details are discussed in I Šlosarčík, 'EU Law in the Czech Republic: From ultra vires of the Czech Government to ultra vires of the EU Court?' (2015) 9 *Vienna Journal on International and Constitutional Law* 417, 418–20.

[32] *Lisbon I* ruling (n 10) para 120 uses the notion 'value identity'.

[33] This case confirmed that the constitutional basis of EU law application in the Czech Republic is the 'transfer of powers' provision of Article 10a of the Constitution rather than its Article 10 regulating the position of ratified treaties agreed to by Parliament in the Czech legal system, which had

> powers flowing therefrom, still remains the Czech Republic, whose sovereignty is still founded upon Article 1(1) of the Constitution of the Czech Republic. It states that the Czech Republic is a sovereign, unitary, and democratic state governed by the rule of law, founded on respect for the rights and freedoms of man and of citizens. In the Constitutional Court's view, the conditional nature of the delegation of these powers is manifested on two planes: the formal and the substantive plane. The first of these planes concerns the power attributes of state sovereignty itself, the second plane concerns the substantive component of the exercise of state power. In other words, the delegation of a part of the powers of national organs may persist only so long as these powers are exercised in a manner that is compatible with the preservation of the foundations of state sovereignty of the Czech Republic, and in a manner which does not threaten the very essence of the substantive law-based state. Should one of these conditions for the transfer of powers cease to be fulfilled, that is, should developments in … EU, threaten the very essence of state sovereignty of the Czech Republic or the essential attributes of a democratic state governed by the rule of law, it will be necessary to insist that these powers be once again taken up by the Czech Republic's state bodies; in such determination the Constitutional Court is called upon to protect constitutionalism (Article 83 of the Constitution of the Czech Republic). That is the case in the formal dimension within the confines of the current constitutional rules. As concerns the essential attributes of a democratic state governed by the rule of law, according to Article 9(2) of the Constitution of the Czech Republic, these remain beyond the reach of the Constituent Assembly itself.[34]

In 2008, the *Lisbon I* ruling of the CCC repeated the holdings of previous main EU-related cases and stressed that its role is to self-restrain and normally employ the principle of EU-friendly construction of the constitutional order, but that in case of a clear conflict, 'the constitutional order, especially its substantive core, must take precedence'.[35] In support, the CCC further cited, inter alia, the German Constitutional Court's *Maastricht* judgment, and confirmed that it views itself as a body whose task 'will (may)' be to assess – as ultima ratio – whether an EU body did not act outside of the transferred powers and added that it considers this eventuality to come up in 'utterly extreme instances' – especially concerning the 'abandoning of value identity or the said transgressing the scope of transferred powers'.[36]

Soon thereafter, in the *Lisbon II* case, the CCC was called upon to identify more clearly where the limits of the possible conferral of powers upon the EU lie but (unlike the FCC) declined to specify them, repeating the thesis from the *Lisbon I* case that

> [t]hese limits should be left primarily to the legislature to specify, because this is a priori a political question, which provides the legislature wide discretion … Responsibility

been a subject of domestic academic debate. M Bobek and Z Kühn, 'What about that "Incoming Tide"? The Application of EU Law in the Czech Republic' in A Lazowski (ed), *The Application of EU Law in the New Member States – Brave New World* (The Hague, TMC Asser Press, 2010).

[34] Ruling of 8 March 2006 File No Pl ÚS 50/04 (*Sugar Quotas III*), part VI. B.

[35] *Lisbon I* ruling (n 10) para 85.

[36] ibid at para 120.

> for these political decisions cannot be transferred to the Constitutional Court; it can review them only at the point when they have actually been made on the political level.[37]

In the cases referred to above, the CCC declared its preparedness to intervene if the EU law obligations contravened the 'power attributes of the Czech Republic's sovereignty' or the essentials of the democratic state governed by the rule of law. However, the possibility that a real conflict vis-à-vis the principle of primacy of EU law arises is, at least in the reasonably foreseeable future, viewed by several Czech commentators who discussed the issue as improbable and, it seems, for good reasons.[38] As regards the protection of the Czech statehood and its sovereignty, they point out that the CCC understands the concepts not in the orthodox absolute fashion but in their modified meaning in the globalised world, as the *Lisbon I* case reveals. The CCC has explicitly referred to the EU as a sui generis entity in which the concept of pooled sovereignty is applied and presented the idea that the membership of the state in the EU can indeed strengthen the protection of the state's external sovereignty, faced with novel geopolitical or economic circumstances.[39] Moreover, it is worth adding that the CCC talks about the instrumental value of state sovereignty for the protection of 'the most crucial constitutional rules and principles of the state governed by the substantive rule of law', for the protection of natural law principles, and rejects that sovereignty of the state could be an aim in and of itself.[40] As to the democratic character of the state, the CCC views the mutual interconnectedness between democracy at the national and supranational levels, as, for instance, the *Lisbon II* or the *European Parliament Electoral Threshold* cases show (the latter case will be dealt with in the following section).[41] Lastly, while EU law is not considered a part of constitutional law per se, the CCC, as already mentioned, has followed the principle that the constitutional order should be construed in a way complying with EU obligations unless it is impossible to do so and the *European Arrest Warrant* case (*EAW*), in particular, confirms that, even in very sensitive constitutional issues, the CCC tries to find such constructions.[42] Again, this case will be analysed in more detail in the following section.

[37] Ruling of 11 March 2009 File No 29/09 (*Lisbon II*), para 111.

[38] Kosař and Vyhnánek (n 2) 102–105 and L Vyhnánek, 'The Eternity Clause in the Czech Constitution as Limit to European Integration: Much Ado About Nothing?' (2015) 9 *Vienna Journal on International Constitutional Law* 240, 248–49.

[39] *Lisbon I* ruling (n 10) paras 102, 108.

[40] ibid at paras 102, 131 and *Lisbon II* ruling (n 37) para 147.

[41] *Lisbon II* ruling (n 37), ruling of 19 May 2015 File No Pl ÚS 14/14 (*European Parliament Electoral Threshold*).

[42] Ruling of 3 May 2006 File No Pl ÚS 66/04 (*EAW*), para 61: 'If the Constitution … can be interpreted in several manners, only certain of which lead to the attainment of an obligation which the Czech Republic undertook in connection with its membership in the EU, then an interpretation must be selected which supports the carrying out of that obligation, and not an interpretation which precludes it'. Moreover, the CCC has increasingly begun referring to the EU Charter of Fundamental

Nevertheless, despite these reasons for why conflicts between the EU and the national constitutional imperatives should not be probable, there are also factors suggesting that the CCC can use its defensive *instruments* mentioned above, developed for the protection of principles deemed constitutionally inviolable, and thus actually employ the jurisprudence of particularism in individual cases if that were considered as required by those principles. The *Slovak Pensions* case, in which the CCC did explicitly, albeit rather fragmentarily, refer to the concept of the 'constitutional identity of the Czech Republic', was such a case.[43] It may be conceptualised as a case in which the *Lisbon* ultra vires jurisprudence joined the question of the interpretation of the 'whose constitution' element of constitutional identity (designation of the state and the constituent subject).

The aim of the following paragraphs is to provide a broader context of this aspect of the identity of the Czech constitution and to try to explain the place of the *Slovak Pensions* case but also of other cases in that context.

III. THE IDENTITY OF THE CONSTITUTION: DESIGNATION OF THE STATE AND THE CONSTITUENT SUBJECT ('WHOSE CONSTITUTION?')

The Constitution designates the Czech state as a republic and as a sovereign, unitary and democratic state governed by the rule of law founded on the respect for rights and freedoms of man and citizen (Article 1(1)). Moreover, it proclaims that it fulfils its obligations flowing from international law (Article 1(2)). As is clear from the above text, the Constitution was not adopted or approved in a referendum but was passed by a legislative body, elected in June 1992 (when the end of Czechoslovak federation arguably was a foreseeable option but still not the only possible solution to the increasingly complex Czech-Slovak relationship within the federation). Despite some opinions which have argued that the original democratic legitimacy of the Constitution was contestable, the Constitution has been in force for almost 30 years now and is generally accepted as fundamental law.[44]

The Constitution is theoretically based on the concept of popular sovereignty and Article 2(1) provides that 'the people' (*lid*) is the source of the entire state authority. The preamble explicitly denotes the constituent subject as 'We, the citizens of the Czech Republic in Bohemia, Moravia and Silesia', deliberately choosing the expression for the political (civic) concept of the constituent subject (*demos*).[45] The civic understanding of citizenship is further underlined

Rights as to a 'component of the reference framework in its review' (eg, ruling of 5 November 2019 File No II ÚS 2778/19, paras 20–25).

[43] *Slovak Pensions* ruling (n 10) part VII.

[44] Jan Kysela refers to this as 'reverse legitimization' in Kysela (n 15) 128.

[45] Filip (n 15) 135. In recent years, there were some academic, extra-parliamentary, proposals to include the more cultural (or ethno) concept of the Czech nation into the Constitution by inserting the provision that 'the Czech Republic is the homeland of the members of the Czech nation and of the

by other provisions in the preamble, stipulating the respect of citizens for the universal values of human rights, civil society, democracy and the rule of law, while also mentioning their determination to 'collectively guard and develop inherited natural, cultural, material and spiritual riches'.

The CCC case law certifies the existence of a strong EU membership dimension of the Czech citizenship and of those constitutional rights that the Czech Charter guarantees to the citizens.[46] This was clearly visible in the *EAW* ruling on the constitutionality of the domestic legislation implementing the European Arrest Warrant.[47] The CCC was required to decide whether the Czech Charter's provision of Article 14(4) which provides that no Czech citizen may be forced to leave his homeland was not violated by the legislation enabling the extradition of a citizen to another Member State on the basis of the EAW. The meaning of the Czech Charter's provision was, in the opinion of the CCC, far from unequivocal. The CCC applied historic and teleological interpretative methods to assess two potential and conflicting interpretative outcomes. Most decisively, even in the context of one of the main citizenship privileges and unlike some of its counterparts in other EU states, the CCC followed the principle of the EU-friendly interpretation of the constitutional order and found a compatible construction of the Czech Charter provision. It held that the temporary extradition to another Member State does not contravene the provision.[48] One of the strong arguments for reaching such a conclusion was the acknowledgement of the changed contents of the Czech citizenship – now citizens do not enjoy the advantages of EU citizenship only but must also accept certain responsibilities.[49]

Another case which might be included in the survey of the CCC's case law reflecting an EU-friendly approach in the context of, inter alia, constitutional rights of Czech citizens protected by the Czech Charter was the *European Parliament Electoral Threshold* case.[50] Here, the CCC, at the initiative filed by the Czech Supreme Administrative Court, dealt with the issue of whether the domestic 5% threshold clause in the elections to the European Parliament violated the principle of electoral equality of all voters and the right of Czech citizens for access to elected offices under equal conditions guaranteed by Articles 21(3) and (4) of the Czech Charter. The CCC, whose approach significantly differed from the way in which the FCC considered the constitutionality

national minorities and entities which are connected with it' but it did not seem to gain wider support within academia and the legal profession, despite being explained as not excluding the civic concept but only complementing it. The new text was proposed by Aleš Gerloch, constitutional lawyer and Vice-Rector of Charles University: Novinky.cz ('Ústavní právník Gerloch chce vrátit do ústavy národ') www.novinky.cz/domaci/clanek/ustavni-pravnik-gerloch-chce-vratit-do-ustavy-narod-40014840.

[46] The quick move from the category of a 'constituent subject' directly to the position of Czech citizens is theoretically questionable, but it is made here for reasons of simplification.

[47] *EAW* ruling (n 42).

[48] ibid at para 61.

[49] ibid at para 71.

[50] *European Parliament Electoral Threshold* ruling (n 41).

of electoral thresholds in its two earlier judgments,[51] justified the constitutionality of the threshold clause by referring to the need to promote 'the creation of a functioning European Parliament capable of generating clear majority will as an expression of the democratic principle', stressing that the rights in question 'have their immanent limits at the point where unlimited application of them would thwart citizens' effective participation in the democratic life of society (the state, the European Union) and markedly limit the possibility, or even make it impossible to connect various particular interests in solutions implementable through practical politics to problems shared by persons with those interests'.[52]

The CCC put an emphasis on the mutual complementarity of democratic processes at the national and European levels and construed Article 1(2) of the Constitution providing that the Czech Republic fulfils its obligations stemming from international law to the effect that even if the real effect of the removal of the Czech threshold clause were in the context of the European Parliament minimal, the state cannot act as a 'free rider' because other states could possibly follow which would already create a stronger disintegrative impact overall. Thus, the interference with the above constitutionally protected rights and principles was upheld.[53]

From another perspective, the CCC also gives weight to the position of citizens of other Member States in the Czech Republic and has, inter alia, referred to them as 'political citizens' of municipalities although under the explicit wording of the Act on Municipalities, the position of municipality citizenship is reserved only to Czech citizens.[54]

On the other hand, when analysing the CCC's case law regarding the 'whose constitution' aspect of the identity of the constitution, it is impossible to omit the notorious *Slovak Pensions* case in which the jurisprudence of particularism seems to be markedly present.[55] In this case, the CCC not only refused to abide by the judgment of the ECJ rendered in the preliminary rulings procedure upon a reference from the Czech Supreme Administrative Court in a similar case, but declared the ECJ's judgment in issue ultra vires, as well.

The case concerned the consequences of the dissolution of Czechoslovakia and the regulation of the administration of pensions for periods of employment before the end of the federation. Under a bilateral treaty between the Czech Republic and the Slovak Republic the pensions for these periods were to be administered by that state on the territory of which their employer had a

[51] H Smekal and L Vyhnánek discuss the case, including the comparison with the cases decided by the BVerfG, in 'Equal Voting Power under Scrutiny: Czech Constitutional Court on the 5% threshold in the 2014 European Parliament Elections: Czech Constitutional Court 19 May 2015, Pl. ÚS 14/14' (2016) 12 *European Constitutional Law Review* 12.

[52] *European Parliament Electoral Threshold* ruling (n 41) paras 67, 65.

[53] ibid at paras 77, 85.

[54] Act No 128/2000 Coll, on Municipalities, as amended, s 16(1) and ruling of 4 June 2019 File No Pl ÚS 48/18, para 28.

[55] *Slovak Pensions* ruling (n 10).

nominal seat at the time of the dissolution of the federation. Due to the different economic situation in the Czech Republic and Slovakia after 1993, the pensions administered by Slovakia were generally lower than pensions for which responsibility lay with the Czech Republic. The CCC held that to guarantee the Czech citizens' right to adequate material security in their old age (Article 30(1) of the Czech Charter) without unjustified differential treatment, those Czech citizens whose pensions were lower because of their former pre-1993 employer's seat in Slovakia were entitled to a compensatory supplement (note: this was not a result of legislation but of the CCC's case law).

The ECJ's judgment did not consider the supplement as such breaching the EU law.[56] Nevertheless, the ECJ found that to apply the criteria of the Czech citizenship and of the residence in the Czech Republic, as conditions for the entitlement to the supplement, amounted to direct and indirect discrimination respectively against those people who enjoyed the right of free movement of persons in the EU. The CCC, however, decided to disrespect this legal opinion and argued that the ECJ's application of the relevant EU law (Council Regulation on coordination of social security systems in the case of migrating workers) in the case was unsubstantiated and misplaced because there was no genuine 'foreign element' involved, upon which the EU regulation rested. In the opinion of the CCC, the ECJ misjudged the legal nature of the problem and failed to adequately acknowledge the specific and unique situation arising from the dissolution of a former state with a uniform social security system from the standard social security situations arising from the free movement of persons in the EC and later the EU. Therefore, the CCC concluded that the ECJ as a body of the EU transgressed the powers transferred to it by the Czech Republic and thus acted ultra vires.[57]

This case is generally considered as an extraordinary case, stepping aside from the CCC's friendly approach towards EU law, and it is usually criticised for the way in which it assessed the relevant EU law.[58] Its background context of a 'guerre des judges' between the Czech Supreme Administrative Court and the CCC over how to tackle the legal problem is often mentioned as a very substantial factor behind the CCC's ruling, which, for purposes of domestic law, expressed the supremacy of the CCC.[59] The influence of judge-rapporteur Pavel Holländer, one of the most prominent constitutional justices and intellectuals

[56] Case C-399/09 *Marie Landtová v Česká správa socialního zabezpečení* ECLI:EU:C:2011:415.

[57] Zbíral (n 4).

[58] J Komárek, 'Playing with Matches: The Czech Constitutional Court Declares a Judgment of the Court of Justice of the EU Ultra Vires; Judgment of 31 January 2012, Pl ÚS 5/12, Slovak Pensions XVII' (2012) 8 *European Constitutional Law Review* 323; P Molek, 'The Czech Constitutional Court and the Court of Justice: Between Fascination and Securing Autonomy' in M Claes et al (eds), *Constitutional Conversations in Europe* (Cambridge, Intersentia, 2012) 155–56., M Bobek, 'Landtová, Holubec, and the Problem of an Uncooperative Court: Implications for the Preliminary Rulings Procedure' (2014) 10 *European Constitutional Law Review* 54.

[59] Zbíral (n 4) 13.

in the entire history of the CCC (he was also the rapporteur in the *Melčák* case), has also been cited as a dominant feature of the case. However, the element of particularism and identity discourse is certainly present in the ruling, founded on the CCC's insistence on the unique particulars of the historic features of the case. The CCC, whose decision was adopted with only one dissenting opinion, explicitly, albeit without further explanation, refers to the 'constitutional identity of the Czech Republic, drawing from the common constitutional tradition with the Slovak Republic, that is from the over seventy years of the common state and its peaceful dissolution, ie, from a completely idiosyncratic and historically created situation that has no parallel in Europe'.

Therefore, when considered from the perspective of the identity of the constitution employed in this chapter, the case may be related to the 'whose constitution' element of the analysis because it impliedly deals with the sensitive question of how to interpret the Czech (Czechoslovak) past and what implications it may have for the constitutional rights of Czech citizens. On the other hand, the arguments employed by the CCC do not seem ethnoculturally based and remain in the sphere of a civic understanding of identity.

It is impossible to overlook here the much older (pre-EU accession) *Dreithaler* case decided by the 'first' CCC[60] in which the CCC firmly upheld the legality and legitimacy of the so-called Beneš decrees issued during and after World War II, including a decree on the confiscation of enemy property which targeted, inter alia, German and Hungarian populations and their property in the territory of Czechoslovakia (in order to escape confiscation, they had to prove some active support of the resistance against the occupation or suffering under the Nazi regime).[61] The petitioner argued that not only did the decrees lack the required legal basis pursuant to the Czechoslovak Constitution of 1920 but also that they violated human rights standards. The CCC resolutely dismissed the petitioner's claim and, while rejecting it mainly by using the argument that the confiscation decree no longer had constitutive effects and did not establish any new legal relationships, it devoted many pages explaining why it rejected the petitioner's assessment of the relevant historical period. Again, a strong perception of the need to define and defend 'who we are' and 'how we lived' is clearly visible in the CCC's argument, with emphasis on continuity with the Czechoslovak statehood.

Despite their different time context, both the *Slovak Pensions* case and the *Dreithaler* case may be considered as part of the 'transitional' case law of the CCC, dealing with sensitive legal issues with important historic and unique features stemming from the past Czechoslovak experience.[62] With this fact in mind, the question arises whether and how much the *Slovak Pensions* constitutional identity remark was influenced by this transitional context and whether

[60] The CCC under the presidency of Chief Justice Zdeněk Kessler (1993–2003).

[61] Ruling of 8 March 1995 File No Pl ÚS 14/94 (*Dreithaler*).

[62] This aspect of the *Slovak Pensions* case was remarked by Katarína Šipulová during the workshop of this monograph's authors.

the CCC will elaborate on this identity discourse – explicitly historically influenced – in its future case law.

All in all, the case law confirms the mutual link between the Czech citizenship and its EU citizenship dimension, which translates to the EU-friendly interpretation of citizens' constitutional rights under the Czech Charter, as cases such as the *EAW* or the *European Parliament Electoral Threshold* rulings showed. On the other hand, the explicit reference to constitutional identity made in the *Slovak Pensions* case and the way the CCC argued in this case may suggest that the 'whose constitution' element of the identity of the constitution is an especially sensitive area in which the preparedness of the CCC to employ particularism may materialise, perhaps in combination with some particular (because historically specific) interpretation of the entrenched principles protected by Article 9(2) of the Constitution.[63]

IV. A FEW NOTES ON THE CONCEPT OF CZECH NATIONAL IDENTITY

Any analysis of constitutional identity in its various understandings presented in political and legal theory should reflect the decision-making of the highest judicial bodies in the relevant constitutional polity. Provided that constitutional identity is analysed as identity of the constitution in the sense of the main legal (set of) norm(s) in the state, such a reflection seems indispensable. The importance of the CCC's case law in this regard is beyond question.

That being said, the CCC's jurisdiction is limited to cases which are filed by subjects authorised to initiate proceedings before the CCC[64] and there are important constitutionally relevant issues which are settled extra-judicially or may not get to the CCC. In addition, the CCC is only one of the participants in the constitutional dialogue, accompanied by other top constitutional bodies – especially the bicameral Parliament, the head of state, the government and top judicial institutions – and, more generally, by the civil society. Therefore, after searching for and analysing the instruments of and elements in the jurisprudence of particularism in the CCC's case law, instances of the *idea* and *policies* of particularism in the other parts of the public domain should be studied

[63] The idea of particularist elements in the otherwise universal 'essentials of the democratic state governed by the rule of law' is studied in Tomoszek (n 6). The unique Czechoslovak historical experience as an important element in the interpretation of citizens' constitutional rights protected by the Czech Charter is linked to the concept of 'constitutional identity' in two dissenting opinions of Judge Kateřina Šimáčková to resolutions of the CCC File No Pl ÚS 10/20 and Pl ÚS 13/20, n 10.

[64] Proceedings before the CCC are regulated by Act No 182/1993 Coll, on the Constitutional Court, as amended. For instance, some of the main cases of the CCC studied in this chapter (eg, the *Melčák* and *Slovak Pensions* cases) were initiated by individuals via the constitutional complaint procedure and, without their initiative, the Court would not be able to deal with the relevant constitutional issues.

because they contribute to the legal and political life in which the CCC operates and may be asked to intervene in the future. Indeed, the contents and directions of constitutional identity have been understood as developing from dialogical (indeed polylogical) processes in a democracy.[65]

Because the central focus of this chapter is on the case law of the CCC, these instances of particularism cannot be explored here in any reasonable detail and in an academically responsible way. However, in light of the suggestion in the previous parts of this chapter that the 'whose constitution' element of the identity of the constitution may reveal as a sensitive area and provide room for the jurisprudence of particularism, the chapter should make at least a few remarks concerning the Czech debate on the concept of national identity (in the sense of the identity of the Czech nation). The debates on how to conceive national identity date back to at least the nineteenth century period of national awakening and the circumstances before and after the establishment of Czechoslovakia in 1918, to the history of the state during World War II and afterwards, as well as the period of federation and its eventual dissolution in 1992. Even this quick overview shows that in the Czech (Czechoslovak) history, the question of 'who we are' (what defines us, what ideals shape us) was always an important issue, as was the issue of possible overlapping or, on the other hand, divergent national identities – especially during the existence of Czechoslovakia.

In modern vocabulary, the question posed is whether the Czech national identity is based (or should be based) on the loyalty to liberal constitutional values (constitutional patriotism) or whether it involves (or should involve) some other unifying (but – on the other hand – also dividing) features such as common history narratives, language, customs, religious traditions.[66] The question gained a new momentum in the context of the 2015 migration wave, in which the Czech Republic participated in the concerted action with Poland and Hungary in refusing the temporary obligatory mechanism for the relocation of applicants for international protection, which resulted in the ECJ's judgment declaring the infringement of these states' EU obligations.[67]

The issue of national identity is narrowly linked to the constituent subject element of constitutional identity and may, therefore, influence the CCC's

[65] GJ Jacobsohn, 'The Formation of Constitutional Identities' in T Ginsburg and R Dixon (eds), *Comparative Constitutional Law* (Cheltenham, Edward Elgar, 2011) 129. See also the introductory chapter in this volume.

[66] J Habermas, *Between Facts and Norms: Contributions to a Discourse Theory of Law and Democracy* (Cambridge, Mass, Polity Press, 1996); J Rawls, *Political Liberalism* (New York, Columbia University Press, 1996); M Seymour (ed), *The Fate of the Nation State* (Montreal, McGill-Queen's University Press, 2004); D Miller, *Citizenship and National Identity* (Cambridge, Mass, Polity Press, 2000); L Orgad, *The Cultural Defense of Nations. A Liberal Theory of Majority Rights* (Oxford, Oxford University Press, 2015). The topic of identity in the European but also Czech and Central European context is a long-term topic of writings of J Přibáň (n 6), and also *Legal Symbolism. On Law, Time and European Identity* (London, Routledge, 2017).

[67] Joined Cases C–715/17, C–718/17 and C–719/17 *Commission v Poland, Hungary and Czech Republic* (2020) ECLI:EU:C:2020:257.

interpretation of the identity of the constitution in this regard. It is a true observation that the concepts of the Czech nation and of Czech national interests (deeply influenced by historic – and therefore also linguistic, cultural, religious and other factors) still have substantial weight for a considerable part of the Czech society (the authors call it 'popular constitutional identity').[68] These views translate to the political representatives and may stimulate *policies* of particularism that can be expressed through *acts* of particularism. It is impossible to foresee how the CCC would react if it were asked to intervene in the name of constitutionality. As emphasised above, the Constitution is based on the civic understanding of the constituent subject. Still, the CCC's answer could be very context sensitive. The legal problem might concern a clear negation of the attained protection of human rights and the CCC would almost certainly reach a holding of unconstitutionality. Or, in a different context, the CCC might consider the matter a 'political question' or a matter in which the discretion of the legislature should be respected and exercise self-restraint.[69]

As regards the EU, the important question is to what extent these positions of particularism have exclusionary effects, how they develop in the process of political communication and how willing society will be to adjust its expectations with the need to accommodate wider European interests, while listening to the relevant arguments and, importantly, while also having the feeling of recognition that it is also heard and listened to. Put very generally, the issue is how the Czech society will coexist with the image of the civic understanding of the constituent subject in the Constitution and, at the same time, the image of a responsible member of the larger supranational EU in the circumstances of our rapidly changing world.

V. SUMMARY AND CONCLUSION

The CCC has only scarcely used the vocabulary of constitutional or national identity so far and has not provided a comprehensive understanding of the concepts. Czech authors who have dealt with the concept of constitutional identity of the Czech Republic, mostly consider it as equivalent to the entrenched principles of the constitutional order – the essentials of the democratic state governed by the rule of law (Article 9(2) of the Constitution) or as an equivalent of the substantive core of the constitution, usually understood as depicting the

[68] Kosař and Vyhnánek (n 2) 94.

[69] J Malíř, 'The Czech Constitutional Court and The Political Question Doctrine: A Contribution to the Debate on The Demise of the Political Question Doctrine' (submitted for publication). For instance, the CCC is of the opinion that changes concerning family, marriage, parenthood or adult-child relationships belong to issues which are better suited for the decision of the legislature than of the CCC (ruling of 19 November 2015 File No Pl ÚS 10/15, para 36 or ruling of 15 December 2020 File No Pl ÚS 6/20, para 32).

main structural features of the constitutional system (some of which are not viewed as entrenched principles). This chapter was methodologically inspired by the three-part analysis of the identity of the constitution proposed by Drinóczi and looked at what the Czech Constitution says about the principle of procedural sameness, the entrenched principles and the designation of the state and of the constituent subject and how the case law of the CCC is relevant in this regard.

The CCC has developed a system of strong defensive tools protecting the 'essentials of the democratic state governed by the rule of law' and the 'power attributes of state sovereignty', as exemplified by the ruling Pl ÚS 36/01 on the position of human rights treaties in the constitutional system (the imperative to construe constitutional amendments always in harmony with Article 9(2)), the *Melčák* ruling (the power of the CCC to review and strike down constitutional statutes) as well as the EU-related cases such as the *Sugar Quotas III* and the *Lisbon I and II* cases. Even though this line of case law can be considered as providing instruments for potential jurisprudence of particularism in the relationship towards EU law in the future, the general approach of the CCC in construing the relevant concepts of state sovereignty, democracy and substantive rule of law is not particularistic and reflects the modified meaning of these constitutional principles in the circumstances of a supranational organisation. Moreover, the CCC understands state sovereignty as not an aim in and of itself but stresses its instrumental role in the protection of fundamental constitutional values and the principle of substantive rule of law.

The CCC's case law relevant for the 'whose constitution' element of the identity of the constitution generally acknowledges a strong EU dimension of the Czech citizenship and civic rights pertaining to it, as shown by the *EAW* or *European Parliament Electoral Threshold* cases. The *Slovak Pensions* case is the most obvious example of the jurisprudence of particularism in this regard, analysed in this chapter as a combination of the exercise of the ultra vires review in combination with a strong identity claim relating to the determination of who we are (were), how we construe our past and what it says about present legal problems. Even though the *Slovak Pensions* case is extraordinary in the CCC's case law concerning the EU law, the chapter suggested that the 'whose constitution' element of the identity of the constitution might reveal a potential space for the jurisprudence of particularism in the future because the CCC defended its approach to the interpretation of the relevant Czech citizens' constitutional right by explicit reference to the concept of constitutional identity drawn from the unique Czech (Czechoslovak) historical experience.

The chapter further briefly noted the ongoing debate about the concept (or rather various conceptions) of the Czech national identity and its historical context and pointed out its potential implications for policies of particularism in the Czech public space. The CCC's approach to possible assertions of particularism in the future, including in the sphere of the Czech Republic's obligations stemming from the EU law, is difficult to foresee. While the Constitution is built on the civic understanding of the constituent subject, the CCC's decision would most probably be context specific and may involve sensitive issues of the constitutional relationships between different branches of the separation of powers.

By way of conclusion, two final remarks must be made. In the context of the Czech legal system's relationship to EU law, the CCC views its role of the protector of the constitutional order as fundamental for the preservation of the state sovereignty (in the *Lisbon I* case the CCC declared that, provided it remains the final interpreter of the constitutional order, it follows that the principle of state sovereignty still holds).[70] In that same case, the CCC's final sentence mentions two determining factors guiding its decision-making: the fact that it is 'responsible to the people of the Czech Republic' but also that the reason behind this responsibility is to guarantee 'the constitutionality of a democratic, law-based state entrusted with the protection of inherent, inalienable, non-prescriptible and unrepealable fundamental rights and freedoms of individuals equal in dignity and in rights'.[71]

[70] *Lisbon I* ruling (n 10) para 216.
[71] ibid at para 217.

5

Constitutional Identity in Poland: Transplanted and Abused

MICHAŁ ZIÓŁKOWSKI

RESEARCH ON CONSTITUTIONAL identity, the identity of constitutions, their narratives, contexts, and methods of analysis fills thousands of pages.[1] A lot of what has been said depicts Polish constitutionalism accurately.[2] The Polish constitutional transformation of 1989–1992 and the long constitution-making process (1992–1997) reflected the nation's axiological and legal 'aspirations'[3] and constitutional 'long-standing commitments and sanctioned practices'.[4] They provided perfect material for building a constitutional identity.[5] However, constitutional identity researchers have to work in a somewhat difficult environment. The Polish Constitutional Tribunal (the Tribunal) explicitly applied the concept of constitutional identity only once: in 2010. It appeared in the context of European integration in a judgment regarding the Lisbon Treaty (the *Lisbon* case).[6] However, as this chapter shows, the Tribunal's understanding of identity was far from clear. In fact, it was a constitutional transplant rather than a genuinely local concept, the meaning having unfolded organically and incrementally. After the *Lisbon* case, the Tribunal has never explicitly revisited the concept of identity and never elaborated on it in case law. Identity had become a dormant concept until the Polish constitutional crisis started. Then, it began to reappear in 2021 and 2022 in the public debate

[1] See eg, the books of GJ Jacobsohn, *Constitutional Identity* (Cambridge, Mass, Harvard University Press, 2010) and M Rosenfeld, *The Identity of the Constitutional Subject* (London, Routledge, 2009).

[2] See more A Śledzińska-Simon, 'Constitutional identity in 3D: A Model of Individual, Relational, and Collective Self and its Application in Poland' (2005) 13 *International Journal of Constitutional Law* 124–55.

[3] Jacobsohn (n 1) 7.

[4] Jacobsohn (n 1) 345.

[5] More about the models, see M Rosenfeld, 'Constitutional identity' in M Rosenfeld and A Sajó (eds), *The Oxford Handbook of Comparative Constitutional Law* (Oxford, Oxford University Press, 2012) 756.

[6] Case K 32/09 [2010] CT.

and in motions submitted to the captured[7] and unconstitutionally composed[8] Tribunal. It became an abusive[9] weapon[10] to limit the EU law.

The chapter is underpinned by the supposition that constitutional case law creates a space in which constitutional identity may be reflected. Instead of theorising about the experience of Polish constitutional identity on a high and abstract level, the chapter takes a bottom-up perspective. It aims to show how the concept of constitutional identity appeared and where it resulted in the Tribunal's case law. It also discusses an attempt by the captured Tribunal to build a new constitutional identity in Poland. Thus, it is predominantly descriptive and interpretive, but it also offers normative suggestions.

Section I briefly recalls the Tribunal's statements in the *Lisbon* case. Section II discusses the constitutional background of the case and explains why the Tribunal did the transplant. Section III discusses the transplant's[11] scope and weakness. Section IV discusses how identity was abused by the captured Tribunal. It refers to the recent case law of the Tribunal concerning freedom of assembly, abortion and the independence of Polish courts. As I am going to argue, the cases represent an exclusionary vision of constitutional identity and follow the pattern of the jurisprudence of particularism.[12]

I. THE *LISBON* CASE

The Tribunal's judgment concerning the constitutionality of the Lisbon Treaty[13] and Polish constitutional identity[14] has been broadly discussed. For the purposes

[7] By the term I mean the unlawfully composed court between 2017 and 2022, and under the presidency of Julia Przyłębska.

[8] *Xero Flor v Poland*, App no 4907/18, Judgment of 7 May 2021, paras 255–75.

[9] I use this term following D Landau and R Dixon, 'Abusive Judicial Review: Courts Against Democracy' (2019) 53 *University of California Davis Law Review* 1313.

[10] Compare with the Hungarian example of abusive use of the identity's concept, K Kovács, 'The Rise of an Ethnocultural Constitutional Identity in the Jurisprudence of the East Central European Courts' (2017) 18 *German Law Journal* 1703–1720; G Halmai, 'Abuse of Constitutional Identity. The Hungarian Constitutional Court on the Interpretation of Article E) (2) of the Fundamental Law' (2018) 43 *Review of Central and East European Law* 23–42.

[11] I use the term 'transplant' in a neutral way as a synonym for borrowing – V Perju, 'Constitutional Transplants, Borrowing, and Migrations' in M Rosenfeld and A Sajó (eds), *The Oxford Handbook of Comparative Constitutional Law* (Oxford, Oxford University Press, 2012) 1308. My criticism concerning the particular transplant of constitutional identity in the *Lisbon* judgment does not imply any pejorative meaning of the term. There could be successful transplants.

[12] I use this term following the introductory chapter in this volume.

[13] See, eg, S Dudzik and N Półtorak, 'The Court of the Last Word: Competences of the Polish Constitutional Tribunal in the Review of European Union Law' (2012) 15 *Yearbook of Polish European Studies* 225–58; K Kowalik-Bańczyk, 'Sending Smoke Signals to Luxembourg – the Polish Constitutional Tribunal in Dialogue with the ECJ' in M Claes et al (eds), *Constitutional Conversations in Europe: Actors, Topics and Procedure* (Cambridge, Intersentia, 2012); K Wójtowicz, *Constitutional Courts and European Union law* (Wroclaw, University of Wroclaw E-Press, 2014).

[14] See the contributions of A Kustra, K Kowalik-Bańczyk, M Laskowska and M Taborowski published in S Dudzik and N Półtorak (eds), *Prawo Unii Europejskiej a prawo konstytucyjne państw członkowskich* (Warszawa, Wolters Kluwer Poland, 2013).

of this chapter, it is important to be reminded of only the following parts of the Tribunal's argumentation.[15]

At first, the Tribunal presented a narrow understanding of constitutional identity, which was portrayed as a list of powers that cannot be transferred to or conferred on any entity or organisation (such as another state, international organisation or the EU). Constitutional identity was directly linked to the concept of sovereignty, which had been interpreted by the Tribunal dynamically following the developments of international law.[16] This identity was considered respected as long as Poland remained a sovereign state within the meaning of international law. In other words, the identity could not be automatically violated by Poland's membership in an international or supranational organisation as long as the core of constitutional powers remained in the hands of the Polish constitutional authorities. The Tribunal did not explain what the core consisted of or what criteria could be applied to determining the core. Instead, it suggested that constitutional identity would be violated if the Tribunal failed to have the last word on the constitutionality of laws in Poland. The hypothetical situation of Parliament losing the power to enact laws became another example of violation of that identity.

Subsequently, the Tribunal offered a more detailed and far-reaching definition of identity[17] as

> a concept which determines the scope of 'excluding – from the competence to confer competences – the matters which constitute … "the heart of the matter", i.e. are fundamental to the basis of the political system of a given state' …, the conferral of which would not be possible pursuant to Article 90 of the Constitution. Regardless of the difficulties related to setting a detailed catalogue of inalienable competences, the following should be included among the matters under the complete prohibition of conferral: decisions specifying the fundamental principles of the Constitution and decisions concerning the rights of the individual which determine the identity of the state, including, in particular, the requirement of protection of human dignity and constitutional rights, the principle of statehood, the principle of democratic governance, the principle of a state ruled by law, the principle of social justice, the principle of subsidiarity, as well as the requirement of ensuring better implementation of constitutional values and the prohibition to confer the power to amend the Constitution and the competence to determine competences.[18]

Moreover, the Tribunal introduced a separate notion of 'Polish national identity', having 'European roots' and derived from the national history, tradition

[15] See also A Śledzińska-Simon and M Ziółkowski, 'Constitutional Identity in Poland: Is the Emperor Putting On the Old Clothes of Sovereignty?' in C Calliess and G van der Schyff (eds), *Constitutional Identity in a Europe of Multilevel Constitutionalism* (Cambridge, Cambridge University Press, 2020).

[16] Śledzińska-Simon and Ziółkowski (n 15) 249–55.

[17] Compare with the judgment on the Accession Treaty issued five years earlier – Case K 18/04 [2005] – or the judgment concerning the European Arrest Warrant – Case P 1/05 [2005], where the Tribunal had ruled substantially the same without references to constitutional identity.

[18] Case K 32/09 (n 6) para III.2.1.

and culture as well as European history.[19] However, the Tribunal's reasoning was terse regarding the specific meaning of this new notion and its potential impact on constitutional review. It referred to the Constitution's Preamble and the political and cultural definition[20] of the nation in the constitutional provisions. It only pointed to respect for national identity, in addition to constitutional identity, being a 'significant constitutional clause'. This might have been a hint that the Tribunal operated with two different but substantially interrelated concepts of identity. First, the legal and narrow concept of constitutional identity covered institutions and powers. Second, the cultural concept of national identity covered Polish historical and cultural commitments and aspirations, as it was expressed in the Constitution's Preamble.[21]

Finally, the Tribunal stressed shared values ('axiological identity' to use the Tribunal's words) between Poland and the EU and found that the concept of constitutional identity corresponded to the concept of national identity under Article 4(2) TEU. The two were not necessarily exact synonyms, according to the Tribunal, but the judicial concept of constitutional identity assumed 'axiological sameness of the Republic of Poland with the European Union as a community of values'.[22]

Following the *Lisbon* case, the Tribunal had several opportunities to clarify the concept of constitutional identity, for instance, in judgments concerning the constitutionality of EU secondary law,[23] provisions on the stability mechanism for the Member States whose currency was the euro[24] or limitations imposed on gambling in breach of EU notification requirements.[25] However, the Tribunal did not reiterate the nebulous formula of constitutional and national identities. It confined itself to a generic formula, according to which constitutional identity is the ultimate limit for conferral of powers upon the EU. Moreover, between 2010 and 2016, there were no other cases in which the constitutional identity formula was invoked. Even in the face of an unprecedented attack of the political majority on fundamental constitutional principles and institutional arrangements,[26] the Tribunal decided not to use the concept of identity again. Striking down the laws hindering constitutional review, introduced by the Law and Justice party in 2015 and 2016, the Tribunal abstained from mentioning

[19] Case K 32/09 (n 6) para III.2.2.

[20] See also Case K 28/13 [2015] CT.

[21] The Preamble in Poland is a part of the normative text. Thus, it has its legal standing. It became the source of several legal norms – Case K 24/02 [2003] CT. Therefore, it is not surprising that the Tribunal referred to the Preamble in the *Lisbon* case, looking for identity. More on Preambles and identity, see Jacobsohn (n 1) 13, 106, 118, 189.

[22] Śledzińska-Simon and Ziółkowski (n 15) 255.

[23] Case SK 45/09 [2011] CT.

[24] Case K 33/12 [2013] CT.

[25] Case P 4/14 [2015] CT.

[26] For more on this, see W Sadurski, *Poland's Constitutional Breakdown* (Oxford, Oxford University Press, 2019).

constitutional identity as a basic structure or constitutional core that could limit the Parliament.[27] Such a change in the Tribunal's narrative cannot be ignored when we consider the Tribunal's regular practice of self-referencing and extensive citations from existing case law. One of the Tribunal's judges even suggested in his concurring opinion that it had been to the Tribunal's disadvantage that it failed to delve into the concept of identity after the Lisbon case.[28]

The Tribunal's understanding of identity in the Lisbon case and the fact that it was abandoned in subsequent cases provoked numerous questions from legal scholars and commentators. The Tribunal seemed to have stopped halfway through the constitutional development of the doctrinal concept. It added a new term to its dictionary, including its possible variations. It linked these variations to pre-existing terms such as sovereignty and conferral of powers, while emphasising their heterogeneity. Finally, it did not offer any criteria for the introduced novelty (other than comparative ones, which are discussed in section II of this chapter).

We might argue that the Tribunal's understanding of identity is equivalent to what was called an absolute limit for the conferral of powers upon the EU in the first judgments concerning Poland's membership in the EU. Consequently, the Tribunal's concept of identity focuses on the division of powers and institutional arrangements in the very particular context of EU integration. The identity would be nothing more than a judicial shield and sword[29] or a rhetorical strategy[30] against transferring too much power to the EU. It should not be extrapolated to other constitutional discourses (such as identity as a basic structure, limits of constitutional amendments, justification of transitional solutions or common constitutional values). However, such a narrow interpretation of the Tribunal's formula of identity would make it redundant because of the well-established doctrine of the conferral of powers. Moreover, this approach would make the Tribunal's concept of 'national identity' an empty vessel.

Yet, we could also argue that the Tribunal attempted to introduce a new concept at the national constitutional level. The well-established understanding of conferral of powers upon a supranational entity (coming from the previous judgments) alone was enough to decide the *Lisbon* case. Nevertheless, the Tribunal decided to introduce a new concept of identity, which involves more 'passion'[31] and politics than technical terms like 'eternity clause', 'substantive

[27] Case K 34/15 [2015] CT; Case K 47/15 [2016] CT; Case K 39/16 [2016] CT.

[28] Case K 33/12 (n 24) (separate opinion of judge Mirosław Granat).

[29] In a broader context, see T Konstadinides, 'Constitutional Identity as a Shield and as a Sword: The European Legal Order within the Framework of National Constitutional Settlement' (2011) 13 *Cambridge Yearbook of European Legal Studies* 195–218.

[30] In a broader context, see D Kelemen and L Pech, 'Why Autocrats Love Constitutional Identity and Constitutional Pluralism: Lessons from Hungary and Poland' (2018) 2 *RECONNECT Europe Working Paper*.

[31] D Kosař and L Vyhnánek, 'Constitutional Identity in the Czech Republic. A New Twist on an Old-Fashioned Idea?', in C Calliess and G van der Schyff (n 15) 112.

core' or 'conferral of powers'. The Tribunal sketched identity, sovereignty and the conferral of powers as three interrelated but substantially separate concepts.

This chapter explores the second possible interpretation of the *Lisbon* case. Trying to rationalise the nebulous understanding of identity offered by the Tribunal (or trying to save it under Article 90 of the Constitution) the contributions of legal scholars have so far neglected at least one alternative interpretation of the *Lisbon* case. The contributions have not explored the possibility of identity being a careless transplant, reflecting the judges' constitutional aspirations and preferences rather than a constitutionally rooted legal concept.

II. WHY THE TRANSPLANT?

Before I unpack this chapter's central argument and discuss the transplant and its output in more detail, it should be explained why the Tribunal made the transplant in the first place. My answer is simple: the Tribunal acted under doctrinally challenging conditions. The concept was well-known in the comparative law literature, but in the domestic context it had not yet been explored. What the Tribunal did seems to be an example of a 'cost-saving'[32] decision rather than an original contribution to the development of domestic constitutional law. Instead of resolving unsettled scholarly disputes or taking a big judicial leap regarding constitutional interpretation to root the concept, the Tribunal used a concept tested by other constitutional courts. The arguments that follow may support this view.

The concept of constitutional identity was not broadly discussed when the Constitution was being made in Poland. The concept did not appear in the debate within the Constitutional Committee of the National Assembly, which was responsible for drafting the new Constitution. Nor had it been explored by the constitutionalists of that time. This does not mean that Poland's prolonged constitutional moment (or lack of the typical constitutional moment[33]) cannot inform us about constitutional identity. It means only that the Tribunal in 2010, when deciding the *Lisbon* case, had no direct legal sources, academic reports or empirical studies in law, coming from the constitution-making moment, on how constitutional identity was understood. The Tribunal refrained from carrying out its own research. As a result, the *Lisbon* judgment did not consider the possible links between the constitution-making moment and constitutional identity.

Neither the constitutional identity of a state nor the constitutional identity of a constitution itself is a concept directly based on the Constitution's text in Poland. This has never been the case, since 1921, when the first democratic

[32] GJ Jacobsohn, 'The Permeability of Constitutional Borders' (2004) 82 *Texas Law Review* 1763.

[33] A Sajó, 'Constitution without the Constitutional Moment: A View from the New Member States' (2005) 3 *International Journal of Constitutional Law* 243.

constitution was adopted in Poland. None of the Polish constitutions (1921, 1935 or 1952) and none of the constitutional laws adopted between 1947 and 1997, referred to the notion of 'identity'; let alone 'constitutional identity'. The notion appeared in Articles 6 (concerning the protection of cultural heritage) and 35 (concerning the protection of minorities) of the 1997 Constitution. However, those parts of the constitutional text have not been elaborated on in the Tribunal's case law so far. Neither the judgments concerning minorities nor the judgments referring to the constitutional concept of the nation[34] explored the notion of identity. The Tribunal used the notion of identity with three different meanings. Identity became a synonym for (i) sameness of two or more institutions, (ii) principle of equality, or (iii) the core of a particular institution (such as 'constitutional identity of a court').[35] None of these references reflected the contemporary discourses on constitutional identity.[36] This does not mean that Article 6 of the Constitution and well-established case law cannot serve as the basis for a fruitful theoretical or doctrinal exploration of the concept of constitutional identity. It only means that the Tribunal, when it mentioned identity for the first time in 2010, had no express constitutional text or previous case law to build on. Since the Tribunal refrained from carrying out its own research regarding Articles 6 and 35 of the Constitution, the notion of 'national identity' in the *Lisbon* case became related to the constitutional text only to a limited extent.

The Tribunal's difficulty in expounding constitutional identity was intensified by a lack of eternity clauses or relatively unamendable constitutional provisions similar to ones included in the Czech, Italian or German constitutions. These are often used on the national and comparative planes to discuss constitutional identity as the constitution's basic structure or as the constitutional order's core elements, which cannot be changed. Constitutional identity as a limit for a substantive constitutional amendment appears in constitutional courts' judgments when they assess the constitutionality of constitutional amendments. However, the text of the Polish Constitution does not necessarily support this way of understanding constitutional identity, and it never did in the past. None of the previous constitutions directly provided substantive limits to constitutional amendments. Such a concept has gained little support from academics in Poland so far.[37] Moreover, the Tribunal has had no opportunity to explore the concept of identity as a limitation to constitutional amendment as there has not been even a single case concerning the unconstitutionality of a constitutional amendment in Poland.

[34] See, eg, case K 18/04 (n 17).

[35] Śledzińska-Simon and Ziółkowski (n 15) 247.

[36] For more on the discourses, see M Polzin, 'Constitutional Identity as a Constructed Reality and a Restless Soul' (2019) 18 *German Law Journal* 1597.

[37] Constitutional identity as the limit for constitutional amendment is suggested by M Granat and K Granat, *The Constitution of Poland. A Contextual Analysis* (Oxford, Hart, 2019) 239–40.

Finally, neither the constitutional law scholarship in Poland nor the Polish constitutional case law developed a historical constitution concept, such as the one developed in Hungary,[38] which could have been an impetus for discussion on constitutional identity.

In sum, when the Tribunal made, back in 2010, the first ever reference to constitutional identity, it had no express (and ready to use) constitutional provisions, nor doctrinal or empirical legal analyses. None of the discourses[39] concerning constitutional identity had been resolved in Poland before the Tribunal decided the *Lisbon* case. If the Tribunal had wanted to root constitutional identity in Polish constitutional history, culture, provisions and developments, it would have made a big judicial leap in constitutional interpretation. The Tribunal would have to either interpret constitutional provisions extensively in a broader socio-historical context, or it would have to take a clear position in one of the doctrinal disputes (such as the disputes concerning the importance of the constitution-making moment, relatively unchangeable constitutional provisions or substantial constitutional core).

We might argue that the Tribunal's concept of identity became constitutionally unrooted. The Tribunal had not taken the opportunities the *Lisbon* case created. Yet, we might say that the Tribunal did not have to take the opportunities since the concept of identity was developed in foreign jurisdictions. In my view, avoiding a deeper constitutional justification for identity and deciding for the transplant was not necessarily good or bad in itself. The assessment depends on the answer to the question about how the Tribunal made that transplant?

III. THE TRANSPLANT

This section discusses constitutional identity as a concept that has been transplanted by the Tribunal from foreign case law and one that was not necessarily well adapted to the Polish constitutional framework.

The Tribunal explicitly admitted that the case law of other constitutional courts concerning the Lisbon Treaty became a point of reference when the Tribunal 'specifi[ed] the constitutional principles concerning the state of Poland's sovereignty in the context of European integration'.[40]

However, when defining constitutional identity, the Tribunal chose only one of the doctrinal studies, mentioned it as a reference, and openly approved the definition provided in an eminent book on conferral of powers upon a supranational organisation, written by Krzysztof Wojtyczek.[41] In the book, Poland's

[38] See chapter six in this volume.

[39] Polzin (n 36) 1604.

[40] Case K 32/09 (n 6), para III.1.3. *in fine*.

[41] K Wojtyczek, *Przekazywanie kompetencji panstwa organizacjom miedzynarodowym* (Krakow, Jagiellonian University Press, 2007) 261–62.

constitutional identity is understood as a set of core constitutional principles of a liberal democratic state ruled by law.[42] And the Tribunal's definition of constitutional identity in the *Lisbon* case is a verbatim repetition of the core constitutional principles recognised by Wojtyczek.[43] It is true that Wojtyczek's book deals primarily with Polish constitutional law, however, comparative research substantially underpins it.[44] A careful examination of Wojtyczek's original and doctrinal contribution reveals an exact understanding of constitutional identity, which was influenced and inspired by German constitutional law.[45] When the Tribunal applied Wojtyczek's understanding of constitutional identity, consciously or unconsciously, it also followed his inspirations from the German Basic Law.

Still, an important part of the justification in the *Lisbon case* concerned constitutional identity in the judgments given by constitutional courts in Germany, Czechia and France.[46] The Tribunal referred to foreign case law for three reasons. The first was to confirm a consensus among constitutional courts regarding the conformity of the Lisbon Treaty with national constitutions.[47] The second was to ensure that the common constitutional traditions of EU Member States were essential premises for constitutional review of the treaties.[48] The third reason was to find a supporting or ready-to-use concept of constitutional identity. According to the Tribunal:

> A common characteristic of those adjudications is the emphasis on the openness of the constitutional order with regard to European integration, and the focus on the significance of constitutional and systemic identity – and thus sovereignty – of the Member States, the respect for which excludes the possibility of any presumed amendment to a national constitution and, in particular, as regards the rules of the conferral of competences which arise from a given constitution.[49]

[42] Wojtyczek was an assistant to one of the Tribunal's judges before the *Lisbon* case was decided. Now he is a constitutional law professor at Jagiellonian University and the Polish judge of the ECtHR.

[43] Compare case K 32/09 (n 6) para III.2.1 Wojtyczek (n 41) 284–302.

[44] Wojtyczek (n 41) 14. The author expressly states that the scope of his book is limited to Polish constitutional law. However, at the same time, the author pointed out that German constitutional law developments concerning Articles 23 and 24 of the GBL could be important inspirations in evaluation and interpretation of the Polish constitutional provisions.

[45] Wojtyczek (n 41) 285, 287, 302, 364.

[46] The Tribunal also referred to judgments of constitutional courts in Austria, Latvia and Hungary. However, the references were so short and descriptive that they cannot be considered decisive.

[47] Case K 32/09 (n 6) para III.3.1.

[48] Case K 32/09 (n 6) para III.3.8. ('Despite such circumstances, arising from the variety of constitutional regulations, the jurisprudence of European constitutional courts concerning the Treaty of Lisbon confirms the solemn character of constitutional traditions, which are common to the Member States, and which constitute a vital premiss of adjudicating in the present case'.)

[49] Case K 32/09 (n 6) para III.3.1. ('European constitutional courts confirm the significance of the principle of sovereignty reflected in the provisions of the state's constitution, due to which the assessment of the Treaty of Lisbon is carried out in the regard indicated by the applicants'.)

The Tribunal's claims based on comparative law should be considered with caution for the following reasons. First, the Tribunal's suggestion that the constitutional courts in Czechia, Germany and France underlined the 'significance of constitutional and systemic identity' and used the concepts in their decisions concerning the Lisbon Treaty was misleading. While the protection of constitutional identity became one of the most important elements of the *Lissabon-Urteil*,[50] the core of the French Conseil Constitutionnel decisions (concerning the treaties) did not develop the concept of constitutional identity.[51] The Conseil Constitutionnel focused on sovereignty instead. Moreover, it did not frame constitutional identity in such an extensive[52] and firm[53] way as the German Federal Constitutional Court (FCC). Similarly, constitutional identity had not been explored in the Czech cases concerning the Lisbon Treaty. It only appeared later, after the Polish case had already been decided.[54] Second, as the national and comparative studies show, the ways constitutional identity is understood in France, Czechia and Germany are slightly different because of the eternity clauses and different historical backgrounds. Moreover, the tone and context of the foreign judgments mentioned by the Tribunal were different. In particular, the Czech CC 'adopted a very euro-friendly interpretation of the Czech constitutional order and by doing so distanced itself from the rather assertive *Lissabon-Urteil* of the *Bundersverfassungsgericht*'.[55] Third, in its comparison the Tribunal took no note of the difference between the constitutional identity of a state and the identity of a constitution,[56] as pointed out by the FCC. The fourth reason is that the Tribunal's use of the comparative argument did not take into account the fact that the constitutions in France, Czechia and Germany refer to the EU, integration and limits of constitutional change, whereas the Polish constitutional text does not. Nevertheless, the Tribunal concluded:

> The jurisprudence of European constitutional courts included the view that the provisions of the Treaty of Lisbon were consistent with the national constitutions. At the same time, the focus was also placed on the significance of the constitutions and

[50] BVerfGE 123, 267.

[51] The 'Conseil has never defined' the identity – F-X Millet, 'Constitutional Identity in France: Vices and – Above All – Virtues' in C Calliess and G van der Schyff (n 15) 146.

[52] The identity review in France does not regard the Treaties itself. As Millet observed 'until recently, identity review was very limited in scope: it only concerned directives and even more specifically the statutes designed to transpose directives. It was recently broadened to include EU regulation and international agreements concluded by the EU'. F-X Millet (n 51) 142.

[53] Kovács (n 10) 1718.

[54] Kosař and Vyhnánek (n 31) 86, observed, 'surprisingly the Czech Constitutional Court did not engage with the concept of constitutional identity adequately in either of these two judgments. In fact, it has not referred to the concept of "constitutional identity" in any decision in its entire body of case-law apart from one sentence in the Holubec judgment'.

[55] ibid at 85.

[56] The Tribunal's distinction between constitutional and national identity did not cover the identity of a constitution (as a normative act on a particular basic structure; fundamental and unchangeable settings).

> statutes of the Member States as regards guaranteeing their sovereignty and national identity, which is clearly reflected in the judgment of the Federal Constitutional Court of Germany (of 30 June 2009). … The constitutional courts of the Member States share – as a vital part of European constitutional traditions – the view that the constitution is of fundamental significance as it reflects and guarantees the state's sovereignty at the present stage of European integration, and also that the constitutional judiciary plays a unique role regards the protection of the constitutional identity of the Member States, which at the same time determines the treaty identity of the European Union.[57]

Reading the comparative part of the *Lisbon* judgment in conjunction with the Tribunal's identity formula and further case law suggests that the references to French and Czech case law were only ornamental.[58] If the Tribunal had indeed sought to compare and find common patterns concerning constitutional identity as a driving force for its judgment, it would have had to notice at least the differences between French and German approaches to sovereignty and substantive limits to constitutional amendment. The Tribunal would have also had to avoid references to 'national identity' since different understandings of 'nation' had appeared in different jurisdictions. The Tribunal's conclusion suggests that the judges had been primarily oriented to the FCC's understanding of constitutional identity. The following observations support that view.

The Tribunal linked constitutional identity with human dignity and the liberal democratic state ruled by law (rather than the sovereignty of people or the rule of law). The Tribunal, however, did not refer to any particular understanding of Polish democracy, like the FCC did when it linked identity to the 'German understanding of democracy'.[59] Moreover, contrary to the FCC, the Tribunal never explored the principle of democracy as a source of the constitutional right to challenge EU law.

The Tribunal underlined that the concept of constitutional identity assumes an openness of the Polish constitutional order towards supranational integration. Therefore, the starting point for the review of constitutional identity should always be an attempt to find an 'EU-friendly' interpretation of the Polish Constitution. Such 'EU-friendly' interpretation is limited by 'the explicit wording of constitutional norms'[60] and 'the minimum of the guarantee functions fulfilled by the Constitution'.[61] The dialogue with the ECJ underpins this approach. However, it does not mean the Tribunal preferred to follow the ECJ's

[57] Case K 32/09 (n 6) para III.3.8. *in fine*.

[58] But see Granat and Granat (n 37) 240. They observed that the definition of constitutional identity 'adopted by the Tribunal is arguably similar to the approach taken by the constitutional courts of France and Germany'. (Mirosław Granat was a judge sitting on the panel of the Tribunal in the *Lisbon* case.)

[59] Kovács (n 10) 1719.

[60] Case K 2/02. Repeated in Case K 32/09 (n 6).

[61] Case K 18/04 (n 17). Repeated in Case K 32/09 (n 6).

interpretations concerning identity.[62] Like the FCC,[63] the Tribunal emphasised that the national and EU notions and concepts have an autonomous nature.

Moreover, the Tribunal hid all possible judicial tools of review in the concept of identity in a similar way as did the FCC. The Tribunal's understanding of identity in conjunction with other parts of the *Lisbon* case[64] suggests that the Tribunal reserved for itself: human rights review, ultra vires review,[65] and identity review.[66] The significant difference is, however, that the Tribunal in the *Lisbon* case had not been linguistically direct like the FCC, when suggesting the scope of the review.[67] Interpreting the *Lisbon* case one year later, the Tribunal directly pointed out that its approach to the constitutional review of the EU law is similar to the FCC.[68]

Finally, the internal logic of the Tribunal in the *Lisbon* case is very close to what the FCC adopted. Since none of Poland's constitutional provisions refers to the EU, integration, constitutional core or eternity clause, the Tribunal hinged the whole concept of constitutional identity on Article 90 of the Constitution. The Tribunal attempted to transform Article 90 in the image of Article 23(1) in conjunction with Article 79(3) of the GBL. In a similar way to the German cases, the Tribunal's interpretation of Article 90 of the Constitution implies: (a) a minimum of an internal hierarchy of constitutional regulations, that allowed the Tribunal to separate what could be the subject of conferral and what could not (covered by identity); (b) a unique position of the Tribunal itself to be an ultimate 'guardian of the constitution' and 'guardian of identity'; (c) a unique ability of the Tribunal to recognise the scope of the identity; (d) a monistic approach to the validity and precedence of the constitution (it always has to be binding and applied) mixed up with the dualistic approach to the validity and precedence of the EU law (it may be valid, but it cannot be applied when the Tribunal rules on its unconstitutionality).

Supposing the suggestion above is correct and will resonate with the pending empirical studies on what the Tribunal's judges think about Polish constitutional identity, the *Lisbon* case could be seen to be less about the new constitutional contribution of the Tribunal and more about what judges read[69] and how judges

[62] Cases K 32/09 (n 6) and SK 45/09 (n 23).

[63] I follow Christian Callies's interpretation that the notion of constitutional identity in *Lissabon-Urteil* covers three review tools. C Callies, 'Constitutional Identity in Germany. One for Three or Three in One?' in C Calliess and G van der Schyff (n 15) 169.

[64] See cases SK 45/09 (n 23) and K 33/12 (n 24).

[65] Case K 32/09 (n 6) para III.2.2. *in fine*.

[66] It should be however underlined that the Tribunal only proclaimed the identity review and has not used it so far.

[67] Case K 32/09 (n 6) para III.2.3. *in principio*.

[68] Case SK 45/09 (n 23) paras III.8.2 and 8.4.

[69] More on that kind of judge's motivations to do comparative argument, see V Jackson, *Constitutional Engagement in a Transnational Era* (Oxford, Oxford University Press, 2013).

became engaged in a debate on identity. Therefore, identity could be analysed more as a dialogical experience of judges.[70]

IV. THE ABUSE

The careless nature of the Tribunal's transplant in the *Lisbon* case opens the door for abusive use of constitutional and national identities to justify particularism. The internal contradictions in the Tribunal's identity formula, lack of a minimum level of substantive precision and criteria left a powerful[71] judicial tool in the hands of the captured Tribunal.

How powerful this tool may be became clear recently from the statements made by Lech Morawski,[72] Mariusz Muszyński[73] and Jarosław Wyrembak[74] – the three unlawfully elected judges of the captured Tribunal. They all explored constitutional identity as justification of Polish constitutional particularism or an absolute exception from the principles of primacy and effect of EU law.

[70] Identity 'exists neither as a distinctive object of invention nor as a heavily encrusted essence embedded in a society's culture, requiring only to be discovered' – Jacobsohn (n 1) 7.

[71] Compare with Kelemen and Pech (n 30).

[72] Polish identity was built on an experience of 150 years of loss of independence, World War II and the communist period. One of the most critical consequences became a division between Poles of those who expected a 'strong', 'independent' state built on traditional values and those who aimed at closer cooperation with other European states and organizations, including the EU. Morawski pointed out that the division had been clearly visible in a dispute between the Law and Justice government (defending state sovereignty) and its opposition (proclaiming the complete dependence on the EU). He argued that the dominant interpretation of TEU had not taken into account that constitutional identity will be based on differently understood common and particular values of national origin. Morawski's understanding of identity was aimed to expose political, cultural and legal differences between the Member States and legitimise acts of the governmental party. Morawski underlined that the European Commission and Venice Commission had not demonstrated an understanding of the Polish constitutional particularism (L Morawski, 'A Critical Response', *VerfassungsBlog*, 2017/6/03, http://verfassungsblog.de/a-critical-response/).

[73] In his separate opinion concerning judicial independence (Case Kpt 1/20 [2020] CT), Mariusz Muszyński referred to Polish constitutional identity as an ultimate limitation for the EU law's primacy principle. He pointed out that the 2017–2020 reform of the judiciary in Poland is in Poland's hands as part of Polish constitutional identity. The EU, particularly the ECJ, have, therefore, no power in this area. Moreover, the unlawful member of the Tribunal claimed that the ECJ could not order or instruct the Polish authorities on how judicial independence and judicial appointment might look. Otherwise, it would be a violation of Polish constitutional identity. Muszyński also suggested that Polish courts, including the Supreme Court, violated Polish constitutional identity following the ECJ's judgment of 19 November 2019. According to Muszyński, the Tribunal has the power to define constitutional identity.

[74] In his separate opinion concerning abortion (Case K 1/20 [2020] CT), Jaroslaw Wyrembak referred to the 'axiological foundations'' and 'identity' of the Constitution. He argued that the 'axiological foundations' and 'identity' in Poland fully protect the life of a foetus. Consequently, identity prevents the Parliament from liberalising the abortion law after the captured Tribunal struck down the right to abortion due to foetal abnormality. Moreover, according to Wyrembak, the 'axiological foundations' and 'identity' prevent courts and scholars from giving a liberal interpretation of the binding law after the captured CT's judgment (paras XII–XIII).

In a very similar way, the Polish Prime Minister used constitutional identity in 2021[75] to question the constitutionality of Articles 4(3) and 19(1) TEU. According to the PM, the Treaty provisions violated Poland's constitutional identity, since they expressed the principle of effective legal protection and interfered with the national institutional arrangements of the judiciary.[76] The PM's aim was to constitutionally protect the reform of the judiciary in Poland and new judicial appointments. (The appointments were made by illiberal authorities and these judges did not give an appearance of independence.) The PM's reference to constitutional identity aimed to prevent courts in Poland from applying the EU standard of judicial impartiality and stop the courts from making references for preliminary rulings to the ECJ.

In November 2021, the captured Tribunal declared Article 19(1) TEU unconstitutional.[77] The core argument of the justification[78] was based on the principle of conferral and constitutional identity as a limitation for the ever-closer Union. According to the Tribunal, Poland's judicial appointment system is part of the basic institutional structure and fundamental constitutional choice. Therefore, the Tribunal found a violation of constitutional provisions since Article 19(1) TEU had been interpreted by the ECJ as a source of binding substantial rules and principles concerning the judiciary structures in the Member States.

The captured Tribunal explored the concept of constitutional identity gradually starting from undercover abuse of essential elements of the concept and ending with an open reference and its own version of identity review. The first way means that the Tribunal avoided direct references to the notion of identity and at the same time it explored the potential of constitutional particularism without calling it an identity review. The second way means that the Tribunal directly referred to the notion of constitutional identity and suggested legal basis and aim of the identity review. I will refer below to four case studies where constitutional particularism became replaced by the Tribunal's direct use of constitutional identity.

[75] The Polish Prime Minister's motion of 29 March 2021 (BPRM.5091.5.2021).

[76] The Prime Minister pointed out that ultra vires, human rights reviews and identity review are three constitutionally rooted and justified judicial tools enabling the Tribunal to review EU law (ibid, 19.). To support this argument, the PM referred to the *Lisbon* case and used comparative references (Italian, Dutch, Czech), emphasising the FCC judgment of 5 May 2020 (ibid at 21–58.). The PM linked constitutional identity to the absolute binding force of the Polish Constitution. Consequently, protection of identity should also be absolute. It creates an exception to the principle of primacy of EU law. The PM concluded that the principle of EU law primacy is unconstitutional when its application interferes with Polish constitutional identity (ibid, 91.).

[77] Case K 3/21 [7 October 2021] CT.

[78] In the written justification published in November 2022, the Tribunal referred to the nebulous Lisbon formula, the FCC's understanding of identity as a static limit for integration, and linked identity to sovereignty. Yet the argument does not go beyond what the Tribunal had said in case P 7/20 (discussed in IV.D).

A. Freedom of Assembly v National Values

The first case concerns the freedom of assembly.[79] The Tribunal ruled on the constitutionality of a new type of public assembly, referred to as periodical assemblies. The new type was to protect the particular type of public assembly (Polish: *miesięcznice smoleńskie*), organised by the governing party after President Lech Kaczynski's plane crash in Smolensk in 2010. Those assemblies consisted of public prayers, political statements made by party leaders, and expressions of support for the government. The true intention behind the new law was to limit anti-government assemblies by giving pro-government assemblies a higher legal status.

The case could be summarised by the following question: is it constitutional to give a conclusive priority to periodical assemblies over other types of assembly (anti-government protests, civic movements rallies, pride marches)? And the Tribunal answered in the affirmative. The case did not concern the application of the concept of identity directly. However, the Tribunal referred to history and national values mentioned in the Preamble of the Constitution (as the formula used in the *Lisbon* case was nebulous when the Tribunal mentioned 'national identity').[80] Periodical assemblies were found to be constitutionally legitimate since they aimed to celebrate the most important historical events (such as the plane crash in Smolensk). The Tribunal pointed out that periodical assemblies might help realise the essential constitutional values (protection of Homeland, common good, 'obligation to bequeath to future generations all that is valuable from our over one thousand years' heritage'). The Tribunal even observed that periodical assemblies might shape 'nationally desirable' patterns of behaviour. Finally, according to the Tribunal, the exclusion of any counter-manifestations clashing with periodical assemblies helps maintain public order.

The nation-values and social-engineering arguments were decisive for the Tribunal. The judgment did not contain a full proportionality test. Thus, it was structurally close to the national identity argument. First, the reference to national values was sufficient to rule on the constitutionality of the law. Second, the Tribunal assumed it was competent to define national values and exercise its review. The Tribunal went even further, claiming that the new law was right for protecting historical memory and the common good of the Homeland. Third, the Tribunal did not provide any criteria for selecting national values relevant to the case. The judgment did not go beyond the very general notions used in the Preamble, which suggests the risk of either a too extensive or homogenous

[79] Case Kp 1/17 [2017] CT.

[80] It may be an illustration how the Tribunal's 'heavy reliance on the constitution's preamble' in the *Lisbon* case provided 'room for a more historical account should future circumstances render such a development politically desirable'. See chapter one in this volume.

interpretation of those values. Finally, when the Tribunal pointed out that periodical assemblies realised 'common good', it completely ignored the protection of ethnic minorities, which may suggest an ethnoculturally homogenous interpretation of the Polish nation.

B. Right to Abortion v Religious Values

The second case concerns abortion.[81] The Tribunal questioned the right to abortion attributable to foetal abnormality. The oral argumentation provided by the Tribunal is simplistic and unsophisticated: the claim is that a foetus is an 'unborn child', which is a 'human being',[82] so the Constitution should fully protect its life.[83] The Tribunal did not recognise the differences between a foetus, a *nasciturus* and a child or mature person. The Tribunal's argument may be summarised: life is life no matter what form or stage, regardless of scientific or moral arguments. Then the Tribunal claimed that a 'foetus' life' might be limited in an extraordinary situation,[84] suggesting only one case when it would be constitutionally justified: when the life and health of the pregnant woman are threatened.[85] The Tribunal indicated that this is the situation when Parliament has the power to limit the life of the foetus and protect that of the woman.[86]

The Tribunal pointed out that: (1) the Constitution does not protect the right to abortion;[87] (2) the Constitution fully protects the dignity of a foetus as a human being;[88] (3) the constitutional protection of women's health does not justify abortion in case of foetal abnormality.[89] The Tribunal did not refer to the international standards of human rights. The justification of the judgment did not even mention that forcing women to give birth in case of foetal abnormalities could be recognised as inhuman treatment. The Tribunal also failed to consider the case from the point of view of the constitutional right to privacy, as other constitutional courts did in similar cases. Instead of doing so, the Tribunal generally underlined positive constitutional obligations of the state to support parents after the child is born.

[81] Case K 1/20 [2020] CT. For criticism, see W Sadurski and A Gliszczyńska-Grabias, 'The Judgment That Wasn't (But Which Nearly Brought Poland to a Standstill): "Judgment" of the Polish Constitutional Tribunal of 22 October 2020, K1/20' (2021) 17 *European Constitutional Law Review* 130.

[82] Case K 1/20 (n 81) paras III.1.2. *in fine*, III.2.3, III.3.3., III.3.4.

[83] ibid at paras III.3.3.1–3.3.2. and III.3.4.

[84] ibid at para III.4.2.

[85] ibid.

[86] ibid.

[87] Case K 1/20 (n 81) para III.3.3.

[88] ibid at para III.3.4.

[89] ibid at para III.4.2.

Again, the judgment does not contain the full proportionality test.[90] It is based on an exclusionary and particularistic interpretation of human dignity. The Tribunal claimed that constitutional protection of the foetus was a consequence of the protection of human dignity as a fundamental constitutional value. No matter whether we agree with that or not, there is a more serious problem with the Tribunal's reasoning. Protection of dignity of one subject cannot lead to the reification of another subject. Protection of a foetus's dignity cannot make a woman an object. The concept of dignity should not be used when one group is dehumanised. Moreover, the judgment ignores comparative arguments and international jurisprudence. Finally, the Tribunal assumed it had the power to define essentially contested concepts, as well as traditional values, and legally enforce them. The understanding of tradition and values that emerges from the judgment is highly exclusionary, since a large part of the society cannot recognise it as their own. The Tribunal's narrative is close to what the introductory chapter of this volume calls 'wall-identity' that 'effectively shuts out "the other"'.[91]

C. EU Law v National Institutional Arrangements

The third case (U 2/20)[92] concerns the resolution decision of the three joint chambers of the Polish Supreme Court,[93] which concerned the application of European and constitutional standards of impartiality and independence of the national judicial authority. The ECJ's judgment of 19 November 2019[94] was in the background.[95] Following that judgment, the Supreme Court ruled that the Polish National Council of the Judiciary and the Disciplinary Chamber of the

[90] The judgment focuses on the foetus as a human being and on limitation of the foetus's 'right to life'. The constitutional rights of women were not even recognised as equal to the constitutional status of the foetus. The Tribunal found women's life and health as a narrow exception that may limit the foetus's 'right to life'. This means that the constitutional protection of the foetus may prevail over the protection of pregnant women in the case of rape. The Tribunal said that when the lives of pregnant women were not at stake, the protection of the foetus prevailed. This conclusion has, however, no evident legal basis, since the Constitution expressly protects women in different situations and does not even mention the 'foetus' or 'unborn child' – Case K 1/20 (n 81) para III.4.2.

[91] See the introductory chapter in this volume.

[92] Case U 2/20 [2020] CT.

[93] Case BSA I-4110-1/20 [23 January 2020] Polish Supreme Court.

[94] Case C-585/18, C-624/18 and C-625/18, *AK and Others v Sąd Najwyższy* [2019] ECJ. M Krajewski and M Ziółkowski, 'EU judicial independence decentralized' (2020) 57 *Common Market Law Review* 1107–138.

[95] The case before the ECJ concerned mainly the issues of independence and impartiality of the National Council of the Judiciary and the Disciplinary Chamber. The ECJ decided that it should be the Supreme Court's task to consider whether national judicial authorities are independent under the Charter and ECJ case-law. At the same time, the ECJ offered a helping hand to the referring court and provided numerous directions on how independence and impartiality might be tested – *AK and Others* (n 94) para 134.

Supreme Court lacked independence (both with members appointed during the constitutional crisis in Poland). Moreover, the Supreme Court pointed out that the newly appointed judges in Poland may not have an appearance of independence since the procedure of their appointments was conducted with the involvement of the non-independent National Council of the Judiciary.

The Tribunal ruled that the decision of the Supreme Court was unconstitutional. The case could be summarised by the following question: is it constitutional for the Supreme Court to protect the judiciary's independence by offering an 'EU-friendly' interpretation of a national law adopted after the ECJ's judgment? And the Tribunal answered it in the negative. The Tribunal ruled that the Supreme Court's decision was unconstitutional because an 'EU-friendly' interpretation became an act of law-making.

The phrase 'constitutional identity' was not expressly used by the Tribunal. However, it did mention 'national identity' as part of Article 4 TEU. The Tribunal also directly referred to the 'common constitutional traditions' and Article 2 TEU (pointing out that the rule of law is common for all EU Member States). Therefore, this case is an example of an indirect use of the identity argument. The Tribunal underlined an absolute primacy of the Constitution over EU law. Moreover, the Tribunal called itself a guardian of the Constitution[96] and reserved for itself a role of 'protecting of the hierarchical structure of the constitutional system of laws by protecting the Constitution and being a guardian of the treaties that constitutionalised the EU'.[97] The Tribunal also pointed out that there could be cases of fundamental contradictions between the ECJ's interpretation of the Treaties and the Tribunal's interpretation of the Constitution. In such cases, the Tribunal reserved for itself the role of the 'court having the last word' to avoid overlapping jurisdiction and any 'incoherent interpretation' between the Constitution and EU law.[98] Finally, the Tribunal portrayed the judicial appointments as a fundamental and historically rooted institutional arrangement on a constitutional level.[99]

As a result, the Tribunal pointed out that the Supreme Court violated the rule of law by following ECJ guidance. According to the Tribunal, neither the Constitution nor EU law and ECJ case law gave the Polish Supreme Court the power to question the results of the reform of the judiciary in Poland (to question the validity of judicial appointments or to question the independence of the Disciplinary Chamber, as well as the independence of the National Council of the Judiciary). According to the Tribunal, the Supreme Court failed to protect Polish constitutional identity and common constitutional traditions

[96] Case U 2/20 (n 92) paras III.4.2–4.3.
[97] ibid at para III.4.3.
[98] ibid at para III.4.2.
[99] ibid at para III.4.1.

(all interpreted according to the Tribunal's whim). The Tribunal admitted that effective protection of judicial independence is an element of the rule of law and common constitutional traditions. However, those common constitutional traditions and the rule of law should be interrelated and interpreted in accordance with the Polish Constitution or, more precisely, following the Tribunal's will. The Tribunal ended with a claim that after its ruling there should be no tensions between the Treaties, ECJ case law, and the Constitution.

The case may serve as a model of an abusive and one-sided narrative about exclusionary identity. The Tribunal, consciously or innocuously, followed the nebulous *Lisbon* case formula. It admitted the ECJ had its own jurisdiction and 'national identity' enshrined in the Treaty, yet the Tribunal used the 'national identity' argument to criticise the Supreme Court, which followed ECJ guidance. Moreover, the Tribunal recognised its own authority to decide what the ultimate institutional arrangement under Polish constitutional law is: it is one that makes it possible to ignore ECJ judgments and effective protection of judicial independence.

Another case on the Law and Justice (PiS) party's judicial 'reform' (Kpt 1/20)[100] concerned a conflict of powers: the power of Parliament to reform the judiciary, the power of the President to appoint judges, and the power of the Supreme Court to question the independence of newly appointed judges. Again, the ECJ's judgment of 19 November 2020 was in the background.

This case was resolved by the Tribunal as a 'dispute' under Article 189 of the Constitution. The Tribunal ruled that the Supreme Court had no power to enforce the judgment of the ECJ, because that judgment infringed the President's power to appoint judges. This particular power, emphasised the Tribunal, is fundamental to Polish constitutionalism, cannot be limited, cannot be subject to judicial review, and cannot be undermined, voided or modified. As a result of the primacy of the Constitution and constitutional arrangements, the new judicial appointments cannot be questioned.

The Tribunal did not refer to constitutional or national identity directly. The Tribunal used the same approach in both cases. Still, the justification is structurally close to the identity argument. According to the Tribunal, since the constitutional arrangements in the judiciary system (including the President's power to appoint judges) are so fundamental and historically rooted, neither EU authorities nor the Polish Supreme Court (following EU authorities' guidance) can refer to EU principles or standards to justify their interventions. The President's power to appoint judges always prevails and should always be effective. And it is the Tribunal's role to decide, as the court having the last word in identity-related issues.

[100] Case Kpt 1/20 [21 April 2020] CT.

D. The ECJ's Ultra Vires Act and an Absolute Approach to Identity

The last case (P 7/20) is an example of direct reference to the identity as a precondition for ultra vires review. For the first time, the Tribunal ruled that the ECJ had acted beyond its scope of competence and violated Polish constitutional identity.

The case was initiated by preliminary reference of the captured Disciplinary Chamber of the Polish Supreme Court. The Disciplinary Chamber was added to the structure of the Supreme Court during the illiberal 'reform' of the judiciary in Poland. It was later recognised by the ECJ not to be impartial within the meaning of EU law. Because the Disciplinary Chamber ignored the ECJ's judgment and continued examining disciplinary cases against judges in Poland, the ECJ imposed an interim measure to stop the Chamber and protect the independence of Polish judges. Thus, the Disciplinary Chamber questioned the constitutionality of the ECJ's power.

The captured Tribunal declared Articles 4(3) TEU and 279 TFEU unconstitutional and recognised the ECJ's interim measure as an ultra vires act that had violated Polish constitutional identity.[101] Consequently, the interim measure could not have an impact on the Polish judiciary system. Moreover, the Tribunal ruled that the EU law cannot force the Polish courts to enforce the ECJ's judgments relating to the lack of independence and impartiality of the Disciplinary Chamber. According to the Tribunal, the EU had no power over the institutional arrangements of the judiciary system (ie, judicial appointments), and such a power could not be conferred upon the EU. The Tribunal also pointed out that its constitutional duty is to protect Polish constitutional identity and the ultra vires review is a suitable tool.[102] The review concerns both the primary and secondary EU law as well as the ECJ's legal interpretation. The Tribunal admitted that it generally has no power over the ECJ's interpretation, which cannot be voided as long as the ECJ follows principles of conferral, subsidiarity and proportionality. However, in case of violation of the principles or any other kind of interference by the ECJ with Polish constitutional identity, the Tribunal is constitutionally obliged to act.[103]

When using the concept of identity, the Tribunal referred to the *Lisbon* case and suggested inspiration from the FCC case law. However, in my view, the Tribunal summarised and pieced together the previously made indirect references to the constitutional identity and symptoms of constitutional particularism. Firstly, the Tribunal's approach to identity is based on a one-sided and arbitrary narrative concerning the Constitution. It creates the risk of a too extensive or homogenous constitutional interpretation since the Constitution has no identity

[101] Case P 7/20 [14 July 2021] CT para III.6.8.
[102] ibid at para III.6.5.
[103] ibid at para III.6.5.

or eternity clauses to build on. The Tribunal did not justify why principles of judicial appointments (or any other constitutional principles) are so special or important to be part of constitutional identity in Poland. Also it did not provide any criteria for selecting constitutional values as covered by identity protection. Secondly, the Tribunal suggested a rather static than dynamic approach to identity. It cannot be deliberated among different actors of constitutional law. It is, instead, proclaimed by the Tribunal. Once it is proclaimed it cannot be changed since the Tribunal reserved for itself an exclusionary power to decide on identity. Thirdly, the Tribunal used the identity in an absolute way by declaring that the protection of the constitutional identity in Poland has absolute and abstract primacy over the EU law. It does not leave any space for balancing or dialogue with the ECJ. Once some principles or institutions (ie, principles of judicial appointments) are covered by identity protection they cannot be proportionally suited to the EU law. Finally, the Tribunal extended the addressees of the identity. The identity limits not only national authorities when they decide on the conferral of powers or when they ratify new treaties, but it also limits the EU authorities when they exercise powers that had been conferred upon the EU.

V. CONCLUSION

If identity had not appeared in the *Lisbon* judgment or if it had been better defined at that time, the captured Tribunal and other illiberal authorities would be in a different position now. The authorities would probably be unable to refer to Polish constitutional identity and use the *Lisbon* case to support their abusive constitutional interpretations. Still, the fluidity of Poland's constitutional identity (as the Tribunal adopted it in the *Lisbon* case) and the serious abuse of this concept by the unconstitutional Tribunal does not mean that identity should be abandoned as a dangerous concept.[104] What should be abandoned is the *Lisbon* formula of identity. The backsliding of constitutional democracy in Poland has shown that almost every concept of constitutional law (including the doctrines of sovereignty or judicial independence) or institution (including the Tribunal or the Supreme Court) can be reversed and used in an abusive way.[105] This does not mean that it is the fault of a given legal concept or institution.[106] It does not imply that prospective and deliberative discussions could not help to override the disgraced label attached to constitutional identity during the constitutional crisis in Poland.

[104] F Fabbrini and Sajó, 'The Dangers of Constitutional Identity' (2019) 25 *European Law Journal* 457.

[105] M Bernatt and M Ziółkowski, 'Statutory Anti-Constitutionalism' (2019) 8 *Washington International Law Journal* 487.

[106] See convincing arguments given by J Scholtes, 'Abusing Constitutional Identity' (2021) 22 *German Law Journal* 545–55.

The chapter has discussed the Tribunal's understanding of constitutional identity as a constitutionally careless transplant. A tension between two desires underpinned it. The first was the desire to be a member of a supranational community of liberal constitutional values. The second desire was constitutional particularism. Therefore, in Poland it was not the concept of constitutional identity itself that was dangerous. The risk of its abuse resulted from the way it was transplanted and how the transplant was linked to national values and history. If it is a convincing interpretation of the Tribunal's understanding of constitutional identity, then two possible solutions will appear for the next (constitutionally composed) Tribunal as well as for academics in Poland. One is to make the transplant again, but in a more thoughtful way. The other is to abandon the transplant and to start looking for sources of identity in the constitution-making moment as well as in global constitutionalism. The Polish Constitution being as young as it is, there is still a lot to unveil.[107]

[107] I.e., the civic definition of the nation in the constitutional provisions; the reception of the 1921 constitution in the binding constitutional provisions; the unique character of constitution-making in Poland; consequences of the minimal popular engagement in constitution-making in Poland.

6

Reconceptualising Constitutional Identity: The Case of Hungary

KRISZTA KOVÁCS

On 9 September 2016, when accepting the Person of the Year Award from the then Polish Prime Minister, Beata Szydło, Hungarian Prime Minister, Viktor Orbán, said:

> The Central European nations must preserve their identities, their religious and historical national identities. … I regret to say that we must [protect these virtues] from time to time not only against the faithless and our anti-national rivals but also from time to time we must do so against Europe's various leading intellectual and political circles. But we have no choice: we must protect our identities – Polish, Hungarian and Central European identities – in the face of everyone because otherwise there will be no room for us under the sun.[1]

Here, I believe, we are presented with a false dichotomy. National identity is portrayed as if it were a thing having DNA that contains all the information necessary to develop a communal identity and as if it were so evident that community members are all familiar with it. If the community does not recognise and protect its 'naturally given' national identity, so the argument goes, it will unavoidably fail.

However, as this book's introductory chapter explains,[2] national identity does not exist naturally, nor does it enjoy timeless validity. It is not a matter of fact; it is a matter of choice. The case of Hungary demonstrates this point unequivocally. There are two powerful claims on communal identity in Hungary, both firmly rooted in centuries of contestation.[3] Hungary's choice of identity

[1] Viktor Orbán's acceptance speech after receiving the 'Person of the Year' award 9 September 2016 www.miniszterelnok.hu/prime-minister-viktor-orbans-acceptance-speech-after-receiving-the-person-of-the-year-award/.

[2] See the introductory chapter in this volume.

[3] One of the examples of this is an embittered political debate on the new coat of arms of Hungary in the early 1990s, which demonstrated the differences in the viewpoints of the political actors. The progressives wanted to replace the Soviet-like emblem with the respected Kossuth coat

either entails a return to an authoritarian tradition or a move to a democratic tradition that looks to the modern universal constitutional commitments to human rights, democracy, and the rule of law.

After successfully transitioning from Soviet-type authoritarianism to democracy, Hungary revised its 1949 constitution significantly. The 1989–1990 amendments (the 1989 constitution) made a commitment to universal constitutional principles while also following the progressive traditions of the Hungarian past. The 1989 constitution gave birth to a constitutional identity based on the core features of constitutionalism – the commitment to the protection of human rights, democracy, and the rule of law. It institutionalised a parliamentary democracy with a government answerable to the legislature and an indirectly elected president with limited powers, following the Hungarian democratic-republican traditions established in the period from the 1848 revolution to the 1946 proclamation of the republic. Parliament was at the heart of this constitutional order, but this order also provided the opportunity for everyone to access the parliament and other democratic institutions (eg, the Constitutional Court). The transformative[4] decisions of the newly established Hungarian Constitutional Court (HCC) reflected this choice of identity, and the constitutional identity developed steadily. Although the 1989 constitution was amended several times during the two decades after the transition to democracy, these were mainly connected to Hungary's membership of NATO and the European Union. The constitutional changes did not affect the core of the constitution, so the constitutional identity remained untouched until 2010.

In the late 2000s, the inexperience of politicians and institutions in managing a democratic regime made consolidating the democracy extremely difficult. Severe political and social tensions were also at work. The internal cold war between the political left and right, domestic political scandals, collapsing state finances, and a global economic crisis that pushed Hungary into an IMF bailout resulted in a deep constitutional and moral crisis. All this made the electorate ready for change in 2010. That year, Viktor Orbán's Fidesz party and its satellite Christian Democratic Party gained a supermajority of parliamentary seats, opening the way for a profound change of direction. The 2010 changes in the constitutional framework went to the very heart of Hungary's constitutional identity.

of arms of the 1948–49 War of Independence. The traditionalists, however, opted for the royal coat of arms with the Holy Crown. A Felkay, *Out of Russian Orbit. Hungary Gravitates to the West* (Westport/Connecticut, Greenwood, 1997) 16.

[4] Transformative in a sense, K Klare introduced this notion. In his understanding, transformative constitutionalism entails 'a long term project of constitutional … interpretation … committed to transforming a country's political and social institutions and power relationships in a democratic, participatory, and egalitarian direction'. K Klare, 'Legal Culture and Transformative Constitutionalism' (1998) 14 *South African Journal of Human Rights* 157. Such transformative decisions were, for instance, the Death Penalty Decision 23/1990 and the Political Speech Decision 36/1994 of the Constitutional Court of Hungary.

One year into its term, the governing coalition passed a new constitution officially called the Fundamental Law (FL). The coalition justified its adoption with the argument that the 1989 constitution was not homegrown or organically evolving, but was something imposed by external forces, such as the international community[5] and that its identity failed to comply with Hungarian national identity.[6] For these reasons, the ruling politicians argued, the country needed a new 'social contract' that provided a 'foundation for the spiritual and intellectual renewal of Hungary'.[7]

The FL does not acknowledge continuity with the previous democratic regime. It explicitly breaks with the essential notion of a republic and changes the country's name from the 'Republic of Hungary' to simply 'Hungary'.[8] The act of renaming the state is important: it suggests that the FL's concept of identity is incompatible with the concept of the republic and that Hungary does not cherish democratic ideals.[9] Instead, it follows the authoritarian tradition, where the assumed common ethnicity of the Hungarian people serves as the core of national identity. A single adjective serves as a fitting representation of the identity offered by the FL: ethnocultural.

The ethnocultural national identity is problematic in many respects. First, it means that only some can believe that they are part of the same political community and not all citizens. Second, as the introductory chapter demonstrates, a national identity that aims at protecting ethnic or religious purity runs counter to EU foundational values and the European Court of Justice's (ECJ) efforts to reconcile the various national identities of the Member States with

[5] '[W]e are writing our own constitution … And we don't want any unconsolidated help from strangers who are keen to guide us.' V Orbán, 'Nem leszünk gyarmat!' [We won't be a colony anymore!] www.2010-2015.miniszterelnok.hu/beszed/nem_leszunk_gyarmat_.

[6] See, eg, T Navracsics, 'A New Constitution for Hungary: Locking in the Values of 1989–1990. Transition, At Last' (2011) 19 *The Wall Street Journal*, 19 April 2011.

[7] Proclamation of the Parliament on Statement of National Cooperation 1/2010. (VI. 16.). A government ordinance was published to make it compulsory that the proclamation be prominently displayed in governmental buildings.

[8] Referencing the country simply as 'Hungary' without any designation of the form of government evokes national imagery associated with the interwar period's cultural visions. Between 1920–1944, the state's official name was the 'Kingdom of Hungary', but the state was practically a 'kingdom without a king', so the name 'Hungary' was used even in international treaties. P Takács, 'Renaming States A Case Study: Changing the Name of the Hungarian State in 2011. Its Background, Reasons, and Aftermath' (2020) 33 *International Journal for the Semiotics of Law* 905–906. The FL also replaced the names of the courts and administrative bodies. For instance, it changed the name of the Supreme Court to Kúria. Notably, Kúria was the name of the highest court before 1945. Act CCI of 2011 replaced the term 'Republic of Hungary' with the word 'Hungary' in the text of hundreds of laws. Government Decree 322/2011 performed the same in hundreds of decrees. Between 1989 and 2012, court judgments used the following performative: 'In the name of the Republic of Hungary'. Act CLXI of 2011 repealed this performative.

[9] Already in 2006, V Orbán noted in one of his speeches as leader of the opposition, 'for us, the republic is an empty word. … Our future is in the nation and not in the republic'. Viktor Orbán, 'Számunkra a köztársaság csak egy szó, az csak egy ruha [For us, republic is an empty word, it is just a dress] www.ma.hu/tart/rcikk/a/0/143121/1.

these values. Hence, this chapter amounts to an exercise in reconceptualising the Hungarian constitutional identity. It aims to present an alternative to the ethnocultural national identity: an inclusive yet distinctive constitutional identity embedded in domestic democratic tradition and consistent with the EU foundational values.

The chapter is structured as follows. The first section opens with an analytical account of the three pillars of the FL's ethnocultural identity: non-inclusive religious considerations, historical myths, and the mythical concept of the 'nation'. This section demonstrates that the FL has a relatively straightforward religious profile; it portrays Hungary as a Christian nation. It also shows that the FL imposes a specific historical narrative based on resentful nationalism, which constitutes an integral part of the national identity and that it invokes the mythical concept of 'the nation' instead of 'the people' as the constitution's originator. The second section outlines the judicial interpretation of identity and demonstrates that the ethnocultural national identity entrenched in the FL determines constitutional court decisions. In 2016, the HCC confirmed that Hungary's identity is equivalent to the FL's identity. Since then, a range of decisions – on the EU refugee relocation scheme, asylum and a criminal provision aimed at NGOs assisting asylum seekers – have reflected this identity's exclusionary aspect. Finally, the third section offers a way to reconstruct constitutional identity supported by three key pillars. The first pillar can be built on the institutional values of the democratic Hungary: representative government, consensual parliamentary democracy, and meaningful constitutional review conducted by an independent judiciary. The universal constitutional principles, as the HCC's transformative decisions interpreted them, can constitute the second pillar. The third pillar can encompass EU laws' crucial achievements as they were implemented in domestic law. Section IV of this chapter concludes.

I. THREE PILLARS OF THE ETHNOCULTURAL NATIONAL IDENTITY

The term 'identity' features prominently in the FL. Among the solemn declarations, we find that safeguarding Hungary's identity is the state's fundamental duty. In Article R(4), we read that every state organ must protect 'Hungary's constitutional self-identity and Christian culture'. Furthermore, the FL explicitly mandates the state to ensure that children receive an 'upbringing based on the value system of Hungary's constitutional self-identity and Christian culture'.[10] The FL suggests that 'Hungary's constitutional self-identity' is distinctively and uniquely rooted in its 'historical constitution',[11] and in 'the Holy Crown, which embodies the state's constitutional continuity and nation's unity'.[12]

[10] XVI(1) of the FL.
[11] National Avowal of the FL.
[12] ibid.

Ostensibly, the qualifier 'constitutional' in the term 'constitutional self-identity' suggests that this identity is closer to a constitutionalist meaning.[13] But in fact, under 'constitutional', the FL understands 'constitutional' to mean the constitution in the empirical sense of the political condition of the state[14] and not a normative framework. Moreover, the FL applies the term 'constitution' only in connection with the so-called 'historical constitution'. Even the official name of the current constitution, 'The Fundamental Law of Hungary', implies that the document is simply a part of this historical constitution, but it is not the country's constitution. The 'constitutional self-identity' entrenched in the FL does not provide concretisations of universal constitutional values; rather, it represents a national-historical ethnic category based on non-inclusive religious considerations, historical myths, and a mythical concept of the 'nation'.

A. Non-Inclusive Religious Considerations

The FL's text and the symbolism around it have a relatively straightforward religious profile. It was Easter Monday of 2011 when the FL was signed into law by the president. The invocation to God in the very first sentence, 'God bless the Hungarians', implies that everyone who wishes to identify with the text also identifies with this opening entreaty.[15] The legally binding preamble to the FL, called the National Avowal, has its foundation in religious considerations. The Avowal, as its name suggests, does not only reflect the historical role of Christianity in founding the state but also expresses that Hungarian constitutionalism today is based upon traditional Christian views.[16] For example, in addition to expressing that the Hungarians are proud that their 'king Saint Stephen built the Hungarian state on solid ground and made (their) country a part of Christian Europe one thousand years ago', the National Avowal 'recognises the role of Christianity in preserving nationhood' and mandates the state organs to protect Hungary's Christian culture.[17] Since both the state's strong attachment to Christianity and religious toleration are deeply rooted in Hungary, the government's decision to select the Christian heritage from this tradition is a clearly values-driven exercise.[18]

[13] To learn more about the constitutionalist meaning, see chapter seven in this volume.

[14] D Gosewinkel, 'The Constitutional State' in H Pihlajamaki, MD Dubber and M Godfrey (eds), *The Oxford Handbook of European Legal History* (Oxford, Oxford University Press, 2018) 947.

[15] A Arato et al, 'Opinion on the Fundamental Law of Hungary (Amicus Brief)' in GA Tóth (ed), *Constitution for a Disunited Nation: On Hungary's 2011 Fundamental Law* (New York, Central European University Press, 2012) 461.

[16] K Kovács and GA Tóth, 'Hungary's Constitutional Transformation' (2011) 7 *European Constitutional Law Review* 198.

[17] Article R(4) of the FL.

[18] R Uitz, 'Freedom of Religion and Churches' in Tóth (n 15) 202.

Yet, the reference to Christianity is more about the national culture than Christianity as faith.[19] Some FL provisions are worded in the spirit of traditional Christian culture. For instance, Article L defines a family according to the traditional Christian view of marriage and family by stipulating that only a man and a woman can marry, and declares that families, which are the foundations of the nation's survival, are based on marriage, parent–child relationships, or both. The provision also clarifies that the mother is a woman; the father is a man. The protection of the traditional marriage is complemented with a provision seeking to 'protect the foetal life from the moment of conception',[20] and another that ensures the children's right to identify with their gender at birth.[21] The latter provision also requires children to be raised with a 'Christian interpretation' of gender roles and have an upbringing based on national identity and Christian culture, thereby mandating that the upbringing should have both a national identity and a Christian component.[22] Another tool the text uses to bolster this vision of 'national consciousness' is the restriction of free speech in the interest of protecting a dominant religious group[23] and the Hungarian nation.[24]

Other provisions that are not worded explicitly in the spirit of traditional Christianity, such as the basic principles (eg democracy or the rule of law) or some fundamental rights provisions (eg freedom of assembly), are to be interpreted following the national-historical narrative and Christian culture. This is because the National Avowal is not just a solemn declaration which signals a certain self-interpretation of the community; it has normative strength. Article R(3) requires that all FL provisions, even those that declare universal constitutional principles like democracy and the rule of law, should be interpreted according to the FL's objectives, the National Avowal and the 'achievements of the historical constitution'. But what exactly is the historical constitution?

[19] O Roy, 'Beyond Populism' in N Marzouki, D MacDonell and O Roy (eds), *Saving the People: How Populists Hijack Religion* (Meridian, Hurst & Company 2016) 186.

[20] Article II of the FL.

[21] Article XVI(1) of the FL.

[22] The explanatory text mentions the 'laws of nature' (the two sexes are created) and explains that the terms (one woman and one man) flow from the order of 'Creation'. It further suggests that raising children according to the national identity and Christian culture gives new generations the chance to learn about Hungarian identity and protect its sovereignty and Christianity's national role. The Hungarian language explanatory text is available at www.parlament.hu/irom41/13647/13647.pdf.

[23] Article IX(5) of the FL allows restrictions on free speech in order to protect a religious group. In 2016, when Poland tightened its abortion law, demonstrators protested it by performing in front of the Polish Embassy in Budapest. The performance included an imitation of the Eucharist, and one protester placed a white tablet from a bag labelled 'abortion pill' on the other protesters' tongue. A handful of Catholics who saw this performance on YouTube turned to the HCC. In its Decision 6/2021. (II. 19.), the HCC held that the performance violated the Catholic petitioners' human dignity because their religious community were offended disproportionately.

[24] For example, the Kúria held that calling Hungarians 'migrants' violates the dignity of the Hungarian nation. Supreme Court Decision of 24 March 2021, Kúria Pfv.IV.20.199/2020/7. For more on this technique of free speech restriction, see GA Tóth, 'Constitutional Markers of Authoritarianism' (2019) *Hague Journal on the Rule of Law* 37.

B. Historical Myths

The doctrine of the historical constitution dates to 1896, the 1000th anniversary of the conquest of Hungary's territory. At that time, a claim appeared[25] that Hungary was the only nation in Central Europe[26] with a tradition of statehood dating back 1000 years.[27] The historical constitution doctrine was built on the 'holy crown' doctrine. The crown in question[28] was the one which the future king (later Saint) Stephen received from Pope Sylvester II as he laid the foundations of the centralised Hungarian Kingdom by converting to Christianity. According to the doctrine, the crown is thus an ancient source of authority, a literal marker of the unity of the king and the noblemen. The scholar and theologian István Werbőczy introduced the holy crown doctrine into Hungarian public law with his work *Tripartitum* (1617). Late-nineteenth-century legal historians and politicians breathed new life into this doctrine by creating the 'myth' of the historical constitution[29] and proposing a continuous constitution in Hungary from the day when Stephen received his crown through the Great Bull of 1222 and other – so-called fundamental – laws[30] that regulated the constitutional order to the nineteenth century.

Since the late nineteenth century, both claims have been used for various political purposes. For instance, at the end of the nineteenth century, they claimed a privileged position for the Hungarians within the Habsburg Monarchy.[31] During Miklós Horthy's national-conservative authoritarian regime (1920–1944), these doctrines shaped Hungary's constitutional system.[32] Around this time, the expression 'Lands of the Hungarian Crown' began to be used in legal texts to

[25] G Andrássy (*Vasárnapi Újság* [Sunday News] 15 June 1884) quoted in JM Bak and A Gara-Bak, 'The Ideology of a "Millennial Constitution" of Hungary' (1981) 15 *East European Quarterly* 307; A Apponyi 'Speech at the Meeting of the Interparliamentary Union' (1904) quoted in J Bak, 'Political Uses of Historical Comparisons: Medieval and Modern Hungary' (2006) 23 *Post-Medieval Studies* 273.

[26] By the second half of the nineteenth century, the view that 'with regard to rank and age the Hungarian constitution could be compared to British constitutionality had become a widely held conviction'. Even the building of the Hungarian parliament was modelled after Westminster. This view, however, cannot be supported by facts of legal development. A Cieger, 'National Identity and Constitutional Patriotism in the Context of Modern Hungarian History' (2016) 5 *Hungarian Historical Review* 129–30, 133.

[27] JM Bak and A Gara-Bak, 'The Ideology of a "Millennial Constitution" of Hungary' (1981) 15 *East European Quarterly* 307.

[28] The original crown was lost, so the crown known today is a replica.

[29] S Radnóti, 'A Sacred Symbol in a Secular Country: The Holy Crown', in Tóth (n 15) 94.

[30] The fundamental laws were enacted laws, but usually, customary law defined their 'fundamental' character.

[31] J Bak, 'Political Uses of Historical Comparisons: Medieval and Modern Hungary' (2006) 23 *Florilegium* 273.

[32] And just like the basis of today's Orbán's regime, the basis of Horthy's regime was mainly a self-professed 'Christian middle class', a social group with traditionalist anti-Communist and anti-Semitic sentiments. J Kis, 'From the 1989 Constitution to the 2011 Fundamental Law' in Tóth (n 15) 17.

integrate the territories detached by the 1920 Treaty of Trianon.[33] Many decades later, the celebration of the millennium of the founding of the state brought the revival of the cult of the holy crown. In 2000, the first Orbán government moved the crown from the National Museum to the parliament and placed it 'in exactly the same place where the first republic had been proclaimed on 16 November 1918'.[34] More recently, the Hungarian government has presented the debate within the EU about migration and multiculturalism as a clash between 'national identity protection' and 'identity destruction'.[35] It claims that Hungary's foundational pillars, as a Christian nation strengthening its historical constitution, are in question. For the Orbán government, the EU is siding with the identity destroyers; thus, the 'fight against Brussels' is an obligation in which Hungary, 'as an experienced nation in identity protection ever since 1920'[36] can lead the way.

Although there are several interpretations of these doctrines, the interpretation according to which the crown is a synonym for royal power remained in use throughout.[37] The core ideas indicate a preference for the ancient territory of the Hungarian Kingdom over the current state borders, hierarchy and noble privileges over the republican traditions of Hungary, and a 'mystic membership' of all ethnic Hungarians over constitutional patriotism.[38]

Reference to Hungary's past greatness by invoking the historical constitution and the holy crown is complemented with victimisation. The FL offers the Hungarian nation a self-understanding as a 'victim of great powers' with the greatness to overcome oppression. It depicts Hungarians as victims, stripped of two-thirds of their lands after World War I, then occupied by Nazi Germany, then invaded by the Soviet troops. The FL insists that the country lost its sovereignty on 19 March 1944, when Nazi troops entered its soil, and that this autonomy was restored on 2 May 1990, with the opening session of the first freely elected parliament. Thus, according to the FL's prevailing

[33] A Cieger, 'Book Review of Hungary's Long Nineteenth Century. Constitutional and Democratic Traditions in a European Perspective. Collected Studies. By László Péter' (2012) 1 *Hungarian Historical Review* 248.

[34] Takács (n 8) 923.

[35] As V Orbán put it, 'There is no cultural identity in a population without a stable ethnic composition. The alteration of a country's ethnic makeup amounts to an alteration of its cultural identity.' www.visegradpost.com/en/2017/07/24/full-speech-of-v-orban-will-europe-belong-to-europeans/.

[36] The year 1920 refers to the Treaty of Peace between the Allied and Associated Powers and Hungary (Trianon, 4 June 1920). The speech delivered by L Kövér, the Speaker of the Parliament. See, ES Balogh, 'László Kövér on "hidden power" and "identity protection"' (*Hungarian Spectrum*, 9 March 2019) http://hungarianspectrum.org/2019/03/09/laszlo-kover-on-hidden-power-and-identity-protection/.

[37] Cieger (n 33) 248.

[38] GA Tóth, 'Hungary' in LFM Besselink et al (eds), *Constitutional Law in the EU Members* (Alphen aan den Rijn, Uitgeverij Kluwer BV, 2014) 791. That is why these doctrines cannot be reconciled with universal constitutional principles as some scholars suggests. See, eg, F Hörcher and T Lorman, *A History of the Hungarian Constitution. Law, Government and Political Culture in Central Europe* (London, Bloomsbury, 2020).

ideology, Hungary was just an innocent victim and not an ally of Hitler, and the Holocaust was an exclusively German crime. Hence, contrary to historical facts, the FL denies that the Hungarian state played a decisive role in the tragedy of the Hungarian Jews during World War II. Furthermore, the constitutional text demonises the communist regime but whitewashes the pro-Nazi Hungarian authoritarian Horthy regime. Although it contains a sentence condemning 'the inhuman crimes committed against the Hungarian nation and its citizens under the national socialist and the communist dictatorship', the rest of the text deals only with the 'communist crimes'.[39]

C. The Ethnic Vision of 'We The Nation'

This chosen narrative of national identity serves as a tool for determining who belongs to 'the people'. In the constitutionalist tradition, the notion of 'the people' serves as a criterion to judge whether the totality of citizens and voters is a legitimate source of authority.[40] In this scheme, the 'people' are the subjects of legal rights and obligations; they are the people who fall under the scope of the acts adopted by parliament and bear the consequences of political decisions. In contrast, the FL invokes the mythical concept of the 'nation' instead of the people as the originator of the constitution. Although it does not explicitly define the notion of the nation, its provisions imply that under the term 'nation', the FL understands a political power located outside the legal order. It is perceived as a naturally given, living and willing entity that is based on genetic affiliation and has existed since time immemorial.[41]

The FL seems to be premised on a distinction between the Hungarian nation and (other) nationalities living in Hungary, who are not part of the people behind the FL's enactment. 'The members of the Hungarian nation' include ethnic Hungarians living beyond the state, even without an effective link to it,[42] but there is no place in this concept of the nation for national and ethnic minorities

[39] For instance, the FL declares the 'Communist constitution' of 1949 'invalid' since it was the basis for 'tyrannical rule', and a voluminous Article U deals only with the communist past.

[40] J Kis, *Constitutional Democracy* (New York, Central European University Press, 2003) 65–66.

[41] 'We must state that we do not want to be diverse and do not want to be mixed: we do not want our own colour, traditions and national culture to be mixed with those of others. … We do not want to be a diverse country. We want to be how we became 1100 years ago here in the Carpathian Basin.' V Orbán's speech at the annual general meeting of the Association of Towns Having County Rights on 8 February 2018. www.miniszterelnok.hu/prime-minister-viktor-orbans-speech-at-the-annual-general-meeting-of-the-association-of-cities-with-county-rights/. 'In the Carpathian Basin we are not mixed-race: we are simply a mixture of peoples living in our own European homeland.' V Orbán's speech in Tusnádfürdő [Băile Tuşnad] on 23 July 2022. https://abouthungary.hu/speeches-and-remarks/speech-by-prime-minister-viktor-orban-at-the-31-st-balvanyos-summer-free-university-and-student-camp.

[42] Article D of the FL refers to the 'one single Hungarian nation that belongs together'. See also Z Körtvélyesi, 'From "We the People" to "We the Nation"' in Tóth (n 15) 111.

living within the country. The nation as perceived by the FL is a homogeneous[43] group: it is constructed through an invocation of trans-border co-ethnics and, in parallel, an exclusion of refugees, ethnic minorities and 'others'.[44] The document thus enshrines an ethnic vision of the 'we the nation' concept because it is not the people in a constitutionalist sense who are the sovereigns but those belonging to the 'Hungarian nation'.[45]

In sum, the non-inclusive religious considerations, the historical myths of origin, and the assumed common ethnicity of the Hungarian people serve as the core of the exclusivist[46] pre-institutional national identity provided by the FL. Its repertoire includes both the doctrines of the historical constitution and the holy crown. Hence, it is no coincidence that the FL forms a mental image of an indivisible and homogeneous ethnic, linguistic, and cultural community consisting exclusively of ethnic Hungarians worldwide and cherishes traditionalist values. Because the FL does not allow an evolution of the national identity,[47] this a worthwhile issue for exploration. The next section examines how the HCC navigates between this constitutionally entrenched national identity and the universal principles of constitutionalism.

II. THE RECENT JURISPRUDENCE OF PARTICULARISM

For a long time, the HCC's working vocabulary did not include the term 'identity'. Even though the HCC was inspired[48] by the FCC's *Lisbon Treaty* decision,[49] which introduced the concept of identity into German public law, the HCC avoided applying this word even in its 2010 *Lisbon Treaty* decision.[50] The Hungarian *Lisbon Treaty* decision recognised the primacy of EU law

[43] 'We regard it to be a value that Hungary is a homogenous country and that it shows a very homogenous face in its culture, way of thinking and customs of civilization.' V Orbán's speech at the European Parliament on 19 May 2019. www.index.hu/kulfold/eurologus/2015/05/19/orban_sosem_voltunk_multikulturalis_tarsadalom/.

[44] In the Hungarian political discourse, the malign 'other' is used to define the groups considered not to belong to the nation because they differ in some key characteristics. The threatening 'other' is the 'migrant', and the 'forces' behind the migrant: the 'financiers', the 'pro-refugee' NGOs and 'Brussels'.

[45] Z Körtvélyesi, 'Nation, Nationality, and National Identity: Uses, Misuses, and the Hungarian Case of External Ethnic Citizenship' (2020) 33 *International Journal for the Semiotics of Law* 777. The nationhood principle trumps the citizenship principle. See chapter three in this volume.

[46] Z Körtvélyesi and B Majtényi, 'Game of Values: The Threat of Exclusive Constitutional Identity, the EU and Hungary' (2017) 18 *German Law Journal* 1721.

[47] As, for instance, the Irish or the Polish constitutions do. For more on this, see chapters one and five in this volume.

[48] J Rideau, 'The Case-law of the Polish, Hungarian and Czech Constitutional Courts on National Identity and the "German Model"' in AS Arnaiz and CA Llivina (eds), *National Constitutional Identity and European Integration* (Cambridge, Intersentia, 2013) 243, 253.

[49] BVerfGE 123, 267. For more on this and other relevant decisions of the FCC, see chapter two in this volume.

[50] Constitutional Court Decision 143/2010. (VII. 14.). In English available at: www.hunconcourt.hu/uploads/sites/3/2017/11/en_0143_2010.pdf.

and underscored that the reforms brought about by the Lisbon treaty are of paramount importance. Still, the HCC emphasised that the Lisbon treaty did not change the fact that Hungary retained its independence and sovereignty. Interestingly, the decision did not mention any inherent limits of the European integration or fields reserved for national legislation. Thus, the idea of identity review did not appear in the judgment – it emerged only in a concurring opinion that emphasised that the primacy of EU law is restricted by the sovereignty and constitutional identity of the Member State.[51] A couple of years later, both concurring and dissenting opinions referred to the concept of constitutional identity,[52] but it was only in 2016 that the HCC picked up this idea and embarked on a new path in identity jurisprudence.

By that time, the HCC was already neutralised as a check on the executive. From 1990 to 2010, the HCC was the most potent check on governmental majorities in Hungary's unicameral parliamentary system. However, immediately after its election in 2010, the Orbán government attacked the independence and competencies of the HCC. The Fourth Amendment to the FL adopted in 2013 marked the final capture of the HCC. It continued to exist on paper, but the governing majority packed it with political allies and clipped its wings.[53]

So, the already seized HCC introduced 'the constitutional self-identity' as a justiciable concept into the domestic public law space with its *identity* decision.[54] The case was about the EU refugee relocation scheme.[55] The ombudsman turned to the HCC, asking it to interpret two FL provisions over the refugee issue.

[51] The concurring opinion was written by Judge L Trócsányi, who later became Minister of Justice in the Orbán government.

[52] In Decision 23/2015. (VII. 7.), a dissenting opinion argued that the differentiation between the legal status of churches, denominations and religious communities follows from Hungary's constitutional self-identity (para 89). In Order 3130/2016 (VI. 29.), a concurring opinion argued for an identity review of EU legislative acts (para 22). Both opinions were written by Judge AZs Varga, who was later picked up by V Orbán to become the president of the Kúria. As the UN Special Rapporteur on the independence of judges and lawyers rightly put it, the election of Judge Varga 'has only been made possible as a result of a series of legal amendments to the Hungarian legislation aimed at facilitating his election, and despite the manifest objection of the National Judicial Council' UN Special Rapporteur AL HUN 2/2021, 15 April 2021.

[53] K Kovács and KL Scheppele, 'The Fragility of an Independent Judiciary: Lessons from Hungary and Poland – and the European Union' (2018) 51 *Communist and Post-Communist Studies* 189.

[54] The 2016 Seventh Amendment to the FL used this term for the first time. It was an amendment personally proposed by the prime minister to define the 'core element of the constitution'. It leaned on 'constitutional self-identity' to gain an exemption from EU law in the area of immigration. Since at that time, the governing majority did not have the necessary two-thirds majority in parliament to amend the FL, Constitutional Court decision 22/2016 achieved the required result. Constitutional Court of Hungary, Decision 22/2016. (XII. 5.)

[55] In September 2015, an EU Council Decision was adopted introducing a quota system for the distribution and relocation of asylum seekers and migrants among Member States (EU Council Decision 2015/1601 on establishing provisional measures in the area of international protection for the benefit of Italy and Greece). Hungary challenged this Council Decision before the ECJ (Case C-647/15: *Hungary v Council of the European Union*). Soon afterwards, the European Commission opened an infringement procedure against Hungary concerning its asylum legislation. In response to this, the ombudsman, nominated and elected by the governing majority, turned to the HCC.

One of the provisions prohibits collective expulsion, stating that foreigners staying in Hungary's territory may only be expelled based on a lawful decision.[56] The other is the 'EU clause', which allows Hungary to exercise some of the competences deriving from the FL jointly with other Member States through the EU institutions.[57] The ombudsman explained this move by saying that he wished to clear up legal concerns around the mandatory transfer of asylum seekers to Hungarian territory. Ostensibly, the ombudsman was protecting the asylum seekers' rights by arguing that the FL secures their rights more than the EU law. But in fact, the ombudsman was questioning the EU Council decision's lawfulness and constitutionality by insisting that the HCC was competent to declare secondary EU legislation inapplicable in the domestic legal order to the extent that it conflicts with national identity. The *identity* decision only interpreted the EU clause and left the EU relocation issue to another decision.

A cursory reading suggests that the *identity* decision is typical for a court decision on constitutional identity. Closer examination reveals this is anything but the case. The identity language used by the HCC bears a superficial resemblance to that of the FCC, but it differs from it in three crucial ways. There is a difference regarding the substance of the elements identified as defining part of the respective constitutional identities, the scope of the identity review and the context in which this type of review is conducted.

According to the FCC's jurisprudence, the non-amendable elements of the German Basic Law constitutes the constitutional identity; thus, the concept is based on an attachment to the universal constitutional values recognised by the GBL.[58] By contrast, the Hungarian *identity* decision declares that constitutional identity corresponds to what the FL acknowledges as 'Hungary's self-identity'.[59] Since the FL does not include a non-amendable clause, the decision lists a couple of values as possible components of this 'self-identity': 'freedoms, the division of powers, republic as the form of government, respect of autonomies under public law, the freedom of religion, exercising lawful authority, parliamentarism, equality of rights, acknowledging judicial power, the protection of nationalities that are living with us'.[60] On the face of it, this catalogue of values is compatible with universal constitutional standards.[61] Yet, as the decision reminds us, the FL requires the judges to interpret these values in the light of the National Avowal and the 'achievements' of the historical constitution.[62] Following this instruction, the HCC remains deferential to the

[56] Article XIV(1) of the FL.

[57] Article E(2) of the FL.

[58] Article 79(3) of the GBL. See chapter two in this volume.

[59] Constitutional Court of Hungary (n 54) paras 64, 67.

[60] ibid at para 65.

[61] The pretence of compliance with universal constitutional standards is a phenomenon typical of the recently emerged undemocratic regimes. For more on this see GA Tóth, 'Authoritarianism' in *Max Planck Encyclopaedia of Comparative Constitutional Law* (Oxford, Oxford University Press, 2017).

[62] Constitutional Court of Hungary (n 54) paras 64–65.

claim entrenched in the FL that Hungary's identity is distinctively rooted in the historical constitution. Hence, the identity offered by the FL is not a dialogic and mutable concept – it is static[63] because both the text of the FL and the judicial deference exclude the possibility to interpret this identity in accordance with universal constitutional principles.

Different possible components of the 'constitutional self-identity' appear in other parts of the decision. These may include areas that influence citizens' living conditions, particularly 'the private sphere of their responsibility, personal and social security, protected by fundamental rights, and cases where the linguistic, historical and cultural traditions of Hungary are affected'.[64] This sentence has been taken from the *Lisbon Treaty* decision of the FCC, which maintains that sufficient space should be left for the Member States to regulate economic, cultural and social living conditions when achieving European unification. According to the German decision, this applies in particular to areas that 'shape the citizens' living conditions, in particular, the private sphere of their own responsibility and of political and social security, protected by fundamental rights, as well as to political decisions that rely especially on cultural, historical and linguistic perceptions'.[65] The sentence, which rephrases and modifies the German wording to encompass historical and cultural traditions, was included as part of the Hungarian decision without any argument justifying its presence in the text. Its presence can nevertheless be explained by pointing out that the addition provides a justification for Hungary to use the 'historical and cultural traditions' as a pretext not to implement certain EU legislative acts.

To protect these components of 'constitutional self-identity', the HCC, which perceives itself as 'the guardian' of this identity, has created different judicial tools: the fundamental rights review and the ultra vires review, composed of a sovereignty review and an identity review.[66] In theory, these reviews are the same as the reviews found in the German legal system. And indeed, the terms 'fundamental rights review', 'ultra vires' and 'identity review' might sound familiar to a reader with good knowledge of the German jurisprudence. But in Germany these concepts have been used to draw red lines relating to further European integration in different periods. In 1986, the German court's *Solange II* judgment introduced the fundamental rights review for this purpose.[67] A couple of years later, the 1993 *Maastricht* judgment used the language of sovereignty as a justification for the state not to implement EU law.[68] Today, the

[63] For more on the static and dialogic nature of the concept of identity, see GJ Jacobsohn, *Constitutional Identity* (Cambridge, Harvard University Press, 2010).

[64] Constitutional Court of Hungary (n 54) para 66.

[65] BVerfGE 123, 267, para 4.

[66] Constitutional Court of Hungary (n 54) para 55.

[67] BVerfGE 73, 339.

[68] BVerfGE 89, 155.

same problem is framed as a constitutional identity problem due to the 2009 *Lisbon Treaty* decision.[69]

All these three reviews appeared at once in the Hungarian *identity* decision. The fundamental rights review concerns the protection of rights ensured by the FL against infringements from European legal acts. The HCC does not address whether there is a difference in fundamental rights protection between the national and EU level, but introducing this review implies that the FL guarantees a higher level of fundamental rights protection than the EU. Second, the *identity* decision introduces the sovereignty and identity reviews as components of ultra vires review.[70] The problem with this categorisation is that ultra vires and identity are two different types of claims. During an ultra vires review, the constitutional court may argue that an EU institution that derives its powers from the consent of the Member States is acting ultra vires, and therefore, the act of the EU institution is unlawful and should not be binding in the EU. It is a criticism of the EU with regards to its own commitments to universal constitutional principles. In this case, there is no divergence of fundamental principles; both the EU and the domestic institutions respect the principle in question (eg, democratic accountability) – there is only a debate between the national and EU court over what would constitute this principle's realisation.[71] In contrast, during an identity review, the constitutional court usually questions a fundamental principle (eg, the rule of law or gender equality) by referring to a particular feature of the domestic legal or political system and the country's 'right' to be accommodated in the EU under constitutional identity. The problem here is that the EU court and the national court are not committed to the same principles.

The context in which these types of reviews are conducted is also different. In the *identity* decision, the HCC empowers itself to examine whether the joint exercise of competencies with the EU infringes Hungary's self-identity based on its historical constitution.[72] The reference to the historical constitution further differentiates the Hungarian concept from its German counterpart, because this reference means that constitutional identity is associated with ethnocultural considerations.[73] The *identity* decision suggests that Hungary's 'constitutional self-identity' is distinctively rooted in the historical constitution and the holy

[69] BVerfGE (n 65).

[70] Constitutional Court of Hungary (n 54) para 54.

[71] A good example is the so-called *PSPP* judgment. BVerfGE 146, 216.

[72] The HCC, in its Decision 2/2019, clarified that Hungary could only be deprived of its 'constitutional self-identity' through the final termination of its sovereignty, its independent statehood. Decision 2/2019. (III. 5.).

[73] This interpretation of identity led the HCC to conclude in its Decision 3/2019 that the criminal provision aimed at NGOs assisting the incoming asylum seekers is in harmony with 'the fundamental duty of the state', which is to protect Hungary's self-identity. Decision 3/2019. (III. 7.). In a similar vein, the Kúria held that calling Hungarians 'migrants' violates the dignity of the Hungarian nation (n 24).

crown doctrine, and these features cannot be found elsewhere. However, a closer look at these two doctrines reveals that both are regional phenomena, not specific to Hungarian history.[74]

Even seemingly specific historical traditions are rarely unique and distinctive because their elements may be detected in other countries' historical pasts, too. As historian Ferenc Eckhart convincingly proved, the Hungarian constitutional development is not extraordinary; on the contrary, it quite resembles the constitutional developments of the neighbouring Slavic peoples. For instance, the Czech and Hungarian constitutional development paths are analogous.[75] It is equally true for the holy crown doctrine. While in Western countries, the invisible crown represented the continuity of the state, in Central Europe, the visible crown concept was adopted, under which the material crown has been seen as a source of authority independent of the king himself. It was true for the crown of Charlemagne, for the crown of Saint Wenceslas of Bohemia, and the crown of Polish Boleslaw the Champion.[76] Thus, the holy crown doctrine has its counterpart in other countries' historical pasts too.

What could be unique in the Hungarian judicial interpretation of identity is how universal constitutional values have been discussed and interpreted by the democratic institutions, including the parliament or the HCC, since the 1989 democratic transition. But the FL brought this democratic dialogue to an end by nullifying the entire HCC jurisprudence between 1990 and 2011. None of the constitutional court decisions before the enactment of the FL can be relied on as legal authority, including all prior constitutional court decisions on democracy, human rights, and the rule of law. And even if the HCC were courageous not to follow the path the FL requires, the FL itself would remain a problem.

The ethnocultural national identity entrenched in the FL in many ways contradicts the egalitarian claim that forms the basis of a constitutional democracy: the protection of the human dignity of free and equal individuals. It privileges those who identify with the prescribed Christian culture and accept the historical myths as a reference point while at the same time failing to integrate the whole population. Ultimately, the ethnocultural national identity provided by the FL allows only some and not all people to believe that they are part of the same political community.

It seems improbable that the ethnocultural national identity entrenched in the FL and approved by the HCC in its *identity* decision[77] would conform with

[74] A Wessely, 'The Shaman and Saint Stephen's Holy Crown' in M Heller and B Kriza (eds), *Identities, Ideologies, and Representations in Post-Transition Hungary* (Budapest, Eötvös University Press, 2012).

[75] L Péter, *Hungary's Long Nineteenth Century* (Miklós Lojkó ed, Leiden-Boston, Brill, 2012) 98.

[76] Radnóti (n 29) 91.

[77] G Halmai, 'Abuse of Constitutional Identity. The Hungarian Constitutional Court on Interpretation of Article E) (2) of the Fundamental Law' (2018) 43 *Review of Central and East European Law* 23.

EU law. Should a case come to the ECJ, it would likely realise that a claim that Hungary's traditions, cultures, and interests are so special that they cannot follow a particular piece of EU law would weaken the authority of the ECJ itself and, therefore, ultimately, the rule of law in the EU. The ECJ would also likely take into account that such a solid ethnocultural national identity claim would negatively affect the European constitutional project and shatter its very foundations.[78] A constitutional identity connected to both the text and values of a democratic domestic constitution committed to universal constitutional values is more likely to comply with universal constitutional principles and EU law. But how might such a constitutional identity be developed?

III. THREE PILLARS OF THE RECONSTRUCTED CONSTITUTIONAL IDENTITY

For Hungary to comply with these principles, which are also the foundational values of the EU, it would need to adopt a new democratic constitution suitable for offering an integrative constitutional identity. When developing this identity, the constitution drafters would have to consider universal constitutional principles. This should not be too difficult in the Hungarian context, where being committed to universal principles is part of the national constitutional culture. The most notable example is the commitment of the 1989 constitution to ensure everyone's inherent right to life and human dignity.[79] Adhering to the local peculiarities of constitutionalism is another tradition deeply embedded in the country's history. Although Hungary only became a democracy for the first time in its history in 1989, the theoretical roots of the struggle for universal constitutional principles like freedom and equality can be discovered in the Hungarian past from the progressive 'April Laws' of 1848, which transformed the Hungarian feudal kingdom to a constitutional monarchy, through the declaration of the first Hungarian republic in 1918 to the proclamation of the second republic in 1946.[80] The 1989 constitutional order followed this tradition when setting up domestic institutions (parliament, courts, ombuds-institution), which then played an essential role in interpreting universal principles and applying them to the local context. The 1989 constitution was not able to safeguard Hungarian democracy, but the universal principles it recognised and the democratic institutions it provided may serve as a reference point for the future constitutional identity.

[78] R Uitz, 'National Constitutional Identity in the European Constitutional Project: A Recipe for Exposing Cover Ups and Masquerades' (*Verfassungsblog*, 11 November 2016) www.verfassungsblog.de/national-constitutional-identity-in-the-european-constitutional-project-a-recipe-for-exposing-cover-ups-and-masquerades/.

[79] Article 54(1) of the 1989 Constitution.

[80] English translation of these primary sources provided in F Hörcher and T Lorman, *A History of the Hungarian Constitution. Law, Government and Political Culture in Central Europe* (London, Bloomsbury, 2018) appendix VII, IX, XII.

Following the two-pronged tradition of the commitment to universal principles and local peculiarities of constitutionalism, the pillars of the constitutional identity can include (1) the emblematic political institutions of the Hungarian democratic period between 1989 and 2010, (2) the universal constitutional principles as they were authoritatively interpreted by the independent HCC, and (3) the crucial achievements of EU law concretising universal principles as they were implemented in domestic law. All three ingredients – institutions, principles, and EU law achievements as contextualised in Hungary – are essential. I will discuss each of them in turn in the following sections.

A. Democratic Domestic Institutions

The first pillar of identity includes a commitment to basic democratic institutions built around the 1989 constitution during the country's two decades of democracy: representative government, consensual parliamentary democracy, and meaningful constitutional review exercised by an independent judiciary.

The ideal of representative government has its roots in Hungarian legal traditions. Although there was only one very brief republican period after World War II, the demand for the representative government was deep in the Hungarian collective memory – one of the central demands of the revolutionaries in the 1848 Hungarian Revolution was a separate national government (and not just branches of the central ministries in Vienna) and annual national assemblies in Buda-Pest.[81] The April Laws set up an 'independent Hungarian responsible ministry' who could be called to account. These laws also extended the right to vote to adult males who met certain property requirements and spoke Hungarian. A year later, in April 1849, a separate Hungarian government was established within the Austro-Hungarian Empire. Thus, when the democratic opposition made constitutional choices in 1989, it followed this constitutional tradition and demanded real popular representation and a parliamentary republic. Although the then ruling party desired a semi-presidential system with a popularly elected president,[82] this alternative was closely identified in the public mind with the *ancien régime*. The introduction of a parliamentary democracy with an indirectly elected president followed the example of the proclamation Act I of 1946 that declared Hungary to be a republic with a president elected by the parliamentarians. Hence, the 1989 Hungarian constitutional structure evolved its own constitutional tradition concerning representative government by establishing an adapted parliamentary system instead of importing a presidential architecture.[83]

[81] Péter (n 75) 143.

[82] G Szoboszlai, *Democracy and Political Transformation: Theories and East-Central European Realities* (Budapest, Hungarian Political Science Association, 1991) 203.

[83] L Garlicki, 'Democracy and International Influences', in G Nolte (ed), *European and U.S. Constitutionalism* (Cambridge, Cambridge University Press, 2005) 264.

Another crucial institutional pillar is the consensual parliamentary democracy native to continental Europe. It assumes the presence of more than two parties in the parliament, a coalition government, and a sufficiently proportional electoral system.[84] The 1989 constitution required a consensus of the governing coalition parties to govern the country properly. The system was consensual in another sense, too. The model demanded that governing parties involve their coalition partners and the opposition, at least in constitutional matters. Hence, the coalition government was required to agree with the opposition on the system of government and foundational values. This was ensured by the two-thirds-majority rule, which was not only a formal requirement but also the proof of a broad political consensus in parliament. The rationale behind incorporating the supermajority statutes (major constitutional organs and fundamental rights) was that the government did not need to reshape the constitutional architecture or limit fundamental rights to govern the state properly. However, the constitution drafters would need to be aware that a two-thirds-majority rule should be built on a sufficiently proportional electoral system; otherwise, a party could secure two-thirds of the parliamentary seats with a little more than fifty percent of the votes.

Furthermore, constitutional review exercised by an independent court is an institutional pillar of constitutional identity. Independent checks are of utmost importance in a unitary state with a consensual parliamentary democracy, as legislative and executive powers are intertwined in such a system. In Hungary between 1990 and 2010, constitutional review provided crucial protections, and the position of the HCC as an important participant in the democratic process had a stabilising effect. Thus, meaningful constitutional review has its roots in Hungarian democratic history, and it may also serve as the primary constraint on the executive power in the future. In 1989, during round table discussions, the democratic opposition had three straightforward demands concerning the HCC: first, judges be elected based upon a consensus; second, everyone should have standing before the HCC (*actio popularis*);[85] and third, the HCC should have the power to review the constitutionality of all legal rules and annul unconstitutional ones. These historical demands can provide a solid basis for the institutional pillar of a constitutional judiciary.

When developing a constitutional identity, the constitution drafter should also consider the 1989 constitution's vital public participatory elements, which gave the people the right to play a meaningful role in the governance process beyond voting in elections. It provided ways to direct exercise of popular

[84] The Hungarian electoral system adopted during the democratic transition and its results were far from proportional. A Lijphart, 'Democratization and Constitutional Choices in Czecho-Slovakia, Hungary, and Poland, 1989–1991' (1992) 4 *Journal of Theoretical Politics* 207.

[85] In a similar vein, M Kumm argues that the right to contest in constitutional review settings is at least as empowering as the right to vote. M Kumm, 'The Idea of Socratic Contestation and the Right to Justification: The Point of Rights-Based Proportionality Review' (2010) 4 *Law and Ethics of Human Rights* 168.

sovereignty (popular initiative, referendum) and ensured the right to appeal to an ombuds-institution, which proved to be an efficient tool against maladministration. All these elements (constitutional review, ombudsperson process and referendum) would give the people a platform to challenge rules that ought to bind them. They would provide with the people the possibility to participate in decision-making processes in a democratic way.

B. Universal Constitutional Principles as they were Contextualised in Hungary

The 1989 Constitution committed itself to universal constitutional principles (human dignity, equality) and granted the courts, including the Constitutional Court, a free hand in interpreting them. The Fundamental Law also proclaims some constitutional principles[86] but recognises them in an equivocal and conditional way and obliges the courts to interpret the universal constitutional principles according to the ethnocultural national identity. The new constitution should recognise and safeguard all constitutional principles and give the courts a free hand in contextualising them. Since Hungary is an EU member state and also member of the Council of Europe, the domestic contextualisation of these universal values should be embedded within the European constitutional context.

Understandings, practices, and interpretations of these values might differ to a certain degree from one Member State to another because the Member States are self-governing polities. We may think of the German doctrine of militant democracy, which aims to protect the democratic state through a variety of laws that ultimately leads to a specific understanding of free speech. In a similar vein, according to the Czech and Polish constitutional jurisprudence, the constitutional right to free speech does not encompass hate speech.[87] Contrariwise, until 2010, Hungarian free speech constitutional jurisprudence embraced the idea of content neutrality and did not restrict speech in the interest of social peace. The free speech interpretation of the HCC took a different path than other European courts did, but it remained consistent with the universal constitutionalist principles. The same is true of some other leading decisions of the HCC. For instance, in the death penalty judgment, the court developed a complete theory of human dignity by saying that it is a value *a priori* and beyond law and is inviolable.[88] Or, to take another example, the HCC famously stated in one of its early decisions that the state was to remain neutral in cases concerning the right to freedom of conscience and that it was required to guarantee the

[86] Some but not all, see eg, K Kovács, 'The Missing Link: Equality' in Tóth (n 15) 171.

[87] Czech Constitutional Court Pl ÚS 5/92, Decision 2943/08 of January 2009, Polish Constitutional Tribunal, 7 June 1994, K 17/93.

[88] Constitutional Court of Hungary, Decision 23/1990. (X. 31.)

possibility of the free formation of individual belief.[89] These are just a few examples of how some crucial fundamental constitutional principles may be defined according to the Hungarian and the European constitutionalist tradition.

C. EU Law Achievements as Domestic Authorities Concretised Them

In addition to the universal principles, there are specific legal safeguards in EU law concretising universal constitutional principles such as freedom and equality that might also serve as pillars of constitutional identity. These include anti-discrimination laws, including the ban on ethnic discrimination and gender equality measures. A significant milestone on the road to equality in the EU was the adoption of the Racial Equality Directive,[90] which prohibits discrimination on the grounds of racial or ethnic origin in both the public and private sectors. Likewise, the equal treatment of women and men in employment, including the principle of equal pay for equal work, is a long-standing EU constitutional tradition.[91] In 2003, Hungary adopted its first anti-discrimination law[92] in line with these directives; however, the drafters constructed the anti-discrimination law such that it was broader in scope. It included other prohibited grounds in addition to those required by the directives and went beyond the employment field by referring to all aspects of social life (housing, access to goods and services, etc).[93] This commitment to equality in everyday life could serve as one of the main pillars of constitutional identity.

Information rights may be another possible component of constitutional identity. The introduction of technology-neutral information rights, including data protection and informational self-determination, was one of the first important steps made by the Hungarian authorities after 1989.[94] There were strong protections on privacy in domestic law, the institutional underpinnings of which were developed in a system composed of ombudsperson-like and judicial protection.[95] However, the FL abolished the data protection ombudsperson's office, discharged the incumbent ombudsman prematurely, and established an administrative agency for data protection. The ECJ later held that Hungary violated the EU law on data protection, but the ombudsman was not reinstated.[96] Since then, privacy and data protection have been at the heart of political discourse.

[89] Constitutional Court of Hungary, Decision 4/1993. (II. 12.)

[90] Council Directive 2000/43/EC of 29 June 2000.

[91] See, eg, Directive 2006/54/EC of 5 July 2006, Council Directive 92/85/EEC of 19 October 1992, and Council Directive 2004/113/EC of 13 December 2004.

[92] Act CXXV of 2003 on Equal Treatment and the Promotion of Equal Opportunities.

[93] ibid at Articles 26, 30.

[94] Constitutional Court of Hungary, Decisions 15/1991. (IV. 13.) and 46/1995. (VI. 30.)

[95] PL Láncos, 'Freedom of Information in Hungary: A Shifting Landscape' in DC Dragos et al (eds), *The Laws of Transparency in Action, A European Perspective* (Cham, Palgrave, 2019) 389–424, 390.

[96] Case C-288/12, *Commission* v *Hungary* [2014].

It should be emphasised that the catalogue of crucial EU law achievements considered in this part is far from exhaustive. These are just examples of how EU law is contextualised and concretised in the domestic system might serve as pillars of constitutional identity.

IV. CONCLUSION

In the past thirty years, Hungary had two constitutions representing two identities. The 1989 constitution eventually was not able to safeguard Hungarian democracy, but it had the potential to facilitate democracy and ensure the self-government of free and equal persons through the law. In 2011, the FL replaced the democratic constitution and introduced an ethnocultural national identity. It uses the term 'constitutional self-identity', but it, in fact, refers to national identity connected to ethnic and religious homogeneity and particularities – the unique history and cultural traditions of the Hungarian community. The HCC has already rubberstamped this identity. Its decisions understand the laws as expressions of this identity and examine the constitutional validity of laws through the prism of this ethnocultural national identity.

The main problem with the ethnocultural national identity is that it is inconsistent with universal constitutional values and incompatible with EU law. Based upon the ECJ's adjudication scheme, it seems that national identity aimed at protecting ethnic or religious purity runs counter to EU law and the ECJ's efforts to reconcile the various national identities of the Member States with EU law.

This chapter presents an alternative to the ethnocultural understanding of identity: a new and overarching sense of constitutional identity that is in accord with universal constitutional principles, which are also the foundational values of the EU. The paper demonstrates how such an inclusive constitutional identity may be developed. It argues that a sufficiently robust constitutional identity may be built on the prominent democratic political institutions set up during the two decades of democracy: representative government, consensual parliamentary democracy, and meaningful constitutional review conducted by an independent judiciary. The second pillar of the new identity may be the universal constitutional principles as interpreted by the HCC's transformative decisions.[97] Finally, the constitutional identity may be built on the crucial EU achievements concretising universal constitutional principles as domestic authorities implemented them. Such achievements include non-discrimination in all aspects of social life and informational self-determination.

[97] But see P Bárd, N Chronowski and Z Fleck, 'Inventing Constitutional Identity in Hungary', *MTA Law Working Papers* 2022/6, 32.

Part III

The European Constitutional Challenge

7

Un-European Identity Claims: On the Relationship between Constituent Power, Constitutional Identity and its Implications for Interpreting Article 4(2) TEU

MATTIAS KUMM

THE IDEA OF constitutional identity has many meanings and has been used in a variety of ways.[1] In Europe, the understanding of the term is of practical significance in particular because Article 4(2) of the Treaty on European Union (TEU), which requires EU law to respect national identities 'inherent in their fundamental structures, political and constitutional'. Whereas Member States are generally under a duty to apply EU law even when it is in tension with national constitutional commitments, this provision has been interpreted to authorise Member States not to apply EU law, insofar they can successfully claim that the application of EU law would be incompatible with their national constitutional identity. In the following, I will refer to 'national identity inherent in their fundamental structures, political and constitutional' simply as 'constitutional identity'.[2] In the context of Article 4(2) TEU, questions relating to constitutional identity thus become questions about

[1] See the introduction and chapter one in this volume.

[2] Whereas the term 'national identity' is of course more capacious, Article 4(2) TEU only protects national identities properly qualified. The qualifier refers to national identities 'inherent to their fundamental structures, political and constitutional'. Since the fundamental structures of the political system are themselves part of the constitution, it is redundant to speak of 'political and constitutional' fundamental structures. That choice of language is best understood to reflect the various degrees in which Member States have made explicit and worked out in formal constitutional texts the norms that define the fundamental structure of the political system. The idea here is that the scope of the protected national identity should not depend on the degree to which these fundamental structures are concretely and explicitly codified in a constitutional text. When speaking of 'constitutional identity' in the following I will refer to a capacious concept of the constitution,

the domain over which Member States can claim to be exempt from the duty to apply EU law.

What is clear and uncontroversial is that national identities inherent in Member States' fundamental structures, political and constitutional, are not already in play anytime a national constitutional provision, as interpreted by a national apex court, is in tension with the requirements of EU law. Article 4(2) TEU does not mean that the primacy of EU law applies only to national sub-constitutional norms and that constitutional norms generally prevail over EU law. Only a qualified set of norms and understandings that connects to Member States' political and constitutional 'fundamental structure' allows Member States to claim exemption from the application of EU law incompatible with them. The question is what that means: what kind of norms can make up the constitutional identity of a Member State and thus provide the grounds for exempting that state from applying EU law when it is in conflict with them?

There is by now a rich literature describing the various positions of Member States, Constitutional Courts and scholars in the European Member States in doctrinal terms.[3] What I will be trying to do here is provide a general, theoretically informed framework for thinking about questions of constitutional identity as they are relevant for engaging Article 4(2) TEU.

I will begin by analysing the basic structure of a widely influential conception of constitutional identity associated with Carl Schmitt (section I), before contrasting it with a competing conception, which I call the Constitutionalist conception, and which, I will argue, is more persuasive (section II). Even though within either conception, there is space for basic principles for liberal constitutional democracy on the one hand, as well as more particular national commitments on the other, the way they operate in constitutional discourse and the way they are identified and circumscribed differs fundamentally. I then argue that the European Union commits the Member States to national identities, including constitutional identities, not in conflict with Constitutionalist principles, presumed to be shared in Europe and grounding all public authority exercised there (section III). Identities at odds with fundamental constitutionalist principles are not to be respected, whereas national constitutional identities compatible with them are generally unlikely to be in conflict with EU law but may exceptionally qualify as a ground not to apply otherwise valid EU law. In other words, any legally persuasive jurisprudence of particularism is circumscribed

which includes as part of it the concrete basic normative understandings and practices that structure, guide and constrain the political process, whether or not those normative understandings are specifically codified in constitutional texts. In this understanding 'national identity inherent to their fundamental structures, political and constitutional' becomes identical with 'constitutional identity'. (Furthermore, the terms 'constitutional identity' and the idea of the 'basic structure' can, as concepts of general constitutional theory, be regarded as coextensive and will be used as synonyms).

[3] See, for example, C Callies and G van der Schyff, *Constitutional Identity in a Europe of Multilevel Constitutionalism* (Cambridge, Cambridge University Press, 2020).

by common European constitutionalist commitments. Un-European identity claims by the Member States are claims that are in conflict with European constitutionalist principles – violating European constitutionalist identity – and can make no claim to be respected.

I. CARL SCHMITT: A FORMAL CONCEPTION OF CONSTITUTIONAL IDENTITY

Under one conception, generally attributed to Carl Schmitt,[4] the idea of constitutional identity is formal: The idea of constitutional identity is not defined in substantive terms. Indeed, there are *no limitations on what the content of constitutional identity might be*. The substantive content of constitutional identity is determined by the basic decision made by the constituent power or *pouvoir constituant*, enacting one kind of constitution – understood as a decision on the form and structure of political unity – rather than another. This makes it possible to speak of the constitutional identity of a fascist dictatorship, a communist one-party state, a liberal constitutional democracy or an ethno-culturally exclusionary nationalist electoral autocracy. These constitutions may differ considerably, but all qualify as constitutions, and all have a constitutional identity. This way of understanding constitutional identity opens the door to the jurisprudence of particularism, conceptually unrestricted and unguided by basic norms of liberal constitutional democracy.

The *function* of the concept of constitutional identity so understood was traditionally to place limits on the constitutional amendment power to protect the results of the exercise of constituent power (1). In the European context, it serves to protect the results of national constituent power against encroachment by supranational institutions (2).

(1) The function of the concept of constitutional identity was to mark the privileged domain of constituent power and distinguish it from and limit the constitutional amendment power. The constituent power, and only the constituent power, has the authority to decide over the general form and structure of political unity by enacting a constitution. The constitutional amendment power is limited to addressing institutional or substantive specifics but may not change the basic structure of the constitution, or, to say the same thing, it may not change a constitution's identity. To the extent that the formal amendment process is used to bring about changes in the fundamental structure of the constitution, such amendments are ultra vires and thus unconstitutional, even if the constitution does not specifically contain a clause that limits the substantive scope of the amendment power. This way of thinking about the amendment power was used, among others, by the Indian Supreme Court in the development of its 'basic

[4] C Schmitt, *Verfassungslehre* 11th edn (Berlin, Duncker & Humblot, 1928) 75–103.

structure doctrine'[5] and has spread across the world to other countries in Asia to Africa and South America.[6]

What norms make up the basic structure or the constitutional identity of a constitution is, of course, not easy to define. Constitutional identity or the basic structure of the constitution is at issue when a constitutional change would bring about a situation where the constitution would stop being the kind of constitution it was before the amendment. This obviously raises many questions and leaves room for much argument and disagreement about how exactly these lines are to be drawn. But the function of the doctrine in a context where apex courts have jurisdiction to interpret and enforce constitutional questions is to authorise courts to draw these lines.

Note that a constitutional provision that does explicitly textually limit the amendment power to exclude the constitution's basic structure – such as the 'eternity clause' found in Article 79(3) of the German Basic Law (GBL) – would provide some authoritative guidance as to how to understand the basic structure of a constitution. But ultimately, such provisions would be of declaratory significance only. If such a clause did not exist, the basic structure of the constitution would still be immune from constitutional amendment legally. An attempt by the constitutional legislature to abolish or amend a positivised basic structure clause like Article 79(3) of the GBL using the amendment procedure specified in the constitution could not effectively enlarge the scope of the amendment power to include the constitution's constitutional identity. In that sense, something like an explicit 'eternity clause' may provide lawyers with a helpful textual basis to work through the limits of the amendment power, but the scope and content of those limits should ultimately be understood to be independent of whether they are explicitly codified or not.

(2) In the European context, the idea of constitutional identity similarly functions to protect the national constituent power's monopoly to determine the constitutional identity of a state. But here, the idea of constitutional identity is not directed against an overreaching constitutional legislature seeking to amend the constitutional text. Here the threat is ultimately supranational and can take two different, more concrete forms: on the one hand, constitutional identity provides a barrier to an overreaching national legislature when that legislature decides in the context of ratifying European Treaties to 'transfer powers' to the European Union. Even when the legislature does so using a procedure that requires supermajorities and is equivalent to the constitutional amendment procedure, the basic structure defines the legal limits of such a transfer. The transfer of powers must never be such that it undermines the constitutional identity of the Member State. On the other hand, those powers transferred to the

[5] *Kesavananda Bharati v State of Kerala* [1973] 4 SCC 225 (Supreme Court of India). See also chapter one in this volume.

[6] Jurisdictions outside of the European Union that have accepted the 'basic structure doctrine' today include among others Bangladesh, Malaysia, Pakistan, Myanmar, Uganda and Columbia.

European Union must not be interpreted and exercised by the European Union in a way that would undermine national constitutional identity. If they are, such an interpretation or exercise cannot be regarded as binding by that Member State. In that way, constitutional identity is a barrier to the progressive development of European law by European institutions.

The German Federal Constitutional Court's (FCC) elaboration of the doctrine of constitutional identity is clearly informed by this understanding of constitutional identity. Even if its jurisprudence is ostensibly focused on the protection of human rights and democracy as the German constitutional identity specifically protected in Article 79(3) GBL's 'eternity clause', the link between constitutional identity and the basic principles of liberal constitutional democracy is contingent only. It is clear that the court's understanding of constitutional identity is shaped by the theoretical presuppositions laid out above. This is apparent in two ways.

First, the FCC emphasises that whatever limitations it is deriving from Article 79(3) of the GBL – the constitutions positively codified constitutional identity as one connected to liberal constitutional democracy – can be overcome by an exercise of constituent power. If one day a new European Union were to be created by way of a European Demos exercising European constituent power, then all restrictions contained in the German constitution – including those defining its identity – would no longer present a barrier. Constituent power both defines and is able to overcome constitutional identity. Constitutional identity claims may be claims justifying limits on the national application of EU law, but they are not absolute, legally insurmountable barriers.

Second, the FCC's understanding of Article 79(3) of the GBL, and of democracy specifically, is refracted through the idea of state sovereignty. This focus is most obvious in the FCC's *Maastricht* decision.[7] But constructively, the court's *Lisbon Treaty* decision[8] and its later jurisprudence did not fundamentally change in this regard, notwithstanding the role that the concept of constitutional identity would play from then onwards. This rhetorical shift of emphasis – it is no more than that – is widely believed to have been influenced by the fact that the newly introduced language of Article 4(2) TEU allowed the court to frame its argument in a way that relates to EU law and makes its claims more palatable. EU primary law does not mention the sovereignty of Member States and certainly provides no proviso that would allow Member States to set aside EU law when it was deemed to be incompatible with sovereignty.

The language of constitutional identity as it relates to constituent power within a Schmittian framework is closely connected to the idea of sovereignty. If we imagine constituent power to be unbound and unlimited, as Schmitt, referring to Abbé de Sieyès, does, then it can only be so because the power of the sovereign is unlimited. In that sense, the idea of constituent power in the French

[7] BVerfGE 89, 155, 190.
[8] BVerfGE 123, 267, 346.

Revolution, as read by Schmitt, takes up the absolutist tradition which insists on the sovereignty of the king. Only now, it vests sovereignty not in the king but in 'the people'. When the people acting together as constituent power decide on the form and content of their political unity when giving itself a constitution, their authority is as boundless as the sovereignty of the absolute ruler was. Constituent power creates the world of positive law in the form of the highest law out of nothing, legally speaking, in much the same way as an almighty god creates the world out of nothing and with no constraints. Given that the almighty gods in the political world are a plurality of territorially separated *demoi* exercising their constituent power, the space for the jurisprudence of particularism appears to be unconstrained. There is, in this way of construing the constitutional universe, no necessary link between liberal constitutional democracy and the exercise of constituent power and constitutional identity. Constitutional identity can have any content, depending on the nature of the constitution that the constituent power has willed into being.

II. A NEW START: CONSTITUTIONALISM, CONSTITUENT POWER AND CONSTITUTIONAL IDENTITY

The Schmittian approach linking the idea of constitutional identity to constituent power and sovereignty, I will argue, is not only a misreading of the eighteenth-century revolutions and Sieyès but, more importantly, also an unpersuasive constitutional theory. It is a mistake to think that constituent power knows no internal limits and that constitutional identity can be divorced from a commitment to human rights, democracy and the rule of law. The space for a jurisprudence of particularism that the idea of constitutional identity invokes is circumscribed by basic principles constitutive of constitutionalism. In the following, I will try to substantiate that claim and, in very broad strokes, develop the general contours and basic arguments for what might be called a constitutionalist conception of constituent power (A) and then discuss what the implications of this alternative account are for the idea of constitutional identity, the interpretation of Article 4(2) TEU and the European jurisprudence of particularism more generally (B).

A. Constitutionalist Conception of Constituent Power

The American Declaration of Independence and the French Declaration of Rights of Man and Citizens did not simply take up the idea that there were some natural law constraints limiting what states could legitimately do. They brought into the political world through revolutionary actions the insistence that public authority, if it is to have the legitimacy it claims to have, must respect the status of each human being as free and equal. The rights that those subject to public authority have are those of persons that have the equal status of being free persons. Not only everything that a government does, but also how it is constituted, has to be justifiable, in the end, as respecting, protecting and helping realise the rights derived from persons having such a status. To put it another way: How the government is structured, the means through which government power is exercised, and the purpose it pursues must be conceived as part of the project of self-government of free and equals. There are three basic requirements conventionally derived from such a starting point: government has to be democratically structured; its rule has to be exercised within and operate through law, and its substantive focus must be to respect, protect and fulfil the rights of its subjects as free and equals. This gives rise to the trinitarian formula that defines the commitments constitutive of constitutionalism properly so called: human rights, democracy, and the rule of law.

How, then, does constituent power come into the picture? Constituent power, in this conception, is the power of those who are to be bound by the constitution to concretise and specify what those principles mean for a particular community at a particular point in time by way of enacting a constitution. The constitutive principles of constitutionalism are highly abstract and indeterminate and require context-sensitive specification, about which there is likely to be serious disagreement. The principle that government be democratic may require, among other things, that regular elections be held, and that universal suffrage be granted, but it does not determine the voting age, the number of years between elections, the role of referenda, or the basic rules governing the elections (a first past the post system, proportional representation) etc. Furthermore, democracy may require that fundamental general decisions are to be made by representatives in a deliberative process which has its centre of gravity in Parliament. But whether the legislative process is structured as a unicameral process or the assent of a second chamber is required, or whether the government is led by an administration that needs the support of the majority in Parliament (a parliamentary system), or is elected independently (like in presidential systems), or something in between, is not determined by the principle. All these questions, along with questions relating to the structure of the judiciary or the list of human rights to enjoy constitutional protection, require concrete and specific legal answers, generally to be provided by a constitutional text. The constituent power is not a general power to decide on the form and structure of political unity. It is the more narrow power to determine the specific constitutional norms through which the self-government of free and equals is to proceed. It is the power to interpret the trinitarian formula of human rights, democracy and the rule of law as it is to apply to a particular community at a particular point in time.

Note the consequence of such a conception of constituent power: if a constitution-giving process leads to the establishment of a theocracy, a communist one-party regime or an ethnoculturally exclusive semi-autocracy, then such a result could not be described as an attempt to interpret, specify and give concrete meaning to the idea of self-government of free and equals for a particular political community in a particular context. It does not qualify valid exercise of constituent power. The resulting document could not be described as a constitution properly so called. This is a position that echoes the famous Article 16 of the French Declaration of Rights of Man and Citizen of 1789, declaring that any community in which the separation of powers is not guaranteed, and rights are not secured does not have a constitution. For constitutional comparativists, such a proposition may seem shocking, even outrageously exclusionary, at first. It would follow, for example, that China or Iran do not have constitutions properly so called. It would also allow us to say that Hungary's 2011 Fundamental Law,[9] insofar as some of its provisions were to be judged as incompatible with the idea of self-government of free and equals, would be constitutionally deficient, even if that deficiency would not be sufficient to deny it the status of a constitution, given the general alignment with constitutionalist ideals of its specific provisions.[10] Of course, the fact that a constitution does not qualify as a constitution properly so called does not mean that it's not worthwhile to study or to take an interest in it.[11] What does follow is that because such 'constitutions' do not reflect a commitment to take seriously the status of each person as free and equal, they do not qualify as grounds for the exercise of legitimate authority, opening up the spectre of legitimate disobedience, resistance and, as a last resort, revolution.[12] This is not the place to make that argument in general philosophical terms. Here it must suffice to point to the fact that this is a position effectively embraced by eighteenth-century revolutionaries, notwithstanding the deeply flawed way they understood this idea as far as its extension to non-whites, women or those without property was concerned. The Declaration of Independence was effectively a political pamphlet seeking to justify a secessionist revolution based on a whole list of grievances, all of which are exemplifications of violations of the general

[9] For more on this, see chapter six in this volume.

[10] For the difficulties involved in identifying authoritarian populist traces in constitutions by going through each of its provisions taking a checklist approach, see KL Scheppele, 'The Rule of Law and the Frankenstate: Why Governance Checklists Do Not Work' (2013) 26 *Governance* 559–62, 559ff.

[11] An excellent example of a recent study of authoritarianism from a constitutional perspective is G Frankenberg, *Authoritarianism: Constitutional Perspectives* (Cheltenham, Edward Elgar, 2020).

[12] Would it be correct to say that at least in the present the fear of revolution is a phenomenon restricted to the world, which under this conception might be called the extraconstitutional world? To put it another way: are there liberal constitutional democracies that face revolutionary threats? Is it a coincidence that the concerns in liberal constitutional democracies are framed as 'democratic backsliding' and authoritarian populists often responsible for it effectively corrupt existing constitutional structures, manipulating them or weaponising them to ensure they do not function like they are supposed to, but rarely display constitutional constructive ambition? And even when they do, like in the case of Hungary's 2011 Fundamental Law effectively enacted by Fidesz under Viktor Orbán, mainly the nationalist exclusionary framing of the preamble provides evidence of a break with liberal constitutional democracy. The core norms associated with constitutionalism, the commitment to the rule of law and independent courts, the democratic process, freedom of speech and association etc are all formally recognised, even when the concrete rules for the operation of these institutions and rights will have been subtly shaped in a way to privilege the dominant party, entrench its policies, and make life difficult for those in opposition.

idea of self-government of free and equals articulated in the second paragraph of the Declaration. Similarly, the claim that a polity that does not respect the basic ideas in the Declaration of Rights of Man and Citizen does not have a constitution – that is the core meaning of its Article 16 – is plausibly read as implying that without such a constitution there can be no legitimate authority. Even the famous text of Sieyès, describing the constituent power, is best interpreted as imagining that power to be limited to fulfil its function to establish a constitution properly so called.[13] In modern constitutional practice, there are constitutions that explicitly write a right to resistance into the constitution to address situations where counter-constitutional movements seek to abolish the constitution and seek to have it replaced with an order that gives up on the basic structure of a free and democratic rule of law based order.[14] Militant constitutionalism, as it developed in the twentieth century defending constitutionalist achievements against backsliding, is the flip side of the revolutionary constitutionalism of the eighteenth century.

B. Constitutional Identity and Article 4(2) TEU

With such a conception of constituent power and the idea of constitutionalism in the background, how then to make sense of constitutional identity?

On the one hand, the constitutional identity of any constitution properly so called consists of the structural features that ensure that it is liberal democratic. If the European Union were to impose requirements on the Member States that are incompatible with Member States' general commitments to human rights, democracy and the rule of law, then states can plausibly invoke Article 4(2) TEU. These types of claims are characteristic of the claims made by the FCC. Even though its general conception of constituent power in its relationship to the eternity clause of Article 79(3) of the GBL is mistaken, as I argued above, its concrete focus are the principles referred to as eternal in the Basic Law, and those include the principle described here as constitutive of constitutionalism. The whole *Solange* saga[15] is a story of insisting on not sacrificing human rights protection on the altar of European integration: for so long as the European Union did not protect human rights itself in a way that was structurally equivalent to national protections, national constitutional courts – to safeguard their constitutional identity – have to step in and review European laws on human rights grounds. But they could and, to simplify somewhat, generally did stop

[13] For such a reading see R Fasel, 'Constraining Constituent Conventions: Emmanuel-Joseph Sieyès and the Limits of Pouvoir Constituant' (2022) 20 *International Journal of Constitutional Law* 1103–29.

[14] Such provisions can be found, for example, in the Portuguese Constitution (Article 21) and German Constitution (Article 20(4)).

[15] BVerfGE 37, 271; 73, 339.

doing that, once the European Union developed its own human rights jurisprudence, with a Constitutional Charter later being included in the EU's body of primary law. Furthermore, according to the FCC, if the European Union acts ultra vires in a way that is clear and has significant structural implications, then such acts are a violation not only of the rule of law but also of the principle of democracy since the authorisation of European Union institutions is ultimately derived from the Treaties ratified democratically by the Member States. Of course, the fact that a national apex court makes critical claims against EU law with regard to constitutionalist bona fides does not mean the court is justified in its claim. It is my view, for example, that the FCC was mistaken in interpreting its role to review whether the European Central Bank was acting ultra vires or not, given that this was a function of the European Court of Justice (ECJ) to assess.[16] In practice, these are questions to be settled in the interaction between the ECJ and apex courts within the context of the preliminary reference procedure. But whatever the case might be, here, claims relating to human rights, democracy and the rule of law are made to safeguard national constitutional identity in a way that, in principle, is plausible.

Note, however, that here an issue is framed as 'respecting a Member State's constitutional identity', that in substance describes and criticises constitutionally deficient practices on the EU level. Since the European Union, too, is committed to human rights, democracy and the rule of law, as spelled out explicitly in Article 2 TEU, national courts, when making constitutional identity claims of this kind, are, in fact, criticising the European Union for not living up to its own constitutional commitments. In practice, these are not situations where the Member States make particularistic claims relating to their history or culture as it is reflected in their constitutions. They are critically castigating the European Union for its deficiencies with regard to constitutionalist standards, effectively pressuring the European Union to change its practice. Invoking constitutional identity in this way is not part of the jurisprudence of particularism. It is the jurisprudence of militant constitutionalism, a kind of official civil disobedience, refusing to implement European legal requirements on the grounds that they are constitutionally deficient and that the European Union should change its ways.

So, is there no space for a genuine jurisprudence of particularism within such an understanding of constitutionalism? There is, but to understand the space for it, it is useful to be clear about what it excludes. Once the idea of constitutionalism is foundationally connected to a commitment to human rights, democracy and the rule of law, then there is no space for a jurisprudence of particularism that is incompatible with such principles. Unlike in the

[16] M Kumm, 'Rebel Without a Good Cause: Karlsruhe's Misguided Attempt to Draw the CJEU into a Game of "Chicken" and What the CJEU Might do About It' (2014) 15 *German Law Journal* 203, 209–15.

Schmittian conception, there is no space for constitutional identities that are connected to authoritarian, illiberal or exclusionary nationalist structures or norms, for example. These structures can simply not be part of constitutional identities properly so called, because they violate constitutionalist principles. They may be claimed to be part of national identities, but if so, then a state which invokes them runs afoul of the Copenhagen accession criteria[17] and is in violation of what Article 2 TEU describes as the foundational values of the European Union that are common to the Member States. Because the European Union is founded on and committed to constitutionalist principles, these could be called Un-European identity claims. They cannot plausibly be made under Article 4(2) TEU to justify the non-application of EU law. On the contrary, to the extent identity claims are connected to norms and practices that are in clear violation of constitutionalist principles, the core issue is what instruments the European Union has available to pressure the Member States to change those practices and align them with common constitutionalist standards.

This leaves two kinds of particularistic claims that can plausibly be made under Article 4(2) TEU. They can only be gestured towards here. The first claim concerns a constitutional identity claim that is tied to a particular interpretation of a constitutional principle. The second category concerns identity claims that are neither interpretations of basic constitutionalist principles nor are they violations of them. This category of cases presumes that not all laws and not even all norms in the constitution are necessarily closely connected to basic constitutional principles. I conclude with an illustration of the first kind of claim: suppose that in the wake of Russian aggression in Ukraine, a new European Security Policy would come about and establish, among other things, an antiterrorism law that authorises the Member States as a last resort, if necessary and proportionate under the circumstances, to shoot down a civilian aircraft captured by and in control of terrorists to prevent them from using the plane as a weapon against civilian targets like high rises or nuclear power plants. Assume the ECJ would hold such a law not to be in violation of the right to life or human dignity because, notwithstanding the expected tragic death of innocent passengers, their claim to life was not an absolute bar to government action in such a situation. The FCC would insist on its own absolutist reading of human dignity in this context[18] and insist that German public officials may never order such a plane to be shot down, no matter how many people's lives might be saved by this. The best case that could be made for the German Court, in my view, is that, given Germany's history of abuse of life by public officials under the National Socialist regime, the intentional killing of innocent civilians by public officials was rightly established as a categorical

[17] The accession criteria (Copenhagen criteria) can be accessed at <https://eur-lex.europa.eu/EN/legal-content/glossary/accession-criteria-copenhagen-criteria.html>.

[18] BVerfGE 115, 118.

taboo and connected to a distinctive German understanding of human dignity. Whatever the security problem might be that German officials are facing, they are required to find a solution that categorically bars them from undertaking any course of action that is sure to involve the death of innocent civilians. Even though human dignity is clearly a universal notion, historical and cultural reasons of this kind might justify deviation from the EU's more permissive, and let's assume, in this case,[19] correct understanding.[20] In these kinds of cases, different interpretations of basic constitutional principles compete. And whereas within the domain of EU law, normally EU human rights standards as interpreted by the ECJ prevail, there are good grounds to permit the Member States to insist on a reasonable differing interpretation if such an interpretation is so deeply connected to national history and culture that it plausibly qualifies as part of its constitutional identity. This is particularly true when that identity is the result of a critical engagement with that country's past in light of its failures. So, in this case Germany would be justified in not applying the law, to the extent it authorises what in Germany is deemed to be a violation of human dignity.

Kriszta Kovács argues in the introduction to this volume[21] that such particularistic interpretations of universal principles can only be invoked when they are connected to national narratives of the historic struggle for universal principles like freedom and equality. Whereas I think that such a limit may be too strict, the fact that a particular interpretation is the result of national historic struggles relating to such principles is a strong presumption to make these identity claims acceptable under EU law. Conversely, when such a historical narrative of struggle and progress for the realisation of constitutional principles is absent, the ECJ may scrutinise more closely the reasonableness (not correctness) of the national claims. If the identity is nothing but the result of inertia, a simple continuation of practices of the past, without ever having faced serious justificatory pressures relating to constitutional principles, then the claim that the existing practice reflects a reasonable context sensitive local interpretation of universal practices deserves closer scrutiny.[22]

[19] For an argument that the argument put forward by the FCC is not a persuasive interpretation of human dignity, see M Kumm, 'Political Liberalism and the Structures of Rights' in G Pavlakos (ed) *Law, Rights, Discourse: The Legal Philosophy of Robert Alexy* (Oxford, Hart, 2007) 155–56.

[20] This is the kind of jurisprudence of particularism with regard to human rights that the ECJ has also accepted in the context of assessing justifications for restrictions on freedoms of goods and services, see for example Case 36/02 *Omega* [2004] ECR I-9609.

[21] See the introductory chapter in this volume.

[22] This would probably mean, for example, that if this became relevant for the enforcement of provisions of EU law one day, French rules relating to *laicite* would be judged more deferentially as interpretations of religious freedom, then say the establishment of an official church in the Scandinavian countries.

III. CONCLUSION

This chapter is mainly a ground clearing exercise. Its ambition is not to resolve or discuss in detail the rich set of cases that have arisen under Article 4(2) TEU and the specific problems they raise but to provide a basic conceptual framework for thinking about constitutional identity claims under Article 4(2) TEU. The chapter makes three core claims.

First, there is no legal space for claims relating to constitutional identity that are illiberal, authoritarian or otherwise exclusionary. All constitutional identity claims must be compatible with the basic principles of constitutionalism. A commitment to human rights, democracy, and the rule of law – the 'holy trinity' of the constitutionalist project – are necessary features of constitutions properly so called. In Europe, they are also explicitly mentioned as foundational values for the European Union and common to all Member States in Article 2 TEU. The principles of constitutionalism circumscribe the limits for any jurisprudence of particularism justified under Article 4(2) TEU.

Second, constitutional identity claims may sometimes take the form of the invocation of basic constitutionalist principles: a commitment to human rights, democracy and the rule of law. Since these are universal norms that define the basic structure of all constitutions properly so called, as well as the basic commitments the European Union claims to be founded on, their invocation is not part of the jurisprudence of particularism. Identity claims of this kind – exemplified by the FCC's *Solange* jurisprudence or its ultra vires review claims – do not seek to justify a national opt out from EU law on the grounds of deeply rooted legitimate national difference. Instead, these claims function as a critique of EU law, which in the concrete case is claimed to justify something akin to a Member State's official disobedience – the refusal to apply EU law – because of the EU law's constitutional deficiency. Here the ultimate goal is for the European Union to change its ways and align its practice with the constitutionalist standards that are declared to be common to the European Union and its Member States.

Finally, there is space for a genuine jurisprudence of particularism, even if the space that it occupies is limited. Constitutional identity claims can plausibly be tied to particular interpretations of a constitutional principle rooted in the history and culture of a nation that diverge from European interpretations of the same principle. Furthermore, there is space for identity claims that are neither interpretations of basic constitutionalist principles nor are they violations of them. A closer exploration of the issues raised by these claims was not the focus of this chapter, but this is where the focus of attention should be.

Carl Schmitt's theory of constituent power and constitutional identity has, I believe, cast a malicious conceptual fog in this area, not least by way of the jurisprudence of the German Constitutional Court. Whereas the more concrete claims made by the FCC were based on the interpretation of a concrete positive provision in the German Basic Law and thus focused on elaborating what are, in fact, basic principles of liberal constitutional democracy, the court's general construction of the relationship between constitutional identity and constituent power is one which opened the door for illiberal authoritarian and exclusionary claims which Central European courts in particular have been happy to draw on. Yet Schmitt's constitutional theory, his voluntarist formal conception of constitutional identity and its relationship to an unbounded constituent power, is a misreading of the constitutionalist project and its eighteenth-century heritage. To the extent the concept of constitutional identity is tied to the jurisprudence of particularism at all, its scope is narrowly circumscribed by the foundational constitutionalist commitments to human rights, democracy, and the rule of law.

8

Constitutionalism Today: The Prospects of the European Constitutional Community

SUSANNE BAER, KRISZTA KOVÁCS AND MAYA VOGEL

IN THE LATE 1940s a consensus emerged: a post-World War II, post-colonial, post-authoritarian, grand consensus in Europe and beyond. Dignity, liberty, and equality should not merely be promises on paper or an elitist privilege for the few, and representative democracy should be the way to run societies.[1] This consensus certainly gave birth to a variety of legal regimes, but it also defined a baseline for the political systems we call constitutional democracies: first, power should be distributed to parliament and representative government via fair elections that ensure equal voting rights and a realistic option of a peaceful change of government and, second, power should be limited by fundamental human rights and by legally enforceable commitments to checks and balances, ie, with separated powers or in a version of federalism. As such, legality is not just a form or a fetish but a substantive notion, and democracy is based on the substantive rule of law.[2] In a constitutional democracy, the law is then *conditio sine qua non* to live together, a safeguard of deliberation, and a foundation of trust. We call this constitutionalism.

Certainly, there are profound assumptions that inform this claim regardless of whatever version of constitutionalism is implemented in real life. The first assumption is the *telos* of constitutionalism itself. Here, the foundational promise of constitutional democracy is, in essence, that people may enjoy their lives as they deem fit, yet no one should ever be permitted to trample over any other because each and every human being deserves the same respect. Normatively speaking, dignity, liberty and equality serve as a foundational triangle of fundamental rights.[3] Often, these normative promises are constructed as separate

[1] K Kovács, 'Parliamentary Democracy by Default' (2020) 2 *Jus Cogens* 237–258.

[2] R Dixon, 'Rule of law teleology: against the misuse and abuse of rule of law rhetoric' (2019) 11 *Hague Journal on the Rule of Law* 461–64.

[3] S Baer, 'Dignity, Liberty, Equality: A Fundamental Rights Triangle of Constitutionalism' (2009) 59:4 *The University of Toronto Law Journal* 417–68.

values, which may inform a hierarchy of importance. But this only results in a partial understanding. For dignity tends to be but a value, liberty a prime interest, and equality a comparative exercise. The foundational triangle leaves the hierarchy behind. To paraphrase a famous claim in legal philosophy,[4] this triangle is based on taking all three rights seriously, and assuming a connection between all three of them and not treating them in isolation from each other. This is because the legal guarantees of dignity, liberty and equality are informed by, and historically result from, struggles that did not separate the three, but demanded emancipation, liberation, respect and equal citizenship as a means of capturing the very foundational recognition of humans as social beings. The normative promises of dignity, liberty and equality are not just mere values; they are rights. As such, they may be claimed in court, and these promises may be delivered by judicial review.

It is this version of constitutionalism that has been attractive to social movements in many rather different settings around the globe and that is alive in the twenty-first century. All over the world there is what Amartya Sen calls a 'democratic commitment',[5] with varieties of what Bruce Ackerman calls 'constitutional moments',[6] producing a wave of constitutional texts that ensure fundamental rights and democracy not merely as a pacifying compromise and rhetoric, but implementing what some call 'new constitutionalism' that features judicial bodies to exercise judicial review.[7] Worldwide, judicial bodies have become an essential means of replacing fascist, colonial, military or otherwise dictatorial rule with democratic governance, from Colombia or South Africa to Central Europe, South Korea or Taiwan. For a while, constitutionalism with that kind of backup looked like the standard.

Yet, in the twenty-first century, constitutional democracy is not well. In fact, it is severely threatened,[8] not only in the wars around the world and in the wake of severe economic and social crises in Latin and South America and Asia, but also in Europe, which proudly conceives itself as the region with the highest standard of democracy worldwide. Rather prominently, the Covid-19 pandemic saw constitutional democracy under stress, when governments constructed and prolonged exceptional measures in states of emergency and when populist politics mobilised around a rallying cry that 'their rights' had

[4] R Dworkin, *Taking Rights Seriously* (Cambridge, Mass, Harvard University Press, 1978).

[5] A Sen, 'Democracy as a Universal Value' (1999) 10 *Journal of Democracy* 3–17.

[6] B Ackerman, *We the People: Foundations* (Cambridge, Harvard University Press, 1991). See also C Klein and A Sajó, 'Constitution-making: process and substance' in *The Oxford Handbook of Comparative Constitutional Law* (Oxford, Oxford University Press, 2012) 419.

[7] M Schor, 'Mapping Comparative Judicial Review' (2008) 7 *Washington University Global Studies Law Review*, 257–87; G Oberleitner (ed), *International Human Rights Institutions, Tribunals, and Courts* (Singapore, Springer Singapore, 2018).

[8] See T Ginsburg and A Simpser (eds), *Constitutions in Authoritarian Regimes* (Cambridge, Cambridge University Press 2014); T Kochi, The End of Global Constitutionalism and Rise of Antidemocratic Politics (2020) 34:4 *Global Society* 487–506.

been taken from them.[9] Yet the crisis of constitutional democracy started before that. During the 'war on terror' after 9/11, many governments prioritised safety and security over liberty and non-discrimination sometimes declaring emergencies, sometimes a new normal.[10] Similarly, after the 2008 financial crisis and after the 2015 wave of migration, public institutions in most European countries were confronted with serious doubts as to their legitimacy and their ability to meet the challenges of the day. In many societies, louder voices challenged, or even denounced, the value and relevance of constitutionalism.[11] Such voices, expressing resentment and emotions of fear and anger, have become worryingly powerful.

In what follows, we will revisit the meaning of constitutionalism, based on the rule of law and backed up by courts, to understand what is at stake and what to do about it. We will first analyse the role of courts within a democratic political system and then revisit what constitutional erosion looks like in some EU Member States. The Hungarian and Polish governments have been the most prominent actors seeking to undermine the very foundations of the EU community itself, but they have not been the only ones. In response to this, the EU launched its rule of law mechanism, which has not been very effective to date.[12] Thus, section III poses the question of whether the European constitutional community is capable of dealing with the challenges to transnational democracy in the region. More specifically, the Court of Justice of the European Union has the mandate to intervene. But domestic courts of Member States, both constitutional and regular, must also contribute to the effort. Yet it is important not to forget that political, social, economic, and academic actors are called upon to revisit their commitments and stand up for them. The concluding section IV summarises the findings.

I. WHY DO COURTS MATTER?

Courts are essential institutions of constitutionalism; they do not just review contracts or tort claims or administer justice to criminals. More fundamentally, courts also review majority decisions, as in legislation, and they make sure

[9] J Grogan and A Donald (eds), *Routledge Handbook of Law and the COVID-19 Pandemic* (London, Routledge, 2022).

[10] In its ruling on the Federal Anti-Terrorism Data Base, the FCC pointed out that even terrorism must be addressed legally and not as an exempt from constitutional requirements based on an exceptional state (*Ausnahmezustand*). BVerfG, Judgment of the First Senate of 24 April 2013 – 1 BvR 1215/07.

[11] P Kratochvíl and Z Sychra, 'The end of democracy in the EU? The Eurozone crisis and the EU's democratic deficit' (2019) 41 *Journal of European Integration* 169–85; J Bast, F v Harbou and J Wessels, *Human Rights Challenges to European Migration Policy (REMAP study)* 2020.

[12] L Pech, 'The Rule of Law' in PP Craig and G De Búrca (eds), *Evolution of EU Law*, 4th edn (Oxford, Oxford University Press, 2021) 307–72.

that fundamental rights guarantee that everyone has a voice in politics via free speech, media and marches, associations and parties, elections and the vote since constitutionalism is a structure for democracies. Thus, in any form of constitutionalism that deserves its name,[13] independent courts have the power of judicial review and are indispensable institutions that stand for a distribution of power that does not allow any majority to trump anyone or leave anyone behind.[14] There is a need for a counter-majoritarian power, ie, courts, to tackle disrespect, oppression, exploitation, or abuse of those not in power, be it a political opposition, manipulated majority, or other people not 'on the agenda'.

Yet, the recent crises in democratic countries have sparked criticism of courts. The British campaign to Brexit was driven not only by a longing for empire or economic gain but also by deliberately manufactured mistrust in European institutions, specifically courts. It was the European Court of Justice (ECJ), the European Court of Human Rights (ECtHR), and ultimately also the UK Supreme Court itself, that were characterised as illegitimate. Along the same lines, the nationalist and ethnonationalist populist parties that have kept gaining momentum in nearly all EU Member States have also challenged courts as truly independent safeguards of democratic procedure and individual human rights. It is noteworthy that even those EU Member States which practice autocracy in corrupt forms try hard to keep a legalistic façade;[15] indeed, it is an indication of the strength of the standard once achieved in constitutionalism. To clear their way, authoritarian leaders take over the judiciary (some examples are discussed in Part II of this volume). When they refuse to play by the rules once agreed to, such countries attack the very foundation of the EU.[16] After all, the EU is a union not based on some essential commonality but has been founded as a 'Rechtsgemeinschaft', a community, then a union, based on law.[17] Therefore, attempts to defend or restore the rule of law are struggles to ensure that this notion of a legal union is not merely a formal one but a substantive key component of constitutionalism.[18]

Certainly, the attacks on the courts target values and European solidarity and undermine representative democracy. But they are also embedded in

[13] We tend to disagree with those who list abusive forms as one version, eg, M Tushnet, 'Authoritarian Constitutionalism' (2015) 100 *Cornell Law Review* 393.

[14] 'LNOB' is Principle 2 of the 2030 UN Agenda for Sustainable Development and its Sustainable Development Goals and has been used widely to frame politics of equal consideration and participation.

[15] GA Tóth, 'Constitutional Markers of Authoritarianism' (2019) 11 *Hague Journal of Rule Law* 37–61.

[16] CJ Schneider, 'Euroscepticism and government accountability in the European Union' (2019) 14 *The Review of International Organizations* 217–38.

[17] In French: *communauté de droit*; in English, often also: the community based on the rule of law. Famously, the term was inspired by Walter Hallstein, eventually picked up by Jacques Delors, the first and eighth President of the European Commission.

[18] S Baer, 'Who Cares? A defence of judicial review' (2020) 8 *Journal of the British Academy* 75–104.

long-established and widespread scepticism. This is the critique of courts known as 'the problem of judicial review' or the 'counter-majoritarian difficulty', thus, more precisely, the problem of 'constitutionalisation'[19] and 'judicialisation' of politics. Thus, even if courts have already contributed to safeguarding and implementing fundamental rights, they are an easy target for attacks since they are confronted by the question of whether they are acting too political or not.[20] They are continuously accused of engaging in (judicial) 'activism' and advised to practice more 'restraint'. These attacks on human rights courts and courts with a constitutional mandate of judicial review force us to rethink judicial review. When is judicial review too much, and for whom, exactly? In protecting fundamental rights and democracy, judicial review forms the basis of constitutionalism in that it holds power accountable. Law without an institution to back it up remains an empty promise, which is why strong judicial review is essential for stable constitutional democracies. Here, strength is not activism. Rather, we suggest considering courage, based on legal skills and institutional wisdom, essential in taking the law seriously even if political pressure points in other directions. In constitutional democracies, the law eventually adjudicated in such courts is the means to defend or, when necessary, to create equal participation in matters of general concern, the *res publica*, in politics. As such, it is a structure of governance with truly independent watchdogs to ensure that it works.[21]

Interestingly, the attacks that threaten such constitutional democracies are often made in the name of the law, subverting its very meaning. Javier Corrales[22] and Kim Scheppele[23] call these attempts to use law in a perfidious way 'autocratic legalism'. András Sajó refers to the phenomenon when laws and institutions are used in a mala fide way to achieve anti-constitutionalist aims 'ruling by cheating'.[24] But how can the law be used as an instrument against these attacks, if the attacks themselves appear legal? The search for an answer should compel us to revisit critical approaches in legal studies. They have consistently exposed the law as a siren call, ambivalent, Janus-faced, sometimes even hydra.[25] In fact, the law is not only repressive but also productive; it may

[19] M Loughlin, 'What is Constitutionalisation?' in P Dobner and M Loughlin, *The Twilight of Constitutionalism?* (Oxford, Oxford University Press, 2010).

[20] M Blauberger and D Sindbjerg Martinsen, 'The Court of Justice in times of politicization: "law as a mask and shield" revisited' (2020) 27 *Journal of European Public Policy* 382–99.

[21] Baer (n 17).

[22] J Corrales, 'The Authoritarian Resurgence: Autocratic Legalism in Venezuela' (2015) 26 *Journal of Democracy*, 37–51. M Neves, 'Lateinamerikanische Verfassungen: Zwischen Autokratismus und Demokratisierung' (1997) 30 *Verfassung und Recht in Übersee/Law and Politics in Africa, Asia and Latin America* 503–19.

[23] KL Scheppele, 'Autocratic Legalism' (2018) 85 *University of Chicago Law Review* 545–83.

[24] A Sajó, *Ruling by Cheating: Governance in Illiberal Democracy* (Cambridge, Cambridge University Press, 2021).

[25] The notion is a classic in feminist legal studies. See C Smart, *Feminism and the Power of Law* (London, Routledge, 1998); discussed by M Drakopoulou, 'Feminism and the siren call of law' (2007) 18 *Law and Critique* 331–60. The ambivalent nature of law is also exposed by critical race theory, critical approaches to international law, etc.

allow for action but also be a means of oppression. To better understand what happens in autocratic regimes, it helps to start by looking at this ambivalence. Then, and based on critical approaches to the law, it seems helpful to look at the realities the law produces, or the realities its absence allows for, and reveal its abuse. Recent attacks on constitutional democracy provoke the question of who suffers, why, and who profits from what. Such an attitude moves beyond the androcentricity of the law and a rallying cry for the rule of law and the primacy of EU law. Instead, it focuses on who constitutionalism is designed to protect, and who will be, or is, left behind or outside when attacks succeed. To uncover the perversion of autocrats, we should focus on the harm done and the question of to whom it was done.

For contemporary autocrats, the law is a means for them to gain power, further their interests and crush those in the way. They 'reform' courts, yet, in fact, destroy the independent institutions with a mandate to limit and exercise control and protect fundamental freedoms, which further endangers the existence of those courts. It is no coincidence that constitutional and international courts are first on the list to be silenced or denied authority and eventually enlisted after 'reform', since they are the institutions with the power to stand in a government's way.[26] Sometimes, minor and seemingly technical changes in procedure amount to an unfriendly takeover.[27] Similarly, modifications of pay, budget, disciplinary power, protocol or even location may, in fact, destroy the institution. There are people who serve in regimes as new 'judges' or 'lawyers' and pervert the law. Likewise, legal academics, lawyers, politicians, media, and other social actors who collaborate and profit from the regime speak out. What they express is not a criticism of courts geared towards improvement, but attacks geared towards dismantlement and destruction, thus categorically different. In such cases, the foundations of constitutional democracy are eroded. Legal protection before independent courts is the domino in governance arrangements throughout Europe that brings everything to fall once it falls itself.

This is worrisome for all of us, although it often targets others, specifically those already stigmatised as different – minorities, such as refugees, those now summarised as LGBTIQ, and other non-conforming women and men – by using established ressentiment and mobilising emotions of fear and anger. But when constitutions only serve as decorum, and when courts are not independent but enlisted in politics, then people suffer and are left without protection. Independent courts may not matter as much to those in the mainstream, but they matter for people in pain. And depending on the autocrat's will, the mainstream

[26] Regarding European law, autocratic regimes are also bothered that each and every court may challenge their ways by referring to the ECJ, which is why this procedure may also be subject to what is then called 'reform'.

[27] K Kovács and KL Scheppele, 'The fragility of an independent judiciary: Lessons from Hungary and Poland – and the European Union' (2018) 51 *Communist and Post-Communist Studies* 189–200.

may change. Certainly, courts that exercise judicial review are particularly important for those not privileged but marginalised or fully excluded. There, the rule of law and the independence of the judiciary are not just concepts but protective devices against the changing moods of political majorities. However, anyone may easily fall into that position at any given moment in time. Autocrats have the power to define at will who belongs to the people and who does not. Today, it may be them, and tomorrow, you.

II. THE EROSION OF CONSTITUTIONALISM

In the 1950s, Walter Hallstein, who was a driving force behind the construction of the European Community and then the Union, said that Europe is a 'community of law' that 'puts the rule of law in the place of power and its manipulation' and 'replaces violence and political pressure'.[28] For Hallstein, the concept of a union based on shared values agreed upon in law was a concept deeply embedded in an attempt to learn from the violent history of the 1940s in Europe. If this is accurate, what happens when the rule of law is destroyed is obvious. If law loses, power and manipulation win and reign again. Taking today's powers into account, this will look different, but there will be suffering for sure. So, when the rule of law is attacked and dismantled or modified into oblivion in the EU Member States in the twenty-first century, this is what is at stake. These attacks on fundamental principles of constitutionalism come in a variety of ways that destroy the fabric of democracy. There has been a forceful resurgence of anti-Semitism, as well as Islamophobia and ethnonationalist racism,[29] and note that this has been orchestrated, inspired, or tolerated by governments once constitutionalism is gone. And constitutional courts, right next to independent media and education, have been dismantled rather quickly in some places.[30] There seems to be a recipe, most prominently associated with Orbán's Hungarian government, for mixing these ingredients into a toxic dish. They serve populism, crude essentialist nationalism, and contempt of democratic institutions, including courts.

As such, populism is not only dangerous in general. It is especially dangerous for the law as the backbone of constitutional democracy. Different versions of populism have, as Nicola Lacey explains, different degrees of systemic or contingent proximity to the rule of law.[31] Nevertheless, it is not by chance that

[28] W Hallstein, *Europe in the Making* trans Ch Roetter (London, Allen & Unwin, 1972).

[29] A Zick, B Küpper, A Hövermann, *Intolerance, Prejudice and Discrimination. A European Report* (Berlin, Friedrich-Ebert-Stiftung, 2011).

[30] Kovács and Scheppele (n 26). This has been described as 'plucking the chicken' by M Albright, *Fascism: A Warning* (New York, HarperCollins, 2018).

[31] N Lacey, 'Populism and the Rule of Law' (2019) 15 *Annual Review of Law and Social Science*, 79–96. S Baer, 'Grundrechte unter Druck', in M Ruffert (ed) *Europa-Visionen* (Baden-Baden, Nomos, 2019). B Bugaric, 'Central Europe's Descent into Autocracy: A Constitutional Analysis

the World Report of Human Rights Watch[32] begins with a description of a human rights crisis that comes along with populism. National populists who seek to turn an ethnoreligious national majority against minorities and individual freedoms do not only have an anti-liberal political agenda. They oppose the very idea of constitutionalism by stating that it is the will of the people that counts and 'a mandate of more than three million voters overwrites everything and gives the right answers to everything'.[33] Populists turn 'we the people', a call for fundamental human rights[34] and democracy in the 'velvet revolution' marches in East Germany before 1989, into a rallying cry of hatred.[35] Once conceived as an associational democratic glue, the 'we' is turned into an ethnically and religiously based concept of a group, defined by exclusion, namely of 'foreigners'. Here, the 'we' is racist, antisemitic, and Islamophobic, as well as sexist and heteronormative that seeks to appeal to a 'natural normal order of things'.

Such populism does not like critics that emphasise diversity over homogeneity. Neither does such populism want its leadership exposed as a group of people who construct the 'we' to simply serve themselves and enrich their families and friends.[36] But when a political programme centred around the 'we' is defined by inequalities, constitutional courts get imminently in the way. This is why human rights and constitutional courts are the first to be attacked, deemed in need of 'reform', and ordered to be dismantled as soon as possible, because they could protect everyone else from being left out and harmed and the commons from being stolen from the people. That is why populists offensively and often very explicitly target courts.

Yet these attacks are, again, complicated. Where courts have a mandate to control branches of government, scholars have warned of a '*gouvernement de juges*',[37] which became a *topos* in constitutional theory.[38] Now, such

of Authoritarian Populism' (2019) 17 *International Journal of Constitutional Law* 597–616. N Walker, 'Populism and constitutional tension' (2019) 17 *International Journal of Constitutional Law* 515–35.

[32] Human Rights Watch (2018), 'The Pushback Against the Populist Challenge' www.hrw.org/world-report/2018/country-chapters/global-4.

[33] S Zsiros cites Judit Varga, the Hungarian Minister of Justice in 'Brussels says Hungary's rule of law situation has deteriorated, as Budapest digs heels in', *Euronews* 23 May 2022.

[34] In 1989, citizens in the then GDR peacefully pressured their government on the Monday marches to hold free elections and ensure human rights. Famously, their rally call was: 'Wir sind das Volk', 'we are the people' – not you, a government that does not have the right to speak in our name.

[35] For instance, recently, the far-right German party (AfD) insists that those who belong to them are 'the people'. Their slogan today, 'Wir sind das Volk' is loaded with nationalist, racialised and gendered meaning. G Dietze 'Rechtspopulismus and Geschlecht: Paradox and leitmotiv' (2018) 27 *Femina Politica* 34–46. S Hark and PI Villa, *Unterscheiden und herrschen* (Bielefeld, transcript, 2017).

[36] A Sajo, *Ruling by Cheating: Governance in Illiberal Democracy* (Cambridge, Cambridge University Press, 2021).

[37] A Stone Sweet, *Governing with Judges: Constitutional Politics in Europe* (Oxford, Oxford University Press, 2000).

[38] Early comparative studies in France warn of a 'gouvernement de juges'. E Lambert, *Le Gouvernement des juges et la lutte contre la législation sociale aux États-Unis, l'expérience américaine du contrôle judiciaire de la constitutionnalité des lois* (Lyon, Persée, 1921).

academic warnings are enlisted by populist autocrats, who can also easily tap into the dissatisfaction of people with lengthy and ever more complicated legal proceedings. Thus, 'those judges' and 'these courts' are easily denounced as 'out of touch', 'not there for us'. Yet courts are precisely the institutions designed to restrain reckless rulers, they are hence intentionally conceived as out of touch with prejudice, intolerance, and ideology, and designed to look after those who lose when the 'we' and only the 'we' rules. If populist parties or actors start abusing the constitution[39] or other forms of law to endanger this very system, it is constitutional and human rights courts that have the task of securing democracy and rights against such threats. This is, again, why constitutional courts or their equivalents are one of the basic pillars of constitutional democracy. A constitutional court is essential for a functioning democracy; it is attacked to destabilise this very power. Therefore, every such court needs 'amici and amicae',[40] as strong supporters taking a clear stand against attacks. When the foundations are at stake, it is crucial to distinguish between critique and attack and to do the former to rebuke the latter. Certainly, there is always a need for critical discussions of what courts do, and friends of the court do not need to applaud any decision taken. But as friends, they need to defend courts as such, to help secure democracy and enforceable protection of fundamental rights. In fact, it is helpful when courts work in contexts that produce critical readings of the law, as criticism helps judges make more informed decisions. Yet it is also necessary to clearly reject the destructive strategies of others. Put differently, the friends of courts are critical companions, but they are not out to destroy a constitutional or human rights court within its system.

When democracy is at risk, the law is desperately needed as a stabilising mechanism, a non-violent means to solve conflicts, a product of deliberation itself that also safeguards deliberation as practice. Again, when the European Community and then Union were designed based on law, this was not an abstract concept, nor a call for bureaucracy or institutionalised authority for the sole sake of status. Rather, the European version of the rule of law was and still is a substantive idea, to restrain power, and especially to organise democracy so that people can live peacefully together. This idea has been heavily informed by the agreements within the larger Europe of the Council of Europe. This Europe included Russia until the Putin government started to wage war against Ukraine.[41] It still includes Turkey, even if Turkey's membership is under severe strain.[42] And it covers the UK, despite highly problematic attacks on

[39] D Landau, 'Abusive Constitutionalism' (2013–14) 47 *University of California Davis Law Review* 189.

[40] S Baer, 'Democracy in peril: a call for amici and amicae curiae and critical lawyering' (2019) 10 *Transnational Legal Theory* 140–62.

[41] On 15 March 2022, because of the Russian invasion of Ukraine, Russia ceased to be a member of the Council of Europe.

[42] IZ Yılmaz, 'Z Erdoğan's presidential regime and strategic legalism: Turkish democracy in the twilight zone' (2020) 20 *Southeast European and Black Sea Studies* 265–87.

the ECtHR during the Brexit campaign calling for a more British version of human rights.[43] Several countries, including Hungary, Turkey, and the UK, have refused to implement ECtHR decisions.[44] The packed yet still so-called Polish Constitutional Tribunal held that Article 6 of the Convention, which guarantees the right to a fair trial, and was recently applied by the ECtHR to punish Poland for firing judges without explanation, was inconsistent with the Polish constitution.[45] Again, we see the same dynamics. The more the Venice Commission and the ECtHR breathe life into a European 'we' committed to democracy and human rights, the more these institutions are attacked by autocrats. Thus, when the authority of the ECtHR is called into question, and when judgments of this court are dismissed or simply ignored, these are attacks on constitutional democracy in general, and it endangers people all around Europe.[46]

As Member States of the Council of Europe, we are in this together; thus, what happens in another Member State cannot be irrelevant to us. And as we are tied together globally, erosion also has a global dimension. If the Council of Europe, founded to provide a set of fundamental values that would be accepted in all Member States and to prevent another European war, loses its power, another building block of peace and democracy will be gone. This is why it is of high importance that not a single one of the European states stops respecting these values and the rulings taken to give them meaning in real life.[47]

The EU consists of substantially fewer Member States than the Council of Europe. But even with a smaller number of states, there have been difficulties agreeing on basic values. By signing the treaties, agreeing to the *acquis communautaire* and profiting from EU laws that organise economics, Member States do agree on the basics of democracy and the substantive rule of law. Yet recently, EU institutions have had to deal with serious breaches of these basic principles. When the Hungarian Prime Minister propagates 'illiberal democracy',[48] it is not a problem of 'another' country but an attack on our shared and agreed upon

[43] See the contributions in M Farrell, E Drywood, E Hughes (eds), *Human rights in the media: Fear and fetish* (New York, Routledge, 2019).

[44] A Cozzi, et al, *Comparative study on the implementation of the ECHR at the national level* (Belgrade, Council of Europe Office in Belgrade, 2016).

[45] 'Constitutional Tribunal' judgment K 6/21 (24.11.2021). E Łętowska, 'The Honest (though Embarrassing) Coming-out of the Polish Constitutional Tribunal', *VerfBlog*, 29.11.2021, https://verfassungsblog.de/the-honest-though-embarrassing-coming-out-of-the-polish-constitutional-tribunal/.

[46] Council of Europe Steering Committee for Human Rights, *The longer-term future of the system of the European Convention on Human Rights* (Council of Europe, 2016) https://rm.coe.int/the-longer-term-future-of-the-system-of-the-european-convention-on-hum/1680695ad4.

[47] S Greer and A Williams, 'Human Rights in the Council of Europe and the EU: Towards 'Individual', 'Constitutional' or 'Institutional' Justice?' (2009) 15 *European Law Journal* 462–81.

[48] Prime Minister V Orbán's Speech at the 25th Bálványos Summer Free University and Student Camp, 26 July 2014, Tusnádfürdő (Băile Tuşnad), Romania. https://2015-2019.kormany.hu/en/the-prime-minister/the-prime-minister-s-speeches/prime-minister-viktor-orban-s-speech-at-the-25th-balvanyos-summer-free-university-and-student-camp.

political and legally secured order. Also, when he announces that an ECJ decision for the relocation of refugees in the EU is not being accepted,[49] it is perilous. And this is a real threat, first and foremost for the refugee but for us as well. We wonder whether there is any room for compromise. What if the refusal to accept the ruling on the distribution of refugees across the EU is accepted? This is the beginning of a very slippery slope that entails accepting or rejecting judgements that fit or do not fit a given political agenda at will. If that becomes precedent, the law – as the foundational structure of Europe – will be destroyed.

Also, when the majority in the Polish parliament has abolished the independence of the courts as part of a campaign named 'justice reform',[50] it is not 'their' problem but 'ours' as well. This is not just the case because the framework for cross-border proceedings, ranging from arrest warrants to trade and to travel, might not be intact anymore. It is also because the legal obligation that protects us is also being destroyed. Even if the law is often still seen as strongly connected to the nation state by 'status-quo lawyers,'[51] the law is by now a transnational phenomenon, a reality of multinormativity. So, if a national legal system betrays the basics, it does not only harm those directly affected, but it is harmful to all of us. There is hence an urgent need to counter these developments.

III. THE PROSPECTS FOR THE EUROPEAN CONSTITUTIONAL COMMUNITY

How can this, and how should this, be done? Although it is not a state or an international organisation, the EU is a legal construct, and with its treaties distributing power and securing rights, it may be conceived as a European constitutional community. But does it have the tools to respond to the challenges arising from attacks? Is this community able to defend itself? Is it a 'militant', or better put, 'defensive' constitutional community?[52] The treaties, including the EU Charter of Fundamental Rights, serve as a legal framework that organises and limits power. Can they prevent or sanction abuse? Also, EU institutions and mechanisms are designed to protect what constitutionalists often call the 'community of values', the bedrock of constitutionalism itself. Are these institutions able and willing to protect it? Finally, domestic courts in all Member

[49] 'Hungary continues to reject migrant quotas'. See the official website of the Hungarian Government: https://2015-2019.kormany.hu/en/ministry-of-justice/news/hungary-continues-to-reject-migrant-quotas.

[50] See, eg, the Position of the Board of the Polish Society of Constitutional Law, 28 October 2020: http://konstytucyjny.pl/zarzad-polskiego-towarzystwa-prawa-konstytucyjnego-krytykuje-rozstrzygniecie-tk-w-sprawie-aborcji/.

[51] Baer (n 39).

[52] The concept by K Loewenstein, 'Militant democracy and fundamental rights' (1937) 31 *American Political Science Review* 417–32, was an argument in the wake of Nazi Germany, by a scholar who had fled Germany, after being removed from his professorship for being Jewish. For comparative material, see N Dorsen et al, *Comparative Constitutionalism* 4th edn (St Paul, West, 2022). See also A Sajó and LR Bentch (eds), *Militant Democracy* (Den Haag, Eleven, 2004).

States have the mandate to implement EU law. Can they serve as safeguards of these common constitutional values?

A. Treaties and the Charter of Fundamental Rights

Historically, the EU started with economic agreements in the West, with what has been called the social dimension ultimately gaining attention. This resulted in several treaties to organise and ensure the fundamental freedoms, most notably, the Lisbon Treaty.[53] But there is an ongoing scepticism, disregard and rejection of the socio-cultural and political dimension of this transnational entity.

In the twenty-first century, the EU is not a community that regularly acts as one entity in the face of international crises, although it must be noted that reactions to the Covid-19 pandemic and the Russian invasion of Ukraine have brought Europe closer together. But there is no European political community across the Member States that serves as an equivalent to the *polis* as the site of democratic deliberation. While 'Brussels' serves as a stand-in for the centrifugal forces, which are often met with snootiness, the diverging forces seem stronger, or at least louder. Europe lacks the cultural mechanisms to underpin it as an economic structure and a cultural and political home. The Erasmus programme by which the EU allows students to develop such a feeling seems like a somewhat singular and privileged activity. Thus, it seems that Europe needs an upgrade rather quickly, specifically to counter the challenges posed by nationalistic populist autocrats.

After 1989, there was a moment of hope that a political, cultural and economic union would eventually evolve. Many people active in public office and in constitutional and EU law believed that the injustices that inspired post-World War II and post-Cold War constitutionalism would not happen again, at least not right here. The rapid emergence of constitutional erosion thus came to many as a shock. The EU seemed not just unprepared but ill-equipped. The treaties were not designed to counter an illiberal and authoritarian trend, and specifically not the destruction of the constitutional order practised by some Member States. For a long time, political actors seemed to wait and see rather than stand up and act persistently. However, appeasement and accommodation did not work.

Currently, Europe is on a learning curve. It has to develop more of a constitutional dimension, not because it desires to but because it needs to. This must include devices of resilience and self-defence. The founding treaties could serve as the starting point. Although the EU is not a state, the treaties are a

[53] I Pernice, 'The Treaty of Lisbon: Multilevel Constitutionalism in Action' (2009) 15 *Columbia Journal of European Law* 349–407.

legal framework with a constitutional function of limiting political power and preventing abuse. Especially the Lisbon Treaty created an 'ever closer' union in Article 1 TEU, with a commitment to values, rights and principles. According to Article 2 TEU, the EU is not just a political or economic community, but a community of values built on the 'respect for human dignity, freedom, democracy, equality, the rule of law and respect for human rights, including the rights of persons belonging to minorities'. The treaty adds that 'these values are common to the Member States in a society where pluralism, non-discrimination, tolerance, justice, solidarity and equality between women and men prevail'. And as the ECJ emphasises, the values contained in Article 2 'define the very identity of the European Union as a common legal order'.[54] Any state that joins the EU must meet these criteria because they were not invented to give birth to the EU but were taken from the constitutions of Member States at the time. Therefore, their respective traditions have to be reconciled as common ground; this is what Article 6 TEU emphasises when guiding the interpretation of the Charter of Fundamental Rights.[55]

To ensure the realisation of the common values, some mechanism is needed. After all, it is difficult to have people, politics, and even courts in all Member States agree on the basics. As the treaties are, formally speaking, not constitutions but international treaties, they are secured by domestic constitutionalism, entangled in the Union, and thus embedded in a shared legal context. This, then, presents the additional challenge that many actors have one job: to protect democracy and fundamental rights in Europe. This calls for a cooperative structure in which responsibilities are shared, entailing a rather specific conversation among courts of equal standing and not a hierarchical order that clearly defines responsibilities. This is called constitutional pluralism by some[56] and multilevel constitutionalism[57] or 'Verbund' by others.[58] This is a challenging situation, both for national courts, who were formerly on their own, and for the ECJ, which is sometimes taken to be the only one out there. Yet they together must ensure that the foundations remain stable in every Member State.

[54] Case C-156/21, *Hungary v European Parliament and Council*, EU:C:2022:97, para 127.

[55] This informs the Right to be Forgotten rulings of the FCC, in which the First Senate emphasised the commonality throughout Europe, as an *in dubio* rule that allows national courts to also interpret the Charter of Fundamental Rights. See BVerfG, Order of the First Senate of 6 November 2019 – 1 BvR 276/17 –, para 57 et seq.

[56] It comes in variations, see N Krisch, 'Beyond Constitutionalism: The Pluralist Structure of Postnational Law' (Oxford, Oxford University Press, 2010); A Stone Sweet, 'The Structure of Constitutional Pluralism: Review of Nico Krisch, Beyond Constitutionalism: The Pluralist Structure of Post-National Law' (2013) 11 *International Journal of Constitutional Law* 491.

[57] I Pernice, 'Multilevel constitutionalism in the European Union' (2002) 27 *European Law Review* 511–29. See also C Callies and G van der Schyff (eds), *Constitutional identity in a Europe of Multilevel Constitutionalism* (Cambridge, Cambridge University Press, 2020).

[58] Most prominently articulated by A Vosskuhle and R Gerhardt, 'Wir leben in einem europäischen Gerichtsverbund' (2015) 48 *Zeitschrift für Rechtspolitik* 61.

B. EU Institutions and Mechanisms to Protect the Community Values

In a system designed by law, courts are most prominently tasked with implementing the Article 2 TEU commitment to a union of common values. However, in a democratic system, several other institutions are responsible for achieving this aim: domestic and EU institutions alike. The EU institutions can be divided into intergovernmental and supranational ones. Intergovernmental institutions like the European Council of Ministers are directly accountable to the national constituencies and cater to the wish for strong nation-states. And there are many politicians and scholars who would like to leave most legislative power and all budgetary competencies with them. In contrast, supranational institutions like the European Parliament are designed to represent the interests of the EU as a whole.[59] To many, they are less accountable because their mandate comes from Europe-wide elections, in which one vote has minimal, albeit not zero, impact on the overall course of European politics. Also, the European Commission has a decisive role and tends to work as a transnational unit. To date, all decisions taken in the EU need both types of institutions so that shared interests and the interests of Member States are equally considered.

For years, and partly based on criticisms that there was a democratic deficit in EU politics and criticism of the pivotal role of the ECJ, there was a trend towards strengthening the supranational EU Parliament. However, recent years have seen a growing demand to return to intergovernmental politics, most radically from the national populist autocrats. This again taps into widespread scepticism regarding the power of supranational institutions, and often, this tends to ignore what such supranational politics did and do for nation states and its citizens. However, the call to 'take back control' over what is considered an internal affair and the rejection of European institutions exercising control over 'domestic measures' is loud. As prominent examples, Hungary and Poland have engaged in such manipulation by launching their 'judicial reforms'.[60] Yet as described above, these 'judicial reforms' are not purely internal affairs. As shown above, constitutionalism only deserves its name if it comes with independent courts committed to democracy and fundamental rights. Likewise for constitutionalism to be truly present, EU law must be implemented in its mix of fully determined normative schemes and room for Member States to find their ways. Yet, in a Union based on law and a commitment to some basic principles, rights and values, domestic judicial reforms are not pure internal affairs but affect us all.

EU institutions thus have reason and have the power to respond to anti-constitutionalist attacks. Article 7 TEU allows for the suspension of voting

[59] RJ Goebel, 'Supranational: Federal: Intergovernmental: The Governmental Structure of the European Union after the Treaty of Lisbon' (2013) 20 *Columbia Journal of European Law* 77–142.

[60] For more on this, see chapters five and six in this volume.

rights and links EU funding to respect for the rule of law and an annual rule of law review. Envisaged by its authors as a means of sanctioning wrongdoing, Article 7(1) TEU should start working when one Member State breaches the rule of law and endangers it within the EU. Consequently, the European Commission has already activated an Article 7(1) procedure against Poland, and the European Parliament has triggered Article 7(1) against Hungary. Eventually, the Council can impose sanctions and suspend voting rights under Article 7(2) TEU, but the Council is restrained as an intergovernmental institution because Member States in the Council do not act against each other.

After its experience with Hungary, the European Commission created a new Rule of Law Framework to give itself the leverage to act the next time when national safeguards are no longer capable of effectively addressing systemic threats to the rule of law. Initially, the framework was meant to ensure that all Member States implemented what they signed in the treaties and just added more cooperation and control. Also, in parallel to the Commission's Rule of Law Framework, the Council launched a new tool called the annual rule of law dialogue.[61] Then, the Commission's annual Rule of Law reporting mechanism was established to look at the key rule of law developments in each Member State. But little is required in a 'peer review' format with a thirty-minute discussion focusing on one state every three years. And as the developments of Hungary and Poland demonstrate, dialogue alone will not be sufficient to get tangible results.[62]

The challenges to constitutional commitments are not limited to Hungary or Poland. Autocratic populism and illiberalism are spreading in several other European societies. Many still democratic legal systems have already applied administrative law in an authoritarian manner.[63] Furthermore, to fight the Covid-19 pandemic, consolidated democratic states have struggled with keeping the rule of law by introducing ill-fated extreme legal measures (eg, declaring state of emergency) justified on the basis of the urgency of the situation.[64] Therefore, more effective measures will be needed to stabilise the rule of law and defend democracy.

If it is to manage the challenges in this transnational democracy, the EU needs to employ robust constitutional mechanisms to safeguard and support the political commitment enshrined in Article 2 TEU. The ECJ has a pivotal role, with much more to handle than European integration. It should gain a constitutional function beyond its role as a supreme court. After all, it is on the ECJ to

[61] Council of the European Union, 'Press Release No 16936/14' (Brussels, 16 December 2014) 20–21.

[62] Pech (n 11) 326–27.

[63] B Schotel, 'Administrative Law as a Dual State. Authoritarian Elements of Administrative Law' (2021) 13 *Hague Journal on the Rule of Law* 195–22.

[64] European Commission, '2021 Rule of Law Report. The Rule of law situation in the European Union' COM(2021) 700 final (Brussels, 20 July 2021).

protect fundamental rights and the separation of powers, democracy and legality, and ultimately declare Member States' legal measures invalid if they do not fit the standards once agreed upon.

C. The Role of Domestic Institutions: Applying the Concept of 'Constitutional Identity'

Yet the ECJ is not alone. Domestic courts also play an essential role in protecting the legal framework of European democracy in the form of principles, rights and values. In addition to genuine EU institutions there are domestic courts, both ordinary and constitutional. Regarding the latter, Article 6 TEU and Article 52(4) of the Charter of Fundamental Rights explicitly require the ECJ to recognise and build on the constitutional traditions of the Member States. At the same time, national constitutional courts or supreme courts with a mandate to review legislation must take Europe into account. As such, national constitutions are entangled with each other and embedded in the larger European frame.

Here, the challenge is obvious, and the concept of 'constitutional identity' illustrates this point remarkably well. In German constitutional jurisprudence, the FCC has developed the doctrine of constitutional identity to protect the core values of the German Basic Law. While this has often been taken to be a creative move, it is based on the explicit 'eternity clause' in Article 79(3) of the GBL, which does not allow for any constitutional amendment ever to change the core content of the constitution. The FCC called this constitutional identity, or '*Verfassungsidentität*'[65] and held that neither domestic law nor any international agreement or institutional arrangement could change this core content.[66] Note that this is ultima ratio to eventually stop the state's participation in European activities and the FCC has not deemed it violated to date. The FCC, like all other actors, has had to try hard to find a European friendly way to solve a problem. Before it stops the state from participating in European activities, the FCC must interpret the act in question in a friendly manner trying to find common ground.

In addition to performing 'identity control', the FCC also checks whether institutions whose competences have been handed to them by the state do indeed act within such limitations or 'ultra vires'. Finally, the FCC also checks whether EU measures respect fundamental rights, first withholding its authority as long as (*solange*) the standard of the GBL is met,[67] and recently, in the *Right to be Forgotten* rulings I and II, moved to reviewing acts itself, based on the EU

[65] For more on this, see chapter two in this volume.
[66] BVerfGE 113, 273; 123, 267; 126, 286; 129, 78; 134, 366; 140, 317.
[67] BVerfGE 37, 271; BVerfGE 73, 339.

Charter if fully determined by EU law, or based on the national constitution whenever EU law leaves room for pluralism.[68] However, these checks are deeply embedded in a constitutional scheme that is predicated on European integration, from the Preamble to clauses on multi-level law-making and conformity with fundamental rights.

Yet the concept of constitutional identity also carries serious risks. Several other constitutional courts have used the concept of constitutional identity to establish limits on European integration.[69] One of the reasons for this might be that not all courts have included the whole concept. Rather, some constitutional courts have tended to load identity with diffuse notions of nationalism[70] rather than applying it based on the respective democratic constitution and the universal constitutional principles. In fact, it seems crucial from a constitutional point of view to limit the notion of identity to a strictly legal claim. Otherwise, those who see the EU primarily as an economic organisation may transform their rejection of EU rights, principles and values into national identity claims. This is especially tempting for autocrats who use legalistic makeup to cover their greed and authoritarian ways – they claim to be 'simply following what others are doing', which is in fact an abuse of comparative constitutional law. Although the legal concept is not per se a nationalist trap, the term 'identity' certainly invites ideological overload.

Thus, it is even more important to point out that the doctrine in German constitutional law is not a theoretical concept[71] but formally doctrinal since it is based on the explicit 'eternity clause' in the constitution. Such an eternity clause is fully compatible with the commitment to European values in Article 2 TEU. Based on an integration clause in Article 23 of the GBL, the FCC had thus held the doors open to European integration when it emphasised European commonalities and not the differences in its rulings on the main treaties and, more recently, on fundamental rights.

No country can take for granted that the internalisation of universal constitutional principles that are legally addressed by fundamental rights will endure. Rather, societies often have to learn the hard way that there must be such limits to governmental power. Yet this learning process is a feature of constitutionalism as such and not a specificity of Europe. In constitutional democracies, the basic legal texts were always promises made in rather specific constitutional moments to turn to a better future. It takes an ongoing commitment to deliver, and it is on all of us to show this commitment.

[68] Order of the First Senate of 6 November 2019 – 1 BvR 16/13 (*Right to be forgotten I*) and Order of the First Senate of 6 November 2019 – 1 BvR 276/17.

[69] See, eg, the Italian Constitutional Court decision: Corte Cost, 27 dicembre 1973, n 183, Giur it 1973, II, 2401 (It) and the decisions of the French Constitutional Council: Conseil constitutionnel decision No 2004-505 DC Nov 19, 2004, Rec 173; Conseil constitutionnel decision No 2007-560 DC Rec 459.

[70] See Part II of this volume.

[71] But see chapter one in this volume and see also GJ Jacobsohn, *Constitutional Identity* (Princeton, NJ, Princeton University Press, 2010).

While the Member States identify with different histories and positions in shared historical events, and while such different developments informed different constitutions, and constitutional identities thus differ, joining the EU means emphasising and working with the overlapping consensus. Differing constitutional frameworks or identities can be in tension with European commitments. Many people first identify as citizens of their nation state, and law alone is not sufficient to change such understandings. Yet legal practice may help us get there. Since constitutional identities have to be brought in line when joining the EU, the option is there, as is the task. Therefore, revisiting what was meant in drafting the treaties and the Charter of Fundamental Rights is like revisiting a national constitution; all of these have to be interpreted in light of their purposes and functions. And the basic assumption of the European project is that Member States are all constitutional democracies that share the commitment to universal constitutional principles.

As contradictory as this may sound, respect for national constitutional identity is key to the European project.[72] There is a reason for the existence of Article 4(2) TEU, which mandates EU institutions to respect the national constitutional identities of Member States. While a literal understanding of this provision may suggest that any domestic interpretation of national identity would be consistent with EU law, Article 4(2) does not give a blank cheque for the Member States to construct whatever national identity they may prefer at a given time. Rather, there is common ground and space for cultural diversity, like the protection of national languages, provided that they are connected to the national constitutional identity embodied by the domestic legal system from the moment of the foundation of the independent and democratic state.[73] So, although Article 4(2) expressly refers to national identity, its concept is a constitutional one. As the ECJ puts it, the values on 'which the European Union is founded' and which 'define the very identity of the European Union as a legal order common to those States'[74] are the bases that have to be agreed on within all Member States. Consequently, the EU has an obligation to respect national identities as long as identity retention does not undermine the EU foundational principles ensured by Article 2 TEU.[75]

This is the spirit that must inform European and domestic institutions and the practices they adopt to align their legal commitments and politics. The idea is to form a common European constitutional identity based on the entangled

[72] For more on this, see the introductory chapter of this volume.

[73] K Kovács, 'Constitutional or Ethnocultural? National Identity as a European Legal Concept' (2022) 8 *Intersections. East European Journal of Society and Politics* 170–190.

[74] C-156/21, *Hungary v Parliament and Council* and C-157/21, *Poland v Parliament and Council*, Judgments of 16 February 2022.

[75] T Konstadinides, 'Constitutional Identity as a Shield and as a Sword: The European Legal Order within the Framework of national Constitutional Settlement' (2011) 13 *Cambridge Yearbook of European Legal Studies* 195–218, W Sadurski, *Poland's Constitutional Breakdown* (Oxford, Oxford University Press, 2019) 223.

national ones, which are in turn deeply embedded in Europe. In the German example, the jurisprudence of the FCC contains several warnings that the court issued to European institutions. In these instances, the FCC called on European institutions to live up to the common constitutional commitments based on treaty law: the principle of democracy (Article 2 TEU and Article 20 of the GBL) and the rule of law (also in Article 2 TEU and Article 20 GBL). These 'warnings' corresponded to Article 23 GBL, which obliges German state institutions to participate in and facilitate the integration process.[76]

In the 1970s, the famous *Solange I and II* decisions of the FCC emphasized that ECJ rulings would be accepted as long as (in German: *solange*) they conformed to the protection of fundamental rights, at a time when there was no such Charter.[77] Yet it is important that there was no divergence of basic values but a debate over what would best realise these values in a given case.[78] Recently, the Right to be Forgotten rulings have given rise to a dialogue between the EU Charter, the European Convention on Human Rights, and the German Basic Law.[79]

By contrast, the national identity concept applied by some constitutional courts in the Visegrád countries is very different. The institutions still called constitutional courts have been dismantled, and they have also applied a hollow copy of the concept of constitutional identity by filling it with the nation's (ethno)cultural characteristics.[80] This leads down a path of dismissing EU law and ECJ rulings on the grounds of nationalistic ideology.[81]

To counter such a trend, European institutions need to act. Accordingly, the ECJ found a Member State to have violated the principle of judicial independence (Article 19(1) TEU) in the cases of the so-called Polish 'judicial reforms'.[82] Since then, the ECJ has seen a 'proliferation of cases' raising judicial independence concerns.[83] Later, the ECJ decided that Poland's Supreme Court's disciplinary chamber must be completely changed in order to guarantee its

[76] Arnold, R, 'Contemporary constitutionalism and integration' in *Constitutional Studies* Vol I (Constitutional Court of the Republic of Bulgaria, 2019) 127.

[77] BVerfGE 37, 271; BVerfGE 73, 339.

[78] BVerfGE 146, 216.

[79] Order of the First Senate of 6 November 2019 – 1 BvR 16/13 (*Right to be forgotten I*) and Order of the First Senate of 6 November 2019 – 1 BvR 276/17.

[80] Kovács (n 72) 176.

[81] F Fabbrini and A Sajó, 'The Dangers of Constitutional Identity' (2019) 25 *European Law Journal* 457–73; G Halmai, 'Abuse of Constitutional Identity. The Hungarian Constitutional Court on Interpretation of Article E(2) of the Fundamental Law' (2018) 43 *Review of Central and East European Law* 23–42; K Kovács, 'The Rise of an Ethnocultural Constitutional Identity in the Jurisprudence of the East Central European Courts' (2017) 18 *German Law Journal* 1703–720.

[82] Case C-192/18 *Commission v Poland* EU:C:2019:924; Case C-619/ 18 *Commission v Poland* EU:C:2019:531. In 2011, the Hungarian government fired judges *en masse* by lowering their retirement age. The Commission brought a procedure against Hungary before the ECJ, but at that time, the ECJ was not yet ready to apply Article 19(1). The ECJ held that the Hungarian government violated the prohibition of age discrimination. Case C-286/12 *Commission v Hungary* EU:C:2012:687.

[83] Pech (n 11) 332.

independence.[84] These are measures to review national regulations and institutions, with a transnational power and instruments to stop further violations of EU foundational principles.

In addition, the ECtHR is not only a protector of individual rights but has a systemic role to play. Confronting the trends of constitutional destruction and the rise of populist autocracies, the Strasbourg Court has also reviewed domestic legislation that violates constitutional commitments shared throughout Europe. As such, it has delivered several judgments on the rule of law violations committed by the Polish authorities.[85] Notably, the first is an example of a human rights court reacting to a misuse of the power of a national constitutional court, when the ECtHR ruled that the Polish tribunal was and still is irregularly composed, and that, therefore, every bench that includes one of the three irregularly appointed 'judges' amounts to an unlawful one under Article 6 of the Convention.[86] Consequently, the largest association of Polish judges decided not to recognise as legitimate the tribunal's ruling when issued by panels that include unlawfully appointed members.[87]

IV. CONCLUSION

Europe still enjoys the highest standard of the rule of law worldwide as a key ingredient of constitutionalism. However, this is a fragile state of affairs. It can neither be taken for granted nor release anyone from the responsibility to defend such a state; these days, it is more of an incentive, a calling, to prevent this achievement from being lost. There is work to be done to maintain the EU as a community committed to constitutionalism, including the rule of law. If the EU is understood as merely a place of cooperation between Member States intended to foster economic progress, it might be questionable how much it can stabilise the rule of law and how much it can protect domestic courts as independent

[84] Case C-791/19 *Commission v Poland* EU:C:2021:596. T Wahl (2020) 'CJEU Rules on Independence of Poland's Disciplinary Chamber of the Supreme Court' www.eucrim.eu/news/cjeu-rules-on-independence-of-polands-disciplinary-chamber-of-the-supreme-court/.

[85] *Xero Flor v Poland*, App no 4907/18, Judgment of 7 May 2021; *Broda and Bojara v Poland*, App nos 2669/18, 27367/18), Judgment of 29 June 2021; *Reczkowicz v Poland*, App no 43447/19, Judgment of 22 July 2021; *Dolinska-Ficek and Ozimek*, App nos 49868/19, 57511/19, Judgment of 8 November 2021; *Advance Pharma v Poland*, App no 43572/18, Judgment of 3 February 2022.

[86] M Szwed, 'What Should and What Will Happen After Xero Flor – The judgement of the ECtHR on the composition of the Polish Constitutional Tribunal' (2021) *Verfassungsblog* www.verfassungsblog.de/what-should-and-what-will-happen-after-xero-flor/. In a follow up, the ECtHR was concerned with the irregularly appointed member of the National Council of Judiciary. *Grzeda v Poland*, App no 43572/18, Judgment of 15 March 2022.

[87] Position of the Polish Judges Association IUSTITIA over the status of the Constitutional Tribunal, 30 October 2020: https://www.iustitia.pl/en/activity/opinions/4022-position-of-the-polish-judges-association-iustitia-over-the-status-of-the-constitutional-tribunal.

guardians of constitutional democracy.[88] Yet the more one revisits common ground, shared commitments, and the embeddedness of each national legal system in Europe, the more obvious it seems that a concerted effort could hinder at least some of the adverse effects of the so called 'reforms' that attacks the foundations of constitutionalism.[89] Then, the power of law is crucial to make Europe a space of equal liberties, peace, and a shared future.

Consequently, we should not underestimate the necessity of investing in the rule of law. No law comes to life on its own. National commitments are needed to back up transnational legal entities like the EU. It seems we need additional measures to deepen this, for EU organs and national institutions, civil society, business and culture, media and academia, and the larger political allies in the world. Everyone can contribute to a politics that may then indeed inform 'identities', yet this must take place in a shared, deep and lasting commitment to safeguarding the spirit of the post-1945 and post-1989 consensus, one that democratic constitutions and the EU treaties embody. This is not a status quo, but a process we are all actively involved in.

[88] C Tomuschat, 'The ruling of the German Constitutional Court on the Treaty of Lisbon' (2009) 10 *German Law Journal* 1259–262.

[89] A Bodnar, 'Strasbourg Steps in', *Rule of Law*, 8 July 2020, https://ruleoflaw.pl/tag/grzeda-v-poland/.

Bibliography

Ackerman, B, *We the People: Foundations* (Cambridge, Harvard University Press, 1991).

Albright, M, *Fascism: A Warning* (New York, HarperCollins, 2018).

Alter, KJ, 'National Perspectives on International Constitutional Review: Diverging Optics' in E Delaney and Dixon, R (eds), *Comparative Judicial Review* (Cheltenham, Edward Elgar, 2018).

Anagnostaras, G, 'Activation of the Ultra Vires Review: The Slovak Pensions Judgment of the Czech Constitutional Court' (2013) 14 *German Law Journal* 959.

Anderson, B, *Imagined Communities: Reflections on the Origin and Spread of Nationalism* (London/New York, Verso, 2016).

Andrássy, Gy, '*Vasárnapi Újság* [Sunday News] 15 June 1884' quoted in JM Bak and A Gara-Bak, 'The Ideology of a "Millennial Constitution" of Hungary' (1981) 15 *East European Quarterly* 307.

Anschütz, G, *Die Verfassung des Deutschen Reichs vom 11. August 1919: Kommentar für Wissenschaft und Praxis*, 14th edn (Berlin, Verlag von Georg Stilke, 1987).

Appiah, KA and Gates, HL, *Identities* (Chicago, The University of Chicago Press, 1995).

Appiah, KA, *The Lies that Bind: Rethinking Identity. Creed, Country, Class, Culture* (New York, Liveright, 2018).

Applebaum, A, *The Twilight of Democracy: The Seductive Lure of Authoritarianism* (New York, Doubleday, 2020).

Apponyi, A, 'Speech at the Meeting of the Interparliamentary Union' (1904) quoted in J Bak, 'Political Uses of Historical Comparisons: Medieval and Modern Hungary' (2006) 23 *Post-Medieval Studies*.

Arato, A, *Post Sovereign Constitution Making: Learning and Legitimacy* (Oxford, Oxford University Press, 2016).

——, et al, 'Opinion on the Fundamental Law of Hungary (Amicus Brief)' in GA Tóth (ed), *Constitution for a Disunited Nation: On Hungary's 2011 Fundamental Law* (New York, Central European University Press, 2012) 455–90.

Arnaiz, AS and CA Llivina (eds), *National Constitutional Identity and European Integration* (Cambridge, Intersentia, 2013).

Arnold, R, 'Contemporary constitutionalism and integration' in *Constitutional Studies* Vol I (Constitutional Court of the Republic of Bulgaria, 2019) 127–54.

Baer, S, 'Who Cares? A defence of judicial review' (2020) 8 *Journal of the British Academy* 75–104.

——, 'Dignity, Liberty, Equality: A fundamental Rights triangle of Constitutionalism' (2009) 59:4 *The University of Toronto Law Journal* 417–68.

——, 'Democracy in peril: a call for amici and amicae curiae and critical lawyering' (2019) 10 *Transnational Legal Theory* 140–162.

——, 'Grundrechte unter Druck', in M Ruffert (ed), *Europa-Visionen* (Baden-Baden, Nomos, 2019).

Bak, J, 'Political Uses of Historical Comparisons: Medieval and Modern Hungary' (2006) 23 *Florilegium* 271.

—— and Gara-Bak, A, 'The Ideology of a "Millennial Constitution" of Hungary' (1981) 15 *East European Quarterly* 307.

Balog, B, *Materiálne jadro ústavy Slovenskej republiky* (Žilina, Eurokódex, 2014).

Bárd, P, Chronowski, N and Fleck, Z, 'Inventing Constitutional Identity in Hungary', *MTA Law Working Papers* 2022/6, 32.

Barker, E, *The Politics of Aristotle* (Oxford, Oxford University Press, 1946).

Barnes, KT, 'Aristotle on Identity and Its Problems' (1977) 22 *Phronesis* 48.

Baroš, J and Pospíšil, I, 'Čl. 112 (Pojem ústavního pořádku)' in P Rychetský et al, *Ústava České republiky. Ústavní zákon o bezpečnosti České republiky: komentář* (Warszawa, Wolters Kluwer, 2015).

Bar-Tal, D, 'Group beliefs as an expression of social identity' in S Worchel et al (eds), *Social identity: International perspectives* (London, Sage Publications, 1998) 93.

Bast, J, v Harbou, F and Wessels, J, *Human Rights Challenges to European Migration Policy (REMAP study)* 2020.

Berlin, I, 'Historical Inevitability' in H Meyerhoff (ed), *The Philosophy of History in our Time* (Hamburg, Anchor, 1959)

—— *Personal Impressions* (London, Pimlico, 1998).

Bernatt, M and Ziółkowski, M, 'Statutory Anti-Constitutionalism' (2019) 8 *Washington International Law Journal* 487.

Besselink, LFM, 'Ilonka Sayn-Wittgenstein v Landeshauptmann von Wien' (2012) 49 *Common Market Law Review* 671.

Bibó, I, 'Miseries of the East European Small States' in I Bibó and Dénes, IZ (eds), *The Art of Peacemaking. Political Essays by István Bibó* (London, Yale University Press, 2015).

Bieber, R, 'An Association of Sovereign States' (2009) 5 *European Constitutional Law Review* 391.

Bilfinger, C, 'Verfassungsfrage und Staatsgerichtshof' (1931) 20 *Zeitschrift für Politik* 81.

——, *Nationale Demokratie als Grundlage der Weimarer Verfassung: Rede bei der Feier der zehnjährigen Wiederkehr des Verfassungstags gehalten am 24. Juli 1929* (Tübingen, Max Niemeyer Verlag, 1929).

——, *Der Reichssparkommissar* (Berlin, W de Gruyter & Company, 1928).

Blauberger, M and Sindbjerg Martinsen, D, 'The Court of Justice in times of politicization: "law as a mask and shield" revisited' (2020) 27 *Journal of European Public Policy* 382–99.

Blisa A, Molek, P and Šipulová, K, 'Czech Republic and Slovakia: Another International Human Rights Treaty?' in M Bobek and J Adams-Prassl (eds), *EU Charter of Fundamental Rights in the Member States* (Oxford, Hart, 2020).

Bobek, M, 'Landtová, Holubec, and the Problem of an Uncooperative Court: Implications for the Preliminary Rulings Procedure' (2014) 10 *European Constitutional Law Review* 54.

—— and Kühn, Z, 'What about that "Incoming Tide"?: The Application of EU Law in the Czech Republic' in A Lazowski (ed), *The Application of EU Law in the New Member States – Brave New World* (The Hague, Asser Press, 2010) 325.

Böckenförde, E-W, 'Die verfassungsgebende Gewalt des Volkes – Ein Grenzbegriff des Verfassungsrechts' in UK Preuß (ed), *Zum Begriff der Verfassung: Die Ordnung des Politischen* (Frankfurt am Main, Fischer, 1994).

Bröstl A, Kľučka, J and Mazák, J, *Ústavný súd Slovenskej republiky. Organizácia, proces, doktrína* (PHARE Foundation, 2001).

Brubaker, R, *Nationalism Reframed: Nationhood and the National Question in the New Europe* (Cambridge, Cambridge University Press, 1996).

—— and Cooper, F, 'Beyond "identity"' (2000) 29 *Theory and Society* 1.

Bryde, O, 'Verfassunggebende Gewalt des Volkes und Verfassungsänderung im deutschen Staatsrecht: Zwischen Überforderung und Unterforderung der Volkssouveränität' in R Widmer and P Widmer (eds), *L'Espace Constitutionnel Européen/Der Europäische Verfassungsraum/The European Constitutional Area* (Zurich, Schulthess Polygraphischer Verlag, 1995).

Brzezinski, MF and Garlicki, L, 'Judicial Review in Post-Communist Poland: The Emergence of a Rechtsstaat' (1995) 31 *Stanford Journal of International Law* 13.

Bugaric, B, 'Central Europe's Descent into Autocracy: A Constitutional Analysis of Authoritarian Populism' (2019) 17 *International Journal of Constitutional Law* 597–616.

Burgorgue-Larsen, L (ed), *L'identite constitutionnelle saisie par les juges en Europe* (Paris, Institut de recherche en droit international et européen de la Sorbonne, Pedone, 2011).

Buštíková, L and Baboš, P, 'Best in Covid: Populists in the Time of Pandemic' (2020) 8 *Politics and Governance* 496.

Bútora, M and P Hunčík (eds), *Slovensko 1995: Súhrnná správa o stave spoločnosti* (Bratislava, Nadácia Sándora Máraiho, 1996).

Çali, B, 'The Two Faces of German Legal Hegemony?' (*Verfassungsblog*, 07 October 2020).

Calliess, C, 'Constitutional Identity in Germany: One for Three or Three in One?' in C Calliess and G von der Schyff (eds), *Constitutional Identity in a Europe of Multilevel Constitutionalism* (Cambridge, Cambridge University Press, 2020) 153–181.

—— and van der Schyff, G, *Constitutional Identity in a Europe of Multilevel Constitutionalism* (Cambridge, Cambridge University Press, 2020).

Castano, E and Yzerbyt, E, 'The Highs and Lows of Group Homogeneity' (1998) 42 *Behavioural Processes* 219.

Cerruti, F, 'Political Identity and Conflict: A Comparison of Definitions' in F Cerutti and R Ragionieri (eds), *Identities and Conflicts* (London, Palgrave Macmillan, 2001).

Chronowski, N, 'The New Hungarian Fundamental Law in the Light of the European Union's Normative Values' (2012) *Revue Est Europe* 111.

Chubb, B, *The Politics of the Irish Constitution* (Dublin, Institute of Public Administration, 1991).

Cieger, A, 'Hungary's Long Nineteenth Century. Constitutional and Democratic Traditions in a European Perspective. Collected Studies. By László Péter' (2012) 1 *Hungarian Historical Review: new series of Acta Historica Academiae Scientiarum Hungaricae* 231.

——, 'National Identity and Constitutional Patriotism in the Context of Modern Hungarian History' (2016) 5 *Hungarian Historical Review: new series of Acta Historica Academiae Scientiarum Hungaricae* 123.

Claes, M, 'National Identity: Trump Card or Up for Negotiation?' in AS Arnaiz and CA Llivina (eds), *National Constitutional Identity and European Integration* (Cambridge, Intersentia, 2013) 109–39.

——, 'Negotiating Constitutional Identity or Whose Identity is It Anyway?' in M Claes et al (eds), *Constitutional Conversations in Europe: Actors. Topics and Procedures (107 Ius Commune Europaeum)* (Cambridge, Intersentia, 2012) 205–33.

Cloots, E, *National Identity in EU Law* (Oxford, Oxford University Press, 2015).

Čorba, J, et al, *Uplatňovanie európskeho práva na Slovensku* (Bratislava, Kalligram, 2002).

Corrales, J, 'The Authoritarian Resurgence: Autocratic Legalism in Venezuela' (2015) 26 *Journal of Democracy*, 37–51.

Coulmas, F, *Identity: A Very Short Introduction* (Oxford, Oxford University Press, 2019).

Cozzi, A, et al, *Comparative study on the implementation of the ECHR at the national level* (Belgrade, Council of Europe Office in Belgrade, 2016).

Dahrendorf, R, 'Germans Lack the Key to Their National Identity', in H James and M Stone (eds) *When the Wall Came Down* (New York-London, Routledge, 1992) 230–33.

Dixon, R, 'Rule of law teleology: against the misuse and abuse of rule of law rhetoric' (2019) 11 *Hague Journal on the Rule of Law* 461–64.

—— and Landau, D, *Abusive Constitutional Borrowing: Legal Globalization and the Subversion of Liberal Democracy* (Oxford, Oxford University Press, 2021).

Dobias, K, 'The Role of Constitutional Identity in the Responses to the Terror Attacks in France and the Refugee Management Crisis in Hungary' (2015) *Annual Review of Constitution Building Processes* 101.

Dorsen, N, et al, *Comparative Constitutionalism* 4th edn (St Paul, West, 2022).

Drakopoulou, M, 'Feminism and the siren call of law' (2007) 18 *Law and Critique* 331–60.

Dreier, H, *Gilt das Grundgesetz ewig?: Fünf Kapitel zum modernen Verfassungsstaat* (München, Carl Friedrich von Siemens Stiftung, 2009).

Drgonec, J, *Ústava Slovenskej republiky s úvodným komentárom* (Vantaa, Heuréka, 2004).

——, *Ústavné právo hmotné* (Munich, CH Beck, 2018).

——, *Ústavné právo procesné* (Munich, CH Beck, 2017).

Drinóczi, T, 'Constitutional Identity in Europe: The Identity of the Constitution. A Regional Approach' (2020) 21 *German Law Journal* 105.

——, 'Hungarian Constitutional Court: The Limits of EU Law in the Hungarian Legal System' (2017) 11 *Vienna Journal on International Constitutional Law* 139.

Drugda, Š, 'Changes to Selection and Appointment of Constitutional Court Judges in Slovakia' (2019) 102 *Právny obzor* 14.

——, 'On Collision Course with the Material Core of the Slovak Constitution' (*Verfassungsblog*, 3 December 2020).

Dudzik, S and Półtorak, N, 'The Court of the Last Word: Competences of the Polish Constitutional Tribunal in the Review of European Union Law' (2012) 15 *Yearbook of Polish European Studies* 225–258.

—— (eds), *Prawo Unii Europejskiej a prawo konstytucyjne państw członkowskich* (Warszawa, Wolters Kluwer, 2013).

Dupré, C, 'Human Dignity: Rhetoric, Protection, and Instrumentalization' in GA Tóth (ed), *Constitution for Disunited Nation: On Hungary's 2011 Fundamental Law* (New York, Central European University Press, 2012) 143–70.

——, *The Age of Dignity: Human Rights and Constitutionalism in Europe* (Oxford, Hart, 2015).

Dworkin, R, 'What Is Democracy?' in GA Tóth (ed), *Constitution for a Disunited Nation: On Hungary's 2011 Fundamental Law* (New York, Central European University Press, 2012) 25–34.

——, *Taking Rights Seriously* (Cambridge, Mass, Harvard University Press, 1978).

——, *Law's Empire* (Cambridge, Mass, Harvard University Press, 1986).

——, *Sovereign Virtue: The Theory and Practice of Equality* (Cambridge, Mass, Harvard University Press, 2000).

——, *Justice for Hedgehogs* (Cambridge, Mass, Harvard University Press, 2011).

Erikson, EH, *Dimensions of a New Identity* (New York, WW Norton and Co., 1979).

European Commission, 'The Development of European Identity/Identities: Unfinished Business' (2012).

Fabbrini, F and Sajó, A, 'The Dangers of Constitutional Identity' (2019) 25 *European Law Journal* 457–73.

Faraguna, P, 'Constitutional Identity in the EU – A Shield or a Sword' (2017) 18 *German Law Journal* 1617.

——, 'Taking Constitutional Identities away from the Courts' (2015) 41 *Brooklyn Journal of International Law* 491.

Farrell, M and E Drywood and E Hughes (eds), *Human rights in the media: Fear and fetish* (New York, Routledge, 2019).

Fasel, R, 'Constraining Constituent Conventions: Emmanuel-Joseph Sieyès and the Limits of Pouvoir Constituant' (2022) 20 *International Journal of Constitutional Law* 1103-29.

Felkay, A, *Out of Russian Orbit. Hungary Gravitates to the West* (Westport/Connecticut, Greenwood Publishing Group, 1997).

Filip, J, 'K formulaci evropských klauzulí v ústavním právu' (2010) 18 *Časopis pro právní vědu a praxi*.

——, *Ústavní právo České republiky. Základní pojmy a instituty. Ústavní základy ČR. Díl 1* 4th ed (Brno, Masarykova univerzita and Doplněk, 2003).

Frankenberg, G, *Authoritarianism: Constitutional Perspectives* (Cheltenham, Edward Elgar, 2020).

Friedman, LM, 'Nationalism, Identity, and Law' (1995) 28 *Indiana Law Review* 503.

Frosini, JO, 'Constitutional Preambles: More than Just a Narration of History' (2017) *University of Illinois Law Review* 603.

Fukuyama, F, *Identity: The Demand for Dignity and the Politics of Resentment* (New York, Farrar, Straus and Giroux, 2018).

Gallie, W, 'Essentially Contested Concepts' (1956) 56 *Proceedings of the Aristotelian Society* 167.

Garlicki, L, 'Democracy and International Influences' in G Nolte (ed), *European and U.S. Constitutionalism* (Cambridge, Cambridge University Press, 2005) 263–79.

Geertz, C, *The Interpretation of Cultures* (New York, Basic Books, 1973).

Greer, S, and Williams, A, 'Human Rights in the Council of Europe and the EU: Towards 'Individual', 'Constitutional' or 'Institutional' Justice?' (2009) 15 *European Law Journal* 462–81.

Ginsburg, T and A Simpser (eds), *Constitutions in Authoritarian Regimes* (Cambridge, Cambridge University Press, 2014).

Goebel, RJ, 'Supranational: Federal: Intergovernmental: The Governmental Structure of the European Union after the Treaty of Lisbon' (2013) 20 *Columbia Journal of European Law* 77–142.

Goldberg Ruthchild, R, 'Women and Gender in 1917' (2017) 76 *Slavic Review* 694.

Gosewinkel, D, 'The Constitutional State' in H Pihlajamaki and MD Dubber (eds), *The Oxford Handbook of European Legal History* (Oxford, Oxford University Press, 2018).

Graber, MA, 'The Nonmajoritarian Difficulty: Legislative Deference to the Judiciary' (1993) 7 *Studies in American Political Development* 35.

Granat, M, 'Konstytucyjność prawa bez sądu konstytucyjnego' in R Balicki and M Jabłoński (eds), *Państwo i jego instytucje. Konstytucja – sądownictwo – samorząd terytorialny* (Wrocław, Wydawnictwo Uniwersytetu Wrocławskiego, 2018).

—— and Granat, K, *The Constitution of Poland. A Contextual Analysis* (Oxford, Hart, 2019).

Grewe, C, 'Methods of Identification of National Constitutional Identity' in AS Arnaiz and CA Llivina (eds), *National Constitutional Identity and European Integration* (Cambridge, Intersentia, 2013).

Grogan, J and A Donald (eds), *Routledge Handbook of Law and the COVID-19 Pandemic* (London, Routledge, 2022).

Grosser, A, 'The Federal Constitutional Court's *Lisbon* Case: Germany's "Sonderweg" – An Outsider's Perspective' (2009) 10 *German Law Journal* 1263.

Grudzińska-Gross, I, *Constitutionalism in East Central Europe: Discussions in Warsaw, Budapest, Prague, Bratislava* (Czecho-Slovak Committee of the European Cultural Foundation, 1994).

Guastaferro, B, 'Beyond the Exceptionalism of Constitutional Conflicts: The Ordinary Functions of the Identity Clause' 31 (2012) *Yearbook of European Law* 263–318.

Gusy, C, '*Demokratische Verfassungsänderung – Selbstschutz oder Selbstpreisgabe der Verfassung*' (2010) 20 *Der Staat* 159.

Habermas, J, 'Citizenship and National Identity: Some Reflections on the Future of Europe' in R Robertson and KE White (eds), *Globalization: Global Membership and Participation* (London, Routledge, 2003) 155.

——, *Between Facts and Norms: Contributions to a Discourse Theory of Law and Democracy* (Cambridge, Mass, Polity Press, 1996).

——, *Eine Art Schadensabwicklung. Kleine Politische Schriften* VI (Berlin, Suhrkamp, 1987).

Halász, I, *Minulosť a symbolika v ústavách štátov strednej Európy* (Bratislava, Ústav státu a práva AV ČR, 2019).

Halberstam, D and Möllers, C, 'The German Constitutional Court Says "Ja Zu Deutschland!"' (2009) 10 *German Law Journal* 1241.

Haller, M and Ressler, R, 'National and European identity' (2006) 47 *Revue Francaise de Sociologie* 817.

Hallstein, W, *Europe in the Making* trans Ch Roetter (London, Allen & Unwin, 1972).

Halmai, G, 'Abuse of Constitutional Identity. The Hungarian Constitutional Court on Interpretation of Article E) (2) of the Fundamental Law' (2018) 43 *Review of Central and East European Law* 23–42.

——, 'Illiberal Constitutionalism? The Hungarian Constitution in a European Perspective' in S Kadelbach (ed), *Verfassungskrisen in der Europäischen Union* (Baden-Baden, Nomos, 2018) 85–104.

Hanley, S and Vachudova, MA, 'Understanding the illiberal turn: democratic backsliding in the Czech Republic' (2018) 34 *East European Politics* 276.

Harris, E, 'Nation before Democracy? Placing the Rise of the Slovak Extreme Right into Context' (2019) 35 *East European Politics* 538.

—— and Henderson, K, 'Slovakia since 1989' in SP Ramet and CM Hassenstab (eds), *Central and Southeast European Politics Since 1989* (Cambridge, Cambridge University Press, 2019).

Hart, HLA, *The Concept of Law* 2nd edn (Oxford, Oxford University Press, 1994).

Hein, M 'Entrenchment Clauses in the History of Modern Constitutionalism' (2018) 86 *Tijdschrift voor Rechtsgeschiedenis* 434.

Herdegen, M, 'Maastricht and the German Constitutional Court: Constitutional Restraints for An "Ever Closer Union" and Document "Extracts from: Brunner v. The European Union"' (1994) 31 *Common Market Law Review.*

Hobsbawm, E, *The Invention of Tradition* (Cambridge, Cambridge University Press, 2012).

Hofmannová, H, '"Small, but Ours": The Czech features of authoritarian methods of governance' (2020) *Charles University in Prague Faculty of Law Research Paper.*

Holmes, S, 'The Identity Illusion' (17 January 2019) *The New York Review of Books.*

Hong, M, *Der Menschenwürdegehalt der Grundrechte* (Tübingen, Mohr Siebeck, 2019).

Hörcher, F and Lorman, T, *A History of the Hungarian Constitution. Law, Government and Political Culture in Central Europe* (London, Bloomsbury Publishing, 2018).

Huber, PM, 'Die Anforderungen der Europäischen Union an die Reform des Grundgesetzes' (1994) 31 *Thüringer Verwaltungsblätter* 1.

Hvížďala, K and Přibáň, J, *Hledání dějin: O české státnosti a identitě* (Prague, Karolinum, 2018).

Ignatieff, M, *Blood and Belonging: Journey into the New Nationalities* (New York, Farrar, Straus and Giroux, 1995).

Ingold, A, 'Die verfassungsrechtliche Identität der Bundesrepublik' (2015) 140 *Anstalt des öffentlichen Rechts* 1.

Ipsen, H-P, 'BVerfG versus EuGH re "Grundrechte": zum Beschluß des Zweiten Senats des Bundesverfassungsgerichts vom 29. Mai 1974' (1975) 10 *Europarecht.*

Jackson, V, *Constitutional Engagement in a Transnational Era* (Oxford, Oxford University Press, 2013).

Jacobsohn, GJ, 'A Lighter Touch: American Constitutional Principles in Comparative Perspective' in K Orren and JW Compton (eds), *Cambridge Companion on the United States Constitution* (Cambridge, Cambridge University Press, 2018) 13–44.

——, *Constitutional Identity* (Cambridge, Mass, Harvard University Press, 2010).

——, 'Constitutional Identity' (2006) 68 *The Review of Politics* 361.

——, 'Constitutional Values and Principles' in M Rosenfeld and A Sajó (eds), *The Oxford Handbook in Comparative Constitutional Law* (Oxford, Oxford University Press, 2012) 777–91.

——, 'The Formation of Constitutional Identities' in T Ginsburg and R Dixon (eds), *Comparative Constitutional Law* (Cheltenham, Edward Elgar Publishing, 2011).

——, 'The Permeability of Constitutional Borders' (2003) 82 *Texas Law Review* 1763.

——, and Roznai, Y, *Constitutional Revolution* (New Haven, Yale University Press, 2020).

Jakab, A, 'What is Wrong with the Hungarian Legal System and How to Fix it' *Max Planck Institute for Comparative Public Law & International Law (MPIL) Research Paper No. 2018–13.*

James, C, 'Céad míle fáilte? Ireland Welcomes Divorce: The 1995 Irish Divorce Referendum and the Family (Divorce) Act of 1996' (1997) 8 *Duke Journal of Comparative and International Law* 175.

Jarass, HD and Kment, M, *Grundgesetz für die Bundesrepublik Deutschland: GG – Kommentar* 16th edn (Munich, CH Beck, 2020).

Jellinek, W, 'Das verfassungsändernde Reichsgesetz' in R Thoma and G Anschütz (eds) 2 *Handbuch des Deutschen Staatsrechts* (Tübingen, Mohr, 1931).

Jeselsohn, S, *Begriff, Arten und Grenzen der Verfassungsänderung* (Heidelberg, Carl Winters Universitätsbuchhandlung, 1929).

Jičínský, Z, 'Ústavněprávní a politické problémy vzniku České republiky a charakteristika sociálnědemokratického návrhu: Ústavy ČR' in A Gerloch and J Kysela et al (eds), *20 let Ústavy České republiky: Ohlédnutí zpět a pohled vpřed* (Prague, Aleš Čeněk, 2013).

Káčer, M and Neumann, J, *Materiálne jadro v slovenskom ústavnom práve. Doktrinálny disent proti zrušeniu sudcovských previerok* (Prague, Leges, 2019).

Kaczorova-Ireland, A, 'What Is the European Union Required to Respect under Article 4(2) TEU?: The Uniqueness Approach' 25 (2019) *European Public Law* 57–82.

Kashyup, SC, *Jawaharlal Nehru and the Constitution* (New Delhi, Metropolitan Book Co., 1982).

Kelemen, D and Pech, L, 'Why Autocrats Love Constitutional Identity and Constitutional Pluralism: Lessons from Hungary and Poland' (2018) 2 *Reconnect Europe Working Paper.*

Kelemen, K, 'The Hungarian Constitutional Court and the Concept of National Constitutional Identity' (2017) 15–16 *Ianus-Diritto e finanza* 23.

Kelsen, H, *Allgemeine Staatslehre* (Tübingen, Mohr Siebeck Lehrbuch, 1925).

Khaitan, T, 'Directive Principles and the Expressive Accommodation of Ideological Dissenters' (2018) 16 *International Journal of Constitutional Law* 389–420.

Khvorostiankina, A, 'Constitutional Identity in the Context of Post-Soviet Transformation. Europeanization and Regional Integration Processes (the case of Armenia)' (2017) 1 *Armenian Journal of Political Science* 45.

Kindlová, M, 'Formal and Informal Constitutional Amendment in the Czech Republic' (2018) 8 *The Lawyer Quarterly*.

Kirchhof, P, '183 Der deutsche Staat im Prozeß der europäischen Integration' in J Isensee and P Kirchhof (eds), 7 *Grundlagen von Staat und Verfassung – Handbuch des Staatsrechts der Bundesrepublik Deutschland* (Heidelberg, CF Müller, 1992) 855–78.

——, 'Die Identität der Verfassung in ihren unabänderlichen Inhalten' in J Isensee and P Kirchhof (eds) *Handbuch des Staatsrechts II*, 3rd edn (Heidelberg, CF Müller, 2004).

——, *Brauchen wir ein erneuertes Grundgesetz* (Heidelberg, CF Müller, 1992).

Kis, J, 'Introduction: From the 1989 Constitution to the 2011 Fundamental Law', in GA Tóth (ed), *Constitution for a Disunited Nation. On Hungary's 2011 Fundamental Law* (New York, Central European University Press, 2012) 1–24.

——, *Constitutional Democracy* (New York, Central European University Press, 2003).

Kitschelt, H, *Post-Communist Party Systems: Competition, Representation, and Inter-Party Cooperation* (Cambridge, Cambridge University Press, 1999).

Klare, KE, 'Legal Culture and Transformative Constitutionalism' (1998) 14 *South African Journal of Human Rights* 146.

Klein, C and A Sajó, 'Constitution-making: process and substance' in *The Oxford Handbook of Comparative Constitutional Law* (Oxford, Oxford University Press, 2012).

Kochenov, D, 'When Equality Directives Are Not Enough: Taking an Issue with the Missing Minority Rights Policy in the EU' in U Belavusau and K Henrard (eds), *EU Anti-discrimination Law Beyond Gender* (Oxford, Hart, 2018) 119–140.

Kochi, T, The End of Global Constitutionalism and Rise of Antidemocratic Politics (2020) 34:4 *Global Society* 487–506.

Kohn, H, *The Idea of Nationalism: A Study in Its Origins and Background* (New York, MacMillan, 1944).

Kohn, M, 'From Lublin to London, Europe's Contested Ideas of National Identity' (12 November 2019) *The New York Review of Books*.

Kokott, J, 'Report on Germany' in A-M Slaughter, A Stone and JHH Weiler (eds), *The European Court and National Courts – Doctrine and Jurisprudence: Legal Change in its Social Context* (Oxford, Hart, 1998) 77–131.

Komárek, J, 'Czech Constitutional Court Playing with Matches: The Czech Constitutional Court Declares a Judgment of the Court of Justice of the EU Ultra Vires; Judgment of 31 January 2012, Pl. ÚS 5/12, Slovak Pensions XVII' (2012) 8 *European Constitutional Law Review* 323.

Konstadinides, T, 'Constitutional Identity as a Shield and as a Sword: The European Legal Order within the Framework of National Constitutional Settlement' (2011) 13 *Cambridge Yearbook of European Legal Studies* 195–218.

Korkut, U, *Liberalization Challenges in Hungary: Elitism, Progressivism, and Populism* (London, Palgrave MacMillan, 2015).

Körtvélyesi, Zs, 'From "We the People" to "We the Nation"' in GA Tóth (ed), *Constitution for a Disunited Nation. On Hungary's 2011 Fundamental Law* (New York, Central European University Press, 2012) 111–42.

——, 'Nation, Nationality, and National Identity: Uses, Misuses, and the Hungarian Case of External Ethnic Citizenship' (2020) 33 *International Journal for the Semiotics of Law* 771.

—— and Majtényi, B, 'Game of Values: The Threat of Exclusive Constitutional Identity, the EU and Hungary' (2017) 18 *German Law Journal* 1721.

Kosař, D, *Perils of Judicial Self-Government in Transitional Societies* (Cambridge, Cambridge University Press, 2016).

—— and Šipulová, K, 'How to Fight Court-Packing?' (2020) 6 *Constitutional Studies* 133.

—— and Vyhnánek, L, 'Constitutional Identity in the Czech Republic' in C Calliess and G van der Schyff (eds), *Constitutional Identity in a Europe of Multilevel Constitutionalism* (Cambridge, Cambridge University Press, 2019) 85–113.

—— and Vyhnánek, L, 'The Constitutional Court of Czechia: A New Twist on the Old Fashioned Idea?' in A von Bogdandy, P Huber and C Grabenwarter (eds), *The Max Planck Handbooks in European Public Law: Volume III: Constitutional Adjudication: Institutions* 3 (Oxford, Oxford University Press, 2020) 119–79.

—— and Vyhnánek, L, 'Ústavní identita České republiky' (2018) 10 *Právník* 854.

Kovács, K, 'Changing Constitutional identity via Amendment' in P Blokker (ed), *Constitutional Acceleration within the European Union and Beyond* (London, Routledge, 2018) 197–214.

——, 'Constitutional or Ethnocultural? National Identity as a European Legal Concept' (2022) 8 *Intersections. East European Journal of Society and Politics* 170–90.

——, 'Parliamentary Democracy by Default' (2020) 2 *Jus Cogens* 237–258.

——, 'The Missing Link: Equality' in GA Tóth (ed), *Constitution for a Disunited Nation. On Hungary's 2011 Fundamental Law* (New York, Central European University Press, 2012) 171–96.

——, 'The Rise of an Ethnocultural Constitutional Identity in the Jurisprudence of the East Central European Courts' (2017) 18 *German Law Journal* 1703–720.

—— and Scheppele, KL, 'The Fragility of an Independent Judiciary: Lessons from Hungary and Poland – and the European Union' (2018) 51 *Communist and Post-Communist Studies* 189–200.

—— and Tóth, GA, 'Hungary's Constitutional Transformation' (2011) 7 *European Constitutional Law Review* 183–200.

Kowalik-Bańczyk, K, 'Sending Smoke Signals to Luxembourg – the Polish Constitutional Tribunal in Dialogue with the ECJ' in M Claes et al. (eds), *Constitutional Conversations in Europe: Actors, Topics and Procedure* (Cambridge, Intersentia, 2012) 267–84.

Kraft-Fuchs, M, 'Prinzipielle Bemerkungen zu Carl Schmitts Verfassungslehre' (New York, J. Springer, 1928) reprinted in (1930) 12 *Zeitschrift für Öffentliches Recht*.

Krajewski, M and Ziółkowski, M, 'EU Judicial Independence Decentralized: A.K.' (2020) 57 *Common Market Law Review* 1107–138.

Kratochvíl, P and Sychra, Z, 'The end of democracy in the EU? The Eurozone crisis and the EU's democratic deficit' (2019) 41 *Journal of European Integration* 169–85.

Krisch, N, 'Beyond Constitutionalism: The Pluralist Structure of Postnational Law' (Oxford, Oxford University Press, 2010).

Krošlák, D, *Ústavné právo* (Warszawa, Wolters Kluwer, 2016).

Kühn, Z and Bobek, M, 'Europe Yet to Come: The Application of EU Law in Slovakia' in A Lazowski (ed), *The Application of EU Law in the New Member States: Brave New World* (The Hague, Asser Press, 2010) 357–78.

Kumm, M, 'The Cosmopolitan Turn in Constitutionalism: An Integrated Conception of Public Law' (2013) 20 *Indiana Journal of Global Legal Studies* 605.

——, 'The Idea of Socratic Contestation and the Right to Justification: The Point of Rights-Based Proportionality Review' (2010) 4 *Law & Ethics of Human Rights* 142.

——, 'The Idea of Thick Constitutional Patriotism and Its Implications for the Role and Structure of European Legal History' (2005) 6 *German Law Journal* 319.

——, 'Who is Afraid of the Total Constitution? Constitutional Rights as Principles and the Constitutionalization of Private Law' (2006) 7 *German Law Journal* 341.

——, 'Why Europeans Will Not Embrace Constitutional Patriotism' (2008) 6 *International Journal of Constitutional Law* 117.

——, 'Rebel Without a Good Cause: Karlsruhe's Misguided Attempt to Draw the CJEU into a Game of "Chicken" and What the CJEU Might do About It' (2014) 15 *German Law Journal* 203.

——, 'Political Liberalism and the Structures of Rights' in G Pavlakos (ed) *Law, Rights, Discourse: The Legal Philosophy of Robert Alexy* (Oxford, Hart, 2007).

Kymlicka, W, *Multicultural Citizenship* (Oxford, Oxford University Press, 1996).
Kysela, J, *Ústava mezi právem a politikou: úvod do ústavní teorie* (Prague, Leges, 2014).
—— and P Ondřejek (eds), *Stát jako kolos na hliněných nohou?* (Prague, Leges, 2016).
Lacey, N, 'Populism and the Rule of Law' (2019) 15 *Annual Review of Law and Social Science*, 79–96.
Lambert, E, *Le Gouvernement des juges et la lutte contre la législation sociale aux États-Unis, l'expérience américaine du contrôle judiciaire de la constitutionnalité des lois* (Lyon, Persée, 1921).
Láncos, PL, 'Freedom of Information in Hungary: A Shifting Landscape' in DC Dragos et al (eds), *The Laws of Transparency in Action, A European Perspective* (Cham, Palgrave, 2019) 389.
Landau, D, 'Abusive Constitutionalism' (2013–14) 47 *University of California Davis Law Review* 189.
—— and Dixon, R, 'Abusive Judicial Review: Courts Against Democracy' (2019) 53 *University of California Davis Law Review* 1313–387.
Láštic, E, *V rukách politických strán: Referendum na Slovensku 1993–2010* (Bratislava, Univerzita Komenského, 2011).
Leško, M, *Mečiar a mečiarizmus: Politik bez škrupúľ, politia bez zábran* (Prešov, VMV, 1996).
Łętowska, E, 'The Honest (though Embarrassing) Coming-out of the Polish Constitutional Tribunal' (*Verfassungsblog*, 29 November 2021).
Lijphart, A, 'Democratization and Constitutional Choices in Czecho-Slovakia, Hungary, and Poland, 1989–91' (1992) 4 *Journal of Theoretical Politics* 207.
Lilla, M, *The Once and Future Liberal: After Identity Politics* (New York, HarperCollins, 2018).
——, *The Shipwrecked Mind: On Political Reaction* (New York, The New York Review of Books, 2016).
Linz, JJ and Stepan, A, *Problems of Democratic Transition and Consolidation: Southern Europe, South America, and Post-Communist Europe* (Baltimore, Johns Hopkins University Press, 1996).
Locke, J, *An Essay Concerning Human Understanding* (Pennsylvania, Pennsylvania State University, 1999).
Loewenstein, K, 'Militant democracy and fundamental rights' (1937) 31 *American Political Science Review* 417–32.
Loughlin, M, 'What is Constitutionalisation?' in P Dobner and M Loughlin, *The Twilight of Constitutionalism?* (Oxford, Oxford University Press, 2010).
Macejková, I, 'Právo Európskej únie v rozhodovacej činnosti Ústavného súdu Slovenskej republiky' in A Krunková (ed), *Európska únia a jej vplyv na organizáciu a fungovanie verejnej správy v Slovenskej republike* (Košice, Univerzita P J Šafárika, 2016).
Malenovský, J, 'O legitimitě a výkladu české Ústavy na konci století existence moderního českého státu' (2013) 152 *Právník* 745.
Malíř, J, 'The Czech Constitutional Court and The Political Question Doctrine: A Contribution to the Debate on The Demise of the Political Question Doctrine' (forthcoming)
—— and J Ondřejková, 'Law-Making Activity of the Czech Constitutional Court' in M Florczak-Wątor (ed), *Judicial Law-making in European Constitutional Courts* (London, Routledge, 2020) 111–27.
Malová, D, 'Slovakia: From the Ambiguous Constitution to the Dominance of Informal Rules' in J Zielonka (ed), *Democratic Consolidation in Eastern Europe* 1 (Oxford, Oxford University Press, 2001) 347–77.
——, 'Slovakia' in J-M de Waele, F Escalona and M Vieira (eds), *The Palgrave Handbook of Social Democracy in the European Union* (London, Palgrave Macmillan, 2013) 550–574.
——, 'The Role and Experience of the Slovakian Constitutional Court' in W Sadurski (ed), *Constitutional Justice, East and West: Democratic Legitimacy and Constitutional Courts in Post-Communist Europe in a Comparative Perspective* (The Hague, Kluwer Law International, 2010).
Maršálek, P, 'Evropská integrace, unijní občanství a česká národní identita' (2014) 2 *Acta Universitatis Carolinae – Iuridica* 73.
Martí, JL, 'Two Different Ideas of Constitutional Identity: Identity of the Constitution v. Identity of the People' in AS Arnaiz and CA Llivina (eds), *National Constitutional Identity and European Integration* 4 (Cambridge, Intersentia, 2013) 17–36.

Marušiak, J, 'Ústavy SR a ČR a ich úloha v procese konštituovania národných identít' in V Goněc and R Holec (eds), *Česko-slovenská historická ročenka 2012. Češi a Slováci 1993-2012: Vzdalování a přibližování* (Warszawa, VEDA, 2013).
Mayer, FC, 'Rashomon in Karlsruhe: A Reflection on Democracy and Identity in the European Union: The German Constitutional Court's Lisbon decision and the changing landscape of European constitutionalism' (2011) 9 *International Journal of Constitutional Law* 757.
——, 'Verfassung im Nationalstaat: Von der Gesamtordnung zur europäischen Teilordnung?' (2015) 75 *Veröffentlichung der Vereinigung der Deutschen Staatsrechtslehrer* 7.
Mazák, J, 'Príspevok Ústavného súdu Slovenskej republiky při uplatňovaní práva plnění povinností na komunitárnej úrovni' (2005) 14 *Jurisprudence* 11.
—— and Jánošíková, M, 'Prienik Charty základných práv Európskej únie do vnútroštátneho práva na príklade Slovenskej republiky' (2016) 2 *Acta Universitatis Carolinae Iuridica* 11.
—— and Orosz, L, 'Quashing the Decisions on Amnesty in the Constitutional System of the Slovak Republic: Opening or Closing Pandora's Box?' (2018) 8 *The Lawyer Quarterly.*
Meessen, KM, 'Maastricht nach Karlsruhe' (1994) 47 *Neue Juristische Woche* 549.
Michnik, A, 'The Trouble with History: Tradition: Imprisonment or Liberation?' (2009) 22 *International Journal of Politics, Culture, and Society* 445.
Mill, JS, *Considerations on Representative Government* (London, Parker, Son and Bourn, 1861).
Miller, D, *Citizenship and National Identity* (Cambridge, Mass, Polity Press, 2000).
——, *On Nationality* (Oxford, Oxford University Press, 1995).
Miller, F, 'Aristotle's Political Theory', in EN Zalta (ed), (2017) *The Stanford Encyclopaedia of Philosophy.*
Millet, F-X, 'Constitutional Identity in France: Vices and – Above All – Virtues' in C Calliess and G van der Schiff (eds), *Constitutional Identity in a Europe of Multilevel Constitutionalism* (Cambridge, Cambridge University Press, 2020).
——, 'Prix de thèse du Conseil constitutionnel 2013: L'union européenne et l'identité constitutionnelle des États membres' (2013) 41 *Les Nouveaux cahiers du Conseil Constitutionnel* 217.
Molek, P, 'The Czech Constitutional Court and the Court of Justice: Between Fascination and Securing Autonomy' in M Claes et al (eds), *Constitutional Conversations in Europe: Actors. Topics and Procedures (=107 Ius Commune Europaeum)* (Cambridge, Intersentia, 2012) 131–60.
——, *Materiální ohnisko jako věčný limit evropské integrace?* (Brno, Muni Press, 2014).
Moliterno, JE et al, 'Independence without Accountability: The Harmful Consequences of EU Policy Toward Central and Eastern European Entrants' (2018) 42 *Fordham International Law Journal* 481.
Möllers, C, *Der Staat als Argument* (Tübingen, Mohr Siebeck, 2011).
Moravcsik, A, 'The Origins of Human Rights Regimes: Democratic Delegation in Postwar Europe' (2000) 54 *International Organization* 217.
Morawski, L, 'A Critical Response' (*Verfassungsblog*, 03 June 2017).
Müller, J-W, *Constitutional Patriotism* (Princeton, Princeton University Press, 2007).
——, 'Militant Democracy and Constitutional Identity' in G Jacobsohn and M Schor (eds) Comparative Constitutional Theory (Cheltenham, Edward Elgar, 2018).
—— and Scheppele, KL, 'Constitutional Patriotism: An introduction' (2008) 6 *International Journal of Constitutional Law* 67.
Murkens, JEK, '"We Want Our Identity Back" – The Revival of National Sovereignty in the German Federal Constitutional Court's Decision on the Lisbon Treaty' (2010) 3 *Public Law* 530.
Navracsics, T, 'A New Constitution for Hungary: Locking in the Values of 1989–1990 Transition, At Last' (2011) 19 *The Wall Street Journal.*
Nawiasky, H, *Die Grundgedanken des Grundgesetzes für die Bundesrepublik Deutschland* (Stuttgart, W Kohlhammer, 1950).
Nettesheim, M, 'Ein Individualrecht auf Staatlichkeit? Die Lissabon-Entscheidung des BVerfG' (2009) 62 *Neue Juristische Woche* 2867.
——, 'Wo endet das Grundgesetz – Verfassungsgebung als Grenzüberschreitender Prozess' (2012) 51 *Der Staat* 313.
Neubauer, Z, *Státověda a theorie politiky* (Prague, Jan Laichter, 1947).

Neves, M, 'Lateinamerikanische Verfassungen: Zwischen Autokratismus und Demokratisierung' (1997) 30 *Verfassung und Recht in Übersee/Law and Politics in Africa, Asia and Latin America* 503–19.

Oberleitner, G (ed), *International Human Rights Institutions, Tribunals, and Courts* (Singapore, Springer Singapore, 2018).

Offe, C, *Varieties of Transition. The East European and East German Experience* (Cambridge, Polity Press, 1996).

Orgad, L, *The Cultural Defense of Nations. A Liberal Theory of Majority Rights* (Oxford, Oxford University Press, 2015).

——, 'The Preamble in Constitutional Interpretation' (2010) 8 *International Journal of Constitutional Law* 714.

Orosz, L, 'Dvadsať rokov Ústavy Slovenskej republiky' (2012) 12 *Roczniki Administracji i Prawa* 35.

——, Grabowska, S and Majerčák, T (eds), *Ústavné dni : tretie funkčné obdobie Ústavného súdu Slovenskej republiky – VII. Ústavné dni* (Košice, Univerzita P J Šafárika, 2019).

Orwell, G, 'Politics and the English Language' 76 *Horizon* 1946.

O'Toole, F, 'Celtic Myths' (7 March 2019) *The New York Review of Books.*

Payandeh, M and Sauer, H, 'Menschenrechtskonforme Auslegung als Verfassungsmehrwert: Konvergenzen von Grundgesetz und EMRK im Urteil des Bundesverfassungsgerichts zur Sicherungsverwahrung' (2012) 289 *JURA* 295.

Pech, L, 'The Rule of Law' in PP Craig and G De Búrca (eds), *Evolution of EU Law*, 4th edn (Oxford, Oxford University Press, 2021) 307–72.

Perju, V, 'Constitutional Transplants, Borrowing, and Migrations' in M Rosenfeld and A Sajó (eds) *The Oxford Handbook of Comparative Constitutional Law* (Oxford, Oxford University Press, 2012) 1304.

Pernice, I, 'Multilevel constitutionalism in the European Union' (2002) 27 *European Law Review* 511–29.

——, 'The Treaty of Lisbon: Multilevel Constitutionalism in Action' (2009) 15 *Columbia Journal of European Law* 349–407.

Péter, L, 'Hungary's Long Nineteenth Century. Constitutional and Democratic Traditions in a European Perspective. Collected Studies' (M Lojkó ed, Leiden-Boston, Brill, 2012).

Peters, A, 'Rechtsordnungen und Konstitutionalisierung: Zur Neubestimmung der Verhältnisse' (2010) 65 *Zeitschrift für Öffentliches Recht* 3.

Pitkin, HF, 'The Idea of a Constitution' (1987) 37 *Journal of Legal Education* 167–70.

Pócza, K, *Constitutional Politics and the Judiciary: Decision-Making in Central and Eastern Europe* (London, Routledge, 2018).

Polzin, M, 'Constitutional Identity as a Constructed Reality and a Restless Soul' (2017) 18 *German Law Journal* 1595.

——, 'Constitutional Identity, Unconstitutional Amendments and the Idea of Constituent Power: the development of the doctrine of constitutional identity in German constitutional law' (2016) 14 *International Journal of Constitutional Law* 411.

——, *Verfassungsidentität: ein normatives Konzept des Grundgesetzes?* (Tübingen, Mohr Siebeck, 2018).

Post, RC, 'The Supreme Court, 2002 Term-Forward: Fashioning the Legal Constitution: Culture, Courts and Law' (2003) 117 *Harvard Law Review* 4.

Preuss, O, 'Demokratický právní stát tesaný do pískovce' (2016) 24:3 *Časopis pro právní vědu a praxis.*

——, 'Slovenský "Melčák", nukleární zbraň jako dar novému ústavnímu soudu' (2019) 6 *Jurisprudence* 1.

Preuss, UK, 'Constitutional Powermaking for the New Polity: Some Deliberations on the Relations between Constituent Power and the Constitution' in M Rosenfeld (ed), *Constitutionalism, Identity, Difference and Legitimacy: Theoretical Perspectives* (Durham, Duke University Press, 1994) 143–64.

Přibáň, J, *Legal symbolism. On Law, Time and European Identity* (London, Routledge, 2017).

Procházka, R, *Ľud a sudcovia v konštitučnej demokracii* (Prague, Aleš Čeněk, 2011).

——, *Mission Accomplished: On Founding Constitutional Adjudication in Central Europe* (New York, Central European University Press, 2002).

Radnóti, S, 'A Sacred Symbol in a Secular Country: The Holy Crown' in GA Tóth (ed), *Constitution for a Disunited Nation. On Hungary's 2011 Fundamental Law* (New York, Central European University Press, 2012) 85–110.

Rapaczyński, A, 'Constitutional Politics in Poland: A Report On The Constitutional Committee Of The Polish Parliament' (1991) 58 *University of Chicago Law Review* 595.

Rawls, J, *Political Liberalism* (New York, Columbia University Press, 1993).

Reschová, J, 'Paradoxy česko-slovenských vztahů' (2018) 3 *Acta Universitatis Carolinae Iuridica* 11.

Rév, I, 'Identity by History', in S Greenblatt, I Rév, & R Starn, (1995) 49 *Representation, Special Issue: Identifying Histories: Eastern Europe Before and After 1989*, 8–10.

Rideau, J, 'The Case-law of the Polish, Hungarian and Czech Constitutional Courts on National Identity and the "German Model"' in AS Arnaiz and CA Llivina (eds), Cambridge *National Constitutional Identity and European Integration* (Cambridge, Intersentia, 2013) 243–62.

Robertson, D, 'A Problem of their Own, Solutions of their Own: CEE Jurisdictions and the Problems of Lustration and Retroactivity' in W Sadurski, A Czarnota, and M Krygier (eds), *Spreading Democracy and the Rule of Law? The Impact of EU Enlargement for the Rule of Law, Democracy and Constitutionalism in Post-Communist Legal Orders* (Dordrecht, Springer, 2006) 73–96.

Rosen, M, *Dignity: Its History and Meaning* (Cambridge, Mass, Harvard University Press, 2012).

Rosenfeld, M, 'Constitutional Identity' in M Rosenfeld and A Sajó (eds), *The Oxford Handbook of Comparative Constitutional Law* (Oxford, Oxford University Press, 2012) 756–76.

——, *The Identity of the Constitutional Subject: selfhood, citizenship, culture and community* (London, Routledge, 2009).

Roy, O, 'Beyond Populism' in N Marzouki, D MacDonell and O Roy (eds), *Saving the People: How Populists Hijack Religion* (Meridian, Hurst & Company, 2016) 186–202.

Roznai, Y, 'Legisprudence Limitations on Constitutional Amendments? Reflections on the Czech Constitutional Court's Declaration of Unconstitutional Constitutional Act' (2014) 8:1 *Vienna Journal on International Constitutional Law* 29.

——, *Unconstitutional Constitutional Amendments – The Limits of Amendment Powers* (Oxford, Oxford University Press, 2017).

——, 'Who Will Save the Redheads? Towards an Anti-Bully Theory of Judicial Review and Protection of Democracy' (2020) 29 *William & Mary Bill of Rights Journal* 327.

Rutherford, J, *Identity, Community, Culture, Difference* (London, Lawrence & Wishart, 1990).

Rychlík, J, 'The "Velvet Split" of Czechoslovakia (1989–1992)' (2018) 15 *Politeja* 169–87.

Sachs, A, 'Grundrechte: Freiheit der Person – Sicherungsverwahrung Urteil vom 04.05.2011 – 2 BvR 2365/09', Besprechung (2011) *Juristische Schulung* 854.

Sachs, M (ed), Grundgesetz Kommentar 6th edn (Munich, CH Beck, 2011).

Sadurski, W, *Poland's Constitutional Breakdown* (Oxford, Oxford University Press, 2019).

—— and Gliszczyńska-Grabias, A, 'The Judgment That Wasn't (But Which Nearly Brought Poland to a Standstill): "Judgment" of the Polish Constitutional Tribunal of 22 October 2020, K1/20' (2021) 17 *European Constitutional Law Review* 130–53.

Sajó, A, 'Constitution without the Constitutional Moment: A View from the New Member States' (2005) 3 *International Journal of Constitutional Law* 243.

——, *Ruling by Cheating: Governance in Illiberal Democracy* (Cambridge, Cambridge University Press, 2021).

—— and LR Bentch (eds) *Militant Democracy* (Den Haag, Eleven International Publishing, 2004).

Scheppele, KL, 'Autocratic Legalism' (2018) 85 *University of Chicago Law Review* 545–83.

——, 'Guardians of the Constitution: Constitutional Court Presidents and the Struggle for the Rule of Law in Post-Soviet Europe' (2005) 154 *University of Pennsylvania Law Review* 1757.

—— The Rule of Law and the Frankenstate: Why Governance Checklists Do Not Work' (2013) 26 *Governance* 559–62.

Scheuerman, B, 'Is Parliamentarism in Crisis? A Response to Carl Schmitt' (1995) 24 *Theory and Society* 135.

Schlesinger, J, 'Der Pouvoir Constituant' (1933) 13 *Zeitschrift für Öffentliches Recht*.

Schmitt, C, *Constitutional Theory* trans J Seitzer (Durham, Duke University Press, 2008).

——, *Die Diktatur* 3rd edn (Berlin, Duncker & Humblot, 1964).

——, *Der Begriff des Politischen* (Berlin, Duncker & Humblot, 1991).

——, *The Concept of the Political* (Chicago, Chicago University Press, 2007).

——, *Verfassungslehre* 11th edn (Berlin, Duncker & Humblot, 1928).

——, 'Zehn Jahre Reichsverfassung (1929)' 58 *Juristische Wochenschrift* 2313 reprinted in: C Schmitt, *Verfassungsrechtliche Aufsätze aus den Jahren 1924–1954* 2nd edn (Berlin, Duncker & Humblot, 1957).

Schmitter, PC and Karl, TL, 'What Democracy Is … and Is Not' (1991) 2 *Journal of Democracy* 75.

Schneider, CJ, 'Euroscepticism and government accountability in the European Union' (2019) 14 *The Review of International Organizations* 217–38.

Schnettger, A, 'Article 4(2) as a Vehicle for National Constitutional Identity in the Shared European Legal System' in C Calliess and G van der Schyff (eds), *Constitutional Identity in a Europe of Multilevel Constitutionalism* (Cambridge, Cambridge University Press, 2020) 9–40.

Scholtes, J, 'Abusing Constitutional Identity' (2021) 22 *German Law Journal* 534–56.

Schor, M, 'Mapping Comparative Judicial Review' (2008) 7 *Washington University Global Studies Law Review*, 257–87.

Schönberger, C, 'Identitäterä: Verfassungsidentität zwischen Widerstandsformel und Musealisierung des Grundgesetzes' (2015) 63 *Jahrbuch des öffentlichen Rechts der Gegenwart* 41.

——, '*Lisbon* in Karlsruhe: Maastricht's Epigones at Sea' (2009) 10 *German Law Journal* 1201.

Schotel, B, 'Administrative Law as a Dual State. Authoritarian Elements of Administrative Law' (2021) 13 *Hague Journal on the Rule of Law* 195–222.

Seymour, M (ed), *The Fate of the Nation State* (Montreal & Kingston, McGill-Queen's University Press, 2004).

Sen, A, 'Democracy as a Universal Value' (1999) 10 *Journal of Democracy* 3–17.

Shaw, J, *The People in Question: Citizens and Constitutions in Uncertain Times* (Bristol, Bristol University Press, 2020).

Šimíček, V, 'Art. 2' in L Bahýlová et al, *Ústava České republiky: Komentář* (Prague, Linde Praha, 2010).

Sládeček V et al, *Ústava České republiky. Komentář* 2nd edn (Praha, CH Beck, 2016).

Śledzińska-Simon, A, 'Constitutional Identity in 3D: A Model of Individual, Relational, and Collective Self and its Application in Poland' (2015) 13 *International Journal of Constitutional Law* 124–55.

—— and Ziółkowski, M, 'Constitutional Identity in Poland: Is the Emperor Putting On the Old Clothes of Sovereignty?' in C Calliess and G van der Schiff (eds), *Constitutional Identity in a Europe of Multilevel Constitutionalism* (Cambridge, Cambridge University Press, 2020).

Šlosarčík, J, 'EU Law in the Czech Republic: From ultra vires of the Czech Government to ultra vires of the EU Court?' (2015) 9 *Vienna Journal on International Constitutional Law* 417.

Smart, C, *Feminism and the Power of Law* (London, Routledge, 1998).

Smekal, H and Vyhnánek, L, 'Equal Voting Power under Scrutiny: Czech Constitutional Court on the 5% threshold in the 2014 European Parliament Elections: Czech Constitutional Court 19 May 2015, Pl. ÚS 14/14' (2016) 12 *European Constitutional Law Review* 148.

Smith, AD, 'Will and Sacrifice: Images of National Identity' (2001) 30 *Millennium: Journal of International Studies* 571.

Spáč, P, 'Slovakia' in V Havlík, et al, *Populist Political Parties in East-Central Europe Vol 49* (Brno, Munipress, 2012) 227.

Spáč, S, Šipulová, K and Urbániková, M, 'Capturing the Judiciary from Inside: The Story of Judicial Self-Governance in Slovakia' (2018) 19 *German Law Journal* 1741.

Stein, E, *Czecho/Slovakia: Ethnic Conflict, Constitutional Fissure, Negotiated Breakup* (Ann Arbor, University of Michigan Press, 2000).

Steiner, U, *Verfassunggebung und verfassunggebende Gewalt des Volkes* (Berlin, Duncker & Humblot, 1966).

Steuer, M, 'Constitutional Court of the Slovak Republic' in R Grote, F Lachenmann and R Wolfrum (eds), *Max Planck Encyclopaedia of Comparative Constitutional Law* (Oxford, Oxford University Press, 2019).

——, 'Constitutional Pluralism and the Slovak Constitutional Court: The Challenge of European Union Law' (2018) 8 *The Lawyer Quarterly.*

——, 'The First Live-Broadcast Hearings of Candidates for Constitutional Judges in Slovakia: Five Lessons' (*Verfassungsblog*, 5 February 2019).

——, 'The Guardians and the Watchdogs: The Framing of Politics, Partisanship and Qualification by Selected Newspapers during the 2018–2019 Slovak Constitutional Court Appointment Process' (2019) 102 *Právny obzor* 34.

——, 'Variácie demokracie v rozhodovacej činnosti Ústavného súdu Slovenskej republiky v treťom funkčnom období: Prípadová štúdia kreačných právomocí hlavy štátu' in L Orosz, S Grabowska and T Majerčák (eds), *Ústavný súd Slovenskej republiky v treťom funkčnom období – VII. ústavné dni* (Prague, Univerzita P J Šafárika, 2019).

Štiavnický, J and Steuer, M, 'The Constitutional Court of the Slovak Republic: The Many Faces of Law-Making by Constitutional Courts with Extensive Review Powers' in M Florczak-Wątor (ed), *Judicial Law-Making in European Constitutional Courts* (London, Routledge, 2020).

Stone Sweet, A, *Governing with Judges: Constitutional Politics in Europe* (Oxford, Oxford University Press, 2000).

——, 'The Structure of Constitutional Pluralism: Review of Nico Krisch, Beyond Constitutionalism: The Pluralist Structure of Post-National Law' (2013) 11 *International Journal of Constitutional Law* 491.

Stückrath, B, *Art. 146 GG: Verfassungsablösung zwischen Legalität und Legitimität* (Berlin, Duncker & Humblot, 1996).

Suk, J, *Labyrintem revoluce* (Prague, Prostor, 2009).

Sunstein, CR, *One Case at a Time: Judicial Minimalism on the Supreme Court* (Cambridge, Harvard University Press, 2001).

Suteu, S, *Eternity Clauses in Democratic Constitutionalism* (Oxford, Oxford University Press, 2021).

Szoboszlai, G (ed), *Democracy and Political Transformation: Theories and East-Central European Realities* (Budapest, Hungarian Political Science Association, 1991).

Szwed, M, 'What Should and What Will Happen After Xero Flor – The judgement of the ECtHR on the composition of the Polish Constitutional Tribunal' (*Verfassungsblog*, 8 May 2021)

Takács, P, 'Renaming States–A Case Study: Changing the Name of the Hungarian State in 2011. Its Background, Reasons, and Aftermath' (2020) 33 *International Journal for the Semiotics of Law* 899.

Tamir, Y, *Liberal Nationalism* (Princeton, Princeton University Press, 1995).

Taylor, C, *The Ethics of Authenticity* (Cambridge, Harvard University Press, 1991).

Thiruvengadam, AK, *The Constitution of India: A Contextual Analysis* (London, Bloomsbury Publishing, 2017).

Thoma, R, 'Das Reich als Demokratie' in R Thoma and G Anschütz (eds), *Handbuch des Deutschen Staatsrechts Vol 1* (Tübingen, Mohr & Siebeck, 1930).

——, 'Die juristische Bedeutung der grundrechtlichen Sätze der deutschen Reichsverfassung im Allgemeinen' in HC Nipperdey (ed), *Die Grundrechte und Grundpflichten der Reichsverfassung, Kommentar zum zweiten Teil der Reichsverfassung* (Berlin, Hobbing, 1930).

——, 'Grundbegriffe und Grundsätze' in R Thoma and G Anschütz (eds), *Handbuch des Deutschen Staatsrechts Vol 2* (Tübingen, Mohr & Siebeck, 1932).

Thym, D, 'Attack or Retreat? Evolving Themes and Strategies of the Judicial Dialogue between the German Constitutional Court and the European Court of Justice' in M Claes et al (eds), *Constitutional Conversations in Europe: Actors. Topics and Procedures (=107 Ius Commune Europaeum)* (Cambridge, Intersentia, 2012) 235–50.

——, 'Friendly Takeover, or: The Power of the "First Word". The German Constitutional Court Embraces the Charter of Fundamental Rights as a Standard of Domestic Judicial Review' (2020) 16 *European Constitutional Law Review* 187.

Tomoszek, M, 'Ústavní identita jako vyjádření ústavní filosofie' in T Sobek, M Hapla et al (eds), *Filosofie práva* (Brno, Nugis Finem, 2020).

Tomuschat, C, 'Die Europäische Union unter der Aufsicht des Bundesverfassungsgerichts' (1993) 20 *Europäische Grundrechte Zeitschrift* 489.

——, 'The Defence of National Identity by the German Constitutional Court' in AS Arnaiz and CA Llivina (eds), *National Constitutional Identity and European Integration* (Cambridge, Intersentia, 2013).

——, 'The ruling of the German Constitutional Court on the Treaty of Lisbon' (2009) 10 *German Law Journal* 1259–262.

Toniatti, R, 'Sovereignty Lost, Constitutional Identity Gained' in AS Arnaiz and CA Llivana (eds), *National Constitutional Identity and European Integration* (Cambridge, Intersentia, 2013).

Tóth, GA, 'Authoritarianism' in *Max Planck Encyclopaedia of Comparative Constitutional Law* (Oxford, Oxford University Press, 2017).

——, *Constitution for a Disunited Nation: On Hungary's 2011 Fundamental Law* (New York, Central European University Press, 2012).

——, 'Constitutional Markers of Authoritarianism' (2019) 11 *Hague Journal on the Rule of Law* 37–61.

——, 'Lost in Transition: Invisible Constitutionalism in Hungary' in R Dixon and A Stone (eds), *The Invisible Constitution in a Comparative Perspective* (Cambridge, Cambridge University Press, 2018).

Tripkovic, B, *The Metaethics of Constitutional Adjudication* (Oxford, Oxford University Press, 2017).

Troper, M, 'Behind the Constitution?' in A Sajó and R Uitz (eds), *Constitutional Topography: Values and Constitutions* (The Hague, Eleven, 2010).

Tushnet, M, 'Authoritarian Constitutionalism' (2015) 100 *Cornell Law Review* 393.

——, *Taking the Constitution Away from the Courts* (Princeton, Princeton University Press, 2000).

Uitz, R, 'Freedom of Religion and Churches' in GA Tóth (ed), *Constitution for a Disunited Nation. On Hungary's 2011 Fundamental Law* (New York, Central European University Press, 2012) 197–236.

——, 'National Constitutional Identity in the European Constitutional Project: A Recipe for Exposing Cover Ups and Masquerades' (*Verfassungsblog*, 11 November 2016).

Urbániková, M and Šipulová, K, 'Failed Expectations: Does the Establishment of Judicial Councils Enhance Confidence in Courts?' (2018) 19 *German Law Journal* 2105.

Vagovič, M, *Vlastnou hlavou* (Bratislava, Premedia, 2016).

van de Heyning, C, 'The European Perspective: From Lingua Franca to a Common Language' in M Claes et al (eds), *Constitutional Conversations in Europe: Actors. Topics and Procedures (107 Ius Commune Europaeum)* (Cambridge, Intersentia, 2012).

Vikarská, Z and Bobek, M, 'Slovakia: Between Euro-Optimism and Euro-Concerns' in A Albi and S Bardutzky (eds), *National Constitutions in European and Global Governance: Democracy, Rights, the Rule of Law: National Reports* (The Hague, TMC Asser Press, 2019).

von Bogdandy, A, 'The European Constitution and European Identity: Text and Subtext of the Treaty Establishing a Constitution for Europe' (2005) 3 *International Journal of Constitutional Law* 295.

—— and Schill, SW, 'Overcoming Absolute Primacy: Respect for National Identity under the Lisbon Treaty' (2011) 48 *Common Market Law Review*.

Vosskuhle, A and Gerhardt, R, 'Wir leben in einem europäischen Gerichtsverbund' (2015) 48 *Zeitschrift für Rechtspolitik* 61.

Vyhnánek, L, 'The Eternity Clause in the Czech Constitution as Limit to European Integration: Much Ado About Nothing?' (2015) 9 *Vienna Journal on International and Constitutional Law* 240.

Waldron, J, *The Harm in Hate Speech* (Cambridge, Mass, Harvard University Press, 2012).

Waluchow, W, 'Constitutionalism', in EN Zalta (ed) (2018) *The Stanford Encyclopaedia of Philosophy*.

Walker, N, 'Populism and constitutional tension' (2019) 17 *International Journal of Constitutional Law* 515–35.

Weiler, JHH, 'Does Europe Need a Constitution? Demos, Telos and the German Maastricht Decision' (1995) 1 *European Law Journal* 219.

——, 'On the power of the Word: Europe's constitutional iconography' (2005) 3 *International Journal of Constitutional Law* 184.

Wessely, A, 'The Shaman and Saint Stephen's Holy Crown' in M Heller and B Kriza (eds), *Identities, Ideologies, and Representations in Post-Transition Hungary* (Budapest, Eötvös University Press, 2012).

Whitman, JQ, 'On Nazi "Honour" and the New European "Dignity"' in C Jourges and NS Gholeigh (eds), *Darker Legacies of Law in Europe: The Shadow of National Socialism and Fascism Over Europe and Its Legal Traditions* (Oxford, Hart, 2003).

Wieland, J, 'Germany in the European Union – The Maastricht Decision of the Bundesverfassungsgericht' (1994) 5 *European Journal of International Law* 259.

Williams, B, *Ethics and the Limits of Philosophy* (London, Routledge, 2006).

Wilson, EO, *The Social Conquest of Earth* (London, Liveright, 2012).

Wójtowicz, K, *Constitutional Courts and European Union Law* (Wroclaw, University of Wroclaw E-Press, 2014).

Wojtyczek, K, *Przekazywanie kompetencji panstwa organizacjom miedzynarodowym* (Krakow, Jagiellonian University Press, 2007).

Wyrzykowski, M, 'Constitutional Changes in Poland 1989–1991' (1992) 17 *Bulletin of the Australian Society of Legal Philosophy* 25.

Yılmaz, IZ, 'Z Erdoğan's presidential regime and strategic legalism: Turkish democracy in the twilight zone' (2020) 20 *Southeast European and Black Sea Studies* 265–87.

Zachalova, K, 'Patriotism by Decree in Slovakia' *Time* 18 March 2010.

Zbíral, R, 'Koncept národní identity jako nový prvek ve vztahu vnitrostátního a unijního práva: poznatky z teorie a praxe' (2014) 153 *Právník* 112.

Zhai, H, *The Constitutional Identity of Contemporary China – The Unitary System and its Internal Logic* (Leiden, Brill-Nijhoff, 2019).

Zick, A and Küpper, B, and Hövermann, A, *Intolerance, Prejudice and Discrimination. A European Report* (Berlin, Friedrich-Ebert-Stiftung, 2011).

Zotééva, A and Kragh, M, 'From Constitutional Identity to the Identity of the Constitution' 54 *Communist and Post-Communist Studies* 176–95.

Index

www.ingramcontent.com/pod-product-compliance
Lightning Source LLC
LaVergne TN
LVHW011757200926
848484LV00003B/725